Islamic Law

ISLAMIC LAW

Theory and Practice

Edited by
Robert Gleave
&
Eugenia Kermeli

I.B.Tauris *Publishers*
LONDON • NEW YORK

Paperback edition published in 2001 by I.B.Tauris & Co Ltd
6 Salem Road, London W2 4BU
175 Fifth Avenue, New York NY 10010
www.ibtauris.com

In the United States of America and in Canada distributed by
St Martins Press, 175 Fifth Avenue, New York NY 10010

First published in 1997 by I.B.Tauris & Co Ltd

ISBN 1 86064 652 2

A full CIP record for this book is available from the British Library
A full CIP record for this book is available from the Library of Congress

Library of Congress catalog card: available

Typeset in Monotype Baskerville by Philip Armstrong, Sheffield
Printed and bound in Great Britain by Mackays of Chatham plc

Contents

Contributors

Eric Chaumont is currently a Chargé de Récherche at CNRS, Aix en Provence, France.

Mohammad Fadel Lectures in Arabic and Islamic Studies at the University of Virginia, USA.

Robert Gleave is Lecturer in Islamic Studies at the University of Bristol, UK

Isaac Hollander is a doctoral student at the Hebrew University of Jerusalem, Israel.

Benjamin Jokisch completed his PhD at the University of Hamburg in 1995

Patricia Kabra is currently a Research Scholar at USIS, Damascus, Syria

Eugenia Kermeli is Lecturer in the Department of History, Bilkent University, Turkey.

Birgit Krawietz lectures in Arabic at the Eberhard-Karls-Universität Tübingen

Ruth Mitchell lectures in Islamic Studies at Manchester Metropolitan University.

Yitzhak Reiter completed his PhD from the Hebrew University Jerusalem in 1995.

Amalia Zomeño is a doctoral student at CSIC, Madrid, Spain.

Introduction

ROBERT GLEAVE

The papers in this collection were originally presented at a conference entitled 'Islamic Law: Theory and Practice' held at Ashburne Hall, University of Manchester in June 1995. The aim of the conference was to provide a forum for emerging scholars in Islamic Law to present their research. The conference was intentionally broad in its scope. Papers on legal theory, legal practice and the relationship between the theory and practice in Islamic Law were presented. Consequently this collection contains articles examining Islamic Law from a variety of approaches, examining different geographical areas and time periods. The articles are quite diverse in their content, and this collection is unlikely to satisfy those who are looking for an integrated examination of theory and practice in Islamic Law. However there are a number of themes that run through the collection which deserve comment at the outset.

First, in many of the papers there is a search for an adequate definition of *ijtihād* and juristic interpretation, and a recognition of the need to clarify its relationship with judicial practice at particular points in time. Though much work remains to be done in this area, some of the papers in this volume are evidence that the nature of *ijtihād* and related interpretative practices will form a principal focus of future research in Islamic Law. The papers of Chaumont, myself, Jokisch and Krawietz all utilise related but different conceptions of *ijtihād* in the modern and classical periods. These papers use works of *uṣūl al-fiqh* and *furūʿ al-fiqh* as well as *fatāwā* collections. The different conceptions indicate that *ijtihād* is a slippery term and the quest for a definitive description of its operation is far from over.

In some papers there is also an emphasis on the importance of *fatāwā* collections as evidence of judicial and juristic activity at particular points in time. In recent years, research has begun on the many *fatāwā* compendia and their supposed link with historical phenomena. This research raises questions concerning the relationship between literature and history and the influence of generic constraints upon the authors of *fatwās*. The studies in this volume demonstrate that the inter-relationship between *fatāwā* and history, *fatāwā* and *furūʿ* literature and *fatāwā* and *uṣūl* literature are complex and can be studied from a number of perspectives. It appears that little consensus is emerging concerning the best way to characterise these relationships. These issues are explored in many of the papers, particularly those by Kermeli, Kabra, Fadel and Zomeño.

Finally, there is a clear awareness of the flexibility, perhaps mutability, of the law, both through time and in differing circumstances. Hollander examines the use of *Sharīʿa* courts by the Yemeni Jewish community; Reiter examines the role of *qāḍīs* in the Israeli *Sharīʿa* judiciary and Mitchell describes how a piece of modern state legislation (the 1984 Algerian Family Law) incorporates and adapts classical conceptions of law in a modern context. In these papers, and in others in the volume, there is an acceptance that though the *Sharīʿa* was classically conceived of as an unchanging nexus of regulations, ideas of God's Law and its implementation have developed in response to particular contextual factors, particularly in the modern period.

Other papers presented at the conference, but not contained in this volume, explored similar themes. These included:

Mohammed Daud Bakr: 'A comparative study of Islamic legal theory (*uṣūl al-fiqh al-muqāran*)'
Ibrahim Moosa: 'Public Interest (*maṣlaḥa*) in theory and in practice'
Kathryn Miller: 'The Mufti as Arbitrator: a case of *shubha*'
Lutz Wiederhold: 'Insulting the Prophet (*sabb al-rasūl*): some remarks on the introduction of the issue into Sunni legal literature'
Soraya Bosch: 'Integrating Muslim Personal Law into the new South African Legal Order'

A number of organisations made the conference itself and the publication of this book possible, and deserve our thanks for their support. The University of Manchester Small Grants Fund, ISESCO, the Spalding Trust and the Joseph Rowntree Trust all provided financial support for the conference. The Spalding Trust provided further support for the preparation of the manuscript of this volume.

Drs Norman Calder and Colin Imber of the Department of

Middle Eastern Studies, University of Manchester gave advice and help before, during and after the conference. Dr John Healey also offered valuable advice at various points. Mrs Judith Willson prepared some of the papers for publication in a most efficient and accurate manner. Finally, my thanks go to Eugenia Kermeli, with whom I organised the conference. With our academic and other commitments it has been hard work, but I hope that the final result will prove useful.

A Note on Transliteration

The transliteration from Arabic in this volume follows the system in the *Encyclopaedia of Islam* with some alterations: ḳ is transliterated as q, dj is j and sh, kh and dh are not underlined. Ottoman Turkish follows the system in the *Encyclopaedia of Islam*. The conventional system is used for Hebrew transliteration.

PART ONE

Legal Theory

ONE

Ijtihād et histoire en islam sunnite classique selon quelques juristes et quelques théologiens

ÉRIC CHAUMONT

A la mémoire de Marie Bernand

Présentation

> ... comprendre d'une manière vivante – *poétique* – que cet endroit ressemblait à tous les autres, qu'il était soudé à l'ensemble de la nature planétaire et qu'il en était une manifestation.
>
> **W. Golding, *An Egyptian Journal***

1) L'idée selon laquelle le Droit musulman, le *fiqh*, tel qu'il existe aujourd'hui, c'est-à-dire tel un héritage fait de normes souvent plusieurs fois centenaires, n'est plus véritablement à même de régir les sociétés musulmanes d'un point de vue juridique et social ni de satisfaire les aspirations légitimes de chacune de ses composantes (les femmes, les minorités confessionnelles ou autres), cette idée est largement répandue parmi nos contemporains, qu'ils soient musulmans ou observateurs des sociétés musulmanes (même si elle n'est pas toujours entendue ni évaluée de la même manière par les uns et par les autres). L'accord est quasi unanime aussi pour considérer que la cause profonde, et peut-être l'unique cause, de l'inadéquation du *fiqh* avec le monde contemporain a partie étroitement liée avec l'*ijtihād*, concept ressortissant à la science des *uṣūl al-fiqh* qui, fait rarissime, a même acquis quelque notoriété en dehors de la sphère très restreinte des spécialistes du Droit ou de la pensée légale islamiques. Si le *fiqh* est, au sens strict du terme, inactuel, c'est, dit-on si souvent, parce que quelque chose 'a mal tourné' du côté de l'*ijtihād*, parce que, en

un mot, il y eut 'fermeture de la porte de l'*ijtihād*' (*insidād, sadd bāb al-ijtihād*).

Cette représentation d'une non-évolution du *fiqh*, de son 'ankylose' qui serait due à l'interdiction faite assez tôt (dès le début du IVème/Xème siècle selon J. Schacht) aux juristes d'exercer librement leur *ijtihād*[1] ne tient plus. De nouvelles recherches fondées sur une littérature jusqu'alors négligée et pourtant essentielle en la matière, la littérature du *'ilm uṣūl al-fiqh* (littéralement: 'la science des fondements de la compréhension', sous-entendu 'de la Loi'), ont prouvé qu'il était au mieux abusif, et au pire franchement faux, de parler de la 'fermeture de la porte de l'*ijtihād*' comme d'une *institution* de l'ordre juridique musulman.[2] Tout au long de mon exposé, ce point sera considéré comme acquis et je me contenterai ici, assez longuement il est vrai et en guise d'introduction (L'*ijtihād* et son rôle ...), de mettre en évidence la fonction véritablement centrale dévolue à l'*ijtihād* dans le *fiqh* par deux juristes shāfi'ites importants, Abū Isḥāq al-Shīrāzi et Abū al-Ma'ālī al-Juwaynī qui vivaient pourtant l'un et l'autre à une époque, le Vème/XIème siècle, où l'*ijtihād* est réputé avoir déjà été muselé.

2) Par ailleurs, et tel est le véritable objet de ce travail, la théorie selon laquelle le *fiqh* doit son immobilisme réputé à la 'fermeture de la porte de l'*ijtihād*' repose implicitement sur une représentation bien particulière de la notion d'*ijtihād* comme principe d'adaptation des normes légales à l'Histoire et aux changements inhérents à son écoulement (puisque l'on tient que si l'*ijtihād* avait pu librement se déployer dans l'Histoire, le *fiqh* serait en adéquation avec cette dernière). C'est cette représentation de l'*ijtihād*, paraissant sans doute évidente pour beaucoup, qui sera ici mise à l'épreuve de textes classiques de la littérature des *uṣūl al-fiqh*, le lieu naturel, rappelons-le, où les juristes et parfois les théologiens, les *mutakallims*, théorisèrent la notion d'*ijtihād* et élaborèrent sa problématique.

La question qui sera ici posée est donc la suivante: 'Peut-on dire de l'*ijtihād* comme il fut théorisé dans les *uṣūl al-fiqh* sunnites classiques qu'il est ce principe conçu pour procurer au *fiqh* la capacité d'évoluer avec le temps, c'est-à-dire, tout en restant le même, de s'adapter aux inévitables changements qu'amène l'écoulement des siècles?'

Je vous propose de traiter cette question en deux moments ; dans un premier temps (*Ijtihād* et variabilité ...), la question sera, si je puis dire, réduite à l'essentiel et théoriquement abordée. On cherchera à déterminer si le principe même de la variabilité d'un statut légal (*ḥukm sharʿī*) concernant un seul et même acte humain est positivement reconnu, admis, toléré ou nié par les théoriciens du Droit. De l'acceptation du principe théorique d'une telle variabilité dépend en effet la possibilité pour le *fiqh* d'évoluer (sans préjuger ni du sens de cette évolution ni des facteurs susceptibles de la provoquer). Cette première partie de mon exposé se fondera sur l'examen d'une question, *hal kull mujtahid muṣīb?* ('Tout chercheur qualifié dit-il juste?'), traditionnellement abordée dans tout traité d'*uṣūl al-fiqh*. Ensuite (La question du 'renouvellement' ...), l'étude d'une question pratique posée par les usûlistes viendra confirmer les hypothèses retenues au terme de la première partie de cet exposé tout en les complexifiant.

L'Ijtihād et son rôle dans l'élaboration du *fiqh* selon les *uṣūl al-fiqh* sunnites classiques

1) Si l'on se réfère aux définitions de l'*ijtihād* et du *fiqh* proposées par Juwaynī (m. 478/1085) et Shīrāzī (m. 476/1083) – l'un et l'autre, faut-il le rappeler, auteurs d'œuvres de référence du *madhhab* shāfiʿite[3] – il apparaît dénué de sens de parler d'une quelconque fermeture de la porte de l'*ijtihād* à moins de faire la supposition, absurde ou dénigrante, que ce sont les œuvres de Juwaynī et de Shīrāzī qui, au moment même de leur composition, étaient déjà obsolètes.

Le *fiqh*, écrivent-ils l'un et l'autre, consiste en 'la connaissance des statuts légaux dont la voie [de connaissance] est l'*ijtihād*' (*al-fiqh maʿrifat al-aḥkām al-sharʿiyya al-latī ṭarīquhā al-ijtihād*).[4] Et l'*ijtihād* est à son tour défini comme 'le fait d'user de toutes ses capacités et de déployer un effort dans la recherche du statut légal' (*istifrāgh al-wusʿ wa badhl al-majhad fī ṭalab al-ḥukm al-sharʿī*).[5] Entre Shāfiʿī (m. 204/820), qui, se posant en adversaire du *raʾy* et de l'*istiḥsān*, proposait d'identifier l'*ijtihād* avec le seul raisonnement analogique (*qiyās*),[6] et nos deux auteurs, un chemin considérable a été parcouru au sein même de l'École shāfiʿite. Il n'y a pas lieu ici de retracer ce chemin[7] mais il convient d'en signaler la direction et l'aboutissement.

Contre toute attente (au vu de ce qu'enseignent les manuels), nous n'assistons nullement à un étranglement de l'*ijtihād* mais, au contraire, à un élargissement considérable de son champ sémantique. Ce qu'affirment en substance Juwaynī et Shīrāzī dans leur définition du *fiqh*, laquelle implique en définitive que toute *masʾala fiqhiyya* est une *masala ijtihādiyya*,[8] est qu'il ne suffit pas d'établir la nécessité d'un effort cognitif de l'homme, l'obligation d'un *ijtihād*, pour mettre au jour un statut légal non-immédiatement révélé par le Législateur, un 'cas inédit' (*ḥāditha*), il faut encore, et peut-être surtout, l'affirmer en ce qui regarde l'herméneutique de ce qu'Il a effectivement dit.[9] Dans cette perspective, qui sera ensuite adoptée par l'immense majorité des usûlistes toutes obédiences confondues, l'homme-*mujtahid* se retrouve, bien plus franchement que la théorie de l'*ijtihād* de Shāfi'ī ne permettait de le penser, l'interprète obligé de la Loi (et pas seulement un obligé devant la Loi) en presque chacun de ses articles. En d'autres mots, l'*ijtihād* n'est plus ici, comme c'était en revanche le cas chez Shāfi'ī, par défaut de Révélation, de *waḥy* ; désormais *waḥy*, *ijtihād* et *fiqh* sont devenus des notions absolument inséparables en tant qu'un *ijtihād* est, dans l'immense majorité des cas, nécessaire pour que la réception et la compréhension, le *fiqh*, de la Loi révélée (*al-sharī'a*) soit possible. En une formule ramassée, on peut dire que dans l'esprit des légistes de l'époque, sans *ijtihād*, il ne peut y avoir de *fiqh* et sans *fiqh*, il ne peut y avoir d'application de la Loi.

2) En y mettant beaucoup de mauvaise volonté, on pourrait encore émettre l'hypothèse que la théorie de l'*ijtihād* venant d'être évoquée cessa à un certain moment d'être d'actualité; les *fuqahā'* auraient alors estimé que rien ne pouvant égaler l'*ijtihād* des grands Imams, il convenait non plus de parvenir à la compréhension de la Loi par l'intermédiaire de leur propre *ijtihād*, mais plutôt de *répéter* le *fiqh* des grands Imams en question (Shāfi'ī, Abū Ḥanīfa etc.) tel que ceux-ci, ou leurs disciples immédiats (Muzanī, Shaybānī, etc.), l'avaient consigné dans de volumineux traités; comme si, dans l'esprit des *fuqahā'*, l'*ijtihād* des 'Pieux Anciens' (*al-salaf*) avaient dispensé les Modernes de cette obligation. Après l'âge de l'effort et de la découverte – l'âge de l'*ijtihād* – serait ainsi venu celui du conformisme et de la répétition – l'âge du *taqlīd*.

Mais un survol, même rapide, de la littérature consacrée à l'*iftā'*[10] par, le plus souvent, des *fuqahā'* invalide une telle hypothèse. Sans du tout entrer dans le détail, on constate tout d'abord que pour la majorité des *fuqahā'* toutes époques confondues, la première exigence à laquelle un mufti doive satisfaire est d'être un *mujtahid* (condition qui serait sans objet s'il devait être entendu que la porte de l'*ijtihād* était fermée). De plus, aux questions traditionnelles du genre – 'Le mufti-*mujtahid* a-t-il le droit de se conformer à un autre savant?', 'Le mufti a-t-il le droit d'émettre une *fatwā* dans laquelle il se contenterait de relater l'avis d'un autre *mujtahid*?', 'Un *mujtahid* décédé peut-il faire l'objet du *taqlīd*?', etc., – cette même majorité de *fuqahā'* répond par la négative. Il y a donc une complémentarité évidente entre théories de l'*ijtihād* et de l'*iftā'*, la seconde étant venue se greffer sur la première afin d'en assurer la pérennité.

3) Il apparaît donc, premièrement, que toute l'architecture du *fiqh* repose sur l'ouverture obligée de la porte de l'*ijtihād*, et, deuxièmement, que la fonction de l'*ijtihād* dans le *fiqh* est protégée par la manière dont les *fuqahā'* ont pensé le rapport devant lier les deux moments 'découverte du statut légal par voie d'*ijtihād*' et 'énonciation du statut légal par voie de *fatwā*' dans l'œuvre juridique. Dans l'esprit des *fuqahā'*, et on pourrait à cet égard multiplier les citations à l'infini, l'idéal était de maintenir l'*actualité* du *fiqh* en faisant en sorte qu'il y ait toujours contemporanéité entre 'découvrir' et 'dire' le *fiqh*, afin d'empêcher qu'il devienne loisible de le 'répéter'.

4) Arrivé à ce point en empruntant de sérieux raccourcis, un malentendu est déjà possible qu'il convient de dissiper immédiatement. L'écueil que les usûlistes cherchèrent à l'évidence et de manière très radicale à éviter est la *répétition* du *fiqh* des Imams du passé et ce souci prit la forme, je l'ai très brièvement indiqué, d'une critique radicale du conformisme juridique (*taqlīd*).[11] Mais, *répétition* n'est pas *reprise*[12] et si tout ce qui vient d'être évoqué prouve de manière me semble-t-il irréfutable que les usûlistes mirent tout en place afin d'éviter l'écueil de la répétition, la *reprise* d'un *fiqh* déjà élaboré n'était quant à elle pas du tout concernée par cette critique du *taqlīd*. En effet, le *taqlīd* se définit en substance comme l'acceptation non-critique de l'avis d'un autre; est *muqallid* celui qui adopte l'avis d'un autre *sans en connaître la preuve* (*al-taqlīd qubūl al-qawl min ghayr dalīl*).[13] En d'autres termes, le mufti-*mujtahid* n'est nullement critiquable lorsqu'*en connaissance de cause*, il reprend l'avis, le *qawl*, d'un autre *mujtahid* et propose au *mustaftī* une consultation finalement identique à celle, précédemment émise, par ce premier *mujtahid*. Négativement, cela signifie que la critique en forme d'interdiction du *taqlīd* n'implique nullement que le mufti-*mujtahid* soit continuellement dans l'obligation de faire œuvre originale par rapport à ses prédécesseurs (une telle exigence serait en-soi absurde); néanmoins, il reste vrai que cette théorie ménage la possibilité d'innover et cherche à la préserver (au cas, par exemple, où concernant une question donnée, un *mujtahid* aboutit à une conclusion différente de celle de ses prédécesseurs, il est légalement tenu d'affirmer sa propre conclusion). Nous sommes ici directement concernés par cette marge d'innovation et il convient

maintenant de chercher à précisément en définir d'une part la nature et d'autre part les éventuelles limites.

Ijtihād et variabilité de la norme en théorie

1) *Hal kull mujtahid muṣīb*? On vient de voir que dans la théorie légale sunnite classique, l'*ijtihād* s'identifie avec l'indispensable instrument de connaissance des statuts légaux. Si ceux-ci sont, d'une manière ou d'une autre, présents dans le discours du Législateur, l'*ijtihād* prendra la forme de l'herméneutique de ce discours et s'ils en sont absents, celle d'un raisonnement analogique (*qiyās*). Une telle reconnaissance du rôle central de l'*ijtihād* avait une conséquence pratique inévitable et immédiate: l'émergence de conflits d'interprétation du discours légal parmi les *fuqahā'*.[14] Qui dit 'ouverture de la porte de l'*ijtihād*' dit en effet aussitôt 'ouverture de la porte de l'*ikhtilāf*'.

Au regard du thème qui nous occupe dans la seconde partie de ce travail, on voit que l'existence de divergences d'avis (*ikhtilāf*) en matière légale au sein de la Communauté s'est présentée à la réflexion des théoriciens sunnites de la Loi tel un fait accompli et qu'il leur appartenait donc de formuler, théoriquement en aval de la question de l'*ijtihād*, une théorie de ce que j'ai appelé plus haut la variabilité de la norme légale. En termes négatifs, cela signifie qu'il n'y a jamais eu, du côté des usûlistes et des juristes de la période classique, de volonté spontanée de poser la question de la variabilité de la norme en tant que telle. Bien plutôt se devaient-ils de poser et de résoudre cette question en raison de l'une des conséquences, apparemment la moins tolérable par rapport à la leçon de différents versets coraniques,[15] de leur théorie de l'*ijtihād*.

La question précise modelée à cet effet par les théoriciens du *fiqh* sera: *hal kull mujtahid muṣīb?* ('Tout *mujtahid* dit-il juste?'); l'*ikhtilāf* au sein de la Communauté sera justifié si, par le truchement d'une réponse efficace (mais pas nécessairement positive) à cette question, les usûlistes parviennent à montrer qu'au regard du 'plan divin' se manifestant dans la révélation de la *Sharī'a*, un seul et même acte est, d'une manière ou d'une autre, susceptible d'être différemment qualifié d'un point de vue légal (auquel cas l'*ikhtilāf* intestin sera le signe que la réception humaine de la *Sharī'a* est conforme au 'plan divin' en question).[16]

2) *Al-ḥaqq fī wāḥid.* Le premier rapport véritablement complet de cette problématique qui nous soit conservé est, à ma connaissance, celui de Shāfi'ī dans la *Risāla*. Shāfi'ī établit tout d'abord l'obligation

de recourir à l'*ijtihād* en se fondant sur Cor. II, 150 (*wa ḥaythu mā kuntum* ...), verset dans lequel l'une des conditions de validité de la prière est énoncée, à savoir que l'orant prie dans la direction de la *Kaʿba*. L'*ijtihād fī l-qibla* (et, par extension, l'*ijtihād* tout court) est, dit-il en substance, une obligation légale puisqu'en certaines situations, il est impossible de prier dans la direction prescrite sans avoir auparavant fait un 'effort' cognitif pour la déterminer.

Aussitôt après cette démonstration, Shāfiʿī entreprend d'explorer le sens du mot 'justesse' (*ṣawāb*) lorsqu'il s'applique à l'activité du *mujtahid*; ce sens, explique-t-il, est double.[17] D'une part, la *qibla* étant toujours unique où que l'on se trouve, le *mujtahid* est dans le vrai s'il aboutit à la seule solution objectivement vraie qui soit (en ce sens, selon la formule que l'usage consacrera après Shāfiʿī: *al-ḥaqq fī wāḥid*, 'le vrai est en un'), mais, d'autre part, on peut également affirmer que 'tout *mujtahid* dit juste' (même s'il a objectivement tort) dans la mesure où la réponse à l'*ijtihād* envisagé comme un *impératif* légal (*amr*) ne peut pas prendre la forme d'un jugement de vérité. Un impératif implique en effet d'abord *conformité* (*imtithāl*); dès lors, chaque personne concernée par l'ordre d'exercer l'*ijtihād*[18] sera dite *muṣīb* aussitôt qu'elle s'y sera conformée. D'ailleurs, selon un *ḥadīth* bien connu et agréé (*idhā ḥakama al-ḥākim fa-ijtahada* ...) que rapporte Shāfiʿī,[19] l'exercice de l'*ijtihād*, quel que soit son résultat, mérite déjà une récompense dans l'Autre-Monde. De la sorte, l'éventuelle erreur objective du *mujtahid* est dépouillée de sa négativité et l'*ikhtilāf* trouve ainsi sa justification dans la Communauté au cœur du discours du Législateur lui-même.

Ce raisonnement Shāfiʿien, qui est très strictement juridique en ce sens qu'il ne fait appel à aucun argument de nature théologique (il suppose d'entrée de jeu, sans en rendre compte, que, pour le Législateur, 'le vrai est en un'), sera repris plus tard, parfois avec quelques variations formelles peu importantes pour notre propos,[20] par un nombre important d'usûlistes dont, notamment, le ḥanbalite Abū Yaʿlā (m. 458/1066), les shāfiʿites Juwaynī, Shīrāzī et Bayḍāwī (m. 685/1286) ou encore le mālikite Bājī (m. 474/1081).[21] Dans cette perspective, le principe de la variabilité de la norme légale est certes admis, mais c'est par la 'force des choses' et presque par défaut. Puisque, avance Shāfiʿī, l'*ijtihād* est une obligation et puisque l'exercice de l'*ijtihād*, quoique faillible, est toujours marqué d'un signe positif par le Législateur lui-même (en vertu du *ḥadīth* précité), on est tenu d'assumer qu'une *masala ijtihādiyya* peut être résolue de différentes manières malgré qu'on sache par ailleurs que sa réponse est *de jure* unique.

3) *Kull mujtahid muṣīb.* Les muʿtazilites,[22] qui tout en étant avant tout des théologiens élaborèrent aussi leur propre système en matière d'*uṣūl al-fiqh*, vont initier une autre doctrine en guise de réponse à la question de la justesse de l'*ijtihād* et cette doctrine sera également adoptée par le théologien Ashʿarī[23] (il continuera à la soutenir après sa défection des rangs muʿtazilites) et par de nombreux ashʿarites, dont notamment le mālikite Bāqillānī (m. 403/1013)[24] et le shāfiʿite Ghazālī (m. 505/1111)[25] qui eurent une influence considérable en matière d'*uṣūl al-fiqh.*

Selon ces auteurs, l'exemple de l'*ijtihād fī l-qibla* invoqué par Shāfiʿī n'est pas pertinent pour illustrer la question de la justesse de l'*ijtihād* dans la mesure où l'invoquer suppose la question déjà résolue: s'il est entendu qu'un statut légal déterminé préexiste toujours à l'*ijtihād* (ce que suppose l'image de l'*ijtihād fī l-qibla*) et sachant qu'il convient par ailleurs d'accréditer l'existence d'*ikhtilāf* au sein de la Communauté, la question posée ne peut en effet être résolue qu'à la manière shāfiʿienne. Mais, précisément, concernant une *masʾala ijtihādiyya*, peut-on affirmer qu'un statut légal déterminé existe *auprès du Législateur* avant même l'intervention du *mujtahid*, qu'une *qibla* préexiste à tout *ijtihād*? Tel est, selon Ghazālī, qui n'a pas tort, l'objet réel du débat et il y répondra, lui, de manière négative.

A nouveau, il n'est pas question d'évoquer ici le détail de l'argumentation mise au service de la thèse 'des théologiens'[26] selon laquelle on peut sans nuance affirmer que 'tout *mujtahid* dit juste' (d'où le nom de *taṣwīb al-ijtihād* donné à cette thèse). Ghazālī écrit: 'Ce que soutiennent les partisans véridiques de la doctrine du *taṣwīb* est qu'à propos d'un événement que ne concerne aucun énoncé formel (*naṣṣ*),[27] il n'existe pas de statut déterminé (*ḥukm muʿayyan*) qu'il faudrait chercher à connaître au moyen d'une présomption (*ẓann*); au contraire, le statut suit la présomption (*al-ḥukm yattabiʿu a ẓann*) et le Dieu Très-Haut a imposé à tout *mujtahid* [d'adhérer] à ce qui s'impose à sa faculté de présomption (*mā ghalaba ʿalā ẓannihi*); telle est l'option juste et celle que soutenait le Qāḍī Abū Bakr al-Bāqillānī'[28]

4) 'Probabilisme du *fiqh*' et 'relativisme de la *Sharīʿa*'. Nous cherchions à savoir si le principe de la variabilité d'un statut légal issu de la *Sharīʿa* se trouvait accepté d'un point de vue théorique dans la théorie légale sunnite classique. Au sein de celle-ci, on a pu repérer deux perspectives différentes qui débouchent en réalité sur un même résultat. Dans l'un et l'autre cas, il est admis qu'un même acte humain peut être légalement qualifié de différentes manières et, toujours dans

les deux cas, il convient d'affirmer, d'un point de vue pratique cette fois, que le statut légal devant être appliqué à tel acte est toujours celui dont tel *mujtahid* a cru en la validité (même si l'on sait que si tel autre *mujtahid* avait été consulté, le statut proposé aurait peut-être été différent). L'interprétation plurielle des choses de la Loi est incontestablement chose acquise en Islam sunnite.

Pourtant, dans le premier cas (*al-ḥaqq fī wāḥid*), c'est dans le cadre de ce qu'on peut appeler, avec B. G. Weiss, une 'théorie probabiliste du Droit' que la pluralité *doit* être tolérée; l'accent, ici, est massivement mis du côté du *sujet* de l'*ijtihād* et non de son objet, du côté du *mujtahid* et non du *mujtahad fīhi*. *De jure*, la Loi révélée est une; *de facto*, sa compréhension humaine est plurielle parce que son agent, le *mujtahid*, est intrinsèquement faillible (mais en l'occurrence, même son éventuelle erreur sera récompensée).

A première vue, la seconde théorie (*kull mujtahid muṣīb*) paraît beaucoup plus féconde. Ici, la variabilité de la norme légale proposée à la Communauté au travers du choix que possède chacun de ses membres d'adhérer à telle doctrine légale plutôt qu'à telle autre s'explique de manière positive et naturelle dans le cadre d'une 'théorie relativiste de la *Sharīʿa*': si le *fiqh* (la compréhension de la Loi) est multiple, c'est parce que la Loi révélée est elle-même le plus souvent indéterminée et relative. Mais, par rapport au thème de ce travail – '*Ijtihād* et Histoire', rappelons-le – cette théorie rejoint la première dans la mesure où le relativisme de la Loi y est réputé, on l'a vu,[29] fonction de 'la présomption du *mujtahid*' ; ce relativisme légal n'est en réalité nullement conséquent à une quelconque prise en considération ni de la réalité humaine, éventuellement changeante, que le *fiqh* est appelé à régir, ni du contexte historique, et de ses éventuels bouleversements, qui constitue la trame de l'existence humaine.[30]

La question du 'renouvellement de *l'ijtihād*' (*masʾala tajdīd al-ijtihād*)

1) En traitant de la question 'Tout *mujtahid* dit-il juste?', le propos des usûlistes n'était pas, on l'a vu, de s'interroger à propos de l'adéquation ou de l'inadéquation des normes légales avec l'Histoire (et, à vrai dire, il eut été un peu naïf de penser qu'un tel souci aurait pu comme tel faire partie de leurs préoccupations); il s'agissait plutôt pour eux de justifier la pluralité en matière légale et c'est à cette fin qu'ils élaborèrent une théorie de la variabilité de la norme légal. Pourtant, toujours dans le contexte de la problématique de l'*ijtihād* et du *taqlīd*,

nous avions déjà vu poindre une autre inquiétude chez les usûlistes, celle de voir le *fiqh* perdre son *actualité* pour la Communauté présente.

Ceci étant acquis, il est une autre question, de nature immédiatement pratique cette fois, dans laquelle s'articulent les deux traits que je viens d'évoquer (variabilité de la norme légale et volonté de préserver l'actualité du *fiqh*); une question, par conséquent, concernant laquelle on est cette fois plus en droit de penser que des considérations se rapportant au temps et, subsidiairement, à l'espace vont enfin avoir voix au chapitre dans l'argumentation des usûlistes. Cette question, 'quantitativement' peu importante dans la littérature des *uṣūl al-fiqh* (elle retient rarement l'attention des usûlistes plus d'un paragraphe) est celle du 'renouvellement de l'*ijtihād*' (*tajdīd al-ijtihād*). Shīrāzī en formule ainsi l'objet: 'Si [le mufti] a exercé son *ijtihād* à propos d'un événement, que son *ijtihād* l'aie amené à tel statut et qu'ensuite le même événement se produise une autre fois, [le mufti] a-t-il besoin d'[exercer] un nouvel *ijtihād* ou bien donnera-t-il un avis conséquent à son premier *ijtihād*?'[31]

2) Cette question, à l'instar de celle de la justesse de l'*ijtihād*, fut, un temps, controversée avant de faire l'objet d'un quasi consensus. La solution la plus souvent retenue -celle que proposait le mu'tazilite ḥanafite Abū l-Ḥusayn al-Baṣrī (m. 436/1044) à la suite, sans doute, du mu'tazilite shāfi'ite le Qāḍī 'Abd al-Jabbār (m. 415/1025)[32] – se comprend parfaitement dans le cadre du 'subjectivisme' dans lequel, nous l'avons vu, baigne l'ensemble de la théorie sunnite classique de l'*ijtihād*. Simple et logique, cette solution est en substance la suivante: si le *mujtahid* se souvient précisément de 'la voie de son [premier] *ijtihād*' (*ṭarīqa al-ijtihād*) et se rappelle avec autant de netteté de l'avis qu'il avait émis concernant l'événement en question, il n'est pas dans l'obligation de renouveler son *ijtihād* 'car il est alors comme un *mujtahid* en acte (*li-annahu ka-l-mujtahid fī l-ḥāl*)'.[33] En revanche, s'il ne se rappelle pas des 'voies' de son premier *ijtihād*, il est obligé de le renouveler. Jamais, dans aucun des textes consultés pour ce travail, n'est évoqué l'argument, quitte à ce que ce soit pour le contester, selon lequel le renouvellement de l'*ijtihād* pourrait en règle général s'imposer car l'objet de l'*ijtihād* est en réalité l'événement *en situation* (auquel cas, il faudrait d'abord s'intéresser de près à l'*objet* de l'*ijtihād* avant de pouvoir affirmer qu'il s'agit bien du même).

3) Plus originale, et à ma connaissance très isolée,[34] est la réponse que Shīrāzī apporte à la question du *tajdīd al-ijtihād* en se réclamant de

l'exemple du grand shāfi'ite Abū l-Ḥasan al-Qaṭṭān (m. 345/956) 'qui ne donnait *jamais* d'avis à propos d'aucune question tant qu'il n'en avait pas scruté la preuve'.[35] En quelques lignes très 'légalistes' et, en vérité, très shāfi'iennes par le choix de l'illustration, Shīrāzī procède par analogie pour affirmer que l'*ijtihād* est et reste *toujours* une obligation avant de statuer. L'analogie est la suivante: 'l'*ijtihād* est une obligation pour cet événement [en chacune de ses occurrences] comme l'*ijtihād* pour déterminer la *qibla* est une obligation pour chaque prière en cas de difficulté:[36] lorsque [le *mujtahid*] a exercé son *ijtihād* pour déterminer la *qibla* de telle prière et qu'ensuite, le jour suivant, vient l'heure de la même prière, il ne lui est pas permis de la prier dans la direction déterminée par [son] premier *ijtihād* mais il lui est nécessaire d'innover (*aḥdatha*), pour cette prière, un nouvel *ijtihād* et d'agir en conséquence de ce à quoi l'amène son *ijtihād*. Il en va de même pour la question qui nous occupe ici.'[37]

Même si la tentation est grande, notre lecture de ce passage serait trop rapide et forcée si nous en concluions que, pour Shīrāzī et quelques autres, il convient bel et bien de prendre le contexte d'un événement en considération pour statuer sur cet événement. Shīrāzī et Abū Ya'lā font partie du groupe de ces *fuqahā'* pour qui 'le vrai est en un' (*al-ḥaqq fī wāḥid*) – la *qibla* est pour eux toujours unique – et, comme on l'a vu, la reconnaissance de la variabilité de la norme légale trouve alors sa place dans une théorie probabiliste du *fiqh*. Dès lors, s'ils soutiennent la thèse de l'obligation du renouvellement de l'*ijtihād*, c'est en réalité, comme l'indique clairement un passage de Juwaynī, parce qu'ils insistent sur le fait que 'l'*ijtihād* est changeant'[38] et que, par conséquent, il convient de le renouveler. Mais une telle affirmation doit être comprise en un sens très précis: 'l'*ijtihād* est changeant' signifie simplement qu'entre les deux occurrences du même événement, le *mujtahid*, en colloque *solitaire* avec le discours du Législateur, est susceptible d'avoir affiné sa connaissance des preuves légales pertinentes et donc de changer d'avis.[39] A nouveau, la considération de l'événement *en situation* n'entre pour rien dans le changement susceptible d'affecter l'*ijtihād*; il en va toujours comme si l'événement était, lui, donné une fois pour toutes, comme s'il s'agissait d'un objet statique, d'un *invariant*, à l'image de la *qibla*.

Pour conclure

1) Le ton de cette communication fut surtout négatif. J'ai cherché, *primo*, à confirmer qu'il *n*'y eut *pas* de 'fermeture de la porte de

l'*ijtihād*' ni rien d'approchant dans l'ordre légal sunnite classique et surtout, *secundo*, à montrer que l'*ijtihād n*'a *jamais* été conçu comme principe d'adaptation du *fiqh* à l'Histoire. L'*ijtihād* classique, en un mot, *n*'est *pas* ce principe d'évolution du *fiqh* dont tout le monde semble aujourd'hui attendre le réveil pour sortir le *fiqh* de son long sommeil. Rien dans les écrits que nous avons parcourus ne permet de penser que les théoriciens du *fiqh* ont jamais imaginé que quelque chose comme l'adaptation (et donc le changement) d'une norme légal à l'Histoire pût un jour s'avérer soit nécessaire soit souhaitable et ils ne firent *a fortiori* pas de l'*ijtihād* l'instrument d'un tel projet. Ceci signifie en clair que la question de l'inactualité du *fiqh* à l'époque contemporaine ne peut être mise en relation ni avec celle de 'la fermeture de la porte de l'*ijtihād*' (qui est imaginaire), ni, plus simplement, avec celle de l'*ijtihād* comme tel. Ce qui, aujourd'hui, demande instamment à être interrogé, c'est toute l'organisation de l'ordre légal musulman, soit le système *Sharī'a-ijtihād-fiqh* et toutes ses articulations (par la force des choses et dans des limites certaines, une telle réflexion est déjà entamée dans le monde musulman contemporain[40]) et on ne peut s'empêcher, parfois, de penser que la question de 'la fermeture de la porte de l'*ijtihād*' *et* toutes les réponses qui lui ont été apportées fonctionnent aujourd'hui comme un artifice idéologique voilant la nature et l'ampleur du questionnement qui s'impose et vis-à-vis duquel les résistances sont encore tenaces. Je pense pour ma part, en utilisant la langue des usûlistes, que l'objet de ce questionnement se situe du côté des 'fondements', des *uṣūl*, et non du 'subsidiaire', des *furū*', et que son instrument ne pourrait être qu'un *ijtihād* fraîchement et audacieusement redéfini. De prime abord, une telle démarche paraît supposer une prise de distance vis-à-vis de l''Héritage' (*al-turāth*), une rupture avec les Anciens (*al-salaf*), qui, il est vrai, n'ont jamais accepté, d'une part, que les *uṣūl* tombent dans le domaine de l'*ijtihād* tel qu'ils les avaient les uns et l'autre définis,[41] ni, d'autre part, que l'*ijtihād* puisse en arriver, au nom du bien commun (de 'l'intérêt de la création'), à prendre la dimension socio-historique de la condition humaine en considération.

2) Les résultats de notre enquête ne sont pourtant pas tous négatifs. On a vu notamment que si le *fiqh* ne fut pas pensé comme un système normatif appelé à évoluer (au sens contemporain commun de ce terme), pour autant ce ne fut pas non plus un corps de doctrine figé et immuable qui se serait imposé comme tel à un *ijtihād* dont le rôle aurait alors nécessairement été très mince. Plus, pour de nombreux théoriciens, la Loi révélée elle-même n'a pas grand-chose

d'un donné qu'il s'agirait seulement de retrouver par voie d'*ijtihād*; pour ceux-là, l'*ijtihād* avait une fonction véritablement *créatrice* de normes. Ceci mérite d'être médité car alors qu'aujourd'hui la *création* de nouvelles normes s'avère tellement nécessaire, il semblerait que l'idée que l'on puisse s'octroyer la moindre liberté législative par voie d'*ijtihād* soulève des tempêtes ...

Par ailleurs, et j'aimerais insister sur ce point, on a vu aussi que la question de l'*actualité* du *fiqh* pour la Communauté présente n'a jamais cessé de faire partie des préoccupations les plus inquiètes des *fuqahā'*, or tel est aussi le principal souci de leurs coreligionnaires contemporains. Mais la question ne se pose résolument plus de la même manière à ces derniers. Pour les Anciens, il s'agissait seulement, si je puis dire, d'éviter l'écueil de la répétition tout en favorisant une reprise continuelle du passé de telle manière à ce qu'il demeure composé avec le présent. L'*ijtihād* classique tel qu'à grands traits nous l'avons reconnu dans ce travail paraît avoir été, sur le plan du système normatif, l'instrument efficace d'une telle dynamique de reprise. Beaucoup de choses semblent indiquer que les diverses cultures musulmanes sont aujourd'hui animées par un projet formellement identique à celui-là: 'reprendre' leur passé afin d'actualiser les valeurs véhiculées par un système normatif auquel elles restent légitimement profondément attachées. Mais l'*ijtihād* des Anciens n'y suffit plus; en d'autres termes, il appartient, je crois, maintenant aux Modernes de 'reprendre' cet *ijtihād* en le rendant, notamment et surtout, un peu moins indifférent à l'état du monde. On aura compris qu'à mon sens, seule une telle reprise, qui suppose, on l'a vu, une rupture, est susceptible d'éloigner les deux avatars sous la forme desquels survit péniblement le *fiqh* dans la majeure partie du monde musulman contemporain: la forme, d'une part, d'un 'modernisme' juridique vaguement teinté d''islam' et coupé des racines de ses sujets et celle, d'autre part, d'un fondamentalisme étriqué coupé de leur réalité.

Notes

1 La version 'canonique', celle qui est reprise dans la plupart des ouvrages consacrés au Droit musulman et à l'islam en général, de cette représentation a été présentée par J. Schacht, voir J. Schacht, *An Introduction to Islamic Law* (Oxford, 1964), 69–75 et 'Classicisme, traditionalisme et ankylose dans la loi religieuse de l'Islam', dans *Classicisme et déclin culturel dans l'histoire de l'Islam* (Paris, 1977), 141–61.

2 Voir W. B. Hallaq 'Was the Gate of Ijtihād Closed ?', *IJMES* 16 (1984),

3–41; J. van Ess 'La Liberté du juge dans le milieu basrien du VIIIe siècle', dans G. Makdisi, éd., *La Notion de liberté au Moyen-Âge* (Paris, 1985), 25-35 et W. M. Watt 'The Closing of the Door of Ijtihad', *Orientalia Hispanica* (Leiden, 1974), 1, 675-678.

3 Voir É. Chaumont, 'al-Shāfi'iyya', EI2, vol. IX, 191–5.

4 Abū al-Ma'ālī al-Juwaynī, *al-Waraqāt* (Le Caire, 1977), 7; Abū Isḥāq al-Shīrāzī, *al-Luma' fī uṣūl al-fiqh* (Beyrouth, 1985), 6.

5 Ibid., p. 129.

6 Muḥammad b. Idrīs al-Shāfi'ī, *al-Risāla*, (Beyrouth, s.d.), 477, § 1323–6.

7 Sur ce point, voir É. Chaumont 'La Problématique classique de l'*ijtihād* et la question de l'*ijtihād* du Prophète', *SI* 75 (1992), 105–12 surtout.

8 La complémentarité des notions de *fiqh* et d'*ijtihād* présente dans la langue technique des juristes est à l'image de celle qui leur appartient 'dans la langue commune' (*fī l-lugha*) où le premier terme désigne la 'compréhension' lorsque son objet est réputé 'subtil et obscur' et le second un 'effort soutenu' (ainsi un *ijtihād* est-il nécessaire pour aboutir à un *fiqh*), voir al-Shīrāzī, *Sharḥ al-luma'* (2 vols., Beyrouth, 1988), vol. 1, 157–8, § 22.

9 Dans cette perspective, la mise en œuvre par le juriste de l'un ou l'autre des principes herméneutiques définis dans la science des *uṣūl al-fiqh* (*takhṣīṣ*, *ta'wīl al-ẓāhir*, etc.) afin de découvrir le *fiqh* relève pleinement de l'*ijtihād*, sur ce point, voir, par ex., al-Juwaynī, *al-Burhān fī uṣūl al-fiqh* (2 vols., Le Caire, 1980), vol. 2, 748, § 685, où al-Juwaynī récuse la définition shāfi'ienne du *qiyās* par l'*ijtihād* et *Luma'*, p. 96, où, dans le même esprit, al-Shīrāzī écrit que 'l'*ijtihād* est plus général (*a'amm*) que le *qiyās*'.

10 La 'consultation' (*al-iftā*) est, en Islam, le mode privilégié d'énonciation de la norme légale. Le *mustaftī* (le 'consultant'), qui se définit par le fait qu'il ne connaît pas 'les voies de l'*ijtihād*' (en d'autres termes, le 'profane' [*al-'āmmī*] en matière légale, soit la grande majorité des membres de la Communauté), se trouve dans l'obligation de 'consulter' un *muftī* (le 'consulté'), lequel se définit inversément comme un savant versé dans la connaissance de la Loi (qualité très codifiée), lorsqu'il ignore le statut légal de la panoplie d'actes qu'il est susceptible d'accomplir en telle ou telle circonstance lui advenant. L'*iftā* a été théorisé, d'une part, dans la littérature des *uṣūl al-fiqh*, et, d'autre part, dans une littérature spécifique (ainsi, par ex., le célèbre *Adab al-muftī wa l-mustaftī* d'Ibn al-Ṣalāḥ).

11 Il est bien entendu qu'il est ici question du *taqlīd al-'ālim li-l-'ālim*, c'est-à-dire du cas où c'est le savant-*mujtahid* lui-même qui adopte l'attitude du *muqallid* vis-à-vis d'un autre savant. Le profane (*al-'āmmī*) quant à lui reste dans l'obligation de se conformer à l'avis d'un *mujtahid*; seule manière pour lui, qui n'est pas versé dans la connaissance de la Loi, d'avoir accès au *fiqh*.

12 J'emprunte cette distinction entre *répétition* et *reprise* à S. Kierkegaard, *La Reprise*, trad. N. Viallaneix (Paris, 1990), 56–8 (les remarques de la traductrice).

13 al-Shīrāzī, *Luma'*, p. 125.

14 C'est sous cet angle *ijtihād*/*ikhtilāf* que j'ai, dans un travail récent, abordé

cette question: "Tout chercheur qualifié dit-il juste?' (*hal kull mujtahid muṣīb*). La question controversée du fondement de la légitimité de la controverse en islam', dans A. Le Boulluec, éd., *La Controverse religieuse et ses formes* (Paris, 1995), 11–27. Je me permets de renvoyer le lecteur à cet article pour une argumentation plus rigoureuse de différentes affirmations reprises ici.

15 Coran 3:19; 4:82; 42:13; 98:4 sont autant de versets mis en évidence par, notamment, le juriste ismaélien al-Nuʿmān b. Muḥammad (m. 351/962) en tant qu'ils paraissent contester la légitimité de la divergence au sein de la Communauté, voir al-Nuʿmān b. Muḥammad (al-Qāḍī), *Ikhtilāf uṣūl al-madhāhib* (Beyrouth, 1983), 28–30.

16 Justifier l'*ikhtilāf* avait une visée pratique importante puisqu'il s'agissait surtout de montrer, face à la critique notamment ismaélienne, que l'institutionalisation de différentes 'voies' (*madhāhib*) réputées également 'orthopraxes' de compréhension et d'application de la Loi révélée était légitime au regard de cette dernière. Le lien entre cette problématique 'théorique' et la question des *madhāhib* apparaît clairement dans, par exemple, un argument développé par al-Shīrāzī en *al-Tabṣira fī uṣūl al-fiqh* (Damas, 1980), 509.

17 al-Shāfiʿī, *Risāla*, pp. 497–503, § 1422–55.

18 Rappelons qu'à l'instar du *jihād* (l'effort guerrier entrepris pour la cause de Dieu), l'*ijtihād* est rangé par la grande majorité des juristes dans la catégorie des 'devoirs communautaires' (*furūḍ al-kifāya*), soit une obligation légale dont la plus grande partie de la Communauté est dispensée dès lors que certains de ses membres la prennent en charge de manière telle que la finalité du devoir en question est 'suffisamment' réalisée (littéralement, l'expression *farḍ kifāya* signifie 'devoir de suffisance').

19 Voir al-Shāfiʿī, *Jimāʿ al-ʿilm* (Beyrouth, s.d.), 33, § 163; al-Shāfiʿī, *Kitāb al-Umm*, 7 vols (Le Caire, s.d.), vol. 7, 85. Pour le *ḥadīth* en question, voir A. J. Wensinck et al., *Concordance et Indices de la Tradition Musulmane* (Leiden, 1936), vol. 1, 20.

20 Pour un exposé plus détaillé des thèses en présence, voir al-Juwaynī, *Kitāb al-ijtihād (min Kitāb al-talkhīṣ)* (Damas/Beyrouth, 1987), 27–31 ou Abū al-Ḥusayn al-Baṣrī, *Sharḥ al-ʿumad* (2 vols., Médine/Le Caire, 1989), vol. 2, 235–9.

21 Voir respectivement Abū Yaʿlā (al-Qāḍī), *al-ʿUdda fī uṣūl al-fiqh* (5 vols, Beyrouth, 1980, [1–3] et Riyad, 1990 [4–5]), vol. 5, pp.1541–73; al-Juwaynī, *Waraqāt*, p. 31; al-Shīrāzī, *Lumaʿ*, p.129–31; ʿAbd Allāh al-Bayḍāwī, *Minhāj al-wuṣūl fī maʿrifat ʿilm al-uṣūl* (Beyrouth, 1985), 269-70; Abū al-Walīd al-Bājī, *Iḥkām al-fuṣūl fī aḥkām al-uṣūl* (Beyrouth, 1986), 707–21, § 768–82.

22 Les autorités les plus souvent citées dans le cadre de ce débat appartiennent à la branche baṣrienne de l'école muʿtazilite: Abū l-Hudhayl al-ʿAllāf (m. 226/840–1 ou 235/849–50), Abū ʿAlī al-Jubbāʾī (m. 303/915–6), son fils Abū Hāshim (m. 321/933) et le Qāḍī ʿAbd al-Jabbār (m. 415/1025), voir par exemple al-Baṣrī, *Sharḥ al-ʿumad*, vol. 2, p. 238.

23 D'aprés, notamment, Ibn Fūrak, *Mujarrad maqālāt al-shaykh abī l-Ḥasan*

al-Ashʿarī (Beyrouth, 1987), 201. Voir aussi pourtant Sayf al-Dīn al-Āmidī, *al-Iḥkām fī uṣūl al-aḥkām* (4 vols, Beyrouth, 1984), vol. 4, 190.

24 Voir al-Juwaynī, *Kitāb al-ijtihād*, pp. 23–72.

25 Voir Abū Ḥāmid al-Ghazālī, *al-Mustaṣfā min ʿilm al-uṣūl* (2 vols, Dār al-fikr, s.l.n.d.; reproduction de l'éd. Būlāq, 1322–4/1904–6), vol. 2, 363–75.

26 Cette doctrine est en effet souvent attribuée, sans autre précision, aux 'théologiens' (*al-mutakallimūn*) alors que la première l'est, de façon aussi peu nuancée, aux 'juristes' (*al-fuqahā*), voir, par ex., ʿAlī et Tāj al-Dīn al-Subkī, *al-Ibhāj fī sharḥ al-minhāj* (3 vols, Beyrouth, 1984), vol. 3, 258. Sur ce point, voir la remarque de D. Gimaret, *La doctrine d'al-Ashʿarī* (Paris, 1990), 519.

27 Un tel fait constitue l'objet d'une *masʾala ijtihādiyya*. A propos du terme technique *naṣṣ* ('énoncé formel', et non 'texte'), voir, par ex., al-Shīrāzī, *Lumaʿ*, p. 48: *fa-l-naṣṣ kull lafẓ dalla ʿalā l-ḥukm bi-ṣarīḥihi ʿalā wajh lā iḥtimāl fīhi* ('le *naṣṣ*, c'est tout énoncé indiquant expressément le statut comme tel de façon qu'aucune indétermination ne le concerne'). Tous les usûlistes s'accordent pour reconnaître que les énoncés-*naṣṣ* sont très rares dans le discours légal.

28 al-Ghazālī, *Mustaṣfā*, vol. 2, p. 363.

29 Voir *supra*, l'énoncé ghazālien de la thèse du *taṣwīb al-ijtihād* (*al-ḥukm yattabiʿu al-ẓann*).

30 On pourrait ici faire l'objection qu'une 'psychologie' (au sens aristotélicien du terme) du *mujtahid*, et plus généralement du sujet musulman, devrait être esquisée avant de s'autoriser ce type de jugement. Il n'en est rien dans la mesure où la qualité de *mujtahid* fut très rigoureusement définie par les usûlistes (voir, par ex., Shīrāzī, *Lumaʿ*, p. 127) et qu'aucune des conditions de cette qualité ne concerne autre chose que la connaissance des preuves légales.

31 al-Shīrāzī, *Sharḥ al-lumaʿ*, vol. 2, p. 1035–6, § 1186.

32 Voir al-Baṣrī, *Sharḥ al-ʿumad*, vol.2, p. 314 et al-Baṣrī, *al-Muʿtamad fī uṣūl al-fiqh*, 2 vols (Damas, 1963), vol. 2, 932–3. Parmi les partisans de cette thèse, citons aussi al-Juwaynī (*Burhān*, vol. 2, pp. 1343–4, § 1517-8), Abū al-Khaṭṭāb al-Kalwadhānī, *al-Tamhīd fī uṣūl al-fiqh* (4 vols, La Mecque, 1985), vol. 4, 394, et Fakhr al-Dīn al-Rāzī, *al-Maḥṣūl fī ʿilm al-uṣūl* (6 vols, Beyrouth, 1992), vol. 6, 69–70.

33 al-Baṣrī, *Muʿtamad*, vol. 2, p. 932.

34 A côté de al-Shīrāzī, seul, à ma connaissance, le Qāḍī Abū Yaʿlā soutiendra également ce point de vue, voir Abū Yaʿlā, *ʿUdda*, vol. 4, p. 1228.

35 al-Shīrāzī, *Sharḥ al-lumaʿ*, vol. 2, p. 1037, § 1187.

36 Le second manuscrit utilisé pour l'éd. du *Sharḥ al-lumaʿ* donne *ʿinda l-imkān*: 'lorsque c'est possible'.

37 Ibid., vol. 2, p. 1036, § 1186.

38 al-Juwaynī, *Burhān*, vol. 2, p.1343, § 1517. La teneur de cet argument ('l'*ijtihād* est changeant') n'était contestée par personne mais la majorité n'y voyait pas un argument probant en la matière, cf. al-Shīrāzī, *Sharḥ al-lumaʿ*, vol. 2, p. 1036, § 1187.

39 Voir al-Āmidī, *Iḥkām*, vol. 4, p. 238.

40 A ce propos, voir le livre récent de B. Botiveau, *Loi islamique et droit dans les sociétés arabes* (Paris, 1993), chap. 3, 4 et 5 (103–89) surtout.

41 Sur ce point, voir, au début soit du chapitre consacré à l'*ijtihād*, soit de celui consacré au *taqlīd* de tout traité d'*uṣūl al-fiqh*, la détermination du champ de l'*ijtihād* dont les *uṣūl* sont invariablement écartés; ainsi, par exemple, al-Rāzī, *Maḥṣūl*, vol. 6, p. 27.

TWO

Akhbārī Shīʿī *uṣūl al-fiqh* and the Juristic Theory of Yūsuf b. Aḥmad al-Baḥrānī

ROBERT GLEAVE

Introduction

The Sunni debates surrounding the existence of *mujtahids* and the closing of the gate of *ijtihād* have not, in general, troubled Shīʿī writers of *uṣūl al-fiqh*. Since the time of ʿAllāma al-Ḥillī, the dominant school of Shīʿī jurisprudence, the Uṣūlīs, have maintained, that unlike the Sunnis, their legal system has continued to develop and avoid stagnation because of the continued use of *ijtihād* by Shīʿī jurists. Such a characterisation of Sunni legal thought operated within a Shīʿī-Sunni polemic and its accuracy is questionable, but this is of minor significance when trying to gain an understanding of the development of Shīʿī jurisprudence. The support for *ijtihād* by Shīʿī jurists was not unanimous. *Ijtihād* was not without its detractors in the Shiʿite tradition. From the seventeenth century, and possibly earlier, there existed a section of the scholarly elite who resisted the practice of *ijtihād*. These scholars did not resist *ijtihād* because they believed that all the substantial legal problems had been solved (as the Sunnis supposedly did). Their resistance arose from a rejection of the necessity of *ijtihād* because the texts of revelation, the Qurʾān and the *sunna* (which in Shiʿism includes the *akhbār* of the Imams), were considered equal to the task of providing rulings for novel situations. The scholars who maintained this position were soon named the Akhbārī school, and between the seventeenth and nineteenth century Uṣūlīs and Akhbārīs argued with each other with an invective that occasionally spilled over into intra-community violence. This paper examines the juristic thought of one of these Akhbārī thinkers, Shaykh Yūsuf b. Aḥmad al-Baḥrānī (d.1186/1772).

Akhbarism has proved difficult to define. Western scholars have given widely differing accounts of the nature of the *akhbāriyyūn*. Madelung[1] and Newman[2] see the dispute as having a long history, stretching back to the earliest twelver Shīʿī thinkers. Akhbarism is seen, by Newman at least, as a 'school' with a distinct set of beliefs, encompassing both matters of law and theology (*fiqh* and *uṣūl al-dīn* respectively). Amongst these beliefs was a rejection of reason, a distrust of interpretative practices and an anti-hierarchical stance. The latter manifested itself in a limitation of the role of *fuqahāʾ* in the collection and distribution of *khums* and *zakāt*, the leading of Friday Prayer and the administration of justice. Associated with these doctrines, there was, it is claimed, a negative view of any government during the occultation of the twelfth Imam. Conversely, Kohlberg[3] and Calder[4] see the dispute as beginning only with the person of Muḥammad Amīn al-Astarābādī (d.1033/1623) and his work *al-Fawāʾid al-madaniyya*. In *al-Fawāʾid*, Astarābādī is said to have criticised Shīʿī scholars who resorted to *ijtihād* in order to discover legal rulings on matters not covered by Qurʾān and *sunna*. *Ijtihād* is considered to be the central element in the dispute between Akhbārīs and Uṣūlīs: Akhbārīs rejected *ijtihād*, Uṣūlīs accepted it.[5]

Baḥrānī was born in Bahrain, travelled throughout the Arabian peninsula, but was forced, at a young age, to leave the area as a result of tribal unrest. He travelled first to Iran, and later settled in Najaf, where he taught in the *madrasas* there. He wrote many works on both law and theology, the most famous being *al-Ḥadāʾiq al-Nāḍira*[6], a twenty-five volume work of *furūʿ al-fiqh*. His position within the dispute is somewhat unclear. Some biographical sources describe him as an Akhbārī, though not an 'extremist' (*mutaʿaṣṣib*), who aimed to reduce tension between the two groups. Other sources describe him as an ex-Akhbārī, who left Akhbarism for a 'middle path' (*ṭarīqa wusṭā*) after becoming dissatisfied with the bitterness of the Akhbārī polemic. In both sets of sources he is viewed in a positive light. This is more likely to be a reflection of the manner in which authors of biographical dictionaries aim to incorporate troublesome but important figures into tradition, than a comment on the validity of his legal system for later thinkers.[7]

Western scholars' definitions of the Akhbārī-Uṣūlī dispute differ significantly from Baḥrānī's own depiction of the conflict. His description of the points of difference between the two parties is found in one of the prologues (*muqaddimāt*) which preface the *Ḥadāʾiq*. In the twelfth and last of these *muqaddimas* he lists the main points of difference between Akhbārīs and *mujtahids*. Throughout the *muqaddimas* he rarely uses the term Uṣūlī or *uṣūliyyūn*, preferring instead the term *mujtahid*. This, it could be argued, demonstrates that Baḥrānī considers *ijtihād* as the central point of difference between the two groups. At times, he also uses the term *muḥaddithūn*, in preference to *akhbāriyyūn*, to describe the opponents of the *mujtahids*. The ambiguity in terminology might indicate a desire to move away from the sterile dichotomies of Akhbārī and Uṣūlī which had dominated Shīʿī thought in the previous two centuries.

Baḥrānī's principal argument involves the claim that Akhbārīs and *mujtahids* have existed throughout Shīʿī history. Though their opinions have differed, they have lived together as mutually acceptable schools (*madhhab*) within the Shīʿī *ikhtilāf*. Baḥrānī does, however, give some preference to the Akhbārīs, since, he claims, the earliest Shīʿī scholars, such as Muḥammad b. Yaʿqūb al-Kulaynī (d.328/939) and Shaykh al-Ṣadūq Ibn Babūya (d. 381/991) were Akhbārīs. This claim to an historical pedigree should not necessarily be taken as proof that Akhbarism existed in the earliest period of Shīʿī history. It is only evidence that Baḥrānī wishes to demonstrate that Akhbarism has such an historical pedigree. As will become clear, he has good reasons for wishing to demonstrate that Akhbarism was the original Shiʿite creed and that the *mujtahid* ideas were a later development, possibly an innovation.

The mutual acceptance of Akhbārīs and *mujtahids* all changed with the work of Muḥammad Amīn al-Astarābādī:

> The voice of dispute was not raised until … the time of the author of *al-Fawāʾid al-Madaniyya.* He let loose the tongue of insult upon the *aṣḥāb* and went on at great length about it; he was constantly [making] extreme statements which were not fitting for one of the great *ʿulamāʾ* such as he – even if he was right in many of the questions he addressed in that book.[8]

For Baḥrānī, then, Astarābādī was correct in much of his juristic theory, and hence is praised as 'one of the great *ʿulamāʾ*'. However, he was guilty of being over-zealous in his criticism of the *mujtahids* and introducing a bitter tone into the productive intellectual debate which had existed previously:

> [The dispute] has caused *ʿulamāʾ* of both sides to insult one another and hold one another in contempt as they slander each other[9] … the earliest period was full of *muḥaddiths* and *mujtahids*, although the voice of dispute was not raised amongst them. They did not insult one another, or call each other these names; even if they disagreed with one another in some matters and in the ordering of proofs.[10]

The differences between the camps were real differences. However, they were viewed as acceptable in the past, and so, for Baḥrānī, they should be viewed as acceptable in the present and future.

Baḥrānī delineates three differences between Akhbārīs and Uṣūlīs:

> The clearest thing that is claimed is that for the *mujtahids* there are four sources of law: *kitāb*, *sunna*, *ijmāʿ* and *dalīl al-ʿaql* – *dalīl al-ʿaql* refers to *al-barāʾat al-aṣliyya at* and *al-istiṣḥāb*. For the Akhbārīs, only the first two [are sources]. In this area there is a clear difference …
>
> Also amongst the differences which they mention is that for the Akhbārīs things are divided into three: *ḥalāl* things are clear, *ḥarām* things are clear and in between them are doubtful things (*shubha*). For the *mujtahids* there are only the first two. On this point there is also real dispute …
>
> Another difference which is often mentioned is that the search for proofs from the Book and the *sunna* was specific to the Akhbārīs. However, the Akhbārīs themselves differ over this. Amongst them is Astarābādī, who was the reviver (*mujaddid*) of the Akhbārī school in the recent period. He, in his book *al-Fawāʾid al-Madaniyya*, says it is not permitted to derive anything from the Book unless it is found in the *tafsīr* of the Imams. Others restrict [themselves] to acting upon the *muḥkamāt* (clear verses) of the Qurʾān; others still oppose this to the point where they are almost like the Imams themselves in terms of explaining the *mutashābihāt* (unclear verses).[11]

There are then differences between Akhbārīs and *mujtahids*, but there are also differences within each camp. Baḥrānī describes only three differences:

1. the number of sources of law (the Akhbārīs say two; the *mujtahids*, four)
2. whether *shubha* is a category (the Akhbārīs say it is; the *mujtahids* say it is not)
3. whether the Qurʾān can be understood only with the *tafsīr* of the Imams (some Akhbārīs say the *tafsīr* of the Imams is necessary, others say that one can understand some verses without the Imams; the *mujtahids* say that if the Qurʾān is unclear one can look to other sources such as *sunna*, *ijmāʿ* and *dalīl al-ʿaql* for alternative proofs).

Interestingly, attitudes towards *ijtihād* are not mentioned as a difference between the two groups. In the other main description of the dispute, the forty points of difference between Akhbārīs and *mujtahids* by ʿAbd Allāh al-Samāhijī (d.1135/1723), *ijtihād* is the first difference[12], and indeed in Baḥrānī's other description of the conflict, in *al-Durur al-Najafiyya*, it is one of eight differences he lists there.[13] The reason for this omission is unclear, though it is possible that

Baḥrānī was attempting to reduce tension by not mentioning *ijtihād*. *Ijtihād* had been the focus of much debate since Astarābādī, not all of it conducted in a manner Baḥrānī felt was helpful. By avoiding the mention of *ijtihād*, he may have hoped to avoid a resurgence in intra-community conflict.

One important reason why these three differences are described by Baḥrānī in *muqaddima* 12 is that the other eleven *muqaddimas* are a clear attempt to describe his own position on these issues.

An analysis of the sources of law is carried out in *muqaddimas* 1 to 3. Here Baḥrānī gives his own opinion on the first difference, that of the number of legitimate sources of law. In *muqaddimas* 4 to 6, the areas of uncertainty (*shubhāt*) are examined, and the means of eliminating this uncertainty are described. These *muqaddimas* are evidence of Baḥrānī's position *vis-à-vis* the second difference. Finally, in *muqaddimas* 7 to 11, he examines how the words in the documents of revelation are to be interpreted and whether any other source apart from the *akhbār* can aid in this interpretation, hence providing a position with regard to the third difference outlined above.

That the three issues of dispute correspond to the three sets of *muqaddimas* is clear. This paper will describe Baḥrānī's *uṣūl al-fiqh*, through an examination of his own position on these three issues. Baḥrānī is subtly presenting his views on the Akhbārī-*mujtahid* dispute, and from these *muqaddimas* we can find an indication of whether Baḥrānī considered himself to be an Akhbārī or not.

The Nature and Use of the Sources of Law.

Muqaddimas 1 and 2 concentrate on *sunna* as a source of law. In Shīʿī *fiqh*, the *sunna* is both the *ḥadīths* of the Prophet and the *akhbār* of the Imams. *Muqaddima* 3 deals with Qurʾān, *ijmāʿ* and *dalīl al-ʿaql*. As becomes clear, the fact that *sunna* receives two *muqaddimas* and the other three supposed sources only one between them is significant. The sequence of *sunna*, Qurʾān, *ijmāʿ* and *dalīl al-ʿaql* also indicates that the *sunna* holds a position of overriding importance compared to the other sources.

In *muqaddima* 1, Baḥrānī seeks to demonstrate that any apparent contradiction between the two or more *khabars* is not due to one being sound and the other weak. The contradictions are due solely to the existence of *taqiyya*, the established Shīʿī practice of dissimulation whereby it is permitted for an Imam or a believer to hide his true faith when revealing it might expose him to oppression.[14]

Baḥrānī's opponents are not given a collective name. They are referred to as 'some of our colleagues (*aṣḥāb*)' or a 'section of our *ʿulamā*''. The opponents trace the contradictions (*taʿāruḍāt*) within the *sunna* to either *taqiyya* or the relative 'soundness' (*ṣiḥḥa*) of the *akhbār*. Baḥrānī accepts only the first cause, and also expands the number of *akhbār* which might be considered *taqiyya*-generated.

The opponents argue that all *taqiyya akhbar* are easily identified: 'Our colleagues favour a *taqiyya*-interpretation when the questioner is from the Sunnis'.[15] Hence the faith of the questioner is the crucial factor determining the classification of a *khabar*. If he is discovered to be a Sunni, then the Imam was practising *taqiyya* and the *ḥukm* contained in the *khabar* is not a true reflection of the *aḥkām sharʿiyya*. It may, however be a reflection of the Imam's advice to a believer who is living in circumstances which require *taqiyya*.

Baḥrānī is clearly dissatisfied with the assertion that the only criterion for determining a *taqiyya ḥadīth* is the faith of the questioner. He quotes five *akhbār* from the collections of Kulaynī and Shaykh al-Ṭā'ifa Muḥammad b. Ḥasan al-Ṭūsī (d.460/1067). In all of these *akhbār* the Imam is asked a question by a succession of Shiʿite believers, and in each case gives a different answer. Since all the answers cannot be correct, some of them must have been revealed under *taqiyya*. The first *khabar* is followed by an exegetical comment:

Khabar:

Amongst the (*akhbār*) which prove this position [vis-à-vis *taqiyya*] is the *mawaththaq* of Zurāra from Abū Jaʿfar. He says: 'I asked [the Imam] a question and he gave me an answer. Then a man came to him and asked the same question. However, he gave a different answer to that which he had given me. Then another man came and he gave yet another answer, different to mine and the first man's. When the two men had left I said: 'Oh descendent of the Prophet of God! Two men from your Shīʿa in Iraq came and you gave them each a different answer.'

He said, 'Oh Zurāra! This is a good deed for us and is for your preservation. If you agree on a matter, then the people will associate you with us [the Imams] and our life and your life will be shortened.'[16]

Exegetical comment:

I see the clear meaning of this *khabar* and the different answers he gave to one question in the same session (*majlis*), and the amazement of Zurāra. If the differences (*ikhtilāf*) only occurred in order that the Imams might agree with the Sunnis, then one answer would have been enough. This was why Zurāra was amazed. He knew that the Imams, from time to time, gave *fatwās* because of *taqiyya*, which were in agreement with the Sunnis.

> Perhaps the secret of this *khabar* is that if the Shīʿa left the Imams with different opinions, each one relating something different from the next person concerning his Imam, then, in the sight of the Sunnis, their *madhhab* would be foolish; they would accuse them of lying in their transmission; they would say 'they are ignorant and irreligious' and in the Sunnis' view, they would be of little importance. On the other hand, if their words agreed, and their statements concurred, then the Sunnis' would take them seriously; their hatred for the Imāmiyya, their Imams and their creed would harden, and this would cause an eruption of enmity.[17]

This, for Baḥrānī, proves that the Imams gave *taqiyya* answers to both Sunni and Shīʿī questions. By proving this, he reduces the number of insoluble contradictions within the *akhbār*, and affirms the position that all the *akhbār* are historically accurate accounts of the Imams' words, but may not be true reflections of the *aḥkām sharʿiyya.*

The other supposed cause of contradictions is that some of the *akhbār* are fabricated:

> They [the unnamed opponents] think that the differences only occur because of the surreptitious inclusion of 'the *akhbār* of liars' in our *akhbār;* hence they use this technique in order to differentiate the *ṣaḥīḥ akhbār* from the faulty ones and the healthy ones from the unhealthy ones.[18]

Whether a *khabar* is *ṣaḥīḥ*, or one of the other categories, is dependent upon the validity of the *isnād*. As in Sunni jurisprudence, *akhbār* required a sound chain of transmission. A chain could be verified by the examination of its members' lives and characters. This information is gained through the consultation of *rijāl* works.

Baḥrānī claims that *isnād* criticism is unnecessary because, in his view, all the books of *akhbār* have their own pedigree which ensures their reliability. According to Baḥrānī, the Imams' utterances were originally committed to writing by the authors of the four hundred *uṣūl* (collections of sayings). These works were checked by the Imams themselves and any errors were eliminated. This is proven by the citation of a *khabar* from Yūnus ʿAbd al-Raḥmān found in Kashshī's *Rijāl*. In the *khabar* it is related how Yūnus used to travel throughout Iraq collecting *akhbār*. He presented his findings to Imam Riḍā who would then reject unsound *akhbār*.

For Baḥrānī, the four hundred *uṣūl* were preserved by the early Shīʿa. They were checked for accuracy by the Imams before the *ghayba* and by the companions after the *ghayba*:

> [The Imams] are the preservers of the *Sharīʿa* ... They have delegates in this [task] from members of the trustworthy *aṣḥāb* and the selected ones

from the transmitters. [The Imams] enlightened them with their secrets of the *aḥkām*, and they set them [the selected ones] right upon the nature of what is *ḥalāl* and *ḥarām*.[19]

Baḥrānī therefore constructs a chain of transmission for the books of *akhbār* as a whole. The Imams verified the four hundred *uṣūl*, and it was these that the *ḥadīth* collectors such as Kulaynī, Ibn Babūya and Shaykh al-Ṭūsī used to compose their collections. In this manner, Baḥrānī nullifies the objections of his opponents who believe that fabricated *akhbār* were 'surreptitiously' included in the *akhbār*. He quotes from the writings of these scholars to support his claim.

According to Baḥrānī's schema, a contradiction between two *khabars* can only be due to *taqiyya*. One must, therefore, determine which are *taqiyya akhbār*, by a process of preference (*tarjīḥ*):

Perhaps, with the help of this [evidence], you can know that the preference between *akhbār* (*tarjīḥ*) on the basis of *taqiyya*, after a comparison with the Holy Book, is the strongest means of making a preference. For most, no all of the *ikhtilāf* that occur in our *akhbār*, after some consideration and examination, have come about because of *taqiyya*. Because of this, doubt is now cast upon [the opinion of] the group of our modern scholars.[20]

Muqaddima 2 continues in the same vein, but with the specific aim of refuting the convention of 'dividing the *akhbār* into four categories' in descending order of soundness from *ṣaḥīḥ* (sound), *ḥasan*, *mawaththaq* to *ḍaʿīf* (weak). According to Baḥrānī, this convention (*iṣṭilāḥ*) was practised by a 'group of modern scholars' including Shaykh al-Bahāʾī, Muḥammad b. Ḥusayn (d.1031/1622) and Ḥasan b. al-Shahīd al-Thānī (d.966/1558). It was introduced into Shīʿī *fiqh* by ʿAllāma and Ibn Ṭāwūs (d.664/1266). Baḥrānī considers all these scholars to be 'modern' (*mutaʾakhkhir*); the modern period for Baḥrānī has an impressive scope, stretching back six hundred years. For him, the thought of the Shīʿī thinkers of the earliest period is given preference over later innovations.

Baḥrānī mentions this as a specific issue of dispute between Akhbārīs and *mujtahids*. He claims that he is following a middle path (*ṭarīqa wusṭā*) though his arguments lead to a rejection of the four-fold classification, and hence concur with the Akhbārī position. In *muqaddima* 2 he re-iterates two of his arguments in *muqaddima* 1. These are the prevalence of *taqiyya* and the sound chain of transmission from the Imams to the collectors of the four books of *akhbār*. His one additional argument is a rejection of the science of *ʿilm al-rijāl*.

The classification of the *akhbār* is based upon the findings of *ʿilm al-rijāl*. *ʿIlm al-rijāl* is unnecessary because the compilers of the four hundred *uṣūl* and subsequently the four books of *akhbār* were scrupulously careful in their selection of *akhbār*. Furthermore, the works of *rijāl*, upon which *isnād* criticism is based, are unavoidably flawed:

> You know that there was a long time between the writers of those books [of *rijāl*] and the *rāwīs* of the *akhbār*. How were they informed about their lives, which are the basis upon which they call them just or unjust?[21]

The time which elapsed between the *rāwīs* lives and the *rijāl* writers is such that, for Baḥrānī, doubt is cast on their reliability. Finally, Baḥrānī argues, the *rijāl* writers contradict one another. One is left in the confusing position where a *rāwī* is sound (*thiqa*) for one and unsound (*kadhdhāb*) for another.

In the arguments in *muqaddimas* 1 and 2, Baḥrānī is constructing an epistemological topology which informs all of his *uṣūl al-fiqh*. *Ḥadīth* are either *ṣaḥīḥ* or *ḍaʿīf*, a *ḥukm* is either certain or it is not. Knowledge of the *Sharīʿa* must belong to the first category and not the second, that is, it must reach the highest level of certainty (*ʿilm*). Dividing the *akhbār* into four categories introduces unnecessary levels of uncertainty for Baḥrānī, and is therefore rejected.

It is also significant that Baḥrānī expands those *akhbār* which can be considered *ṣaḥīḥ* to include those not found in the four canonical books. In the final section of *muqaddima* 2, he describes as sound *akhbār* from other early books of *akhbār*. He quotes from Niʿmat Allāh al-Jazāʾirī (a reputed Akhbārī d.1112/1700) as evidence of this:

> The truth is that the four *uṣūl* [the four canonical books] do not contain all the *aḥkām* in their totality. Rather we have found many *aḥkām* in other [books], like the *Akhbār al-Riḍā*, *al-Āmālī*, *kitāb al-Iḥtijāj* and others.[22]

He also cites Muḥammad Bāqir al-Majlisī (d.1111/1700) as supporting this position, since he used such extra-canonical sources in his compilation of the *Biḥār al-Anwār*.

The *akhbār* are, for Baḥrānī, a much wider corpus of material than for his opponents. All the *akhbār* in the four books are sound and the criticism of *isnāds* has been rejected. There are also *akhbār* not found in the four books which are considered sound. By defining this portion of revelatory material in as wide a manner as possible, Baḥrānī restricts those areas of the law for which there is no *dalīl*. These areas had previously been the domain of the other sources of law, i.e. the domain of *ijtihād*, where *ẓann* took over from *ʿilm*. By reducing these areas and by expanding revelatory material, Baḥrānī is restricting the possibility of engaging in independent reasoning or using reason (*ʿaql*) to discover *sharʿī* rulings.

Muqaddima 3 contains Baḥrānī's arguments concerning *kitāb* (i.e. the Qurʾān), *ijmāʿ* and *dalīl al-ʿaql*. His thoughts on *kitāb* involve a rejection of three other positions: one held by the *mujtahids* and two held by different groups of the Akhbārīs. For *mujtahids*, the Qurʾān is a limited source of the *Sharīʿa* because it only contains five hundred verses which refer to legal rulings (*aḥkām*); on matters beyond these five hundred verses, the other sources – *sunna*, *ijmāʿ* and *dalīl al-ʿaql* – are employed. The Akhbārīs divide into two groups. First, there are those who say that the Qurʾān can only be understood with reference to the *akhbār*. It is not an independent source, but can only be viewed through the prism of the *akhbār*. The other Akhbārī position is that the Qurʾān can be understood directly and the *akhbār* are unnecessary. The scholars who claim the ability to understand the Qurʾān directly are arrogant, considering themselves as equal to the Imams in explaining the *mutashābihāt* (unclear verses) of the Qurʾān. Baḥrānī states that both of the Akhbārī positions are excessive (*bayn ifrāṭ wa tafrīṭ*), and that the *akhbār* themselves give differing indications about the issue.

Baḥrānī's own position is actually a compromise between the two Akhbārī positions. The verses in the Qurʾān divide into a number of different categories. He claims to be following Shaykh al-Ṭūsī in this division. The Shaykh, in his commentary, *Tafsīr al-Tibyān*, divides the verses of the Qurʾān into four categories:

(i) those verses of which only God knows the meaning
(ii) those which anyone who knows the language can understand
(iii) those which cannot be understood without the *sunna* of the Prophet
(iv) those which can have two (or more) meanings – for which we need the *tafsīr* of the Imams.

This categorisation is harmonised, rather ingenuously, with a *ḥadīth* from Imam ʿAlī in which he describes three types of Qurʾānic verse:

(a) one which any person, learned or ignorant, can understand
(b) one which someone with a pure mind can understand
(c) one which only God and his Prophets can understand.

(a) is identical to (ii). Baḥrānī declares (iv) and (b) to be identical because the Imams are the only ones who have a pure mind. The Imams are also essential to (c), though not by virtue of having pure minds, but by being 'inheritors' to the Prophets (*wirātha min al-anbīyā'*). (iii) and (c) are identical since one knows the *sunna* of the Prophet only through the *tafsīr* of the Imams. The first category of the Shaykh (verses which only God can understand) is not mentioned by Imam 'Alī because they are so few in number. The verses which can be understood by anyone, (ii) and (a), are also few and, according to Baḥrānī, do not refer to legal affairs.

Baḥrānī's final position is then a compromise between the two Akhbārī positions. He limits the number of *āya*s which can be understood directly, and locates understanding of the *āya*s concerned with the *aḥkām*, uncompromisingly, through the *tafsīr* of the Imams (i.e. the *akhbār*). As in his analysis of *sunna*, the *akhbār* are the only means available to a believer with which to understand the *Sharī'a.*

Historically, *ijmā'* has been a limited source for Shī'ī jurists. *Ijmā'* is only valid because unanimity must include the opinion of the hidden Imam. Majority opinion is not sufficient because the Imam's opinion could be omitted. Baḥrānī quotes Muḥaqqiq al-Ḥillī (d.676/1277) to support this view:

> As for *ijmā'*, it is a proof, in our opinion, when it includes the opinion of the Imam. If a hundred of our *fuqahā'* disagree with his words, then it is not a proof. If this [agreement] occurs with only two [of our *fuqahā'*] then their words constitute a proof.[23]

Baḥrānī, however, considers *ijmā'* as only reaching the level of *ẓann*, not *'ilm*, and therefore rejects it as a source. Theoretically, the Imam is permitted to practice *taqiyya*, and hence, Baḥrānī claims, one can never know if his opinion is included. Practically, the Shī'a are in diaspora and gaining everybody's opinion is impossible. *Ijmā'* was possible, Baḥrānī claims, in the period immediately after the *ghayba*, when the community was small and opinions could be gained easily. He admits that *ijmā'* was reached, and does confer validity upon matters such as the authority of Shaykh al-Ṣadūq's *fatāwā*. In his own period though, *ijmā'* has become an impossibility:

> If (the Imam's) inclusion is known, then there is no doubt and no dispute in calling it *ijmā'*, and verifying it as a proof. If not, then it is *ẓann*.[24]

Even if some Shī'ī scholars have accepted *ijmā'*, they have done so merely in imitation of the Sunnis:

> In sum, there is no ambiguity, and no doubt that there is no support for this '*ijmā'*' in *kitāb* or *sunna*. It is only derived from the whims of the *Sunnis*

> and their conclusions; however, a group of our *aṣḥāb* have, through negligence, followed them in this.[25]

The criterion for judging the validity of a claim of the *Sharīʿa* is certain knowledge (*ʿilm qaṭʿī*). *Aḥkām* which reach only the category of *ẓann* cannot be binding. Baḥrānī's epistemology here implicitly rejects *ijtihād*, since the conclusions of a *mujtahid* are only ever *ẓannī*.

The final section of the *muqaddima* concerns *dalīl al-ʿaql*. Baḥrānī distinguishes three elements of *dalīl al-ʿaql*: *al-barāʾat al-aṣliyya*, *al-istiṣḥāb* and linguistic rules concerning the meanings of words.[26] These *ʿaqlī* principles were designed to enable the scholar to fill lacunae in the areas where Qurʾān and *sunna* were silent. Baḥrānī rejects all three elements of *dalīl al-ʿaql*.

Al-barāʾat al-aṣliyya is the idea that if the texts are silent over a matter, then that matter is presumed to be free (*barāʾa*) from prohibition, and hence permissible. *Istiṣḥāb al-ḥāl* is a related concept. If a ruling is given at a particular point in time, under *istiṣḥāb* it is presumed to continue as valid until certain knowledge is gained that the circumstances have changed and the ruling must be modified. Both principles are widely used by *mujtahids*.

Baḥrānī's argument against both these deductive processes is that the *mujtahid* is making a ruling without a *dalīl*. By presuming a thing to be *mubāḥ* (permitted), the *mujtahid* is elevating his own opinion (*ẓann*) to that of a ruling (*ḥukm*). By assuming that a state of affairs continues to be the case, when it might have changed, the *mujtahid* is acting recklessly, and is in danger of directing the believer in ways contrary to the *Sharīʿa*. Furthermore, by presuming an action or an item to be *mubāḥ* because there is no explicit *dalīl* in the texts of revelation is to imply that God has failed to provide a ruling on this issue, which in turn implies that the *Sharīʿa* is incomplete. This for Baḥrānī is heresy since God, the Prophet and the Imams all bear witness that the *Sharīʿa* is comprehensive and that God has a ruling for every situation. Baḥrānī argues that the *akhbār* are quite clear about the acceptable procedure on occasions when the texts seem unclear:

> The *akhbār* have been passed down through time and decree, in cases like this, that it is *wājib* to exercise *tawaqquf* (suspension of decision) and *iḥtiyāṭ* (caution).[27]

I return to the implications of *iḥtiyāṭ* and *tawaqquf* below.

In summary, with regard to the first area of dispute between Akhbārīs and *mujtahids*, Baḥrānī is clearly advocating an Akhbārī position. There are two sources of law, Qur'ān and *sunna. Ijmā'* and *dalīl al-'aql* are rejected as producing rulings that are uncertain (termed *ẓannī* by Baḥrānī). Furthermore, Baḥrānī's legal epistemology is established. It consists of rigid dichotomies between certainty and doubt, truth and falsehood.

The Categorisation of Actions

In his refutation of *al-barā'at al-aṣliyya,* Baḥrānī gives an indication of his position concerning the second area of dispute between the Akhbārīs and the *mujtahids*:

> All the Sunnis, and most of our *aṣḥāb* support [this] conception [of *al-barā'at al-aṣliyya*], and hold fast to denying *aḥkām* on its basis ... just as it is clear to anyone who examines their books of proofs, like the *Masālik,* the *Madārik* and others like it. Things for them are only *ḥalāl* or *ḥarām.* A group of *muḥaddiths,* and a party of Uṣūlīs advocate the necessity of *tawaqquf* and *iḥtiyāṭ.* Things for them are divided into three categories: *ḥalāl* is clear, *ḥarām* is clear and the *shubhāt* are between them ... The most accurate position (*al-ḥaqq al-ḥaqīq*), which is supported by the *akhbār* of the Imams, is the second position.

This is clear support for the Akhbārī position on the second of the differences between the disputing parties examined in *muqaddima* 12.

Muqaddima 4 is a detailed examination of how *iḥtiyāṭ* (caution) and *tawaqquf* (suspension of decision) operate. Baḥrānī's position is encapsulated by the phrase:

> The obligation [to practice] *iḥtiyāṭ* is in action, and [the obligation to practice] *tawaqquf* is in making rulings.[28]

By this Baḥrānī means that when a scholar is asked for an opinion on a matter which has no clear *dalīl* from the texts, he should first declare that he does not know the nature of the true *ḥukm* (*tawaqquf*). Then he should decide which is the most cautious (*al-aḥwaṭ)* course of action, which will ensure a believer fulfils the *Sharī'a* (*iḥtiyāṭ*). The questioner should then follow this most cautious course. Hence *iḥtiyāṭ* applies to action and *tawaqquf* to making rulings. For Baḥrānī then, knowledge of the *Sharī'a* is of two types, each equally certain. First, there are *aḥkām* which have direct indications (*adilla*) from the texts. Second, there are areas where the ruling is *shubha.* One does not know the *ḥukm* itself; the Imams failed to reveal it because of *taqiyya.* Nevertheless, the Imams did reveal a general rule as to the procedure in such cases – *tawaqquf* and *iḥtiyāṭ*. As we shall see, practising *iḥtiyāṭ* brings certainty in fulfilling the *Sharīʿa*, since it decrees performing actions about which there is doubt as to their necessity.

At the outset of *muqaddima* 4, Baḥrānī locates the practice of *iḥtiyāṭ* within the Akhbārī-*mujtahid* conflict. The *mujtahids* dispute with one another over whether *iḥtiyāṭ* is only *mustaḥabb* (recommended) or illegitimate. The Akhbārīs claim that in some circumstances *iḥtiyāṭ* is *wājib* (obligatory).[29]

In the second part of *muqaddima* 4, Baḥrānī elucidates his theory. *Iḥtiyāṭ* is necessary in cases where there is uncertainty (*shubha*). However, Baḥrānī considers that in these cases, it is not that the texts give contradictory rulings (a process of *tarjīḥ* will be described for such cases). Neither is it that revelation is silent on the issue (revelation, for Baḥrānī, can always be made to have some bearing on a problem). Instead, *shubha* cases occur when it is unclear from revelation under which of the five categories (*wājib*, *mustaḥabb* etc.) an action should be classified.

Baḥrānī's first example concerns the situation where one is unclear whether an action is *wājib* or *mustaḥabb*. In such cases, caution decrees that one should perform the action:

> Amongst the times when *iḥtiyāṭ* is *wājib* concerning the legal ruling, meaning one should act, is when the *ḥukm* is unclear from the *dalīl*, [i.e.] whether it refers to *wujūb* and *istiḥbāb*. It is *wājib* to do *tawaqquf* concerning a *ḥukm*, and *iḥtiyāṭ* in performing that action.[30]

The reasoning here, though not explicitly stated, would seem quite logical. If one neglects the action because one considers it only *mustaḥabb*, then, if the action is in fact *wājib*, one has failed to perform the *Sharīʿa*. If, however, it turns out to be *mustaḥabb*, then one has performed a recommended action, and there is benefit in performing such actions. The only way to ensure that one can fulfil the *Sharīʿa* is by treating the action as *wājib*, even though one is unsure as to its status. This ensures that there is no risk of transgressing God's Law.

Similarly, if the texts are unclear as to whether an action is *makrūh* (disapproved) or forbidden (*ḥarām*), then logic would dictate that one should avoid the action. Baḥrānī argues that if it turns out to be *ḥarām*, one has not transgressed the *Sharīʿa*. If it is only *makrūh*, one has avoided a reprehensible act, which in itself is a good thing.

If one knows that an action is not *wājib*, but is unsure in which of the other four categories it might fall, Baḥrānī declares that one should avoid the action:

> Amongst the times when *iḥtiyāṭ* is *wājib* concerning the *sharʿī* ruling, but [this time] meaning one should refrain from acting, is when the action is between *wājib* and *muḥarram* (forbidden).[31]

It is, therefore, better to risk failing to perform a recommended action than it is to risk performing a forbidden action. This course of action, even if it results in a failure to perform the *mustaḥabbāt*, at least avoids any chance of performing the *muḥarramāt*.[32]

Baḥrānī gives examples of *iḥtiyāṭ* being advised by the Imams. He cites a question which Imam ʿAlī was asked about two men who go hunting together whilst on *ḥajj* and between them kill one animal. This is not permitted and in order for the men's *ḥajj* to be valid, they must perform a penance (*kaffāra*). The question is whether one penance (performed by one of the men) is sufficient since only one act of hunting occurred (i.e. one animal was killed). Imam ʿAlī's reply was that both should perform the penance in accordance with *iḥtiyaṭ*. Baḥrānī elaborates:

> This *riwāya* demonstrates that *iḥtiyāṭ* is *wājib* when one is ignorant of the details of a *ḥukm sharʿī*, and it is not possible to ask [the Imam]. This is because the clear meaning of the *riwāya* is that the questioner knows the *aṣl* [that it is *wājib* to perform the penance]. He only doubts whether one penance is to be placed on both of them, or whether they should perform one penance each.[33]

One does not know the details of the *ḥukm* i.e. it is *shubha* – in such cases *iḥtiyāṭ* is *wājib*. Baḥrānī interprets this *khabar* as a direct injunction from the Imam to perform *iḥtiyāṭ*.

Baḥrānī's theory of *iḥtiyāṭ* occupies similar ground to the mainstream theory of *ijtihād*. The *mujtahid* uses *ijtihād* to discover rulings in cases where the texts are uncertain. He does this through techniques such as *al-barāʾat al-aṣliyya*, *istiṣḥāb al-ḥāl*, the distinction of *ʿumūm* and *khuṣūṣ* and other methods of manipulating the words in the revelatory texts. The *mujtahid's* conclusions are only ever his opinion (*ẓann*), though the *muqallid* is bound to follow them. From Baḥrānī's perspective, there is a danger here of a wrong *ḥukm* from the *mujtahid* leading the *muqallid* astray. If, however, one follows *iḥtiyāṭ* in cases where the texts of revelation are unclear, then one can reach certainty that the *Sharīʿa* has been fulfilled, even though one does not know God's ruling on a particular case. Why rely on the *ẓann* of the *mujtahid*, when one can gain *ʿilm* through following the Imams' commands to perform *iḥtiyāṭ*?

For Baḥrānī, *iḥtiyāṭ* is the correct procedure when there is a lack of clarity in the texts. *Tarjīḥ* is the procedure when the texts are contradictory (*taʿāruḍ*). In *muqaddima* 6, Baḥrānī outlines the process whereby one can discover which of two contradictory texts is *taqiyya*, and therefore to be rejected. With respect to the contradiction within the Qur'ān, he lists the common method of *nāsikh* and *mansūkh*. On the contradictions between *kitāb* and *akhbār*, he advocates seeing the *akhbār* as *muqayyid* or *mukhaṣṣiṣ* of the general (*muṭlaq, ʿumūm,*) rulings in the Qur'ān. However, the contradictions within the body of *akhbār* are his major concern. After an extensive discussion of the famous Maqbūla of Ibn Hanẓala and Marfūʿa of Zurāra, Baḥrānī concludes that there are three 'rules' in performing *tarjīḥ*. These are outlined by Kulaynī:

> I know, oh brother, that the only factors, when pin-pointing matters over which the Imams differ, are those which the Imam himself has said:
>
> 'Refer the two *ḥadīth* to the book of God and whatever agrees with it, obey that, and whatever disagrees with it, reject.'
>
> and [he also said]:
>
> 'Obtain what agrees with the general population [i.e. the Sunnis], and indeed the right path lies in opposing them.'
>
> and [he also said]:
>
> 'Take what is agreed upon (*al-mujmaʿ ʿalayhi*), for there is no doubt in that which is agreed upon.' (108)

The issue of the reliability of the *rāwīs* is not an issue for Baḥrānī, since for him all the *akhbār* are true accounts of the Imams' words. These three tests are merely means whereby *taqiyya akhbār* can be distinguished from non-*taqiyya akhbār*.

However, Baḥrānī's analysis of these rules demonstrates that he considers them to be of little use. Comparison with the Qur'ān is limited to the few verses which refer to the *aḥkām*. Second, Baḥrānī recognises that the Sunnis differ so much amongst themselves that it is difficult to see how it is possible to take an opposing view. Finally, the test of 'what the people agree on' is difficult (*taʿaṣṣur*) because the Shīʿa are scattered and live under dissimulation (*zāwiyat al-taqiyya*). *Ijmāʿ* as a source in itself was rejected as impractical; this is also the case with *ijmāʿ* as a means for deciding between two contradictory *khabars*. The redundancy of these rules leaves the jurist in a difficult situation. Baḥrānī though has a recommended course of action:

> When it is impossible to do *tarjīḥ* by these three principles, then the preferred option is to stop on the shore of *iḥtiyāṭ*.[34]

Theoretically the *ta'āruḍ* in the *akhbār* can be solved by the three means of *tarjīḥ*. In effect, though, most cases will end up with *iḥtiyāṭ*. Another area which under *ijtihād* theory the *mujtahid* would give his opinion is eliminated by Baḥrānī and replaced by the doctrine of *iḥtiyāṭ*.

The Means of Interpreting *Kitāb*

Baḥrānī's conception of the legitimate means whereby the Qur'ān can be interpreted were found in *muqaddima* 3, an account of which has already been given above. His conclusions were that, apart from the few verses that can be understood by anyone who understands the Arabic language, the Qur'ān (including all the verses relating to *aḥkām)*, can only be understood through an acquaintance with the *akhbār*. In effect, the *akhbār* are the only *tafsīr* of the Qur'ān; it is the *akhbār* that occupy the position of exegetical power. *Muqaddimas* 7 to 11 contain a detailed rejection of other exegetical techniques, utilised by other jurists to interpret *kitāb*.

Muqaddimas 7 to 9 are brief examinations of matters relating to the linguistic interpretation of the Quranic text, concerning the meaning of words in revelation. *Muqaddima* 7[35] is concerned with obligation and prohibition. If an order is given in the Qur'ān, does this imply that it is *wājib* upon the believers to carry out that order? Similarly, if a prohibition is found, does this imply that it is *ḥarām* for the believers? Baḥrānī's opponents had attempted to reduce the potency of commands and prohibitions, by relegating them to *mandūb* or *mustaḥabb* (optional but recommended) or *makrūh* (discouraged). Baḥrānī's position is that for a command (*amr*) to be anything less than *wājib*, or for a prohibition (*nahy*) to be anything less that *ḥarām*, it needs textual evidence (*qarīna*, pl. *qarā'in*). A *qarīna* is an indication that the words of command or prohibition are being used metaphorically (*majāz*) and implies that the ruling is *mustaḥabb* or *makrūh* respectively. *Muqaddimas* 8[36] and 9[37] deal with legitimate *qarā'in*. Opponents have argued that when interpreting words in revelation, one can use common, everyday meanings (*al-'urf al-'āmm*), or strictly linguistic meanings (*al-ḥaqīqat al-lughwiyya*). Baḥrānī rejects these possible interpretations. When interpreting words, such as commands and prohibitions, one must assume that the meaning is literal (*ḥaqīqa*, i.e. a command implies obligation), unless one has a *qarīna* taken from the *akhbār* which shows that this verse of revelation can be interpreted other than literally (i.e. in a *majāz* fashion). A *qarīna* may, for example, take the form of an occasion when an Imam interpreted the verse in a non-literal manner. In sum, the commands and prohibitions in the Qurʾān and in the *akhbār* are to be taken literally (*ḥaqīqa*) unless there is a valid indication (*qarīna*) that an other than literal meaning is permissible. This *qarīna* can only be taken from the *akhbār* – general usage of words by ordinary people and strict linguistic definitions are unacceptable. Hence the *akhbār* are, once again, the only true *tafsīr* of the Qurʾān.[38]

Muqaddima 10 is concerned with *al-dalīl al-ʿaqlī*. By *al-dalīl al-ʿaqlī*, Baḥrānī is not referring to *al-barāʾat al-aṣliyya* and *istiṣḥāb*, as discussed in *muqaddima* 3. In this *muqaddima* Baḥrānī is discussing whether 'reason' can be a source of the *Sharīʿa*, alongside Qurʾān and *sunna*. What one can (and cannot) know by reason alone, outside of revelation, is a familiar *topos* in Muslim literature. Shīʿa thought, by incorporating Muʿtazilī ideas, gave reason an independent role in discovering *sharʿī* rulings.[39] Baḥrānī accepts that reason can give rise to knowledge (*ʿilm*) of the *Sharīʿa*. However, it is a specific type of reason:

> There is no doubt that natural sound reason is one of God's proofs and a clear ladder leading from him. It agrees with the Law, rather it is a law from the inside [of a person], just as the other is a law from the outside [of a person], but [only] as long as it is not altered by the preponderance of evil imaginings and affected by extremism or the love of pride or evil intentions … Perhaps it attains things before the coming of the Law, and Law comes to confirm it. On the other hand perhaps it does not prove things before the Law, the essence of things is hidden and the Law comes to clarify and illuminate them …[40]

For reason to bring knowledge it must be 'pure', 'natural' and 'free from evil imaginings'. This is not reason as is commonly (*muṭlaqan*) understood. This pure natural reason is, however, a scarce commodity. Baḥrānī states, 'it is, for certain, rarely found among the people'.[41] If one cannot utilise this level of reason, then Baḥrānī leaves the reader in no doubt as to the correct course of action:

> There is no doubt that legal rulings concerned with *ʿibādāt* and other things, all of them are arbitrary [i.e. not justified by reason], and in need of a proof of revelation from the preserver of the *Sharīʿa*. Because of this, the *akhbār*, just as has been shown to you in the passages of *muqaddima* 3, make clear that [i] it is forbidden to pronounce a legal *aḥkām* without a saying from the Imams and [ii] knowledge originates [only] with them and [iii] *tawaqquf* and *iḥtiyāṭ* are necessary when there is no easy way to [attain] knowledge and [iv] that one must refer to them [the Imams] in all *aḥkām*

> ... If an independent role for reason was established in this way, then the sending of Prophets and revealing of books would be futile.[42]

There is then no source of the *Sharīʿa* apart from revelation. Reason is given a theoretical role, but the standards attached to it are strict, preventing any potential role from becoming a reality. Unsurprisingly, the *akhbār* are seen as the supreme source of *Sharīʿa* knowledge.[43]

The conclusion the reader is forced to reach is that for Baḥrānī only the *akhbār* can be used as *qarīna* for *majāz* and as the sure guide for the believer when his reason fails to reach the strictures laid out in *muqaddima* 10. On the final distinction between Akhbārīs and *mujtahids*, that of the legitimate means of interpreting *kitāb*, Baḥrānī maintains an Akhbārī position.

Conclusion

The above analysis enables us to determine that if one uses Baḥrānī's own definition of the fundamental issues in the Akhbārī-*mujtahid* dispute, he was an Akhbārī. However, at times he avoids labelling himself as such. At the beginning of *muqaddima* 12, he says:

> I was, at first, someone who championed the Akhbārī school. I argued with some of my contemporary *mujtahids* and wrote my book *al-Masāʾil al-Shīrāziyya*, which is a wide-ranging work containing all the great arguments ... However, it became clear to me, after giving much thought to the matter and by examining the opinions of the learned *ʿulamāʾ*, that the positions on this matter were confused and I should remove the veil and curtain covering it.[44]

His reason for avoiding associating himself with the Akhbārīs, even though his *uṣūl al-fiqh* leads one to the conclusion that he was an Akhbārī, may have been irenic. He was attempting to lessen the tensions between the groups and present himself as an intermediary, especially in his claims to be following a middle path (*ṭarīqa wusṭā*). It should be noted that on other definitions of the Akhbārī-Uṣūlī dispute, such as those by Samāhijī, Baḥrānī can also be considered an Akhbārī.[45]

What is clear, however, is that there is no place in Baḥrānī's *uṣūl al-fiqh* for the practice of *ijtihād* as a means of discovering rulings. *Ijtihād* is rejected because its results are epistemologically inferior to rulings which can be gained through reliance on the *akhbār* and following the procedures associated with *iḥtiyāṭ*. The real issue at stake in Baḥrānī's discussions is knowledge. How can one know that one is fulfilling God's law? He finds the theories of *ijtihād* propounded by other jurists, both Sunni and Shīʿī, unsatisfactory answers to this question.

Baḥrānī's pleas for an understanding to be reached between Akhbārīs and *mujtahids* went unheard. In the years following his death, the *mujtahid* Muḥammad Bāqir al-Bihbahānī (d.1205/1791) rose to a position of power in the ʿAtabāt. His pupils became the established scholarly elite in Iran and elsewhere, and the heresy of Akhbarism was extinguished. The successors to Bihbahānī went on to dominate Shīʿa legal thought throughout the Qajar period and into the twentieth century.

Notes

1 See W. Madelung, 'Imamism and Mu'tazilite theology' in Colloque de Strasbourg, *Le Shīʿisme Imamate* (Paris, 1970), 21, n. 1.

2 A. Newman, 'The Nature of the Akhbārī/Uṣūlī Dispute in Late Ṣafawid Iran. Part 2: The Conflict Re-assessed', *BSOAS*, 55 (1992), 250–61.

3 E. Kohlberg, 'Aspects of Akhbārī Thought in the Seventeenth and Eighteenth Century' in J.O. Voll and N. Levtzion ed., *Eighteenth Century Renewal and Reform in Islam* (New York, 1987), 133–60.

4 N. Calder, 'Doubt and Prerogative: The Emergence of an Imāmī Shīʿī Theory of *Ijtihād*,' *Studia Islamica*, 70 (1989), 68, n. 1.

5 Calder argues that the Akhbārī polemic aimed to discredit the developed Shīʿī legal theory of *ijtihād*. This theory only came into being with ʿAllāma al-Ḥillī (d.726/1325) and hence cannot predate his work. For a full discussion concerning whether Akhbarism necessitates a rejection of state power and a reduction in the authority of the jurist, see R. Gleave, 'Akhbārī Shīʿī Jurisprudence in the Writings of Yūsuf b. Aḥmad al-Baḥrānī (d.1186/1772)' (Unpublished Ph.D. thesis, University of Manchester, 1996).

6 Yūsuf al-Baḥrānī, *Al-Ḥadāʾiq al-Nāḍira* (25 vols, Qum, 1377).

7 For the Arabic and Persian biographies of Baḥrānī, see Muḥammad Bāqir al-Khwānsārī, *Rawḍāt al-Jannāt* (8 vols, Qum, 1970-72), vol. 8, 203; Muḥammad Tanukābānī, *Qiṣaṣ al-ʿUlamāʾ* (Tehran, n.d.), 201; Muḥammad al-Hāʾirī, *Muntahā al-Maqāl* (Tehran, n.d.), 334; Muḥammad ʿAlī Kashmīrī, *Nujūm al-Samāʾ* (Lucknow, 1303/1885), 283; see also my analyses of these texts, R. Gleave, 'The Akhbārī-Uṣūlī Dispute in *Ṭabaqāt* Literature: An Analysis of the Biographies of Yūsuf al Baḥrānī and Muḥammad Bāqir al-Bihbihānī', *Jusur*, 10 (1994), 79–109.

8 al-Baḥrānī, *al-Ḥadāʾiq*, vol. 1, p. 170.

9 Ibid., p. 168.

10 Ibid., p. 169.

11 Ibid., pp. 168–9.

12 See A. Newman, 'The Nature of the Akhbārī/Uṣūlī Dispute in Late Ṣafawid Iran. Part 1: 'Abdallāh al-Samāhijī's '*Munyat al-Mumārisīn*", *BSOAS*, 55 (1992), 22–51.

13 al-Baḥrānī, *al-Durur al-Najafiyya* (Qum, n.d.), 253–6.

14 See E. Kohlberg, 'Some Imāmī Views on *Taqiyya*', *JAOS*, 95.3 (1975), 395–402.

15 al-Baḥrānī, *al-Ḥadā'iq,* vol. 1, p. 5.

16 Ibid., pp. 5–6.

17 Ibid., p. 6.

18 Ibid., p. 8.

19 Ibid., p. 10.

20 Ibid., p. 8.

21 Ibid., p. 22.

22 Ibid., p. 25.

23 Ibid., p. 35.

24 Ibid., p. 36.

25 Ibid., p. 39.

26 For a full examination of the rules concerning the meaning of words, see Gleave, 'Akhbārī Shī'ī jurisprudence', pp.33–34. Here I deal only with Baḥrānī's arguments concerning *al-barā'at al-aṣliyya* and *istiṣḥāb.*

27 Baḥrānī, *al-Ḥadā'iq*, vol.1, p. 55.

28 Ibid., p. 66.

29 The first part of *muqaddima* 4 is a detailed refutation of the *mujtahid* position and I do not deal with it here. For an examination of Baḥrānī's arguments, see Gleave, 'Akhbārī Shī'ī Jurisprudence', p. 38–40.

30 al-Baḥrānī, *al-Ḥadā'iq*, vol.1, p. 69.

31 Ibid., p. 70.

32 Unfortunately Baḥrānī does not deal with the interesting question of the situation where a person fails to act cautiously in a case of textual uncertainty. Hence he has failed to perform *iḥtiyāṭ*. However, the action that he chooses to perform, in fact, turns out to be a recommended action. Is he both punished (for failing to perform *iḥtiyāṭ*) and praised (for performing a *mustaḥabb* action) simultaneously? Baḥrānī also does not tackle the issue which would inevitably arise under a schema such as his: that different scholars would differ over whether they feel *iḥtiyāṭ* was necessary in a certain case. Even if they agreed over the need for *iḥtiyāṭ,* they may differ over which course of action is the most cautious.

33 Ibid., p. 73.

34 Ibid., p. 110.

35 Ibid., pp. 112–18.

36 Ibid., pp. 118–21.

37 Ibid., pp. 121–5.

38 This process of separating the language of revelation from everyday speech, might be seen as a means of further sanctifying revelation. The

language used in revelation is unique, and understanding revelation requires reference to other parts of revelation – not to the outside world. Revelation becomes an internally validated set of texts, which require no external justification.

39 See Madelung, 'Imamism and Mu'tazilism' for a general account of the incorporation of Muʿtazilī thinking into Shiʿite thought.

40 al-Baḥrānī, *al-Ḥadāʾiq*, vol.1, p. 131.

41 Ibid., p. 133.

42 Ibid., p. 131.

43 *Muqaddima* 11 mentions a series of principles whereby the *Sharīʿa* can be interpreted. These principles are, in the most part, vague and ambiguous, though it might be argued that they give scope to the jurist to interpret without the aid of the *akhbār*. However, the principles are themselves attributed to the Imams, and Baḥrānī does not concede that there is any possibility of differences of opinion arising from them. For a fuller discussion of these principles see Gleave, 'Akhbārī Shīʿī Jurisprudence', pp. 82–90.

44 al-Baḥrānī, *al-Ḥadāʾiq*, vol.1, p. 167.

45 See Gleave, 'Akhbārī Shīʿī Jurisprudence', pp.91–7 and A. Newman, 'The Nature of the Akhbārī/Uṣūlī Dispute in Late Ṣafawid Iran. Part 1'.

PART TWO

Iftāʾ, *Fatwās* and *Muftīs*

THREE

Rules, Judicial Discretion, and the Rule of Law in Naṣrid Granada: An Analysis of *al-Ḥadīqa al-mustaqilla al-naḍra fī al-fatāwā al-ṣādira ʿan ʿulamāʾ al-ḥaḍra*

MOHAMMAD FADEL

Introduction: Theory and Practice in Islamic Law

While the dichotomy between theory and practice has been a favourite theme of Western writers on Islamic law since the time of Weber,[1] it remains a subject fraught with difficulties. One of these difficulties has been confusion regarding what constitutes Islamic law for a given time and place. Obviously, before one can postulate a contradiction between theory and practice, one must know what the theory is that governed the practice under consideration. Unfortunately, many studies of the this complex issue have not devoted sufficient attention to what constitutes the 'theory' against which practice should be judged. As a result, the contradictions that are asserted often rest on an implicit assumption of what constitutes the legal standard rather than what the local Muslim legal establishment considered to be the legal standard.

Likewise, not much consideration is given to defining what is meant by 'practice'. Is it the behaviour of individuals and groups within societies governed by Islamic law, or is it exclusively a problem of the administration of the law? While Weber discussed this theme mainly in regard to his concept of *Kadi*-justice, i.e., as an issue affecting the administration of the law, Orientalists have often confused the problematic of theory and practice with the behaviour of individuals and groups, a problem that is more properly termed the efficacy of the law.[2] Because of these ambiguities, rarely does the genre of 'theory versus practice' present us with the practice of Muslim legal authorities as they grappled with the issues identified by Western scholarship as legally problematic.

A single example should be sufficient to demonstrate the incomplete nature of previous studies. Coulson mentions that in West Africa a woman is free at any time during her marriage to return half of her dowry and gain a divorce without the agreement of her husband. According to Coulson this is a blatant violation of Islamic law which gives power to divorce exclusively to the husband. Furthermore, he says that any attempt to treat it as a *khul'*[3] divorce is mistaken, because this requires the husband's consent.[4] Coulson, in judging this divorce to be illegal, fails to enlighten us, however, in regard to the legal consequences of this act. Some of the more obvious questions that would need to be answered if Coulson's conclusion is true include the following:

1. If this is not a legitimate divorce in law, does this mean that a husband who does not consent to the divorce has no legal remedy protecting his interest in the marriage?
2. Could the wife who paid this money subsequently enter a claim for unpaid maintenance on the grounds that she was never legally divorced from her husband?
3. Do they each continue to enjoy rights of inheritance in the event of either party's death, or only during the wife's waiting period (*'idda*)?

In brief, Coulson, when recording this custom, enriches us anthropologically, but not legally. Most surprisingly, we are also left ignorant of the local juridical interpretation of this act. This is particularly ironic given Coulson's consistent criticism of Muslim jurisprudence as being only concerned 'with the law as it ought to be', and failing to produce a jurisprudence concerned with prediction of judicial acts.[5]

In contrast to the method outlined above, the basic premise of this paper is inspired by Legal Realism: the law is what its authoritative spokesmen declare it to be. From the perspective of Legal Realism, the relationship of theory to practice is a problematic common to any system that claims to follow rules. To the extent that external observers are able to predict the declarations of these authoritative spokesmen, one can say there is no contradiction between theory and practice.[6] The issue of theory versus practice is thus another way of posing the question of the efficacy of the ideal of a rule of law in a given society. For this reason, we shall try to study the extent to which legal officials in Muslim states could be said to be following the rules of Islamic law.

Ideally, a study of the efficacy of the rule of law in Muslim societies would concentrate on the practice of the two most important officials in the administration of Islamic law: the judge and the *muftī*. Given the fact that for the pre-Ottoman period, however, the sources do not preserve court decisions, any study will necessarily have to be limited to *fatwās*.[7] It is the action of *muftīs* then that will provide the 'practice' that will be judged against 'theory.' What, however, constitutes 'theory' for the Mālikī school of the eighth–ninth/fourteenth–fifteenth centuries? There can be no doubt that the most important statement of Mālikī law for the post-eighth Hijrī century was the *Mukhtaṣar Khalīl*. This work was the third in a series of *mukhtaṣarāt* written by Egyptian Mālikīs that represented the most important literary achievements of their school in the seventh–eighth/thirteenth–fourteenth centuries: *al-Jawāhir*, *Jāmiʿ al-ummahāt*, and *Mukhtaṣar Khalīl*.[8] Historians of the Mālikī school have regarded these works as representing successive generations' efforts to 'summarise' (*ikhtiṣār*) the school's doctrine.[9] The appearance and the rapid spread of these 'summaries' (*mukhtaṣars*), however, have conventionally been understood by Western and Arab historians of Islamic law as both a cause and an effect of the 'decline' of Muslim legal creativity in the post-fifth/eleventh century.[10]

Instead of viewing these works as signs of decadence, however, I propose to view them as the product of the legal system's need for a set of uniform rules. Since Islamic law was a jurists' law,[11] meaning that it was the product of the interpretive labours of succeeding generations of jurists, legal indeterminacy was a particularly acute problem.[12] Since the *mukhtaṣars*, as they appeared initially in the seventh/thirteenth century, preserved competing opinions of the law, they only partially resolved the problem of indeterminacy within the Mālikī school. *Mukhtaṣar Khalīl*, in contrast to these previous *mukhtaṣars*, provided an unequivocal rule in the vast majority of cases, even if that rule itself was actually controversial. Furthermore, if the genre of the *mukhtaṣar*, at least as it appeared in the seventh– eighth/thirteenth– fourteenth centuries, is taken to be representing a desire to codify the positions of the school, then the *mukhtaṣar* also appears as a logical development of issues raised by sixth/twelfth-century jurists such as Ibn Rushd the Grandfather (d. 520/1126) and al-Qāḍī Abū Bakr Ibn al-ʿArabī (d. 543/1148) surrounding what kind of opinions may legitimately be used by a judge or a *muftī* who has not reached the rank of *ijtihād*.[13] Their resolution to the practical problem of legal indeterminacy and its deleterious effect on the legitimacy of the law was essentially political: restrict the legitimacy of interpretation, even within the legal establishment, to a certain group of highly trained jurists. This was often represented in a tripartite division of the legal community into *muqallid*, *mujtahid-fatwā*, and *mujtahid-madhhab*.[14] The role of the *mukhtaṣar* within such a hierarchy would have been to promulgate the 'rules' of the school known as *naṣṣ* or *manṣūṣ* for the lowest ranking jurists whom Ibn al-ʿArabī and Ibn Rushd wished to bind to explicit rules. Taking *mukhtaṣars* to be the functional equivalent of a legal school's code, and therefore, the authoritative source of 'theory,' seems to be a plausible hypothesis. For the purposes of this paper, then, *Mukhtaṣar Khalīl* will be treated as representing authoritative Mālikī doctrine.[15]

Al-Ḥadīqa al-mustaqilla al-naḍra fī al-fatāwā al-ṣādira ʿan ʿulamāʾ al-ḥaḍra[16]

Once the decision to use *fatwās* as data to test the theory/practice problematic is made, however, the researcher is faced with a series of problems relating to the selection of his sample. While collections such as *al-Fatāwā al-hindiyya*[17] and *al-Miʿyār al-muʿrib*[18] are both well known and published, their very size precludes them from analysis for several reasons. The first is that the researcher would have to develop some criteria which would guide his selection of *fatwās* so that he could not be accused of 'stacking the deck' in favour of his thesis. The second stems from the diachronic nature of these works which contain opinions from the most ancient authorities of the school to the most contemporary. The third is the lack of the geographical specificity which is necessary if the opinions analysed are to increase our understanding of a particular legal culture. Thus, it would be hazardous to assume that a fifth-century Mālikī *muftī* of Ifrīqiyya followed the same criteria in answering questions that his Cordovan contemporary followed simply because they were both Mālikīs. If we were to use the opinions of a single *muftī*, on the other hand, we would gain geographical and temporal specificity and insight into that *muftī*'s legal thought, but perhaps at the cost of a wider knowledge of the surrounding legal culture.

In choosing our sample we have attempted to steer a middle course. The collection we have chosen, *al-Ḥadīqa al-mustaqilla al-naḍra fī al-fatāwā al-ṣāḍira ʿan ʿulamā al-ḥaḍra*, contains the responses of twelve *muftīs*, but at the same time is small enough that we were able to include all the opinions in our sample. However, for practical reasons we chose to exclude all *fatwās* dealing with ritual law and its relationship to the doctrine elaborated in the *Mukhtaṣar.*[19] Likewise, we also chose to exclude questions 89–96 for formal reasons: the manuscript describes them as *ajwiba*, 'answers' (sing., *jawāb*). This signified to us that if they are formally distinguished from *fatwās*, they could possibly be misleading in regard to the practice of *fatwā*-giving. Another advantage of this collection is that all the *muftīs*, with the exception of one, are from one city – Granada. Additionally, the time frame of the opinions is approximately 100 years, from the mid-eighth/fourteenth to the mid-ninth/fifteenth century, which would place them all within the reign of the Naṣrid dynasty. Therefore, this collection gives us the opinions of a plurality of *muftīs*, while at the same time guaranteeing geographical and historical specificity. Another advantage of this collection regards its timing: it comes at the culmination of the efforts of codification in the Mālikī school and is contemporaneous to the introduction of *Mukhtaṣar Khalīl* into the Maghrib.[20]

Analysis of the *fatwās*

At the first level of analysis, we divided the *fatwās* into two categories – judicial and non-judicial. The basic difference between the two is that the subject of the latter does not allow for the initiation of judicial proceedings under any circumstances. A clear example of this would be *fatwā* 10, in which the questioner seeks to know the ruling regarding the validity of a particular act that the populace has introduced into the prayer for rain (*ṣalāt al-istisqā'*).[21] Other cases are not necessarily so clear. For example, the issue of the proper way of slaughtering animals for food is clearly a matter of ritual, and therefore should be clearly non-judicial. On the other hand, it involves property, and could conceivably lead to a lawsuit if a butcher failed to follow proper procedures and thus rendered the animal both inedible and useless for other purposes.[22] Because of the potential for a lawsuit arising from improperly following the law, we chose to consider cases of this type to be judicial.

The category 'judicial' was then further subdivided into two categories, judicial and quasi-judicial. The former is used for any *fatwā* that emerged in the course of a lawsuit. The latter category is reserved for cases for which, while there is no explicit evidence of an actual lawsuit, it seems likely that an actual event, or an intended event, prompted the petitioner's question. Furthermore, cases classified as quasi-judicial inevitably involve legal rights which are potentially enforceable in a court of law. These cases are judicial in so far as they deal with a legal issue within the competence of a court, but they are only quasi-judicial in that they may or may not have been asked within the context of a dispute in front of a court.[23] The results have been summarised below in Table 1.

The last level of analysis is a comparison of the rules[24] used by the *muftīs* in their *fatwās* with the doctrine of the *Mukhtaṣar Khalīl*. We have divided the rules into four categories: (1) rules found in the *Mukhtaṣar*; (2) rules contrary to the rule provided by the *Mukhtaṣar*; (3) rules implicit in the *Mukhtaṣar*; (4) rules with no textual basis in the *Mukhtaṣar*. An example from the first category is *fatwā* 1, in which the petitioner wishes to know whether or not the person who was entrusted with something and then subsequently lost it, is liable or not. An example of a *fatwā* which contradicts the rule of the *Mukhtaṣar Khalīl* is *fatwā* 6, where the questioner wishes to know what the rule is regarding the purity of oil into which a dead mouse has fallen. By replying that the oil may be cleansed and then sold, the *muftī*'s opinion was directly opposed to the text of Khalīl which says, 'The sold item, [in order for the sale to be valid] must be pure, unlike dung and [unlike] oil which has been polluted.'[25] An example of a *fatwā* whose rule is implicit in the language of the code is *fatwā* 32. The question involves a man whose garden adjoins the land of another. The owner of the garden wishes to plant grapes in the *ḥarīm*[26] of his garden which lies in his neighbour's property. By replying that the neighbour can prevent the owner of the garden from doing this, the *muftī* declares that while the garden's *ḥarīm* provides protection to the garden from any adverse action by the neighbour, this does not mean that the owner of the garden can introduce positive changes to land which remains the property of his neighbour. That the *ḥarīm* provides only defensive rights is no more than implicit in Khalīl's discussion of this topic, however. An example of a *fatwā* which is not covered by the code is *fatwā* 16 in which there is a dispute between a government-owned bakery and a privately owned one regarding the division of customers in a village. The results are presented below in Table 2.

The next level of interpretation centered around identifying the extent to which particular *muftīs* exercised discretion in their opinions, and the extent to which they clung to the established doctrine of their school. The results are presented below in Table 3.

Table 1

Name of *muftī*	judicial	quasi-judicial	non-judicial	total fatwās
Muḥmmad b. ʿAbd al-Malik al-Mantūri[1]	0	2	0	2
Abū al-Qāsim Muḥammad b. Sirāj[2]	23	73	49	145
Abū ʿAbd Allāh Muḥammad b. Muḥammad al-Saraquṣṭī[3]	16	30	6	52
Abū Isḥāq Ibrāhīm b. Fatūḥ[4]	3	5	1	9
Abū ʿAbd Allāh Muḥammad b. Yūsuf al-Ṣannāʿ[5]	0	4	0	4
Abū ʿAbd Allāh Muḥammad al-Ḥaffār[6]	17	23	16	56
Abū ʿAbd Allāh Muḥammad b. ʿAlī ʿAllāq[7]	2	3	0	5
Abū ʿUthman Saʿd al-Albīrī[8]	1	3	2	6
Abū Isḥāq Ibrāhīm b. Mūsā al-Shāṭibī[9]	4	12	25	41
ʿAbd Allāh b. Muḥammad b. Mūsā al-ʿAbdūsī[10]	1	0	0	1
anonymous *muftī* al-ḥaḍra	2	0	1	3
Aḥmad b. Qāsim b. ʿAbd al-Raḥmān al- Qabbāb[11]	0	0	1	1
Total	70	153	102	325

Note: these numbers include fatwās whose subject matter is ritual law.

1 d. 834/1430, Muḥammad b. Muḥammad Makhlūf, Shajarat al-nūr al-zakiyya (Beirut, 1930), 248.

2 d. 848/1444. He served as chief justice (qāḍī al-jamāʿa) of Granada and wrote a commentary on Khalīl. His student, al-Mawwāq, quotes from Ibn Sirāj extensively in his own commentary on Khalīl. Many of Ibn Sirāj's opinions were transmitted in the Miʿyār.

3 d. 865/1460. Al-Mawwāq quoted some of his opinions in his commentary on Khalīl. Ibid., p.260.

4 d. 867/1462. Some of his opinions were transmitted in the Miʿyār. Ibid., p. 260–1.

5 Abū ʿAbd Allāh Muḥammad b. Yūsuf al-Ṣannāʿ. He seems to have been of the same generation as Ibn Siraj although his death date is not known. Aḥmad Bābā al-Tumbuktī, Nayl al-Ibtihāj bi-taṭrīz al-dībāj (Tripoli, 1989), 527.

6 d. 811/1408. Some of his fatwās have been transmitted in the Miʿyār. Ibid., p.247.

7 d. 806/1403. He was one of the leading scholars of Granada, having served as qāḍī al-jamāʿa. He also wrote a commentary on Ibn al-Ḥājib's Jāmiʿ al-ummahāt. Some of his fatwās have been preserved in the Miʿyār, and al-Mawwāq quotes from him in his commentary.

8 d. 750/1349, al-Tumbuktī, Nayl al-Ibtihāj, p.188.

9 d. 790/1388. He is best-known for his work in uṣūl al-fiqh, al-Muwāfaqāt. He also has many fatwās preserved in the Miʿyār. Ibid., p.231.

10 d. 847/1443 or 850/1446. He was the muftī of Fez. Ibid., p.255

11 d. 778/1376 or 779/1377. Ibid., p.235

Table 2

Rules found in the Mukhtaṣar	Rules contrary to those in the Mukhtaṣar	Rules implicit in the Mukhtaṣar	Rules with no text in the Mukhtaṣar
138	46	26	44

Table 3

Name of muftī	Rules in Mukhtaṣar	Rules contrary to Mukhtaṣar	Rules implicit in Mukhtaṣar	Rules with no text Mukhtaṣar	Total
al-Manṭūrī	2	0	0	0	2
Ibn Sirāj	59	28	9	14	110
al-Saraquṣṭī	32	5	6	8	51
Ibn Fatūḥ	5	0	2	1	8
al-Ṣannāʿ	2	2	0	0	4
al-Ḥaffār	22	4	3	6	35
Ibn ʿAllāq	3	1	2	2	8
al-Albīrī	2	2	0	0	4
al-Shāṭibī	9	3	4	2	18
al-ʿAbdūsī	1	0	0	1	2
Anonymous	2	0	0	0	2
Total	138	46	26	44	254

Contradicting the Rules of the School: Justifications Used by the *muftīs*

Of the *muftīs* mentioned in Table 3, only four have enough *fatwās* to justify a closer look. The rules used by Ibn Sirāj, who has by far the most *fatwās* in the collection, are in accord with the explicit wording of the *Mukhtaṣar* approximately 54 per cent of the time, are in conflict with the explicit wording of the *Mukhtaṣar* 25 per cent of the time, are implied in the wording of the *Mukhtaṣar* 8 per cent of the time, and are outside of the *Mukhtaṣar's* scope 13 per cent of the time. Al-Saraquṣṭī's opinions are in accord with the explicit rules of the *Mukhtaṣar* approximately 63 per cent of the time, are in conflict with the explicit wording of the *Mukhtaṣar* approximately 10 per cent of the time, are implied approximately 12 per cent of the time, and are outside of its scope approximately 16 per cent of the time. Al-Ḥaffār's percentages are almost equivalent to those of al-Saraquṣṭī: 63 per cent, 11 per cent, 9 per cent, and 17 per cent. Al-Shāṭibī's opinions break down approximately into 50 per cent, 17 per cent, 22 per cent, and 11 per cent. The overall percentages for the rules analysed are 54 per cent, 18 per cent, 10 per cent and 18 per cent.

At first glance, the preliminary results suggest that legal indeterminacy was a significant problem facing Granadian legal culture, as the answers for only slightly over one half of the cases represented could have been predicted from Khalīl's *Mukhtaṣar*. At the same time a significant percentage of the answers given are not even covered by the code. These facts require closer inspection, and it is to their analysis that we turn presently.

We have seen that in the *fatwās* analysed, there were forty-three instances where the *muftī* departed from the explicit rule given by the code. Twelve of the instances in which the *muftīs* contradicted the *Mukhtaṣar* occurred in the law of divorce and nine involved the ritual slaughter of animals. In these two cases, i.e., divorce and the slaughter of animals, the local Mālikī legal practice as recorded by the *Ḥadīqa* had departed from the established rule of the school as reported by Khalīl. There is no doubt, moreover, that in both of these instances, the *muftīs* were aware that they were contradicting established doctrine. Thus, Ibn Sirāj says in *fatwā* 101, in reply to a question regarding a man who said to his wife that she was as unlawful to him as the meat of the pig:

> The scholars have held different opinions in ancient and contemporary times regarding the one who says to his wife 'You are forbidden to me', and Ibn al-ʿArabī mentioned fifteen opinions [on the matter], of which five are in the school. Mālik and Ibn al-Qāsim said in the *Mudawwana* that where the wife had been taken to her husband's home, it is a three-fold divorce, and his intention is of no effect. If she has not dwelled in her husband's home, then the husband's intention is effective, whether one or more ... Ibn Khuwayz Mindād transmitted that Mālik said it was one [divorce] of separation for both the wife who has been taken to her husband's home and the one who has not. One of the masters, may God have mercy on them, who had the authority to issue legal opinions in this our town, used to rely on this transmission and issue opinions based upon it. Moreover, he believed it to be in accord with the rule of the *Mudawwana* which has been mentioned previously because he (Mālik) distinguished in it (the *Mudawwana*) between the wife who had been taken to her husband's home and the one who had not because it was their (the Medinese) practice that separation did not occur without a three-fold divorce if the wife had been taken to her husband's home. As for us, she is separated from her

> husband after [only] one divorce. Thus, the wife of today who has been taken to her husband's home is the equivalent of the wife at that time (the time of Mālik) who had not been taken to her husband's home. Therefore, the rule [governing them] is one. Al-Lakhmī referred to this in one of his discussions, and Ibn Rushd gave preponderance to the opinion accepting the [word] of the one who claims that he did not intend by this statement divorce, and declared it to be correct. There is a transmission to this effect in the 'Utbiyya. Thus, *a fortiori*, he (the husband) should be believed when he claims he intended other than a three-fold divorce. Therefore, whoever uses this last opinion is secure, God willing.[27]

Two things from Ibn Sirāj's *fatwā* especially deserve comment. The first is that despite the authoritative statement of the *Mukhtaṣar*, we learn that the school actually has five opinions on this case. The fact that the rule is itself controversial no doubt is important in giving the *muftī* greater freedom in abandoning the established rule. The second is that it is the change in social practice which necessitated the change in the legal rule.[28] It is for this reason that Ibn Sirāj quotes a Granadian predecessor to the effect that in reality the rule has not changed; it is only the practice of the people which has changed.

The claim of this unnamed jurist seems to be confirmed by the practice of the other *muftīs* in this collection: when faced with a similar question they all reply, contrary to Khalīl, that this type of statement has the effect of initiating one divorce of separation unless the husband intends more than one divorce. Likewise, al-Mawwāq mentions the same reasoning in his commentary on Khalīl.[29] For this reason, then, all divorce cases in the *Ḥadīqa* (a total of twelve) which are contrary to Khalīl's rule, are in fact instances of the local rule mentioned by Ibn Sirāj. For this reason they should not be considered instances of judicial discretion, or instances of *ad hoc* rule making. If we then included these cases under a more general category of rule following, as opposed to our original category of following rules found in the *Mukhtaṣar*, then the number of decisions governed by previously existing rules would increase from 138 to 150, or from 54 per cent to 59 per cent.

As for the cases involving ritual slaughter, four involve what is called *al-dhabīḥa al-mughalṣama*. The law requires a butcher, when slaughtering an animal, to cut the throat so that it remains entirely connected to the head of the slaughtered animal. When a part of the throat remains attached to the body, the slaughtered animal is called *mughalṣama*. The standard doctrine of the Mālikī school is that an animal slaughtered in this manner is carrion (*mayta*), and therefore, its meat cannot be used as food nor can the carcass be used for any other purpose.[30] Once again we are faced with a local change in the rule recognised by the school. This case, however, is distinguished from that above in that in this instance, the controversy centres on the rule itself; the practice of the people is not an issue. Because the controversy is over which opinion is the correct rule, Ibn Sirāj does not hesitate to justify his reply solely on the basis of his own reasoning. His replies regarding the *mughalṣama*, then, represent a more clear-cut case of judicial rule making. Ibn Sirāj says in *fatwā* 62:

> As for the *ghalṣama*, there has been much controversy regarding it in the school, and its prohibition has been attributed to Mālik. However, Ibn Waḍḍāḥ rejected the accuracy of this transmission. Ibn Rushd reported that the prevailing [opinion of the school] is that eating from it is forbidden. However, the correct position upon reflection is its permissibility.[31]

The other cases involving ritual slaughter of animals are similar to the *mughalṣama* in that they represent a shift of doctrine based on the *muftī*'s own evaluation of the strength and weakness of the different opinions. Thus, in *fatwā* 64 Ibn Sirāj explicitly contradicts the rule of the school that forbids eating from an animal which has had only one jugular vein cut, using the same reasoning quoted above.[32]

Ibn Sirāj, based on the evidence of the *Ḥadīqa*, is significantly bolder in relying on his own personal reasoning than the other *muftīs* represented in the collection. For example, al-Saraqusṭī, in *fatwā* 86, when asked the same question put to Ibn Sirāj in *fatwā* 64, says that if only one jugular vein is cut, then the animal cannot be eaten.[33] Again, in *fatwā* 68, when asked about a cow which had escaped while being slaughtered, he is content to remark that if it had been captured shortly after its escape, and the slaughter had been completed immediately, then the validity of eating from this cow is controversial (*ukilat bi-khilāf*), without expressly revealing his personal opinion. Ibn Sirāj, however, when asked about a similar case, allowed eating from it unhesitatingly.[34]

This manifests itself rather clearly in Ibn Sirāj's willingness to contradict the established doctrine of the school. While al-Ḥaffār and al-Saraqusṭī contradict established doctrine in only about 10 per cent of their replies, roughly a quarter of Ibn Sirāj's opinions conflict with established Mālikī doctrine. While al-Shāṭibī's answers also contain a significant number of opinions which contradict established doctrine, a little more than one in five, his sample size is not large enough to justify any generalisations about his personality as a *muftī*. That is not the case, however, with Ibn Sirāj, whose opinions are well represented in the collection. Moreover, we find that he contradicted doctrine not just in matters of divorce and the slaughter of animals: he also offered opinions contradictory to the school's prevailing doctrine in partnership,[35] sale,[36] debts,[37] exchange of currency (*ṣarf*),[38] marriage,[39] pledge (*rahn*),[40] and loan.[41]

In most of these cases, Ibn Sirāj has elected to follow an already existing opinion within the school, but one that is contrary to established doctrine. At times he justifies his choice by simply saying that this contrary opinion has a sound basis (*hādhā al-qawl lahu wajh*), as he does in *fatwā* 6 regarding the sale of impure oil. In *fatwā* 8, which deals with the validity of a sale payable in installments where the purchaser stipulated that the installments are maintained even should he die before completion of payment,[42] he points out that since Mālik's opinion was not based on a revelatory text, it is permissible to contradict it. In *fatwā* 11, he chooses the rule which he considers to be sounder in reason (*al-ṣaḥīḥ min jihat al-naẓar*). In *fatwā* 134, where a man married a woman before she completed the waiting period that follows fornication (*istibrā al-zinā*), he allows him to remarry her after she completes the legally prescribed waiting period, also because it is an opinion whose basis is sound (*qawl lahu wajh*). In 155, he based his *fatwā* allowing the mortgagee (*murtahin*) to stipulate that he has the right to sell the pawned item if the mortgagor (*rāhin*) fails to pay the debt at the agreed-upon date based upon a rule identified by Ibn Rushd as controversial.[43] In arguing in *fatwā* 274 that the unit of measurement to be used in the loan of fungible items (*qarḍ*) should be those used in sale, and not that which is used in barter (*mubādala*), he resorts to analogy. It is not, however, a strict instance of the extrapolation of a new rule, because in his *fatwā* he simply uses the analogy to support his *choice* of a rule against the prevailing opinion.

In *fatwā* 3, however, we do have an instance of true extrapolation. The question before Ibn Sirāj was the legitimacy of a partnership between two men for the manufacture of cheese from milk. According to the rule of the school, this was an invalid partnership because Mālik forbade partnerships whose capital was food.[44] What seemed to concern Mālik was the inevitable uncertainty attendant to the division of the manufactured product, since the output would differ depending on the quality of the foodstuffs used as capital. Hence, it would be difficult, if not impossible, to distribute the product equitably among the partners.[45] This objection is also true in the case of manufacturing cheese from milk: some milk will produce more cheese than others, and division based on the original contribution of milk would have to ignore this fact, with the subsequent cause of harm to one of the partners.

Ibn Sirāj, however, finds a precedent in the school for allowing this labour partnership. He notes that this case is the equivalent of the controversy regarding the permissibility of mixing olives and sesame seeds at an oil press (*maʿṣara*). Having made a connection based on the common factor of the uncertainty in assigning the shares of the product, in this case the oil produced from the olives and the sesame seeds, and in the case of the *fatwā*, the cheese from the milk, he extrapolates that this agreement is most likely permissible because of need. He adds, of course, that they must divide the cheese in accord to the quantities of milk contributed by each.[46]

Legal Controversy *(khilāf)* and the Administration of the Law

While Ibn Sirāj's wide use of personal discretion is no doubt important, his use of the expression '*lam yuʿtaraḍ*' or '*lam naʿtariḍhu*' also deserves comment. It seems that the purpose of this expression is to put a limit on state intervention (*ḥisba*) into the acts of individuals. When Ibn Sirāj says that selling impure oil after washing it is lawful, he is merely selecting among the opinions of the school. However, when he adds after that the statement '*fa-man qalladahu lam yuʿtaraḍ*', he is in all likelihood signalling that this case is outside the domain of the market inspector (*muḥtasib*). The same is true in *fatwā* 64, where the import of the statement is that those supervising the slaughter of animals should not intervene in cases where the butcher has cut only one of the jugular veins. Finally, in *fatwā* 134 the effect of his statement '*fa-man qalladahu lam naʿtariḍhu*' is to proclaim that such marriages will be outside the review powers of public authorities.

From these *fatwās* we can extrapolate that the legal machinery of the Naṣrid state was concerned to maintain and enforce the legal standards of the Mālikī school in regard at least to the purity of foodstuffs sold in the markets, the conditions for valid marriages, and the slaughter of animals. A possible unforeseen consequence of the positivisation of Mālikī rules was that it increased the powers of the *muḥtasib* by creating rules in areas of the law which, even within the school itself, were controversial. It is possible that Ibn Sirāj wanted to decrease the regulatory powers of the state by pointing out that many of the rules in the school, although valid when applied within the context of a dispute or in giving legal advice prior to an act, were not valid grounds to justify the intervention of regulatory powers prior to the occurrence of a legal dispute. This policy of limiting the police powers of the state that we find in some of his *fatwās* seems to be in line with what his student, al-Mawwāq, attributes to his teacher in his commentary on the *Mukhtaṣar* :

> My master, Ibn Sirāj, may God have mercy upon him, in regard to this type of case [i.e. controversial cases] would not issue opinions based on them [rules contradictory to the established doctrine of the school] before an act, but he would not be critical of those acting in accord with them. All that can be said is that the individual who does it [acts using a rule contrary to the rule of the school] has abandoned the dictates of piety, and wherever controversy is well known, there can be no intervention, especially if there is a need justifying that action.[47]

Thus, it seems that the proper interpretation of Ibn Sirāj's *fatwās* which are contrary to the doctrine of the school is not to take them as representing a desire to change established doctrine. Rather, it was in all probability an effort to restrict the use of controversial but established rules to dispute situations, and to deny them the status of absolute rules, violation of which could invite state intervention.

In contrast to Ibn Sirāj, we find that al-Ḥaffār and al-Saraquṣṭī do not use expressions like '*lam yuʿtaraḍ*' in contexts where there are competing positions within the school. Al-Shāṭibī, however, does make a reference in one of his *fatwās* to the effect of legal indeterminacy on the enforcement of such a rule:

> The more appropriate course of action in every case for which the scholars of the school have two opinions and the people have followed one of these two, even though it (one of the two) may be considered weak upon reflection, is that they should be left alone, and treated as though they have followed it from ancient times, and that their practice had been governed by it. For, if they were forced to use the other rule, that would create confusion in [the minds of] the populace, and would encourage lawsuits.[48]

In this opinion al-Shāṭibī points to another difficulty involved in the attempt to apply the rules of the school uniformly. While it is possible that a current generation of jurists are able to reach agreement about what is the rule of the school regarding a particular case, that agreement cannot erase a *history* of disagreement and legal indeterminacy. In these cases, al-Shāṭibī argues, strict legality must retreat in the face of material considerations, namely confusion of the populace, and the risk of increased law suits. This differs from the argument of Ibn Sirāj, who wished to use the history of controversy only to limit the regulatory powers of the state. He would still, however, rely on the established opinion of the school in other contexts. Al-Shāṭibi insists that a local legal tradition must be respected even if it is against the established doctrine of the school, implying that the *muftī* should base his *fatwā*, when faced with this situation, upon the local rule, and not the rule of the school.

This does not mean that al-Shāṭibī is a legal pragmatist. Indeed, the texts of his *fatwās* display the conservatism that is typical of all legal writing. Thus, he is usually much more careful than Ibn Sirāj in providing a reasoned argument justifying his diversion from the established doctrine of the school. A good example of this is *fatwā* 265. This is the same question – a partnership for the production of cheese from milk – that was put to Ibn Sirāj.[49] In contrast to Ibn Sirāj who answered in no more than two lines, al-Shāṭibī takes almost two pages of argumentation to justify his opinion. What is most revealing about his personality as a jurist, however, is that despite reaching his conclusion independently of any texts in the school, he refused to respond before coming across a text which he could use as a precedent:

> This [its permission] is what appeared to me without a text regarding this particular case upon which I could base it [my opinion]. For that reason I refrained from answering, although a number of people had asked me about it. Then, I found in the *'Utibyya* a case resembling it, and it is from the transmission of Ibn al-Qāsim from Mālik. He [Ibn al-Qāsim] said: 'I asked Mālik about oil presses, sesame oil and radish seed oil, this man comes with *arādib*,[50] and that one with others, so that when they meet at the press, they press [their seeds] together?' Mālik said: 'This is to be avoided [or: this is detested] because some of it will produce more than the other. However, if the people are in need of that action , I hope that it is a trivial matter, because the people must have what improves their condition. And the thing for which the people find no alternative or substitute, I hope that there is room for that, God willing, and I see no problem in it.' Ibn al-Qāsim said: 'Olives are like that above.' Ibn Rushd said: 'He deemed it to be a small matter because of the necessity involved, for it is impossible to press a small amount of sesame or radish seeds by themselves. Likewise, he also took account of the opinion of those scholars who permit unequal exchange of these things.' ... All of this is some of which points to the validity of what appeared to me in regard to milk, and God knows best.[51]

This opinion exhibits the traits of what Watson terms 'law making by interpreters'. Describing the structure of arguments made by legal interpretation, he says:

> Only some kinds of argument are respectable, above all argument by analogy from existing rules in a similar context, or from authority, such as precedent in one's own system or an opinion expressed for another system that is held in esteem. These arguments have in common that they are of necessity backward looking. Even if the interpreter is in fact bringing about a legal revolution he must justify it with such arguments. This can only reinforce conservative tendencies, and it is notorious that the pace of reform by interpretation is slow.[52]

Thus, we find al-Shāṭibī using each of the three elements mentioned by Watson: an analogy based on the mingling of orphans' property with the property of their guardians in his own attempt to reach a solution to the question, and then an analogy based on a similar ruling attributed to Mālik; for precedent, he quotes Ibn Rushd as approving this ruling; as for an outside opinion, he quotes Ibn Rushd as saying that Mālik ruled in this manner out of his regard for the opinion of other scholars who do not consider the unequal exchange of oil illegal.

Al-Shāṭibī also declares explicitly his allegiance to the basic principle which guided the creation of Khalīl's code – that in controversial cases, the *mashhūr* opinion is the default rule of the school.[53] The *Ḥadīqa*, in *fatwā* 276, preserves an explicit declaration of his fidelity to the rules of the school. Thus, when asked by a petitioner to explain the Mālikī methodological principle of taking cognizance of a weak opinion (*murāʿāt qawl ḍaʿīf*), he takes it as a pretext to scold his colleagues for not sticking to the doctrine of the school closely enough, saying:

> 'Taking cognizance' of other opinions, weak or otherwise, is the affair of *mujtahids* in the law, for 'Taking cognizance of the controversy' means nothing else than taking cognizance of the opponent's evidence … and taking cognizance of the evidence or not doing so, O group of followers (*maʿshara al-muqallidīn*), is not our affair! Therefore, it suffices us to understand the opinions of the scholars, and issue opinions based on the prevailing of these [opinions]. And would that that be sufficient that we may escape with nothing for us and nothing against us![54]

After looking at more detail into the *fatwās* that contradict Khalīl, then, we discover that at the most these represent small divergences in the interpretation of the legacy of the Mālikī legal corpus, of which the *Mukhtaṣar* is just one element, albeit the most authoritative.[55] These divergences from the doctrine of the *Mukhtaṣar*, moreover, are not done out of an anti-codification stance; rather, they represent the right of a *muftī* who is a *mujtahid-fatwā* to choose among the different positions within the school. By itself, this does not represent a challenge to the basic belief that permitted the Mālikī school to create positive rules in the first place: the *mashhūr* position of the school must be followed in cases of controversy.

The Limits of Codification: Cases and Rules not governed by *Mukhtaṣar Khalīl*

We have identified four types of rules which lie outside of the scope of the *Mukhtaṣar*:

1. Secondary rules associated with an existing rule in the code;
2. Rules dealing with the relationship of individuals to the government and other social institutions;
3. Rules governing novel cases;
4. Civil cases governed by no explicit rules in the code.

Category 1

Fatwā 21 presents a typical example of a case which only partially falls under the code. Ibn Sirāj is asked about the validity of a gift given by a father to his son on the occasion of the latter's wedding. The father, however, had the gift witnessed before the marriage contract had been completed by a few days. The *muftī* replied that the gift is valid, but becomes binding only if the son takes possession while the father is alive and healthy. If not, then the gift must be approved by the father's heirs. Up to this point in his *fatwā*, Ibn Sirāj is transmitting standard Mālikī doctrine regarding the conditions by which a gift becomes valid and binding. It is only the last part of the answer which adds a new rule to the doctrine. Ibn Sirāj, after explaining the law of gifts, then adds that had the father included the gift to his son as a part of the son's marriage contract, the gift would have been binding not only against the father, but also against his heirs had the father died before the son took possession of the gift:

> The gift is valid and binds the father if the son takes possession of it while the father is alive and healthy. If the father had died before the son takes possession of it, then the gift is not valid for the son without the permission

> of the heirs, because it preceded the marriage. [This is] in contrast to the situation had it been in the marriage contract, in which case he would not need [their permission].[56]

This last rule, while not mentioned in the *Mukhtaṣar*, does not appear to be a result of the *muftī*'s personal discretion. In all likelihood it is a case of a rule created by the document writers (*ahl al-wathāʾiq, al-muwaththiqūn*). At least two other *fatwās* found in the collection support this conclusion. Al-Shāṭibī notes in *fatwā* 238 that a woman's wearing of clothes is sufficient to prove that the clothes are hers in the context of a dispute with the husband's heirs. In the next *fatwā* al-Shāṭibī attributes this rule to *ahl al-wathāʾiq*.[57] Likewise, in *fatwā* 155, when Ibn Sirāj was asked if the mortgagee (*murtahin*), based on a stipulation in the contract, could sell the pawned item (*rahn*) without the permission of either the mortgagor (*rāhin*) or the approval of a judge, he replied that the mortgagee could do so only if the contract contained a clause making him the mortgagor's agent in life, and his executor on death in regard to the sale of the pawned item:

> If the mortgagor has made the mortgagee, in regard to the pawn's sale, his agent during his [the mortgagor's] life, and his executor after his death, then he [the mortgagee] has the right to sell it. If he did not do this in the mortgage contract, then he cannot sell it without consulting the mortgagor or the judge.[58]

Ibn Salmūn, however, mentions this clause explicitly, attributing it to 'one of the document writers', saying that 'One of the document writers said, 'It is not permissible for him to sell the pawned item without consultation or the [intervention] of the government … unless he said in the document 'He made him his agent in his lifetime and his executor after his death.''' [59]

This circumstantial evidence gives us strong reason to suppose that what was true in *fatwās* 155 and 238 is also true in the other *fatwās* which mention a secondary rule associated with a subject in the *Mukhtaṣar*. For example, in *fatwā* 164 the *muftī* mentions that a sale by estimate of the quantity (*bi-l-taḥarrī*) is valid either if both the purchaser and the seller are skilled in estimation, or they bring in a professional estimator.[60] In all likelihood, the introduction of an estimator was probably introduced in social practice and then given legal recognition, first by those writing contracts, and then finally by *muftīs* and judges. This allows us to see the relationship between the legal genre of *wathāʾiq* and the legal codes: while the latter provide a broad framework for the exercise of legal rights, the former's function is to provide formulae which remove doubt as to the intention of the parties to the agreement as well as providing procedural steps for the exercise of the rights recognised by the law.[61]

Their relationship in this respect is dialectical, for through the exercise of legal powers, new rules are created to govern unanticipated contexts created by the very use of these same legal powers. This is implied in al-Mawwāq's discussion of Khalīl's rule regarding the validity of the mortgagee's sale of the pawned item.[62] On the one hand, Ibn ʿArafa (d.680/1281) is quoted as saying that when the mortgagor gives the mortgagee the right to sell the pawned item without stipulating that it be a good sale (*ṣawāb*), this has the effect of creating a relationship of agency (*maḥḍ tawkīl*). He adds that on the other hand when the mortgagor stipulates this right on the condition that he fails to pay the mortgagee on the agreed-upon date, this creates the possibility for a conflict regarding the fact of payment or non-payment. This possibility of conflict requires the intervention of a judge.

It is not difficult to imagine that the rule mentioned by the *muftī* was originally introduced by the document writers to remove the ambiguities involved in this type of sale. We can speculate regarding the development of the rule. At first there is the recognition of the right of the mortgagee to sell the pawned good if the mortgagor fails to pay on the agreed-upon date. As a result of this latter condition, mortgagors begin to challenge the validity of some sales on the grounds that they had made payment. Legal theory attempts to limit these disputes by requiring that the mortgagee can sell only after consulting a judge who will make sure that the mortgagor failed to pay the money at the due date. The mortgagees counter by requiring that the mortgagors appoint them to be their agents in the sale of the pawned good. This, which began in fact as nothing more than an attempt by mortgagees to avoid the hurdle of judicial intervention, ends as a general rule demanding from all mortgagees that if they wish to exercise the right to sell the pawned good in their possession, they must stipulate this relationship of agency explicitly in the contract. If they fail to do so, the sale cannot proceed without a judge's approval.

Category 2

It is not surprising that rules regarding the relationship between the individual and the state should not be codified. These issues require solutions based more or less entirely on substantive considerations rather than on formal legal ones. This is not to say that legal knowledge is not important in the interpretation of these opinions; rather, it is to point out that in these cases a much fuller knowledge of the historical context of these questions is necessary for a meaningful interpretation of the opinions to be given. In other words, these *fatwās* are of possibly more significance to the social historian than the *fatwās* discussed above.

An example of a dispute involving an individual and a branch of the state occurs in *fatwā* 16. The questioner narrates what amounts to an economic dispute between a privately-owned bakery and a publicly-owned bakery. We are told that there is a village which has two bakeries (*furnān*), one controlled by a certain section of the town, and the other controlled by a mosque (*aḥaduhumā li-l-jānib wa al-ākhar li-l-masjid*). According to the questioner, there was a customary agreement between the two regarding which sections of the village each would serve: *li-kulli furn jiha maʿlūma min diyār al-qarya*. This did not mean that occasionally individuals from one section of the village did not use the facilities of the other section of the village. This, however, was limited to particular individuals and happened by chance: *ʿāriḍ yaʿriḍ lahu*.

The conflict began when a group of people who customarily took their business to the bakery of the *jānib*, took their business to the endowed bakery controlled by the mosque (*furn al-aḥbās*). Somebody opposed this and said that this was not permissible. Furthermore, he added that if the Imām took the flour generated by those who transferred their business, his probity would be affected (*akhdhuhu li-dhālika al-daqīq … qādiḥ fīhi*). The *muftī* rejected these charges and said that this action was perfectly legal. That the *muftī* took the implications of these charges seriously, however, is revealed in the implied threat directed to those making the accusation:

> There is no violation of the law here either on the part of the Imām or any other person, and it is [entirely] legal. As for the one claiming that it is illegal, he is ignorant and making false claims about the law. He must repent from what he says [and cease and desist].[63]

Although the explicit issue in the question concerns the probity of the local prayer leader, it obviously also entails a conflict regarding the distribution of local economic resources. Likewise, the legitimacy of the established religious authority is at stake, and for that reason it seems that Ibn Sirāj responded to the accusations against the Imām sternly.

In *fatwā* 193, there is another case illustrating a conflict between an individual and an agent of the state. Al-Ḥaffār was asked about a sale in which the purchaser was to pay the vendor 100 dinars. On his way to deliver the cash, the purchaser was stopped by a government agent (*mushrif*), who forced him to pay a duty (*thiqāf*) of eleven dinars. The purchaser was seeking a rebate from the vendor in compensation for the duty paid, while the vendor was seeking his money in full. Al-Ḥaffār replied that the purchaser must pay the amount specified in the sale, and that the question of compensation for the purchaser was to be referred to the ruler.[64]

Category 3

At this point in our analysis we shall direct our attention toward solutions to novel cases. What, however, is the distinction between a novel case and any other case not explicitly falling under the province of the code? Often this is an ambiguous distinction. However, we have chosen to make a distinction between the novel cases which arise from the exercise of already existing rights, e.g., the secondary rules mentioned above, and cases which are *generically* a new topic for the law. Because of this distinction between a novel case and a case not governed by an explicit rule, we have not found many instances of novel cases in the *Ḥadīqa*. The one we do have, however, is extremely important as an example of how new social facts help to create new legal rules.

As is well known, the production of silk was a pillar of the economic success of the Naṣrid regime in Granada.[65] What may not be as well known is the extent to which this production depended upon labour partnerships which were irregular according to standard Mālikī doctrine. According to the evidence of the *Ḥadīqa*, the preferred mode of investment took the name of *'alūfa*. This arrangement entailed a partnership between the labourer and the owner of the mulberry trees (*tūt*). Once the mulberry leaves had matured to the point where they could be fed to silkworms, the owner of the tree would hire the labourer to harvest the leaves and feed them to the silkworms. The labourer would also contribute a portion of the silkworms to the partnership. The owner of the mulberry trees and the labourer would then divide the silk produced according to the proportions agreed upon at the outset of the partnership.

The legality of this arrangement was at the very least questionable. If it was viewed as a contract of hire (*ijāra*), then it would be invalid due to the unknown nature of the labourer's wage. It could only be deemed a partnership, however, if it was made analogous to other contracts such as sharecropping (*muzāra'a*). Yet, because this latter contract is itself based on a special dispensation (*rukhṣa*) which overrides the normal principles of the law, there was great reluctance to admit the legality of an arrangement which widened the scope of a dispensation.[66] Nevertheless, the five *fatwās* regarding the *'alūfa* all agree that this arrangement is legal, and therefore binding.

There are five *fatwās* in the collection whose subject is the permissibility of the *'alūfa* contract. These five *fatwās*, 127(g) and 139–42, were authored by three *muftīs*: al-Shāṭibī, al-Ḥaffār, and Ibn Sirāj.[67] Al-Shāṭibī, although he recognised the tenuous nature of the contract, suggests that an arrangement which is similar to 'the practice of the people' is permissible because of its similarity to the *muzāra'a*.[68] Al-Ḥaffār's analysis did not differ too greatly from al-Shāṭibī's except that he made explicit the grounds on which the customary arrangement was invalid as well as noting that most contracts, since they followed customary arrangements, were invalid.[69]

Ibn Sirāj addressed this question in 127(g), 141, and 142. Of these three *fatwās*, the first two are both lengthy discussions regarding the validity of this contract. His discussion of the issues highlights the problematic nature of the case – on the one hand the *muftī* has a responsibility to be loyal to his legal tradition, while on the other hand he cannot ignore economic realities. In the first of the two, he is asked about the legality of the *'alūfa* as it has been practised by the people (*'alā mā jarat bihi 'ādat al-nās*).[70] It is clear from his response that he accepts the solutions of his predecessors, al-Shāṭibī and al-Ḥaffār, as representing the school's position on this matter. He is more explicit in revealing, however, that this solution was contrary to the practice of the people:[71]

> If a person can find someone who will agree with him to an acceptable arrangement, e.g., that the labourer inspects the leaves, he buys half of them from the their owner with his labour… if he finds someone willing to work [under these stipulations], then it is impermissible for him to act in the manner of the custom of the people according to the opinion of Mālik and the majority of scholars. It is permissible, however, according to the opinion of Aḥmad b. Ḥanbal and some scholars of the pious ancestors, by analogy to *qirāḍ* (commenda) and *musāqāt*.[72]

Ibn Sirāj is clearly concerned about the fact that a large number of these partnerships fell outside of the Mālikī legal norm which was to govern the case. His solution, in effect, is to limit the scope of this rule to people who are willing to follow it, and legitimise the 'practice of the people' in all other cases. How does he do this? He provides two arguments, the first is taken from comparative jurisprudence (*'ilm al-khilāf*). The effect of this argument is to show that although the 'practice' is contrary to Mālikī doctrine, and indeed is contrary to the doctrine of most of the scholars, it is, nevertheless, a valid arrangement in the eyes of a small, but important, minority of scholars. The second argument is taken from the principles of the Mālikī doctrine itself, and has the effect of overturning the old opinion and creating a new rule:

> If the person cannot find someone who will work [under these] terms, and [will accept] only the customary arrangements, and if not following that [the custom] leads to their [the trees] non-use, harm [to their owner], and the waste of [his] property, then it becomes permissible according to Mālik's statement allowing that thing which is needed by all.[73]

While he does not state explicitly what the custom of the people is, when this issue is read in the light of al-Ḥaffār's *fatwā* mentioned above, and al-Mawwāq's discussion of lease,[74] we can deduce that it probably entailed hiring the labourer for a wage to be taken from the output, i.e., the silk. Moreover, Ibn Sirāj's last argument implies that the owners of the trees are unable to find labourers willing to accept the terms of the partnership as outlined by Mālikī law.

To summarise, the eighth–ninth century Granadian legal establishment was faced by the novel case of partnership in the manufacture of silk. Investment in this type of partnership seems to have become so common that it required the creation of a specific rule governing it. This seems to have begun with al-Shāṭibī, was developed slightly by the time of al-Ḥaffār, and had become systematic legal doctrine by the time of Ibn Sirāj. The rule that was developed by the school to govern this case was based on a controversial mode of legal reasoning, but this was justified because of economic necessity. The extent to which this rule was followed by citizens of Granada, however, is questionable, for the evidence of the *fatwās* indicates that they had their own customary arrangement. Because this practice was recognised as being valid by at least some jurists in Islamic law, however, the customary arrangement was granted limited recognition.

Category 4

Our last category is defined negatively – we have reserved it for cases which we felt were neither secondary developments of already existing rules, nor were they novel cases. At the same time, however, they are matters that must be considered civil, and therefore should have had a place in the code, but for one reason or another, they were not. Some of the cases, as we shall see, can be extrapolated from other sections of the code. Others, however, seem to be governed by well-established rules, but these rules are not part of the *Mukhtaṣar*.

The first two cases, 169 and 171, involve the economic relations of individuals in a family.[75] They represent actual lawsuits in which the children are suing the father for money owed to their deceased mother. In both cases the father, over the duration of the marriage, had exploited his wife's properties, apparently keeping the produce for himself. We are told that the marriage in the first case had lasted a long time, and in the second it had endured thirty years. The implicit claim of the father in both is that his wife had forgiven him these debts, while the children deny this. What is being contested then is the size of the estate. If the father wins his claim, the estate is essentially limited to the real property of the deceased wife. If the children win, the estate increases dramatically to include all the output of these lands from the moment the husband began farming them to the time of the mother's demise. Al-Ḥaffār, however, rejects the claim of the children, saying:

> If this marriage has endured for a long time, and the wife never claimed from the husband what she was owed of the crops during her lifetime, then her silence over such a lengthy time is cause for cancellation of her right. Thus, her son has no claim on that [money].[76]

In a similar question before Ibn Sirāj, however, he gives the children the right to sue their father for the rent owed to their mother with the exception of that from the domicile. At the same time, however, he gives the father the right to sue the estate for the unpaid wages stemming from his management and farming of his deceased wife's agricultural lands.[77]

The issue in these two cases before the judge is simple: does a wife's non-collection of rent from her husband really amount to a forgiveness of the assumed obligation? Al-Ḥaffār said yes, while Ibn Sirāj said no. Unfortunately, the *Mukhtaṣar* does not address the length of time necessary to pass before a debt is considered to be forgiven. While it does give the amount of time necessary for possession (*ḥiyāza*) to become property (*milk*), and distinguishes between the possession of a stranger (*ajnabī*) and a relative (*qarīb*), it provides no rule for our case. This does not mean that the *muftīs* quoted above were facing entirely unprecedented cases, for there are a number of opinions in the school regarding length of time which must pass before a debt is taken to be forgiven. What seems strange, however, is that Khalīl made no reference to this issue at all.[78]

One reason for Khalīl's silence could be the numerous opinions expressed on this issue. In other words there was a failure to reach enough of a consensus that would allow for a rule to emerge. Thus, this issue was left to discretion, as we see in *fatwā* 298, where al-Ḥaffār was asked about a Jew who was owed some money by a Muslim from a transaction dating back eleven years. Despite the fact that the Jew had documents supporting his claim, al-Ḥaffār ruled that the Muslim was to be believed with his oath in his claim that the Jew had forgiven the debt based simply on the length of time between the debt and the claim.[79]

Our next cluster of questions deals with water law, questions 188–90,[80] a topic of obvious importance for an economy such as Granada's which depended heavily upon irrigated agriculture. Despite this, however, there is no chapter on this topic in the code. This does not mean that it is unregulated and left to the pure discretion of the *muftī*, however. In the three answers of Ibn Sirāj, we see that water law was governed by two basic principles: irrigation water is not subject to ownership, and its use is governed by the principle of prior usage. This meant that if anyone chose not to use his share of irrigation water for a given growing season, he could not 'sell' it to a neighbour. At the same time, however, those who invested in establishing the irrigation network had the exclusive right of determining the shares each person would take from that water. Therefore, if a village built a water wheel (*sāqiya*), they establish prior usage rights to that water, even if they are further away from the stream than another village.[81] Once they have satisfied their need for water, however, they cannot prevent others from using the remainder. Other than these two principles, then, the details of the law are left to the people themselves to work out. It is possible that this was not included in the *Mukhtaṣar*, then, because it is essentially a matter of customary law.

General Rules and Particular Rulings in the *Mukhtaṣar Khalīl*

The only category which we have not discussed at length is that category representing the opinions which are explicitly included in the code. Perhaps this category deserves at least passing comment. It has been asserted that Islamic law, because of its casuistic method, is very 'concrete,' meaning that it provides very specific rules for specific acts. The price of this, however, was that it failed, or more charitably, was not interested in developing abstract rules of general applicability.[82] If one looks at the code of Khalīl, however, one realises that the two types of rules, the very specific and the very general, exist side by side. It would be very surprising indeed if one were to find a code that could be described as 'concrete.' Such a code would be obsolete upon its very completion. The very fact that *Mukhtaṣar Khalīl* survived hundreds of years in locations as different as Andalusia, sub-Saharan Africa and Egypt, indicates that it must have had sufficient generality to allow it to withstand changes in both time and place.

Indeed, one cannot accurately describe the 'concrete' rules in Khalīl as actually being rules: instead, Khalīl may cite concrete examples as instances of a general rule, especially if that example's inclusion within the general rule has been controversial, or if that case is likely to recur in front of a judge or *muftī*. A clear example of this is in the chapter of sale, where Khalīl says: 'The sold item, [in order for the sale to be valid] must be pure, unlike dung and [unlike] oil which has been polluted.'[83] As a matter of fact, this question came up several times in the course of the *fatwās*: is it permissible, and if so, under what conditions, to sell oil which has been polluted by the body of a dead mouse?

Another example should make this point clear. In the chapter on hire (*ijāra*), for example, Khalīl mentions explicitly that hiring a labourer to harvest olives for a percentage of what he picks, if the labourer is obligated to work for a certain time, is invalid. Thus, in *fatwā* 257 the *muftī* is presented with a case which is almost the exact equivalent of the example cited by Khalīl to illustrate his rule that any hire contract is invalidated if a *juʿl*[84] contract is appended to it. Khalīl states the rule, as is his custom, very succinctly, saying 'It [the hire] becomes invalid if … like its inclusion of a *juʿl*.'[85] Upon mentioning that a *juʿl*, if included along with the hire contract, will invalidate it, he mentions several examples of hire contracts which were legally invalid because they also contained within it a *juʿl*. Of these examples provided by Khalīl, the fifth, which is a hire-contract whose '[wage is] what falls or is pressed from the harvest of an olive [tree],' is found in the collection of *fatwās*.[86]

A more accurate description of the language of the code, then, would be that it contains general rules illustrated by examples of particular rulings derived from those general rules.

Conclusion

Are we justified in making any general comments about the nature of Granadian legal culture based on our one collection of *fatwās*? To generalise based on this limited number of *muftīs* and *fatwās* would obviously be dangerous, especially given the fact that there are countless untapped *fatwās* which could be used to answer the same types of questions asked in this study. It goes without saying that the results for eighth–ninth/fourteenth–fifteenth century Granada cannot be, even if they were accepted with certainty, taken to be representative of Islamic legal culture as a whole, or even for that matter, Mālikī legal culture. In order to make these kinds of generalisations many more micro-studies similar to that presented in this study must be conducted. Only then will we have a solid empirical basis upon which we may make reliable statements regarding theory and practice as it affected the application of Islamic law.

Despite this caveat, however, we would like to offer some observations about the *muftīs* represented in our text, *al-Ḥadīqa*. The first is that they are conscious of the fact that they, despite being at the apex of their legal hierarchy, are still no more than interpreters of their legal tradition. On the one hand, this restricts the type of arguments they can deploy, for although they are not required to accept standard Mālikī doctrine in every case, they are bound to take it seriously and argue why the opinion they support is superior. The *fatwās* of the collection reflect this fact rather obviously in their length: almost inevitably, the longer a *fatwā*, the more likely it is to be either a departure from received doctrine, or an attempt to provide a new rule. The converse is also true: the shorter an opinion is, the more likely it is simply a recapitulation of standard doctrine. As a general rule a *muftī* only mentions a source when he is departing from the accepted rule in some way and is completely silent on the source of a rule when it is the standard doctrine of the school. Based on the conventions of these *fatwās*, then, there are no grounds for believing that the brevity of *fatwās*, and their lack of detailed justification, was a device used strategically by the jurists to change legal doctrine, as had been suggested by some writers on Islamic law.

Being a member of a *madhhab* was not just restricting, however. It also gave the jurist greater freedom in other respects because he was freed from the need to justify every step in his argument according to the requirements of *uṣūl al-fiqh*. Instead, he could extrapolate rules directly from the rules developed by the school itself, a privilege none of the great founders of Islamic law enjoyed. To sum up, then, following a *madhhab*, at least at its upper echelons, did not mean that one accepted a mere body of rules; instead, it contained within it as well a series of concepts and principles that allowed for the revision of old doctrine as well as the creation of new. We saw this process at work in the course of a number of *fatwās* within the collection. In some ways, then, the presence of a *madhhab* acted more as a catalyst of legal change than as a hindrance to it.

Another important issue is the question of whether or not the jurists were faithful to a vision of law as being a means to a social Utopia, or as a means to best bring about justice in this world. If all we had to judge by was *al-Ḥadīqa*, we would have to settle decisively for the latter. Roughly two-thirds of the *fatwās* in this collection were either judicial or quasi-judicial. While it is possible that some of these questions were hypothetical, meaning that the question was not occasioned by a dispute, this does not mean the subject of the question was an implausible event. The stereotype that Muslim jurists, out of their lack of connection to the 'fallen world', amused themselves solving cases that never occurred is not supported by the opinions in this collection.

This brings us to the question of using *fatwās* as a source of social history. After this study, we have complete confidence that the vast majority of cases discussed were instanced by real individuals in need of legal advice to further their own private interests. Furthermore, it is relatively easy to distinguish what is an academic question from a question arising from a legal dispute. This does not necessarily mean that they can be used to reconstruct the social history of Granada for the period mentioned. This is due to the fact that these are essentially legal documents, very abstract and apersonal, with only rare references to actual quantities of money involved in financial disputes. This is a result of the fact that *muftīs* only had jurisdiction over law and not fact, and therefore, these quantitative figures were of little use to them. As a result, then, we are given much qualitative information about Granadian social life. For example, we know that children sued their father for debts owed to their deceased mother, or at least tried to, which indicates that at least some women owned significant amounts of agricultural land. We also know that the state tried to protect its share in estates when an individual died without heirs, but we have no idea how often such an event occurred.[87] Beyond that, however, we cannot say much.

Perhaps the most important conclusion we can make about Granadian society based on these *fatwās* is that it had a sophisticated legal culture which took its obligation of administering the law seriously. That it suffered from a measure of legal indeterminacy should not cause us to doubt their commitment to an ideal of rule of law. In any case it is doubtful that the law as administered in Granada was any more indeterminate than the laws of any other advanced legal system. Nevertheless, it would be interesting to do a comparative study of Granadian legal decisions with decisions from the law courts of Castille and Aragon so that we could have a better empirical basis for judging the degree of legal indeterminacy in both societies. At the same time it is imperative to continue studies of other Muslim cities in different times and places using the methodology suggested here so that we can enrich our understanding of Muslim legal history as practised by its representatives.

Notes

1 Bryan S. Turner, *Weber and Islam* (London, 1974), 11. Orientalists subsequently have followed Weber on this point until it has become a recognised *topos* of Western studies on Islamic law: Aziz al-Azmeh, 'Islamic Legal Theory and the Appropriation of Reality', in *Islamic Law: Social and Historical Contexts*, ed. Aziz al-Azmeh (New York, 1988), 50. Udovitch half-jokingly refers to the Hurgronje–Goldziher–Schacht link as providing Western studies of Islamic law the 'golden *isnād*' for this theme: Abraham Udovitch, 'Theory and Practice of Islamic Law', *Studia Islamica*, 32 (1970), 89. Also, see R. Stephen Humphreys, 'Islamic Law and Islamic Society' in *Islamic History: A Framework for Inquiry* (revised ed., Princeton, 1991).

2 H. L. A. Hart, *The Concept of Law* (Oxford, 1961), 100. Hart notes that a rule can remain valid even if it is not efficacious, where efficacy is taken to mean more people obey it than not. However, this must be distinguished from 'a general disregard of the rules of the system. This may be so complete in character and so protracted that we should say, in the case of a new system, that it had never established itself as the legal system of a new group, or, in the case of a once-established system, that it had ceased to be the legal system of the group.'

3 *Khulʿ* is a type of divorce in Islamic law in which the wife pays a certain sum of money to her husband in exchange for a complete (*bāʾin*) divorce. Subsequently, the wife can only return to her husband after a new contract is drawn up and a new dowry is paid.

4 N. J. Coulson, *A History of Islamic Law* (Edinburgh, 1964), 137–8. See also N. J. Coulson, 'Muslim Custom and Case-Law', *Die Welt des Islams* 6 (1959–61), 13–24.

5 Coulson, *A History*, p. 47. In fact, it is not so difficult to reconcile this practice with the Mālikī law of *khulʿ*. The first step is to recognise that the prevalence of this custom makes it necessarily an implicit condition in any marriage contracted among this group of people. If it were to be explicit, it would be something like, 'If you (the wife) pay me (the husband) half of your dowry, then you are divorced.' According to Mālikī doctrine as established by Khalīl, if the husband makes *khulʿ* conditional upon delivery of a certain amount of money, then that condition continues to apply into the future unless he restricts it to a certain period of time, either explicitly or implicitly. According to Khalīl, for a *khulʿ* divorce to take effect 'Simple exchange is sufficient and if he [the husband] makes [it] conditional on payment or delivery, it is not limited to the session unless there is evidence [to the opposite] (*wa kafat al-muʿāṭāh wa in ʿallaqa bi-l-iqbāḍ aw al-adāʾ lam yakhtaṣṣ bi-l-majlis illā li-qarīna*)', Muḥammad b. Muḥammad al-Ḥaṭṭāb, *Mawāhib al-jalīl li-sharḥ Mukhtaṣar Khalīl*, 6 vols (Beirut, 1992/1412), vol. 4, 37. In short, if a man in West Africa seeks to deny his wife this option, the law would seem to oblige him to stipulate this condition expressly at the time of the contract. Unfortunately, we are unable to confirm the accuracy of this reconstruction of legal doctrine because Coulson neglected to tell us what the reaction of the legal community to this practice actually was.

6 Jerome Frank, *Law and the Modern Mind* (Gloucester, Ma., 1970), p.x.

7 For the relationship of *fatwās* to positive law, see Wael Hallaq, 'From *Fatwās* to *Furūʿ*: Growth and Change in Islamic Substantive Law', *Islamic Law and Society*, 1, 1 (1994), 29–65.

8 The author of the first work is Ibn Shās, d. 616/1219, and the second is Ibn al-Ḥājib, d. 646/1248. Both works remain in manuscript. The author of the third work is Khalīl b. Isḥāq al-Jundī, (d. 749/1348 or 767/1365).

9 Burhān al-Dīn Ibrāhīm b. ʿAlī b. Muḥammad Ibn Farḥūn, *Kashf al-niqāb al-ḥājib min muṣṭalaḥ ibn al-ḥājib*, Ḥamza Abū Fāris and ʿAbd al-Salām al-Sharīf eds, (Beirut, 1990), 38–9.

10 Coulson, *A History*, p. 84. Coulson's description of the jurisprudence of this period as slavish both in form and content is representative of the positions of the best-known Western historians of Islamic law. Schacht, however, vacillates on this issue, at times stating that Muslim legal thought basically ceased at the beginning of the fourth/tenth century, while on the other hand claiming that later jurists were just as creative as earlier ones: Joseph Schacht, *An Introduction to Islamic Law* (London, 1964), 70–3. The opinions of Muslim legal historians on this genre scarcely differ from those of Western historians. See, for example, Muḥammad b. al-Ḥasan al-Ḥajawī, *al-Fikr al-sāmī fī tārīkh al-fiqh al-islāmī*, ʿAbd al-ʿAzīz b. ʿAbd al-Fattāḥ al-Qārī ed. (al-Madīna, 1396), 12–13; ʿUmar al-Jīdī, *Muḥāḍarāt fī tārīkh al-madhhab al-mālikī fī al-gharb al-islāmī*

(al-Rabāṭ, 1407/1987), 133; and Muṣṭafā Aḥmad al-Zarqā, *al-Fiqh al-islāmī fī thawbihi al-jadīd: al-madkhal al-fiqhī al-'āmm, al-juz al-awwal* (6th ed., Damascus, n.d.), 122–3.

11 Schacht, *Introduction*, p. 209.

12 Take, for example, the issue known as 'the infallibility of the *mujtahid*' (*taṣwīb al-mujtahidīn*). While jurists differed in their answers regarding this question, in practice the result was a solipsistic view of legal reality. See Aron Zysow, 'The Economy of Certainty' (Ph.D. diss., Harvard University, 1984), 460–1.

13 al-Ḥaṭṭāb, *Mawāhib*, vol. 6, pp. 92–5.

14 See Aḥmad b. Muḥammad al-Ṣāwī, ed. Muṣṭafā Kamāl Waṣfī, *Bulghat al-sālik*, on the margin of *al-Sharḥ al-ṣaghīr* (4 vols, Cairo, 1986), vol. 4, 188.

15 It should also be noted that this is the claim made by Khalīl himself. He states in the introduction that his work was limited to those rules used in giving *fatwās* (*mā bihi al-fatwā*), al-Ḥaṭṭāb, *Mawāhib*, vol. 1, p. 4. Also, see Hallaq, 'From *Fatwās* to *Furū'*', p. 58.

16 *al-Ḥadīqa al-mustaqilla al-naḍra fī al-fatāwā al-ṣādira 'an 'ulamā al-ḥaḍra*, Arab League Manuscript Institute, Fiqh Mālikī, no. 5. This collection contains 298 separate questions. Some *fatwās* contain more than one question. In cases where there are more than one question, we have counted them separately using letters, e.g., 1(a), 1(b), etc., if the subsequent questions are thematically independent of the first question. I will refer to the *fatwās* by number in the text, and provide the folio citation in the notes. This collection of *fatwās* has been the subject of an article by José López Ortiz. The author, however, was more concerned in this article with questions of social history than with questions of legal history: José López Ortiz, '*Fatwās* Granadinas de los Siglos XIV y XV', *al-Andalus*, 6(1941), 73–127.

17 al-Shaykh al-Niẓām, *al-Fatāwā al-hindiyya* (6 vols, repr. Beirut, 1980).

18 al-Wansharīsī, Aḥmad b. Yaḥyā, *al-Mi'yār al-mu'rib wa-al-jāmi al-mughrib 'an fatāwā ahl ifrīqiyyah wa-l-andalus wa-l-maghrib* (13 vols, Rabat, 1981–83).

19 There is no methodological reason, however, that would prevent someone from subjecting the *fatwās* dealing with ritual law to the same type of analysis.

20 According to al-Ḥajawī, the *Mukhtaṣar Khalīl* was introduced into the Maghrib in the year 805/1402. Muḥammad b. al-Ḥasan al-Ḥajawī, *al-Fikr al-sāmī fī tārīkh al-fiqh al-islāmī* (4 vols, Rabāṭ, 1340; completed at Fās, 1345), vol. 4, 76. We also have one explicit reference to the *Mukhtaṣar*, in *fatwā* 88, which refers to the powers of the unrestricted agent (*al-wakīl al-mufawwaḍ*), 12a.

21 2a.

22 al-Qarāfī mentions the dual nature of slaughter. See Shihāb al-Dīn Aḥmad b. Idrīs al-Qarāfī, *al-Umniyya fī idrāk al-niyya* (Beirut, 1404/1984), 9. According to Mālikīs, an animal which is not slaughtered according to the standards of Islamic law is considered carrion (*mayta*). Under Mālikī *fiqh*, moreover, it is not only illegal to eat from a cow which had been incorrectly

slaughtered, it would also be illegal to use its hide or to sell it.

23 An example of what we have chosen to call quasi-judicial is *fatwā* 20, 4r. In this case, a farmer came to an agreement with a shepherd regarding compensation for crops of the farmer damaged by the shepherd's flocks. This agreement stipulated certain conditions that the *muftī* found to be invalid. It is quite likely that after having reached the agreement with the farmer, the shepherd learned that the agreement was illegal and could therefore be challenged. This *fatwā* was solicited in all likelihood, then, in the context of either the shepherd's attempt to gain more favourable terms from the farmer, or in a law-suit to have the agreement voided. It could have been asked either by the shepherd himself or by the judge hearing the case. Because of this ambiguity regarding the questioner and the context of the question, however, we were content to call it quasi-judicial. We have also chosen to classify many questions as quasi-judicial even if there is no suggestion of a dispute. Thus, if there is a question regarding the legally valid way to measure grain for sale, we have chosen to believe that the question was not asked by a disinterested seeker of knowledge. In all likelihood the question was asked so that the questioner could know the probable legal consequences of a certain act under contemplation. In fact, providing high-quality legal advice to lay persons as a guide to help them achieve their goals is an important function of any legal system. For that reason, many of the questions which seem to be 'hypothetical' have been classified by us as quasi-judicial simply on the basis of the question's subject: if it involves a potential legal right protected by a court, then it is quasi-judicial.

24 We are using the term 'rule' instead of '*fatwā*' because a single *fatwā* may turn on the application of several rules. Therefore, a *fatwā* may be made up of more than one rule, some of which may be taken from the text of the *Mukhtaṣar*, while others may only be implicit or non-existent in the text. It is also for this reason that the number of the rules analysed is not the same as the number of judicial and quasi-judicial *fatwās*.

25 *wa sharṭ al-maʿqūd ʿalayhi ṭahāra lā ka-zabl wa zayt mutanajjis*, al-Ḥaṭṭāb, *Mawāhib*, vol. 4, pp. 258–9.

26 The *ḥarīm* of a plant is that area around a plant necessary for its well being. In Mālikī doctrine it is illegal for a third party to introduce anything which would harm the plant within the area of its *ḥarīm*.

27 *Qad ikhtalafa al-ʿulamāʾ qadīman wa ḥadīthan fī man yaqūl li-zawjatihi ʿanti ʿalayya ḥarām' ʿalā aqwāl kathīra dhakara ibn al-ʿarabī minhā khamsata ʿasharata qawlan yataḥaṣṣal minhā fī al-madhhab khamsata aqwāl fa-qāla mālik wa ibn al-qāsim fī al-mudawwana hiya thalāth fī al-madkhūl bihā wa lā yunawwā wa fī ghayr al-madkhūl bihā lahu niyyatuhu min wāḥida aw ghayrihā … wa rawā ibn khuwayz mindād ʿan mālik annahā wāḥida bāʾina fī al-madkhūl bihā wa ghayrihā wa kāna baʿḍ al-ashyākh raḥimahum allāh mimman lahu al-fatwā fi-baladinā hādhā yaʿtamid hādhihi al-riwāya wa yuftī bihā wa yarā anna dhālika jārin ʿalā madhhab al-mudawwana al-mutaqaddim dhikruhu li-annahu innamā farraqa fīhā bayna al-madkhūl bihā wa ghayrihā li-anna al-*

baynūna lam takun ʿindahum illā bi-l-thalāth fī al-madkhūl bihā ammā ʿindanā fa-innahā tabīnu bi-al-wāḥida fa-l-madkhūl bihā al-yawm naẓīr ghayr al-madkhūl bihā idh dhāka fa-ḥukuhumā wāḥid wa qad ashāra ilā hādhā al-lakhmī fī baʿḍ abḥāthihi wa qad rajjaḥa ibn rushd al-qawl bi-taṣdīq man yazʿam annahu lam yurid bi-l-ḥarām al-ṭalāq wa ṣaḥḥaḥahu wa jāʾat bihi riwāya fī al-ʿutibyya wa min bāb awlā taṣdīquhu idhā zaʿama annahu arāda ghayr al-thalāth fa-man akhadha bi-hādhā al-qawl al-akhīr fa-huwa mukhallaṣ in shāʾ allāh, 14r. The established rule of the school according to Khalīl is that any apparent figure of speech (*kināya ẓāhira*) used for divorce produces a three-fold divorce in the case of a wife who has been taken to her husband's home. The expression '*anti ʿalayya ḥarām*', qualifies as a *kināya ẓāhira*, al-Ḥaṭṭāb, *Mawāhib*, vol. 4, p. 54.

28 Thus, al-Qarāfī says, 'The ruling of everything in the law that is subject to customs changes when the custom changes according to that required by the new custom. This is not new *ijtihād* on the part of the *muqallidīn*, so they do not have to meet the requirements of *ijtihād* [to make this kind of change]. Indeed, this is a rule which has resulted from the *mujtahids*' reasoning and to which they all agreed.' Shihāb al-Dīn Aḥmad b. Idrīs al-Qarāfī, *Kitāb al-iḥkām fī tamyīz al-fatāwā ʿan al-aḥkām wa taṣarrufāt al-qāḍī wa al-imām* (Aleppo, 1387/1967), 231–2.

29 Muḥammad b. Yūsuf al-ʿAbdarī al-Mawwāq, *al-Tāj wa al-iklīl* on the margin of *Mawāhib al-jalīl* (6 vols, Beirut, 1412/1992), vol. 4, 54. If we take the statement of Ibn Sirāj in conjunction with Mawwāq's quotation of al-Muṭayṭī (d. 478/1085), then the rule in Andalus changed some time between the time of the latter and a generation prior to Ibn Sirāj.

30 See ʿAbd al-Bāqī al-Zurqānī, *Sharḥ al-zurqānī ʿalā khalīl* (4 vols, Beirut, n.d.), vol. 3, 2–3.

31 *ammā al-ghalṣama [fa-qad] kathura fīhā al-khilāf fī al-madhhab wa ruwiya ʿan mālik manʿ aklihā wa ankara ibn waḍḍāḥ ṣiḥḥat hādhihi al-riwāya wa rawā ibn rushd anna al-mashhūr manʿ aklihā wa al-ṣaḥīḥ min jihat al-naẓar jawāzuhu*, 9a. Al-Mawwāq attributes to Ibn ʿArafa the claim that for one hundred years in Tūnis the opinion given by the legal establishment had been its permissibility. Likewise, al-Mawwāq claims this as the position of his teachers. Al-Mawwāq, *al-Tāj*, vol. 3, p. 207.

32 'The rule of Mālik's school and his colleagues is that it is not eaten, but permission to eat it is attributed to Mālik, and it is the opinion of the majority of the scholars outside of the school. Therefore, whoever acts upon this opinion will not be opposed, because it is correct from the point of view of study and reflection (*inna al-mashhūr min madhhab mālik wa aṣḥābihi annahu lā yuʾkal wa yurwā ʿan mālik jawāz aklihi wa huwa qawl jumhūr al-ʿulamāʾ khārij al-madhhab fa-man akhadha bi-hādhā al-qawl lam yuʿtaraḍ li-annahu ṣaḥīḥ min jihat al-baḥth wa-l-naẓar*). 10r.

33 'The slaughtered animal, if one of its jugular veins has had nothing cut from it, then it [the animal] is not eaten (*inna al-dhabīḥa in baqiya wadj min wadjayhā lam yuqṭaʿ minhu shay lam tuʾkal*). 12a.

34 al-Saraquṣṭī said, 'If the cow is caught nearby, and the slaughter is

completed after having cut from the organs [required] for its [valid] slaughter at the time of the first [attempt] at slaughter that without which it could not continue living, then eating from it is controversial (*in udrikat al-baqaratu bi-l-qurb fa-utimmat dhakātuhā wa kāna qad quṭiʿa min aʿḍā dhakātihā fi-l-dhabḥ al-awwal mā lā taʿīsh maʿahu ukilat bi-khilāf*)', 10a. Compare his statement to Ibn Sirāj's *fatwā* 197: 'He was asked, may God have mercy upon him, about a man who was compelled to raise his hand [i.e. by implication his knife as well] while slaughtering [an animal], after he had cut one of its jugular veins, after which he returned his hand immediately and finished it. He answered 'It is controversial, but the correct opinion is the permissibility of eating from it, (*suʾila raḥimahu allāhu fīman irtafaʿa yaduhu ʿan al-dhabḥ maghlūlaban ʿalayhi wa qad qaṭaʿa baʿḍ al-awdāj thumma aʿāda yadahu fī al-fawr fa-ajhazahā fa-ajāba ukhtulifa fīhā wa-l-ṣaḥīḥ jawāz aklihā*)." 27a.

35 *Fatwā* 3, 1r.

36 *Fatwā* 6, 1a.

37 *Fatwā* 8, 2r.

38 *Fatwā* 11, 2a.

39 *Fatwā* 134, 20r.

40 *Fatwā* 155, 23r.

41 *Fatwā* 274, 43a.

42 The established rule of the school is that all debts mature upon the death of the debtor. Thus, if an obligation is due at the first of the year, but the debtor dies prior to that date, death cancels the date at which the debt was to mature, and the obligation matures immediately, Aḥmad b. Muḥammad b. Aḥmad al-Dardīr, *al-Sharḥ al-ṣaghīr*, ed. Muṣṭafā Kamāl Waṣfī (4 vols, Cairo, 1986), vol. 3, 53.

43 al-Mawwāq, *al-Tāj*, vol. 5, p. 22. The fact that Ibn Sirāj did not seek to justify this latter opinion suggests, however, that this rule had become accepted by his legal culture.

44 Ibid. vol. 5, pp. 125–6.

45 This in turn would lead to the forbidden transaction of *ribā faḍl* – exchange of an unequal amount of one type of food.

46 *ammā al-masʾala al-ūlā (al-sharika fī ikhrāj al-jubn min al-laban) fa-tajrī ʿalā al-khilāf fī khalṭ al-juljulān wa-l-zaytūn fī al-maʿṣara wa alladhī yatarajjaḥ wa allāhu al-muwaffiq jawāzuhā li-l-ḥāja lākin bi-sharṭ an yukāla al-laban ʿinda al-khalṭ wa yuqsama al-jubn ʿalā ḥasabihi*, 1r.

47 *wa kāna sīdī ibn sirāj raḥimahu allāhu fīmā huwa jārin ʿalā hādhā lā yuftī bi-fiʿlihi ibtidāʾan wa lā yushanniʿ ʿalā murtakibihi quṣārā amr murtakibihi annahu tārik li-l-waraʿ wa mā al-khilāf fihi shahīr lā ḥisba fīhi wa lāsiyyamā in daʿat li-dhālika ḥāja.* al-Mawwāq, *al-Tāj*, vol. 5, p. 390.

48 *al-awlā ʿindī fī kull nāzila yakūn fīhā li-ʿulamāʾ al-madhhab qawlān fa-ʿamila al-nās fīhā ʿalā muwāfaqat aḥadihimā wa in kāna marjūḥan fi-l-naẓar an lā yuʿraḍa lahum wa an yujraw ʿalā annahum qalladūhu fi-l-zamān al-awwal wa jarā bihi al-ʿamal fa-innahum in ḥumilū ʿalā ghayri dhālika kāna fī dhālika tashwīsh li-l-ʿāmma wa fatḥ li-*

abwāb al-khiṣām, 34a.

49 See above note 15.

50 A quantity used to measure grain and other foodstuff.

51 *hādhā (jawāzuhu) mā ẓahara lī fīhā min ghayr naṣṣ fī khuṣūṣ al-mas'ala astanid ilayhi wa li-dhālika tawaqqaftu 'an al-jawāb fīhā wa qad sa'alanī 'anhu jumla min al-nās thumma wajadtu fī al-'utbiyya mas'ala tushbihuhā wa hiya min samā' ibn al-qāsim min mālik qāla fīhā: 'wa sa'altu mālikan 'an ma'āṣir al-zayt zayt al-juljulān wa al-fijl ya'tī hādhā bi-arādib wa hādhā bi-ukhrā ḥattā yajatmi'ū fīhā fa-ya'ṣirūn jamī'an?' qāla (mālik): 'innamā yukrah hādhā li-anna ba'ḍahu yukhrij akthara min ba'ḍ fa-idhā iḥtāja al-nās ilā dhālika fa-arjū an yakūna khafīfan li-anna al-nās lā budda lahum mimmā yuṣliḥuhum wa-l-shay' alladhī lā yajidūn 'anhu buddan wa lā ghinan fa-arjū an yakūna lahum fī dhālika sa'a in shā' allāh wa lā arā bihi ba'san.' qāla (ibn al-qāsim) 'wa-l-zaytūn mithlu dhālika.' qāla ibn rushd: 'khaffafahu li-l-ḍarūra ilā dhālika idh lā yata'attā 'aṣr al-yasīr min al-juljulān wa al-fijl 'alā ḥidatihi murā'ātan li-qawl man yujīz al-tafāḍul fī dhālika min ahl al-'ilm.' … fa-hādhā kulluhu mimmā yadull 'alā ṣiḥḥat mā ẓahara lī fī-l-laban wa allāh a'lam*, 40a.

52 Alan Watson, *The Nature of Law* (Edinburgh, 1977), 95.

53 'Judicial practice, in controversial cases, should be governed by the prevailing opinion' (*al-'amal innamā yakūn fī al-masā'il al-khilāfiyya 'alā mā huwa al-mashhūr*), 41r.

54 *murā'āt al-aqwāl al-ḍa'īfa aw ghayrihā sha'n al-mujtahidīn min al-fuqahā' idh murā'āt al-khilāf innamā ma'nāhā murā'āt dalīl al-mukhālif … wa murā'āt al-dalīl aw 'adam murā'ātihi laysa ilaynā ma'shara al-muqallidīn fa-ḥasbunā fahmu aqwāl al-'ulamā' wa al-fatwā bi-l-mashhūr minhā wa laytanā nanjū ma' dhālika ra'san lā lanā wa lā 'alaynā*, 45r.

55 At least one contradiction of the code, however, appears more in the nature of a mistake than a conflict of interpretation. Ibn Sirāj is asked in *fatwā* 154 what a wife whose husband dies before taking her to the marital home deserves. He replies she gets half of her advance dowry and half of her delayed dowry, 23r. According to Khalīl, however, she should get the entire dowry. See al-Mawwāq, *al-Tāj*, vol. 3, pp. 506–7. Ḥaṭṭāb attributes to Mālik another opinion, but it says she merely gets her share in the inheritance, and gets nothing from the dowry. See al-Ḥaṭṭāb, *Mawāhib*, vol. 3, p. 107. One must conclude that the opinion is either an error on the *muftī*'s part, or on the part of the copyist.

56 *al-niḥla ṣaḥīḥa lāzima li-l-ab in kāna ḥāzahā al-ibn fī ṣiḥḥat wālidihi wa ḥayātihi wa in kāna al-ab qad māta qabla an yaḥūzahā fa-lā taṣiḥḥ lahu illā bi-taslīm al-waratha li-annahā taqaddamat al-nikāḥ bi-khilāf mā huwa fī 'aqd al-nikāḥ fa-lā yaftaqir*, 4r.

57 al-Shāṭibī says: 'If one were to argue that the document writers have said in regard to the clothes which the husband dresses his wife, who then wears it and uses it for a year or less, that she has [by this use] become its owner, so he cannot ask her to return it …', (*fa-in iḥtajja muḥtajj bi-anna ahl al-wathā'iq qālū fī al-thawb yaksūhu al-rajul zawjahu fa-talbasuhu wa tamtahinuhu 'āman aw aqalla annahā qad malakathu fa-lā yarji' bihi 'alayhā …*), 34r.

58 *inna al-marhūn ʿindahu in jaʿala lahu al-rāhin annahu aqāmahu fī bayʿihi maqām al-wakīl al-mufawwaḍ ilayhi fī al-ḥayāt wa al-waṣī baʿda al-mamāt kāna lahu bayʿuhu wa in lam yafʿal lahu hādhā fī ʿaqd al-rahn fa-lā yabīʿuhu illā bi-mushāwarat al-rāhin aw al-qāḍī*, 23r.

59 *qāla baʿḍ al-muwaththiqīn: lā yajūz lahu bayʿ al-rahn wa in juʿila lahu dhālika dūna mushāwara wa lā sulṭān … illā an yaqūla fī al-wathīqa ʿaqāmahu maqām al-wakīl al-mufawwaḍ ilayhi fī al-ḥayāti wa al-waṣī baʿda al-mamātʾ*, Abū Muḥammad ʿAbd Allāh b. ʿAbd Allāh b. Salmūn al-Kinānī, *al-ʿIqd al-munaẓẓam li-l-ḥukkām* (2 vols, Beirut, n.d.), vol. 2, 225.

60 'It is permissible … by estimate if the buyer and seller are knowledgeable in estimation or they bring a knowledgeable estimator whose word they accept' (*yajūz taḥarriyan idhā kāna al-bāʾiʿ wa al-mushtarī ʿārifayn bi-l-taḥarrī aw qaddamā ʿārifan yarkunān li-qawlihi*), 23a. Khalīl says that the validity of this sale (*bayʿ al-juzāf*) is conditional on the estimation of the parties to the sale, without mentioning the possibility of using a professional estimator. See al-Mawwāq, *al-Tāj*, vol. 4, pp. 285–7.

61 Wael Hallaq, 'Model *Shurūṭ* Works and the Dialectic of Doctrine and Practice', *Islamic Law and Society*, 2 , 2 (1995), 1–26.

62 al-Mawwāq, *al-Tāj*, vol. 5, p. 21.

63 *laysa ʿalā al-imām junāḥ fī dhālika wa lā ʿalā ghayrihi wa huwa ḥalāl wa man iddaʿā taḥrīmahu fa-huwa jāhil mutaqawwil ʿalā al-sharʿ yajib ʿalayhi al-tawba min kalāmihi*, 3r.

64 'He delivers the price of the properties in its entirety to the heirs, just as it was testified to [in the document of sale]. The problem of the duty is referred to the ruler, may God give him victory. His opinion on this question is final' (*thaman al-amlāk yuʾaddīhi bi-jumlatihi li-l-waratha ḥasbumā waqaʿa ʿalayhi al-ishhād bihi wa qaḍiyyat al-thiqāf yarjiʿ fīhi li-l-mawlā naṣarahu allāhu yantahī fīhi li-mā yamur bihi fī al-qaḍiyya*), 27a.

65 L. P. Harvey, *Islamic Spain 1250–1500* (Chicago, 1990), 13; Levi Provençal, 'al-Andalus', *EI2*.

66 For example, in his discussion of *commenda*, al-Dardīr notes that '*Commenda* is a special dispensation, so it (i.e., its stipulations) is limited to that which has been transmitted. As for [arrangements] other than these [that have been transmitted], they continue to be governed by the original rule prohibiting it', al-Dardīr, *al-Sharḥ*, vol. 3, p. 684.

67 Ibn Sirāj has three, 127(g), 19r, 141, 21r and 142, 21a. Al-Shāṭibī's *fatwā* is 140, 20a, and al-Ḥaffār's is 139, 20a.

68 'It appears that raising silkworms is not permissible in principle if it is a hire contract whose wage comes from that which is being produced. However, raising [them] does become valid under [other] arrangements, two of which Aṣbagh b. Muḥammad (d. 300/912) mentioned… . Another resembles that which is the practice of the people. That is when the owner of the mulberry tree contributes a part of the silkworms, for example, one half, and the labourer the other half. The owner of the tree hires the labourer after he (the labourer)

views and inspects them for half of his (the owner's) [mulberry] leaves to gather the leaves, feed the silkworms, and prepare the tools needed until the work ends and they divide the silk according to the proportion [of ownership] of the silkworms, if the value of the labour approximately equals the value of half the [mulberry] leaves. This arrangement appears to be permissible, and it bears a resemblance to sharecropping (*yaẓhar anna tarbiyat dūd al-ḥarīr lā tajūz aṣlan 'alā an takūna al-ijāra mimmā yakhruj minhu lākin tajūz al-tarbiya 'alā awjuh dhakara minhā aṣbagh ibn muḥammad wajhayn* … . *wa minhā wajh shibh mā yaf'aluhu al-nās wa dhālika an yukhrija ṣāḥib al-tūt juz'an min al-zirrī'a ka-l-niṣf mathalan wa al-'āmil al-niṣf al-ākhar wa yasta'jira ṣāḥib al-tūt al-'āmil bi-niṣf waraqihi ba'da naẓarihi wa taqlībihi 'alā jam' al-waraq wa al-qiyām 'alā 'alf al-dūd wa i'dād al-ālāt allatī yuḥtāj ilayhā ḥattā yantahiya al-'amal wa yaqtasimān lawz al-ḥarīr 'alā nisbat al-zirrī'a idhā tasāwat qīmat niṣf al-waraq aw taqārabat fa-hādhā wajh yaẓhar annahu jā'iz wa fīhi shabah min al-muzāra'a*)'. 20a.

69 20a.

70 19a.

71 *fa-in kāna yajid al-insān man yuwāfiquhu 'alā wajh jā'iz mithl an yuqalliba al-'āmil al-waraq wa yashtariya niṣfahā mathalan min ṣāḥibihā bi-'amalihi* … *fa-in wajada man ya'mal hādhā fa-lā yajūz lahu an ya'mala mā jarat bihi 'ādat al-nās 'alā madhhab mālik wa jumhūr ahl al-'ilm wa yujūz 'alā madhhab aḥmad ibn ḥanbal wa ba'ḍ 'ulamā' al-salaf qiyāsan 'alā al-qirāḍ wa al-musāqāt*, 19a.

72 *Musāqāt* is a type of agricultural partnership between the owner of land and a labourer. Instead of the labourer receiving a wage, however, he gets a percentage of the crop. See al-Dardīr, *al-Sharḥ*, vol. 3, p. 711.

73 *wa ammā in lam yajid al-insān man ya'maluhā illā 'alā mā jarat bihi al-'āda wa tarku dhālika yu'addī ilā ta'ṭīlihā wa laḥq al-ḥaraj wa iḍā'at al-māl fa-yajūz 'alā muqtaḍā qawl mālik fī ijāzat al-amr al-kullī al-ḥājī*, 19a.

74 al-Mawwāq, *al-Tāj*, vol. 5, p. 390.

75 24a.

76 *in kānat hādhihi al-zawjiyya qad ṭālat wa lam taṭlub al-zawja mā yajib lahā fī al-istighlāl fī ḥayāt al-zawj fa-sukūtuhā mūjib li-isqāṭ ḥaqqihā bi-ṭūl al-mudda wa laysa li-ibnihā min dhālika shay'*, 24a.

77 'The children can sue their father for the rent and the produce which he took from the properties [of the wife] with the exception of the domicile, if the wife owned a home. He, however, can seek the wage of his labour (*li-l-awlād ṭalab abīhim bi-l-kirā' wa bi-ghallat mā akhadha min al-amlāk mā dūna dār al-suknā in kānat li-l-zawja dār wa yarji' huwa bi-ijārat khidmatihi*), 24a.

78 See al-Ḥaṭṭāb, *Mawāhib*, vol. 6, pp. 28–30; al-Dardīr, *al-Sharḥ*, vol. 4, pp. 324–5.

79 *yuqḍā fī qaḍiyyat al-yahūdī an yaḥlifa al-muslim annahu khallaṣahu min dhālika al-ḥaqq fa-idhā ḥalafa usqiṭa ḥaqq al-yahūdī*, 48a. This decision was based on two considerations: the first that it is not customary for people to leave their money in the possession of strangers so long, and second, that Jews, because of their enmity to Muslims, consider Muslims' property to be lawful to them (*istiḥlāl*

amwāl al-muslimīn). This latter is an unfortunate entry of prejudice in the exercise of legal discretion.

80 26a–27r.

81 'The decision of the Prophet, may God bless him and grant him peace, regarding water, that it should be distributed to the highest, then the next highest [i.e. closest to the source of the water], this is in regard to water in which no person has a legal right nor is owned, like the water of a flood and other such things ... also not falling under that [rule] is the people of a village who raise a water wheel from the valley. Their rights are equal. Indeed, they water according to their custom, and in this case, the lower [i.e. the further] might water before the higher [the closer], and the higher before the lower, depending on their needs (*ḥukm al-nabī ṣallā allāhu ʿalayhi wa sallama fī al-māʾ an yusqā bihi al-aʿlā fa-l-aʿlā huwa fī al-māʾ alladhī lā ḥaqq fīh wa lā mutamallak li-aḥad ka-māʾ al-suyūl wa shibhihā ... wa lā yadkhul fī dhālika ahl qarya yarfaʿūn sāqiya min al-wādī wa ḥuqūquhum fīhā mustawiya bal yasqūn ʿalā mā jarat bihi ʿādatuhum wa yasqī fī hādhihi al-masʾala al-asfal qabla al-aʿlā wa al-aʿlā qabla al-asfal ʿalā ḥasab ḥājatihim*)'. 27r.

82 See for example, Humphreys, 'Islamic Law and Islamic Society', p. 213.

83 *wa sharṭ al-maʿqūd ʿalayhi ṭahāra lā ka-zabl wa zayt mutanajjis*, al-Mawwāq, *al-Tāj*, vol. 4, pp. 258–9.

84 A *juʿl* contract is similar to a hire contract except that it is non-binding, and the worker can cease whenever he wishes. However, he does not deserve his wage except upon completion of the agreed upon job. See al-Dardīr, *al-Sharḥ*, vol. 4, pp. 79–80.

85 Khalīl's text reads: *wa fasadat ... ka-maʿ juʿl*, al-Mawwāq, *al-Tāj*, vol. 5, pp. 394–400.

86 Ibid., vol. 5, p. 400. The *fatwā* reads: 'The first case, and it is about harvesting olives for a share in the oil produced from it, is not permissible, and it is an invalid hire or *juʿl* contract, and it is not lawful to hire [someone] with it (this wage of oil) (*al-masʾala al-ūlā wa hiya laqṭ al-zaytūn wa nafḍuhā wa taḥrīkuhā bi-juzʾ min al-zayt al-khārij minhu ghayr jāʾiz wa hiya ijāra fāsida aw juʿl fāsid lā yaḥillu al-istiʾjār bihi*), 37a.

87 *Fatwā* 113, 16r.

FOUR

Kafā'a in the Mālikī School: A *fatwā* from Fifteenth-Century Fez

AMALIA ZOMEÑO

Introduction

Generally, according to Islamic law, an adult male has complete freedom to choose his wife. However, the majority of jurists agree that a woman cannot choose her husband. They say that she should be assisted by her father or a male relative on her father's side who acts as her guardian (*walī*). Furthermore, if she has no guardian, she must ask for the *qāḍī*'s permission to marry.[1] The major task of the *walī*, usually the father, is to represent his daughter in her marriage contract, and to choose a suitable (*kuf'*) husband for her. The doctrine of *kafā'a* (equality in marriage) is intended to regulate the legal considerations which must be taken into account when declaring that a man is a suitable husband for a particular woman.

This doctrine was developed in different ways by the four *sunnī* schools.[2] In his study of the *kafā'a* doctrine in Islamic law, Farhat J. Ziadeh gave particular emphasis to the origin of the different accounts given by the Ḥanafi and Mālikī schools. According to Ziadeh, Abū Ḥanīfa (d.150/767) extensively developed the concept of *kafā'a* whereas Mālik (d.179/795) practically ignored it:

> Mālik's denial of the social distinctions upon which *kafā'a* is built is due to the fact that his milieu of Medina and Ḥijāz had not developed such distinctions, while that of Abū Ḥanīfa in Kufah and Iraq, which was more cosmopolitan and socially complex, had.[3]

Thus, he concluded that there is very little in the Arabian tradition, and much more in the Persian/Sasanian tradition, to constitute an origin for the doctrine of *kafā'a*.[4] Later, the doctrine spread to other localities, was adopted by the other schools and applied in other societies.

Y. Linant de Bellefonds has observed that the different emphasis of the two schools is not only justified by social reasons, but also by the fact that Ḥanafi law gives almost complete freedom to the adult woman to marry within the complex structure of its *kafāʾa* doctrine without the intervention of her *walī*. The Mālikī school, on the contrary, with a less complex *kafāʾa* doctrine, demands the presence of the *walī* in a marriage contract as the guarantor of the suitability of the future husband. Linant de Bellefonds considered therefore, that the restricted nature of *kafāʾa* in the Mālikī school is due to the fact that the marriage laws developed by this school already control the suitability of spouses without the need of the *kafāʾa* doctrine.[5]

It is quite clear that the Mālikī school never matched the enthusiasm established by Abū Ḥanīfa's disciples concerning the question of *kafāʾa*. As we can read in the *Mudawwana*,[6] Mālik was asked about the validity of a marriage between a woman and a man who was inferior to her in nobility (*ḥasab*) and dignity (*sharaf*), but equal to her in piety (*dīn*). The woman agreed to that union but the *walī* rejected it. Mālik's answer was clear: the authority (*sulṭān*) should allow the marriage and the pretension of the *walī* was dismissed.[7] On the other hand, Mālik was asked about marriages between Arabs and *mawālī* and about those who invalidated these marriages because of the lack of *kafāʾa*. His answer was also clear: neither a man's *ḥasab* nor a *sharaf* of inferior degree would reduce the status of the husband concerning his wife. In these cases Mālik quotes the Quranic verse 49:13: 'The noblest among you in the sight of God is the most godfearing of you.'[8] This is the foundation of Mālikī arguments against the introduction of lineage (*nasab*) and nobility (*ḥasab*) criteria among the elements of *kafāʾa*. His words are always clear concerning this point: 'All Muslims are equal'.[9] Likewise, when he was asked about the lack of material means (*māl*) of a poor man who was, nevertheless, of an appropriate level of piety for his future wife, Mālik also denied the value of a wealth criterion.[10] Additionally, he said nothing (*lam asmaʿ min Mālik fi-hi shayʾan*) about marriage between a free woman and a slave.[11] In the light of these answers, we can conclude that Mālik considered piety (*dīn*) as the only relevant criterion to use in the *kafāʾa* theory. Subsequent developments in the Mālikī texts, however, indicate greater complexity in the application of the *kafāʾa* doctrine.

The purpose of this paper is two-fold: first, to present several references that I have found in western Mālikī sources reflecting different perceptions of the concept of *kafāʾa*, principally among later jurists; and second, to analyse a particular case in fifteenth-century Fez, taken from the *Miʿyār* of Aḥmad b. Yaḥyā al-Wansharīsī (d. 914/1508) which addresses the legal concept of *kafāʾa*. Most importantly, this case clarifies the fact that there are two aspects of the theory of *kafāʾa*: the legal elements of which it consists and the function which *kafāʾa* plays in the Mālikī matrimonial system as a duty which the *walī* must perform, and which, in the Mālikī texts appears only when the validity of its enactment is put into doubt. In my conclusion, I will emphasise the fact that the function served by the *kafāʾa* doctrine within the Mālikī matrimonial system has survived the centuries practically unchanged, whilst the legal elements used by jurists and which actually constitute the doctrine have changed significantly in theory and in practice through the centuries. These legal elements ceased to bear solely the weight of their historical jurisdiction, and came to be redefined according to contemporary social and political conditions.[12]

The Elements of *kafāʾa* in the Mālikī School

Two very different works in the Mālikī school explore the question of *kafāʾa* with some depth: the *Bidāyat al-mujtahid* of Ibn Rushd 'the Grandson' (d. 595/1198)[13] and the *Kitāb al-qawānīn al-fiqhiyya* of Ibn Juzayy (d. 741/1340).[14]

In the *Bidāya*, the doctrine is discussed in the chapters devoted to the *walī*'s mandate, particularly in the section dealing with the opposition of a *walī* to his ward's marriage (*fī ʿaḍl al-awliyāʾ*). In the opinion of Ibn Rushd, there was an agreement among the jurists of the different schools about the question of a woman who marries a man without her *walī*'s consent. They agreed that he cannot oppose the marriage as long as the man she chooses is adequate for her (*kufʾ la-hā*) and a standard dower (*ṣadāq al-mithl*) is established. On the other hand, the woman must agree to a marriage arranged by her guardian if he chooses a man adequate for her and establishes a standard dower. Ibn Rushd pointed out that the disagreements emerge when jurists try to understand how the *kafāʾa* must be considered, that is to say, to establish the criteria to be used when declaring a man as suitable for his future wife.[15]

Following Ibn Rushd, all the schools agree on the importance of piety (*dīn*) as a *kafāʾa* criterion. Accordingly, a judge can annul a marriage if a woman goes to him arguing that her husband drinks wine (*shārib al-khamr*), has wealth from illicit sources (*mālu-hu ḥarām*) or swears frequently to divorce her (*huwwa kathīr al-ḥalaf bi-l-ṭalāq*).[16] No agreement, however, is found among the schools concerning lineage (*nasab*).[17] According to Ibn Rushd, it is well known (*mashhūr*) that Mālik thought that the marriage of an Arab woman with a *mawlā* man should be allowed, based on his interpretation of the Quranic verse (49:13). Ibn Rushd felt that the differences among the schools also emerged from the interpretation of the *ḥadīth*: 'Marry a woman because of her piety (*dīn*), beauty (*jamāl*), wealth (*māl*), and nobility (*ḥasab*), but you will be damned if you do not choose the most pious.'[18] The interpretation of this last sentence is the source of the disagreement: should all qualities but piety be disregarded, as in Mālik's point of view, or should other qualities that are mentioned in the *ḥadīth* be considered, as in the point of view of Abū Ḥanīfa?

Ibn Rushd indicated that others held the opinion that the criteria of *ḥasab* and *māl* are of the same level of importance as that of *dīn*.[19] Concerning the physical defects of the spouses, those in favour of the dissolution of marriage for this reason include health (*ṣiḥḥa min al-ʿuyūb*) as an element of *kafāʾa* .[20] In the Mālikī school, all jurists agree that poverty (*fiqr*) could dissolve a marriage if the husband is not able to afford the maintenance due to his wife's status (*nafaqa*), and that therefore economic status (*yasār*) and material means (*māl*) must be considered as elements of *kafāʾa*.[21] The state of slavery, on the other hand, could not be considered as an element of *kafāʾa* since a female slave married to another slave could choose between remaining married or divorcing her husband once she obtained her freedom.[22] Consequently, the criteria that Ibn Rushd included in his interpretation of *kafāʾa* are mainly three: piety (*dīn*), wealth (*māl*), and lack of physical defects (*ṣiḥḥa min al-ʿuyūb*).

In the eighth/fourteenth century, Ibn Juzayy developed, in the second chapter of the section on marriage in the *Kitāb al-qawānīn al-fiqhiyya*, the *kafāʾa* theory as one of the qualities of spouses (*awṣāf al-zawjayn*) which must be met prior to the marriage taking place.[23] In his highly structured work, he claims that *kafāʾa* is one of the seven qualities (*awṣāf*) that spouses must have when they marry: (1) the confession of Islamic religion (*islām*); (2) the state of freedom (*ḥurriyya*); (3) the state of having passed puberty (*bulūgh*); (4) the state of mental maturity (*rushd*); (5) *kafāʾa*; (6) good health (*ṣiḥḥa*); and (7) not being in a sacred state (*iḥrām*). Moreover, the confession of Islamic religion and the state of freedom, are required attributes within the *kafāʾa* elements,[24] which, in Ibn Juzayy's work are discussed as five individual points: (1) Islam,[25] (2) the state of freedom, (3) piety (*ṣalāḥ*), (4) wealth (*māl*) and (5) the absence of physical defects (*salāmat al-khalqa min al-ʿuyūb*).

To be a Muslim is a pre-condition for a man to marry a Muslim woman, and this is directly linked by Ibn Juzayy with the *dīn* criterion, although he uses the term *ṣalāḥ*, which might also be translated as 'piety', 'honesty', or 'good behaviour'.[26] Concerning wealth (*māl*), Ibn Juzayy pointed out that the future husband's material means should not determine the union, but that the wife could disclaim her marriage if her husband is not able to afford her rights (*ḥuqūq*).[27] On the issue of physical defects (*ʿuyūb*) of the husband, he described those that would give the wife the right to divorce.[28] Differences between the spouses in terms of lineage (*nasab*) or nobility (*ḥasab*) are of no value from Ibn Juzayy's point of view. He finally refutes the opinion of al-Shāfiʿī who considered it desirable that a husband does not practise a base or vile occupation (*ʿadam al-ḥirfa al-daniyya*).[29] Therefore, five criteria were considered by Ibn Juzayy, three of them already being established requirements for marriage (Islam, freedom and health) and the other two being criteria for the *kafāʾa* (wealth and pious behaviour or piety).

These two legal works, the *Bidāyat al-mujtahid* and the *Kitāb al-qawānīn al-fiqhiyya*, developed the *kafāʾa* doctrine in a theoretical way. In both, the authors adopted an all-inclusive concept that could be explained only by including or disregarding several criteria according to the legal tradition they studied. These two works are also considered by scholars as *ikhtilāf* works and this fact could explain their more extensive treatment of the *kafāʾa* problem.

Turning to two other works of *furūʿ*, one finds very different perceptions of the *kafāʾa* doctrine. In his *Mukhtaṣar*,[30] Khalīl (d. 776/1374) judges the suitability of spouses according to their level of piety and state of physical well-being.[31] Unusually, Khalīl gives the mother the right to approach a judge (*takallum*) in opposition to the father, if he (her husband) wants to arrange a marriage for their daughter to a poor man.[32] Other elements which Khalīl uses as criteria for *kafāʾa* are discused in the *Mukhtaṣar*, including his view that a freed man is considered inferior to a free woman, thus reflecting Saḥnūn's opinion.[33] He also judged that a man without a noble origin (*ghayr sharīf*) is not suitable for a noble woman (*sharīfa)*. In his *Tuḥfa*, Ibn ʿĀṣim (d. 829/1426) mentions the function of *kafāʾa* in the chapters devoted to the *walī*s, without distinguishing any individual criteria.[34]

Likewise, I have found several references to the concept of *kafāʾa* in works of model documents (*wathāʾiq* or *shurūṭ*). For example, in the model dedicated to a marriage contracted by the *waṣī* (and not by the *walī*) Ibn al-ʿAṭṭār (d. 399/1009), indicated that the witnesses of a marriage contract must investigate the suitability of the husband in terms of physical and economic conditions (*fī ḥāli-hi wa-māli-hi*) as well as ensuring that the dower established is the standard dower.[35] Ibn Mughīth (d. 459/1067)[36] and later Abū Iṣḥāq al-Gharnāṭī (d. 579/1183)[37] also consider these two criteria (*wa-l-kafāʾa fī l-ḥāl wa-l-māl*) and Ibn Mughīth quotes Ibn al-Mājishūn (d. 164/781)[38] who adds the piety (*dīn*) criterion as relevant.

There are also differences of opinion regarding whether or not *kafāʾa* is a necessary pre-condition for the validity (*ṣiḥḥa*) of a marriage. Ibn Juzayy felt that *kafāʾa* served only to consolidate (*istiqrār*) marriage, given that when the conditions of the *kafāʾa* are met, the marriage cannot be broken.[39] However, according to Ibn Mājishūn and al-Matīṭī, *kafāʾa* is treated as a mandatory pre-condition (*sharṭ al-nikāḥ*) and thus it has remained so in the practice of the courts.[40]

From this selection of juridical opinions, it is clear that later Mālikī works reflect a lack of agreement with regard to the theoretical criteria which must be included in the evaluation of the *kafāʾa* doctrine. These differences can be summarised in the following manner:

1. Piety only, according to Mālik in the *Mudawwana.*
2. Piety, health and physical well-being, according to Ibn al-Mājishūn and Ibn Rushd.
3. Piety and wealth, according to Ibn Juzayy.
4. Piety and physical well-being, according to the *Mukhtaṣar* of Khalīl.
5. Economic and physical conditions (*al-ḥāl wa-l-māl*), according to Ibn al-ʿAṭṭār, Ibn Mughīth, Abū Isḥāq al-Gharnāṭī,[41] and al-Matīṭī,[42] who attributed this opinion to Ibn al-Qāsim.[43] It was this model which was followed in the practice of the courts (*ʿamal*), and which is usually linked to the concept of *kafāʾa* , even if it is not the opinion shared by two of the most important authorities within the school, Khalīl, and Mālik himself.[44]

A Case from Fifteenth-Century Fez

Aḥmad b. Yaḥyā al-Wansharīsī (d. 914/1508) compiled approximately 6000 *fatwās* of the Western Islamic world and classified them according to the chapters of the *fiqh.*[45] His purpose was to compile a useful work which gathered together all of the legal questions of his time and those of previous *ʿulamāʾ* widely dispersed in works which were not easily accessible.[46] This work is considered as a major source for the study of the economic, social and legal history in North Africa and al-Andalus.[47]

However, in the *Miʿyār*, *fatwās* which address the concept of *kafāʾa* are scarce. Among them, I have chosen a *fatwā* from Fez which is particularly relevant. This *fatwā* is the only case, as far as I know, that addresses the question of *kafāʾa* as the main problem not only in the *mustaftī*'s question but also in the *muftī*'s answer. It also contains all the points included in the development of *kafāʾa* theory; points which are mentioned in other *fatwās* only tangentially. And, furthermore, it raises a number of questions about a particular case of *kafāʾa* which allow us to study the judicial practice with more depth.

The *fatwā* I have chosen can be traced to Fez in the first half of the fifteenth century.[48] The *muftī* responding was one of the best known North African figures of his time, Abū ʿAbd Allāh Muḥammad al-ʿAbdūsī, who died around 1443–46. He belonged to a prominent Fāsī family, the Banū Muʿṭī. He was a *muftī* in the Qarawiyyīn mosque and, during the last years of his life a *khaṭīb*. He was one of the masters of al-Wansharīsī's masters and some of his *fatwās* are included in the *Miʿyār*.[49]

In fact, this particular case is discussed in two *fatwās*. In his first answer, the *muftī* complains about the lack of clarity in a document provided by the litigants. In the second question, this issue was clarified by the *mustaftī* and consequently another answer was required. The way in which these two *fatwās* were recorded and exposed leads me to assume that this *fatwā* can be considered as 'primary'.[50]

The First Question

Al-ʿAbdūsī was asked about an honest, healthy and generous merchant who carried out his duties in a respectable manner. This man and his ancestors had obtained a Qaysī *nisba* some time ago.[51] He requested a marriage with a woman of the Berber Awraba tribe.[52] As the *mustaftī* explains, in spite of being a Berber, her family boasted a generation of men occupying the position of *khaṭīb* (*illā anna ahla-hā min nasal khuṭabāʾ*) and her own father was a *ṭālib*. They were an old family in the town of Tāzā (close to the Marinid capital of Fez). The woman was a virgin and probably an orphan since she was under the tutelage of her brother who fulfilled the function of her *waṣī*. He had the right to contract a marriage for her with whichever husband he preferred and with whatever dower he wanted to established. The brother decided, with the consent of his sister,[53] to contract the marriage with the merchant and he established the standard dower or a superior one. However, the woman's other brothers, those who had no right of guardianship on her, wanted to anull (*faskh*) the marriage, claiming that the husband was not suitable for her (*al-rajul laysa bi-kuf'in la-hā*). They presented a legal document (*rasm*) but no details were given therein about dissolving the marriage contract according to the *Sharīʿa*. The *waṣī* and his ward insisted that the marriage contract was drawn up correctly, taking into consideration that the bride had no wealth. The exact question was: 'Must the opinions of those who try to nullify the marriage because of the lack of *kafāʾa* be considered?'[54]

It is said that the *mustaftī* could be anyone who wants to know the solution of a legal problem that he faces; however, in practice the *mustaftī* used to be a judge (or a jurist) who has doubts in applying the law or who considers neccesary to consult a legal authority before he gives his sentence. I assume that in this case the *mustaftī* is a jurist. In his description of the litigation he considers all the legal questions that the *muftī* will need to consider in a *kafāʾa* case, that is to say: description of the spouses, the presence of a *waṣī* on behalf of the *walī* (thus the consent of the wife was required) and a correctly established dower. Another legal question arose in this matter: the litigants were obliged to present a written proof in which they had to explain why they believed that there was no *kafāʾa*.

Al-ʿAbdūsī's Answer

The text of the *fatwā* of al-ʿAbdūsī, is well structured. For the sake of analysis, I divided the answer into five points (that can be followed in the text):[55]

1. Firstly, he gives a direct and clear statement: 'If the husband fulfills the mentioned qualities (*awṣāf*), then *kafāʾa* has been considered in a correct way (*fa-hiya kafāʾa ṣaḥīḥa muʿtabira*)'.
2. He mentions the legal authorities upon which he makes his statement:

> According to Ibn al-Qāsim, the *kafāʾa* should be considered taking into account the physical and economic conditions (*fī l-ḥāl wa-l-māl*). Jurisprudence and the practice of the courts apply the law according to this (*bi-hi al-qaḍāʾ wa-ʿalay-hi al-ʿamal*).[56] This opinion is shared by Abū al-Ḥasan al-Matīṭī[57] and others. The *qāḍī* must not sentence without taking into account what is commonly accepted by the school (*al-mashhūr*)[58] or according to what makes valid the practice among the people in whose

knowledge and piety we trust (*bi-mā maḍā al-ʿamal min al-mawthūq bi-ʿilmi-him wa-dīni-him*).[59]

3. In al-ʿAbdūsī's opinion, there is no doubt that, if lineage is to be considered, the man is a Qaysī Arab and the woman is a Berber of the Awraba tribes and Arabs are preferable to Berbers (*al-ʿarab afḍal min al-barbar*), so he is appropriate for her. The criterion of economic status (*māl*) also indicates, if the information the *muftī* has is correct, that the man is appropriate for her, because she does not have even a moderate fortune.

   Nasab was the criterion that the *mustaftī* had strongly emphasised in his description of the litigation. In my opinion, given this emphasis, the *muftī* cannot but have taken it into account, even if this is not an acceptable criterion for the Mālikī school. This appearance of the *nasab* criterion could be interpreted as reflecting a social and political[60] situation that could change the general meaning of the Mālikī theory on *kafāʾa*.
4. Using the particle *thumma*, the *muftī* shifted the emphasis to the problem of the testimony provided by the litigants, because those who testified against the suitability of this marriage had expressed their opinions in general terms (*ajmalū wajh dhālika*). However, an explanation was demanded and the witnesses were obliged to explain how they understood that there was no *kafāʾa*. In fact, according to al-ʿAbdūsī, later jurists (*mutaʾakhkhirūn*) were already questioned about the acceptability of an explanation in general terms (*ijmāl*); as, for example, in the *Aḥkām* of Ibn Ziyād[61] and in other sources. These differences among jurists, added al-ʿAbdūsī, emerged not only because of the questioned acceptability of the writing testimony (*shahāda*), but also the credibility of the witnesses and the strength of their opinions when they explain the lack of *kafāʾa* in the husband. Al-ʿAbdūsī complains about the ignorance of many of those who claim knowledge that they do not have.

   In my opinion, it would be desirable that, given the time when we live, there must be no differences in this question. So, there is no other way but to ask them [the witnesses] and they should explain why they think that there is no *kafāʾa* (*wa-l-wājib istifsāru-hum ʿan wajh ʿadam al-kafāʾa*).[62]

5. Finally, al-ʿAbdūsī uses some conditional sentences that posit the legal possibilities which might emerge in the case. 'If the witnesses cannot explain their position, for whatever reason [because they are dead, or absent or it is impossible for them to do so], then their testimony will be annulled.' If, on the contrary, they more

specifically testify, for example, that the husband is a drunkard (*sakīr*) or that he has done something forbidden or if they present any other factor that diminishes the *kafā'a* according to the law (this example represents clearly a lack of piety in the husband), then the means should be given to the *walī* to defend his position. If no defence can be shown, the marriage will be annulled. If witnesses claim something that is immutable in the husband's status regarding *kafā'a* (and is thus irrelevant) then the marriage will continue to be valid.

'He was asked again'

Al-Wansharīsī compiled next the continuation of this case with the second question which was made to al-'Abdūsī with respect to the same legal problem. This second question is much more technical and detailed and also brings into greater focus the contemporary social reality. The description of the conjugal couple is shorter (almost non-existent) and includes only necessary information. The future husband, we read, is a young merchant (*walad bāligh tājir*) who asks for the hand of a woman who is under the tutelage (*waṣī*) of her brother, who retains this responsibility on behalf of their father. Because of this, he can marry her off before or after she reaches the state of puberty. The *waṣī* decides to contract the marriage, and does so.

This being so, the *mustaftī* on this occasion, in response to the demand of al-'Abdūsī, represented the claim of the other brothers of the woman and transmitted their own words as, 'We are disgraced by that [the marriage], and we will not give her in marriage to him because we do not know his *nasab*, and he is not a suitable match for us.'[63] In this petition, the *mustaftī* added, the *fuqahā'* and pious men (*ṣulaḥā'*) of the area have testified and they indicate in the petition that the husband is not adequate for the young woman in regard to three criteria: nobility, lineage and piety (*ghayr kuf'un la-hā fī ḥasabi-hā wa-nasabi-hā wa-dīni-hā*). Furthermore, they express that they are in absolute disagreement with this marriage. Their desire is to annul what the first brother contracted, and they ask again if their claim should be heard.

A Second Answer

In spite of the second question and the evidence submitted in it, al-'Abdūsī does not change his answer significantly and insists on the necessity of the wisdom of the witnesses when deciding if a man is equal or worthy for his wife.

The Function of *Kafāʾa*

The *kafāʾa* doctrine in the Mālikī school has the function of controlling the role of the *walī*. In legal treatises, it always involves the issue of the suitability of spouses in the chapters devoted to the laws pertaining to the *wilāya*. I have found a *dictum* attributed to Mālik which Abū Saʿīd b. Lubb (d. 782/1381) the Granadan *muftī*, mentioned in one of his *fatwā*s which illustrates the point well: 'The purpose of the presence of *walī* in the marriage is to guarantee its suitability' (*al-qaṣd fi'l-wilāya fi'l-nikāḥ al-naẓar fi'l-kafāʾa*).[64]

Thus it is clear that in the moment of contracting the marriage of his daughter or ward, the *walī* takes into account his own interests, and those of his family and must manage to come into agreement with these interests. This moment, which is necessarily previous to the marriage, is not captured in the juridical texts;[65] matrimonial strategies are not reflected in the legal theory of *kafāʾa*. However, as I have illustrated, legal sources do reveal cases in which the criteria of the *walī* do not coincide with those of other masculine members of the bride's family. Practically all of these cases are brought into the realm of legal dispute in the moment after the marriage is contracted when the litigants attempts to annul (*faskh*) the marriage.

The litigants place in doubt the role of the *walī* by attacking one of his principal tasks, the consideration of the *kafāʾa*, claiming that it could disgrace the family.[66] However, when the father or the grandfather have the responsibility for contracting the marriage, their role appears to have been practically uncontestable, thus, most frequently the litigation arises when the *wilāya* is exercised by another male member of the family. In Mālikī law, it is well known that legislation was developed so as to establish an order by which the male relatives of the bride hold authority to exercise the *wilāya*: first her father, second a person to whom he delegates the task (*waṣī-hi*) and in the third place, the order of succession (*ʿaṣaba*) is applied.[67] According to this hierarchy, there are nearer *walī*s (*aqrab*) and distant *walī*s (*abʿad*).

One case which has particular significance for the issue of doubt concerning authoritative role of the father involves a *fatwā* from Cordoba from the end of the tenth century which was presented to Ibn Zarb (d. 381/991).[68] In this case, the *mustaftī* described the father of the bride as an 'Arab of corrupt condition' (*fāsid al-ḥāl min al-'arab*), who marries off his daughter with a man who is not her equal (*min ghayr kuf'*). The *walī*'s brother negated (*ankara*) this marriage and brought the issue to court, where he obtained the favourable opinion of the *muftī* who placed the guardianship under the authority (*sulṭān*), removing the *wilāya* of the father.[69] Al-Wansharīsī compiled this case in the *Mi'yār*, copying it almost exactly from its original source (the *Aḥkām* of al-Sha'bī),[70] and adding a reference from the *Nawādir* of Ibn Abī Zayd (d. 386/996) from which he cited the opinion of Aṣbagh about a man who married his daughter to another who was not appropriate for her;[71] the authority (*imām*) had to annul the marriage, although the girl or in this case, the *waṣī* was in agreement with the marriage.[72]

More frequently, the litigations among various *walīs* (that is, male members of a woman's family) arose when the nearer *walī* (*aqrab*) is absent or dead and thus, the *wilāya* is exercised by another member of the family (*ab'ad*). For example, Ibn Rushd 'the Grandfather' (d. 520/1126) discussed a case which involved a woman who was married by her maternal uncle when she should have been married by the sons of her paternal uncle (who, according to the Mālikī hierarchy of *walīs*, had more right to her guardianship). The marriage took place without their being informed or consulted as they were two days' journey away.[73] When they learned of this marriage, they tried to annul it, claiming that the husband was not suitable for her (*kuf' la-hā*). According to Ibn Rushd, this marriage was considered valid, except if the *walī* could bring to bear a convincing proof (*bayyina 'ādila*) which demonstrated that the husband was not suitable and that the marriage with this man might disgrace the woman, whose interests, in my opinion, had not been taken into account (*ghayr naẓar bi-hā*). Thus, Ibn Rushd understood that the possibility of annulment depended on the petition presented, and that it must contain the terms by which the woman might become disgraced by the lack of *kafā'a* .

On the other hand, al-Māzarī (d. 536/1141), the *muftī* of Qayrawān,[74] described the same legal procedure: if one expressed the desire to annul a marriage because of the lack *kafā'a* , a proof (*bayyina*) must be presented. The case which al-Māzarī faced contained the same characteristics as that solved by Ibn Rushd, and his response is parallel.[75] It similarly involves a woman whose marriage was contracted against the opinion of the family of her father, who were not in agreement with the match. Her paternal uncle approached the judge, claiming that the husband was not appropriate for her (*lā yalīq bi-hā al-zawj*). Al-Māzarī indicated similarly that the marriage would remain valid until he who tried to annul the match brought foward a legal proof (*bayyina*) in which he testified that there was the threat of disgrace or harm (*maḍarra*) and that the husband was not appropriate (*kufʾ*) for her. As in the case of the *fatwā* of al-ʿAbdūsī, the anulment of the marriage would remain deferred until the petition with legal proof was presented by the litigants.[76]

Therefore, when the validity of the decision of the *walī* is put into doubt, it is clear that the *muftīs* demand that the litigants, those who try to annul the marriage, present a written proof in which they explain, as al-ʿAbdūsī requested, the manner in which they understand the absence of *kafāʾa* and why the marriage is disgraceful, as much for the family of the bride as for her. The *fatwā* of al-ʿAbdūsī clearly indicates that the issue of annulment does not only depend of the acceptability of the petition and its validity, but also on the circumstances of the witnesses and their credibility. According to him, they must be individuals who by their learning and piety are trustworthy. The *mustaftī* therefore clearly indicated their qualities with regard to their knowledge of *fiqh* and their piety (*ṣulaḥāʾ*).

One notes that the use of this type of document appeared early in the Western Mālikī texts, in that it was always demanded by the jurists. However, we do not find any indication that in the petition documents, the litigants necessarily limited themselves to the criteria or considerations as they were defined and accepted theoretically in Mālikī law. Nonetheless, the documents must have reflected, to a greater extent, the interests of the fathers in the moment of contracting the marriages of their daughters, or likewise the family interests which ought to have been defended, against a possible fault in the *wilāya* system. However, it is equally interesting that we have not found any case in which the contents of this type of document is expressly reproduced in the *fatwās* except an aside which was made in the second question asked of al-ʿAbdūsī.

Conclusions

The doctrine of *kafāʾa* is applied in Mālikī matrimonial law in two instances:

1) At the moment which fathers or guardians contracted the marriages of their daughters or wards. The juridical texts do not reflect this moment and thus do not contain, in our view, sufficient

information for an understanding of social stratification, as is sometimes assumed. This is not because *fatwās* do not reflect real problems, but because, the social criteria used by fathers (or other *walīs*) were not a subject of interest to the jurists when they compiled their texts.

2) In the moment immediately after the marriage contract. This moment represented the most opportune time for the bride's family to recall *kafā'a* as a mechanism to annul a marriage. The resultant litigation of this mechanism of redress is reflected in juridical texts and thus can provide insight into contemporary legal procedures and indirect evidence of social structures.

In general, we can conclude that, although it was not the only criterion of *kafā'a* the Mālikī school gave predominance to the quality of religious piety.[77] The economic status of the husband was considered important when determining the nature and amounts of the payments he had to give his wife according to the social status she maintained before her marriage. The concept of the standard dower is a major one in marriage laws and was, likewise, on more than one occasion, linked to the concept of *kafā'a*. The *nasab* and *ḥasab* criteria, although theoretically not regarded, become legally valid under certain social circumstances in certain periods. The major reason for this was that the criteria of the fathers and *walī*s, appear to have been respected by the Mālikī jurists, who in later texts renounced the legal theory of *kafā'a* in order to accommodate concrete situations, especially to avoid marriages which might be disgraceful for the family of the bride.

In my opinion, the application of the *kafā'a* continued to serve the useful function of controlling the actions of the *walī* and was applied in practice without theoretical legal considerations which might have resulted in the annulment of too many marriages. That is to say, that the function of the *kafā'a* doctrine did not change, but its criteria and constituents did, and its application by jurists became more a social than a legal question.[78]

Notes

This paper was written within the Spanish research programme no. PB92-0009 funded by the CGICYT

1 M. Abu Zahra, 'Family Law', in M. Khadduri and H. J. Liebesny, eds, *Law in the Middle East* (Washington DC, 1955), 137.

2 For the development of the doctrine of *kafāʾa*, see F. J. Ziadeh, 'Equality (*kafāʾah*) in the Muslim Law of Marriage', *The American Journal of Comparative Law* 6 (1957), 503–17; Y. Linant de Bellefonds, *Traité de Droit Musulman Comparé* (Paris/La Haya, 1965) vol. 2, 171–81; Linant de Bellefonds, 'Kafāʾa', *EI2*, vol. 4 , 421–2 and M. Abu Zahra, 'Family Law', pp. 132–78. I have not had the opportunity to consult M. A. Ajetunmobi, 'An Analytical Survey of *Kafāʾah* (Equality in Islamic Marriage) at the Dawn of Islam', *Journal of Arabic and Religious Studies* 1 (1984), 86–101.

3 Ziadeh, 'Equality', p. 506.

4 The Arabian tradition recognized lineage as socially distinguishing, however Ziadeh argues that these distinctions had not given rise to the legal concept of *kafāʾa*, Ibid., pp. 507–8.

5 'Kafāʾa', *EI2*, vol. 4, p. 422.

6 I have found no mention of a *kafāʾa* doctrine in Mālik's *Muwaṭṭaʾ*.

7 *Al-Mudawwanat al-kubrā*, 16 vols (Cairo, 1905), vol. 4, p. 13.

8 *Inna akrama-kum ʿinda Allāh atqā-kum.* I quoted the English translation, *The Koran* (Oxford, 1983) by A. J. Arberry. The Arabic verbal root *k-f-ʾ* only appears in Qurʾān 112:4 '*kufʾ*' applied to God. Linant de Bellefonds observes that Ḥanafis argue that this verse should not be considered in *kafāʾa* theories because it concerns only the Hereafter where God will judge according to personal qualities, whereas in this world human inequalities are unavoidable. See Linant de Bellefonds, *Traité*, p. 173.

9 *ʾAhl al-islām kullu-hum baʿḍu-hum li-baʿḍin akfāʾ*, Saḥnūn, *Mudawwana*, vol. 4, p. 14.

10 Ibid., vol. 4, p. 29.

11 Ibid., vol. 4, p. 13. However, according to Saḥnūn (d.240/854) a slave is not suitable for a free woman, Ibid., vol. 4, p. 14. For more details about slaves in the chapters of marriage in the *Mudawwana* see C. de la Puente, 'Esclavitud y matrimonio en *al-Mudawwana al-kubrā* de Saḥnūn', *al-Qanṭara* 16 (1995), 185–208.

12 As Ziadeh mentioned in 'Equality', p. 517.

13 Ibn Rushd, *Bidāyat al-mujtahid wa-nihāyat al-muqtaṣid* (Cairo, 1960) vol. 2, 15–17. I also used the French translation by A. Laïmèche, *La Bidaya: Manuel de l'interprète des lois et traité complet du juriste. Du Mariage et de sa Dissolution* (Algiers, 1926), 52–5.

14 Ibn Juzayy, *al-Qawānīn al-fiqhiyya* (Tunis, 1982).

15 Ibn Rushd, *Bidāya*, p. 15.

16 Ibid., p. 16; the same question can be found in the Ḥanbalī school, see S. A. Spectorsky, *Chapters on Marriage and Divorce: Response of Ibn Ḥanbal and Ibn Rāhwayh* (Austin, 1993), 147.

17 On *nasab* as a constituent of *kafāʾa* in the Ḥanafi law, see Ziadeh, 'Equality', pp. 10–11; Linant de Bellefonds, *Traité*, p. 174.

18 El-Bujārī, *Les Traditions Islamiques*, trans. O. Houdas (Paris, 1943) vol. 3, 552.

19 Ibn Rushd, *Bidāya*, p. 16. Ḥanafis on the other hand, understand *ḥasab* and *bayt* (family) within the *dīn* criterion. See Ziadeh, 'Equality', p. 509.

20 Ibn Rushd, *Bidāya*, p. 16. The physical defects were emphasized elsewhere as an important impediment to marriage.

21 See also, Ziadeh, 'Equality', p. 512; Linant de Bellefonds, *Traité*, p. 176.

22 Ibn Rushd, *Bidāya*, p. 16.

23 Ibn Juzayy, *Qawānīn*, p. 202.

24 Ibid.

25 In the Ḥanafi school, *islām*, as *kafāʾa* element, means a period of affiliation to Islam for at least three generations, see Ziadeh, 'Equality', p. 11; Linant de Bellefonds, *Traité*, p. 175.

26 Linant de Bellefonds found in Ḥanafi sources the term *diyāna*, meaning 'tout à la fois le comportement religieux et la conduite strictement morale de l'individu, le Fiqh ne pouvant séparer ces deux aspects d'un même problème', *Traité*, p. 176.

27 As I understand it, *ḥuqūq* refers to maintenance (*nafaqa*) and dower (*ṣadāq*).

28 Ibn Juzayy judges as reprehensible a marriage contracted with a deformed (*damīm*) or decrepit (*haram*) man, but states that beauty (*jamāl*) should not be a conditioning attribute; I assume that he refers to permanent defects in husband's body; Ibn Juzayy, *Qawānīn*, p. 202.

29 The question of the trade of the husband, in the Ḥanafi school, led to intense discussions and its resolution changed significantly over time; see Ziadeh, 'Equality', pp. 12–4; Linant de Bellefonds, *Traité*, p. 75; see also R. Brunschvig, 'Métiers vils en Islam', *Studia Islamica* 16 (1962), 41–60.

30 I have used the French translation by G.-H. Bousquet, *Abrégé de la Loi Musulmane selon le Rite de l'Imām Mālek* (Paris/Algiers, 1958), 28–9 and the Italian translation by I. Guidi and D. Santillana, *Il 'Mukhtaṣar' o Sommario del diritto Malechita di Khalīl b. Isḥāq* (Milan, 1919), vol. 4, p. 17.

31 *Al-kafāʾa al-dīn wa-l-māl.* Bousquet translates 'la foi et l'état moral et physique'. Santillana and Guidi understand the same meaning.

32 This is also the opinion of Ibn al-Qāsim, reflected in the *Mudawwana*; Saḥnūn, *Mudawwana*, vol. 4, p. 5.

33 See above.

34 *Traité de Droit musulman: La Tohfat d'Ebn Acem*, trans. O. Houdas and F. Martel (Algiers, 1882), 190–1.

35 Ibn al-ʿAṭṭār, *Kitāb al-wathāʾiq wa-l-sijillāt*, ed. P. Chalmeta and F. Corriente (Madrid, 1983), 2. However, al-Sijilmāsī, in his commentary on the *ʿamal al-fāsī* reiterated the opinion of Ibn al-ʿAṭṭār with the criteria of *ḥāl* and *dīn*, citing Mālik as the authority, a reference which I have not found in any of the models which he presents in his formulary. See Henry Toledano, *Judicial Practice and Family Law in Morocco: The Chapter on Marriage from Sijilmāsī's al-ʿAmal al-Muṭlaq* (Boulder, 1981), 91.

36 Ibn Mughīth al-Ṭulayṭulī, *al-Muqniʿ fī ʿilm al-shurūṭ*, ed. F. J. Aguirre Sádaba (Madrid, 1994), 2. The chapters on marriage have been translated

into Spanish by S. Vila, 'Abenmoguit: Formulario Notarial', *Anuario de Historia del Derecho Español* 8 (1931), 5–200.

37 Abū Isḥāq al-Garnāṭī, *Al-Wathāʾiq al-Mukhtaṣara*, ed. Muṣṭafā Nājī (Rabat, 1987), 20.

38 Ibn Mughīth, *al-Muqniʿ*, p. 2. Ibn al-Mājishūn's opinion is also recorded in the *ʿamal* commentary; see H. Toledano, *Judicial Practice*, p. 91.

39 Ibn Juzayy, *Qawānīn*, 202–3. See Linant de Bellefonds, *Traité*, pp. 173–4.

40 On this question, see Toledano, *Judicial Practice and Family Law*, pp. 89–90.

41 al-Garnāṭī emphasized the fact that the *kafāʾa* linked with the criteria of *ḥāl wa-l-māl* is one of the questions about which the Andalusians differed from the school of Ibn al-Qāsim; al-Garnāṭī, *al-Wathāʾiq*, p. 52.

42 As quoted by al-ʿAbdūsī, see below.

43 I did not find this opinion of Ibn al-Qāsim in the *Mudawwana*, however, it is attributed to him by al-Matīṭī, according to al-ʿAbdūsī, Sijilmāsī and according to Ibn Rāshid in *Kitāb lubāb al-lubāb*, p. 89.

44 See H. Toledano, *Judicial Practice*, p. 91.

45 This work is *al-Miʿyār al-muʿrib wa-l-jāmiʿ al-mughrib ʿan fatāwā ahl Ifrīqiya wa-l-Andalus wa-l-Maghrib*, ed. M. Ḥajjī et al. (Rabat/Beirut, 1981–3). More details about the life and works of this jurist can be found in F. Vidal Castro, 'Aḥmad al-Wansarīsī (m. 914/1508): Principales aspectos de su vida', *al-Qanṭara* 12 (1991) 351–62; Vidal Castro, 'Las obras de Aḥmad al-Wansarīsī (m.914/1508): Inventario analítico', *Anaquel de Estudios Arabes* 3 (1992), 73–112 and Vidal Castro, 'El Miʿyār de al-Wansarīsī (m. 914/1508), I: Fuentes, manuscritos, ediciones, traducciones', *Miscelánea de Estudios Arabes y Hebraicos* 42–3 (1993–4), 317–61. There is a well-known selection made by E. Amar, 'La pierre de touche des Fétwas de Aḥmad al-Wanscharīsī (Choix de consultations juridiques des Faqīhs du Maghreb, traduites et analysées)', *Archives Marocaines* 12 (1908); 13 (1909). Also well-known are Hady Roger Idris' works on marriage in the *Miʿyār*, 'Le mariage en Occident Musulman d'après un choix de Fatwàs médiévales extraites du *Miʿyār* d'al-Wansharīsī', *Studia Islamica* 32 (1970), 57–67; *Revue de l'Occident Musulman et de la Méditerranée* 12 (1972), 45–62; *ROMM* 17 (1974), 71–105 and *ROMM* 25 (1978), 119–38. See also, V. Lagardère's monograph with a large selection of *fatwās* from the *Miʿyār*, *Histoire et société en Occident musulman au Moyen Age: Analyse du 'Miʿyār' d'al-Wansharīsī* (Madrid, 1995).

46 Wansharīsī, *Miʿyār* vol. 1, p. 1. The short introduction made by al-Wansharīsī to his *Miʿyār* was translated into French by E. Amar, 'La Pierre des Touches de Consultations juridiques', *Archives Marocaines* 12 (1908), XI–XIII.

47 The fact that primary *fatwās* emerged from real problems 'outside the jurists' minds' is, in my opinion, sufficiently proved by Wael B. Hallaq in 'From *Fatwā* to *Furūʿ*: Growth and Change in Islamic Substantive Law', *Islamic Law and Society* 1, 1 (1994), 31–9. For a stimulating approach to *fatwās* as a source for social and legal history, see David S. Powers, '*Fatwās* as Sources for Legal and Social History: A Dispute over Endowment Revenues from Fourteenth-Century

Fez', *al-Qanṭara* 11 (1990), 295–341.

48 The *fatwā* is located in the third volume of the *Mi'yār* (pp. 84–6) dedicated entirely to marriage questions (*nawāzil al-nikāḥ*). Hady Roger Idris gives a brief extract of this *fatwā* in 'Le mariage en Occident Musulman. Analyse de fatwās médiévales extraites du 'Mi'yār' d'al-Wansharīsī', *ROMM* 17–18 (1974), 75.

49 For more details about his biography, see Ibn al-Qāḍī, *Jadhwat al-iqtibās fī dhikr man ḥalla min al-a'lām madīna Fās* (Rabat, 1974) vol. 2, 425; Makhlūf, *Shajarāt al-Nūr al-Zakiyya fī ṭabaqāt al-Mālikiyya* (Cairo, 1350) vol. 1, 255; Aḥmad Bābā, *Nayl al-ibtihāj bi-taḥrīz al-Dībāj* (Beirut, n.d.), 157–8; Fernando R. Mediano, *Familias de Fez (ss. XV–XVII)* (Madrid, 1995), 203–7.

50 A primary *fatwā* is the one in which 'the question and answer are preserved more or less in their original form and content', see Wael B. Hallaq, 'From *Fatwās* to *Furū'*', p. 2. However not all the *fatwās* preserved in the *Mi'yār* could be considered as 'primary'. A study on the sources of this compilation and the way in which the author gathered the *fatwās* is one of the studies that I will follow in the future.

51 About this tribe see A. Fischer, 'Qais-'Ailān', *EI2*, pp. 692–8.

52 P. Morizot, 'Awerba', *Encyclopedie Berbère* vol. 8, pp. 1192–6.

53 al-Wansharīsī, *Mi'yār*, vol. 3, p. 84: *min fuṣūli-hi an yuzawwiju-hā mimman yarā wa-bi-mā yarā*. When it involves a woman who is a virgin, only her father has the right to marry her without her consent; when it involves a *waṣī*, he must wait for her to come of age and then ask for her consent, see Ibn Abī Zayd Qayrawānī, *La Risāla ou Epître sur les éléments du dogme et de la loi de l'Islām selon le rite mālikite* 5th ed., ed. and trans. Léon Bercher (Algiers, 1968), 172–3.

54 al-Wansharīsī, *Mi'yār*, vol. 3, p. 84.

55 Ibid., vol. 3, pp. 84–5.

56 It was later reflected in *'amal* as in H. Toledano, *Judicial Practice*, p. 90.

57 Abū'l-Ḥasan 'Alī b. 'Abd Allāh b. Ibrāhīm al-Anṣārī, known as al-Matīṭī (d.570/1174) is the author of a *shurūṭ* work entitled *al-Nihāya wa-l-tammām fī ma'rifat al-Wathā'iq wa-l-aḥkām* that remains unpublished in El Escorial. See M. García-Arenal, 'Algunos manuscritos de *fiqh* andalusíes y norteafricanos pertenecientes a la Real Biblioteca de El Escorial', *al-Qanṭara* 1 (1980), 13. For more details about his biography, see: Aḥmad Bābā, *Nayl*, p. 99; Majlūf, *Shajarat*, p. 163.

58 For an explanation on the *mashhūr* concept, see Ibrāhīm b. 'Alī b. Farḥūn, *Kashf al-niqāb al-ḥājib min Muṣṭalaḥ Ibn al-Ḥājib*, ed. Ḥamza Abū Fāris and 'Abd al-Salām al-Sharīfa (Beirut, 1990), p. 62ff; see also Wael B. Hallaq, 'Murder in Cordoba: *Ijtihād*, *Iftā'* and the Evolution of Substantive Law in Medieval Islam', *Acta Orientalia* 55 (1994), 55–83, note 2.

59 al-Wansharīsī, *Mi'yār*, vol. 3, p. 84.

60 For details in this political situation that reflects a revaluation of Arab lineages, see H. L. Beck, *L'image d'Idris II, ses descendants de Fās et la politique Sharīfienne des sultans marīnides (656–869/1258–1465)* (Leiden, 1989) and M. García-Arenal, 'The Revolution of Fās in 869/1465 and the Death of Sultan

'Abd al-Ḥaqq al-Marīnī', *BSOAS* 41, 1 (1978), 43–66.

61 A reference to Aḥmad b. Muḥammad b. Ziyād (d.312/924–5). His biographer Abū Faḍl 'Iyāḍ, *Tartīb al-Madārik wa-taqrīb al-masālik li-ma'rifat a'lām madhhab Mālik* (Rabat, 1983), vol. 5, 189, did not mention the work entitled *al-Aḥkām*. His opinions on this issue were also quoted in Ibn Mughīth (p. 40) and al-Sijilmāsī, (H. Toledano, *Judicial Practice*, pp. 68–9) where the *walīs* produce evidence to support their claims against the suitability of the husband.

62 al-Wansharīsī, *Mi'yār*, vol. 3, p. 85.

63 *'Alay-nā ma'arra fī dhālika, fa-lā nuzawwiju-hā min-hu li-anna-nā lā na'rif nasaba-hu, wa-lā huwa kuf'un la-nā*, Ibid.

64 Ibid., vol. 3 p. 29, repeated in vol. 3, p. 228. Ibn Lubb's biography can be found in Mukhlūf, *Shajarat al-nūr*, p. 230–1.

65 If we make an exception of *al-Qawānīn al-fiqhiyya* in which the *kafā'a* is one of the necessary qualifications which must be met prior to marriage taking place.

66 The legal consensus in the Mālikī school is that a woman of low condition (*daniyya*) did not need a *walī* to find a husband for her since any mate would be valid to her and to her family. See Saḥnūn, *Mudawwana*, vol. 4, p. 20; Ibn Abī Zayd, *Risāla*, p. 74; Ibn Juzayy, *Qawānīn*, p. 204; Khalīl, *Mukhtaṣar*, p. 19; H. Toledano, *Judicial Practice*, p. 76–7. Several *fatwās* illustrate this consensus, for example Wansharīsī, *Mi'yār*, vol. 3, p. 315 (al-Māzarī) and Ibid., vol. 3, p. 30–2 (Ibn Lubb).

67 If the woman has no *walī*, the *qāḍī* must exercise this function, taking into account the suitability. See for example *Mi'yār* vol. 3, p. 110–1 (Ibn Rushd, d.520/1126) Cordoba. To follow this rank in the *walī*'s function see Ibn Abī Zayd, *Risāla*, p. 74; Ibn Mughīth, *Muqni'*, p. 31; Ibn Juzayy, *Qawānīn*, p. 204; J. López Ortiz, *Derecho musulmán* (Barcelona, 1932), 157; J. Schacht, *An Introduction to Islamic Law* (Oxford, 1964), 161–2.

68 al-Sha'bī al-Mālaqī, *al-Aḥkām* ed. al-Ṣādiq al-Ḥalawī (Beirut, 1992), 464.

69 In other *fatwās*, Ibn Zarb emphasized the fact that the marriage only could be annulled before the consummation had taken place. See Wansharīsī, *Mi'yār*, vol. 3, p. 114.

70 al-Wansharīsī began the *fatwā*, with the sentence *wa-su'ila ba'ḍa al-'ulamā'*. Hence only by reading the original source can it be located, see Wansharīsī, *Mi'yār*, vol. 3, p. 114 (bottom)..

71 *Sakīr fāsiq lā yu'minu 'alay-hā*, *Mi'yār*, vol. 3, p. 114.

72 al-Wansharīsī follows a *ḥadīth* where it is explained that when a girl is married off by her father to a dissolute man, the father is supposed to renounce his daughter and her descent.

73 Ibid., vol. 3, p. 377.

74 al-Wansharīsī often compares the opinions of Ibn Rushd and al-Māzarī when he collected their answers in the *Mi'yār*.

75 Ibid., p. 311 (al-Māzarī) to be compared with vol. 3, p. 377 (Ibn Rushd).

76 Even if he did not mention a document, Ibn Lubb also indicates that

a marriage remains deferred (*mawqūf*), until the proof of the presence of *kafā'a* Ibid., vol. 3, p. 29.

77 Several *fatwās* reflect an annulment of marriages because of the lack of pious behaviour (in the husband and in the wife), without taking into consideration the *kafā'a* doctrine.

78 The Moroccan Code of Personal Status includes some considerations about *kafā'a* but no mention can be found about any particular criteria; they must be explained in the light of the *'urf* (*fi tafsīri-hā ilā al-'urf*), see Arts. 13–14b. These two articles could be seen as a result from the development of the classical Mālikī rules on this question. Cf. Linant de Bellefonds 'Kafā'a', p. 422.

FIVE

Water Rights and Irrigation Practices in the Medieval Maghrib

PATRICIA KABRA

Access to water determines the survival of individuals and communities in the semi-arid regions of North Africa. Since prehistoric times, the raising of crops and animals in the Maghrib has relied on the management and exploitation of scarce water resources. This has required a special water technology to deal with controlling and directing water resources, as well as a legal framework to establish and maintain water rights. During the Islamic period, the importance and divisiveness of water management was referred to by Muslim travellers, geographers, and legal scholars who described many of the technological and the legal issues. In a colourful account in the anonymous twelfth-century *Kitāb al-istibṣār*, the author exclaimed that if you hear people debating in loud voices – you know that it must be about water! In response to the numerous disputes which arose over access to water, Mālikī legal scholars developed a set of criteria for deciding water rights issues. These criteria are presented in the ninth-century work of Saḥnūn, *al-Mudawwana*, the later *Mukhtaṣar Khalīl* and a variety of *fatwā* collections and other legal sources.[1] It is evident from studying the *fatwās* in Wansharīsī's *Miʿyār*,[2] one of the few Maghribī *fatwā* collections to be published, that legal scholars during the period from the tenth through the fifteenth century balanced community and individual rights in an effort to resolve disputes. Their opinions were influenced by an understanding of legal precedents as well as a knowledge of environmental conditions.

From archaeological and historical accounts it is evident that the technology of water control systems in the Maghrib pre-dates the Greek and Roman period. Over 2000 years ago, water systems in the region were constructed and designed in such a way as to provide sufficient water to support agriculture in the arid and semi-arid regions of North Africa. 'Dry farming techniques of controlling and conserving runoff from streams and rains through the use of earthen terraces, multiple-tiered cropping, and flood zone systems of embankments and levees developed' quite early.[3] Archaeologists working in the Libyan pre-desert near Ghirza have attributed the development of agriculture in the region to Punic influence, or even earlier periods.[4] An elaborate water control system in the *wādī* regions of walls, channels, and cisterns, similar to those still to be found in southern Tunisia today, was first constructed in the pre-Roman period.[5] In the mountain and coastal regions, diversion walls, terraces and dams were used by early farmers to control water flow and to conserve moisture.[6] Documents from the late Roman period attest to the types of irrigation arrangements made in some of the northern coastal regions where a scheme of water distribution was based on day and night units, channel and collection basins, and water rights sold with property deeds.[7] Thus, irrigation technology was already in place in North Africa by the time the Arabs arrived in the seventh century AD and local practices of water management were well entrenched.

During the Islamic period these irrigation systems were maintained and improved through the use of new and old technologies. Mechanical devices for lifting water (*sāniya*),[8] water wheels (*irḥa)*, aqueducts (*qantara mā'*), underground channels (*qanāt)* and elaborate canals (*sāqiya)* were used to convey and direct water. All of this required community or group management: construction, maintenance, and allocation. Water distribution was often arranged according to custom by informal *ad hoc* groups, syndicates, or officials appointed by local authorities. The amount of water and the length of time it was allowed to flow were measured by a variety of techniques. Among these was the *qadūs*, a system where water dripped from a container to mark the time allotted for water to flow. In Tozeur, in southern Tunisia, according to al-Bakrī, four *aqdās* of water cost a *mithqāl* for one year. Both al-Bakrī in the eleventh century and al-Tijānī in the fourteenth described Tozeur as having a complex system of irrigation comprised of three rivers divided into six channels, and each main channel was subdivided into many stone canals.[9] The complexity of such a system was described by Penet in 1913 in his study of irrigation in Tunisia. He noted that Tozeur had a system of water distribution which rotated every seven days, some fields being watered at night and others during the day. This became a problem in a situation where garden A had water from sun up to sun down and bought an additional 48 units of water from neighbour B on Thursday after sun up. Then he died and the garden was divided between two brothers (each getting one third) and two sisters (each with one sixth) and the widow (one eighth). The question of how to allocate the water then had to be negotiated again.[10] This system required both the landowner and the *amīn* overseeing the water distribution to be familiar with these technologies and measurements. According to the *Kitāb al-istibṣār*, the irrigation technology of Gafsa, near Tozeur, was an art of engineering and precision. Even the field workers knew how to tell the time of day. The author of this work claimed that if a not very intelligent worker was asked the time of day, he would stop, look at the sun and measure his shadow. Then he would determine the time to the exact sixtieth of an hour![11] However, disputes often arose as to the allocation and ownership of water, often leading to feuds and bloodshed.

Islamic law played an important role in the Maghrib in the resolution of disputes, and in the formalisation of traditional practices by absorbing them into a Mālikī legal framework. A wide variety of literary and documentary sources refer to the existence of water technology and management in the medieval Maghrib. However, few of them discuss the social, economic, or legal aspects of water distribution. In Mālikī legal texts from North Africa, especially in collections of legal opinions (*fatāwā* or *ajwiba*) relating to *aḥkām al-miyāh* or water laws, it is possible to find detailed descriptions of water technologies and disputes. But, these collections pose several difficulties as source materials. First, with rare exceptions, most notably the *Ajwiba* of ʿAzzūm from sixteenth-century Tunis, these collections often contain abbreviated *fatwās* with the date, litigants, and sometimes even the *muftī*'s names omitted. Collections, such as Burzulī's *Nawāzil* or Wansharīsī's *Miyʿār* contain a variety of *fatwās,* some of which have been reduced to three or four lines containing only the significant legal principle which was applied in the specific case.[12] Thus, the historical context, as well as important descriptions of water systems, may be entirely lost. Second, in the *Nawāzil* and the *Miʿyār* these *fatwās* are grouped by topic, and represent both what the collecter considered significant and a summary of major trends in legal thinking. The very process of selection means that no accurate assessment of the number of cases related to a particular issue in any given time can be easily determined. And, the significance of these cases or the historical context may be difficult to determine. Third, the vast majority of these *fatwā* collections are still in manuscript form, such as the works of 'Azzūm and Burzulī which are housed in the national library in Tunis. There are no detailed studies of their contents, or sources.[13] One of the few *fatwā* collections from the Maghrib to be edited and published is that of the Mālikī jurist, Aḥmad al-Wansharīsī (d. 914/1508), entitled *al-Miʿyār al-muʿrib.* Keeping in mind the problems mentioned above, an examination of the cases in the *Miʿyār* related to *aḥkām al-miyāh,* specifically those involving disputes over water used for irrigation, will demonstrate the way in which the law was used to solve real economic and social problems..

The *Miʿyār* consists of twelve volumes plus an index, and is organised according to subject. About 128 *fatwās* concerning water are collected in the *Miʿyār*; 81 of these cases are in volume eight in two chapters of questions regarding water. The other 47 are distributed in the following volumes:

volume 5: 10 cases in the chapter on contracts and sales
volume 6: 7 cases in the chapter on *qism* (division)
volume 7: 12 cases in the chapter on *ḥubus* (*waqf* properties)
volume 9: 10 cases in the chapter on *ḍarār* (damage)
volume 10: 6 cases in the chapter *daʿawa wa īmān* (propaganda and faith).

There are also a few cases scattered in other sections of the *Miʿyār*. Over half of these *fatwās* concerning water were issued by Maghribī legal scholars during the period from the eleventh to the fifteenth century; the rest are from Andalusia. These *fatwās*, of course, provide only a partial picture of issues related to water rights in the Maghrib and must be placed within the broader traditions in Islamic law.

Water in Islamic law is generally classified according to source, use, and ownership.[14] In principle, water as a whole is *mubāh* and cannot be owned and should be available to those who need it. However, in practice, water is subject to ownership and sale just as in the case of land. The possibility of ownership depends upon the source, the location, the purpose to which it is put, and the process by which it was developed. This is clearly laid out in Saḥnūn's *Mudawwana,* where the opinions of Mālik ibn Anas, as related by Ibn al-Qāsim, and the sayings of Ibn al-Qāsim and sometimes, Saḥnūn himself, are all recorded. Their opinions on water rights are generally contained in the *Mudawwana* in the sections relating to *ḥarīm, shifā, qism, ijāra,* and *bayʿu.* This division differs somewhat from Wansharīsī's *Miʿyār,* and the *Mukhtaṣar Khalīl,* an important source for Mālikī legal scholars after the fourteenth century. In the *Mukhtaṣar Khalīl* almost all references to water for agriculture appear under the sections of *qism, biyʿu,* and *iḥyā al-mawāṭ*.[15]

In these works, three basic categories of water are distinguished according to source: running, stored, and underground water. Running water, like rivers, and streams, was not owned and could be used without restriction, if they were sufficient for those who lived nearby. If the water was not sufficient, or it required the construction of a dam, canal, water wheel, *sāqiya,* or *qanāt* or some other structure to control it, then the water was to be used by those who lived nearby or participated in the construction of the water system. This division of water occurred according to an established system of priority. According to the *Mukhtaṣar*, drawing upon the *Mudawwana* as a source, the occupier of the land closest to the source (*al-ʿalā*) takes precedence over others lower down (*al-asfal*). However, if the one lower down developed his land first, then he has first right to the use of the water.[16] In the case of water accessed by a structure, like a canal, the cases in the *Miʿyār* show that those who participated in its construction had the right to use the water according to the level of their participation. It is this issue of priority in water rights which led to many disputes. In the second category – stored water – resevoirs, cisterns, or wells which have been built to serve the public can be used by all. The water from private wells or cisterns can be restricted or sold. In the *Mudawwana*, Mālik was related to have disapproved of the sale of water of *mawājil*, and rain water, especially for drinking by people or animals; but, excess water from flooding or irrigation water from wells located on someone's property, and irrigation water from springs and sources was permissable to sell.[17] But, the owner had the obligation to give water to anyone in extreme need, especially for drinking.[18] The owner of the water could either be the renter or the property owner of a piece of land with a well or cistern. In a case recorded in the *Miʿyār*, the use of water in a *mājil* was the object of a dispute between a renter and landowner. In this case, al-Māzarī, the tenth-century Qayrawānī legal scholar, was asked about a man who rented a house with a *mājil* and whether he or the owner had the right to use the water. Al-Māzarī concluded that, as in the case of other utilities, the renter had the right to use the water.[19] The third source of water, springs, also was available to all if the water was sufficient. If it was not sufficient, then it was for the use of those who lived nearby or for those who uncovered it and caused it to flow. These texts also discuss techniques for dividing water. Water could be distributed by turns, hours, days; by regulating volume; or by lot. The divisions might vary according to the season, the time of day, the type of crop, or the condition of the land.

One important legal principle in regards to water rights is particularly pertinent to cases involving irrigation: the issue of ownership. Not all sources could be owned – and none of them exclusively. Ownership of water does not imply unlimited rights of usage. In Islamic law, it is incumbant upon the owner of a water source to provide for people or animals in need even if they cannot pay. Ownership of a water source does not mean that it is permissible to flood your neighbours's garden or to let waste water run into his house. And, in a case where water is not owned, those who use it have the responsibility of owners in its management. However, serious problems often arose over how to detrmine and who determines access and the responsibility for control or upkeep of water systems. *Fatwās* relating to these questions in connection with irrigation water are particularly significant because they show both the adaptation and change of Islamic law in light of local conditions, and the way in which members of society attempted to deal with notions of property rights. The problems faced by Maghribi legal scholars in resolving disputes were often exacerbated by the economic or social status of the litigants, or the harshness of local environmental conditions.

One of the most common disputes presented in the cases in the *Miʿyār* concerns the first right of use of flowing water, such as rivers, streams, or springs. Normally, those closest to the source had precedence over those further away. This principle was applied by the Fāsī legal scholar, Misbāḥ (d.705/1305). He was asked about an *ʿayn māʾ* (spring) belonging to the people of a specific region who had irrigated with it and watered their mounts and animals from it for generations without exclusive rights for anyone to all or part of it. But some of the inhabitants of this locale had lands and gardens downstream of this spring and others of them did not have any land. Those who had land downstream wanted to profit from the overflow of water to irrigate their gardens and vegetables which were located in barren land. But those who didn't have gardens or land downstream wanted to use the excess water, either to sell, or to give to others. Should the excess go to profit all of the inhabitants of the locale or only those which have property or lands downstream from the spring? And if to those who are downstream, should it be divided in equal portions, or according to the extent of their lands, or the highest first? Misbāḥ replied that the people who had land and gardens had more rights to the excess water than anyone else. And the highest was first, according to the tradition of the Prophet. And those who planted first had more rights than those who planted later but were higher up (precedent of al-Bājī d.1012–41).[20] In this case, the basic principle of proximity, which was attributed to the saying of the Prophet, was modified to include the case of people who had settled before others, but perhaps were further away from the source. However, those who worked their land had precedence over those who did not, or those who had no agricultural land. The productive use of property becomes more important in this case, and in others, than the mere fact of rights of proximity in time or place.

Another divisive issue was the problem of repair and upkeep of water systems. How was responsibility to be shared? Misbāḥ was asked, in another case, about some people who had a *sāqiya* (channel) passing through their land, and everyone along it had rights to its water. It had been divided with no disagreement about each person's share. However, when rain fell and the *sāqiya* flooded there was a dispute over who was responsable for preventing the *sāqiya* from overflowing.[21] Was it the responsibility of the one with first access to the water higher up to open the channel to his land to relieve the flooding? Or was it the responsibility of the last one to leave a route open for drainage? Or should all share equally? In some cases this question was decided as al-Sāigh (d. 486/1093) did in the case of a *qantara mā'* (aqueduct) which had fallen down and needed repair. He was asked whether its repair was to be at the expense of those who profited from it according to the size of their properties or according to the value of their wealth. He replied that property owners should pay based on the profit drawn from it and the repairs were to be divided among them.[22]

The divisions of repairs and maintenance could possibly put a heavy burden on those who could least afford it – the owners of small plots of agricultural land. Often those with no land, even if they used the water for a craft or business did not have to pay. This inequity was recognised by al-ʿAbdūsī (d. 849/1445–6) when he decided the case of a small village which had water brought to it by a large *qadūs* from about four miles away for the use of the people of the region. They used the water for their mosques, irrigation, baths, and homes. It was in need of repair in many places, but the *ḥubus* which managed it could not afford it and the *bayt al-māl* could not be counted on to do it either. So, he was asked, did the repairs have to fall on all the people of the village, and in the case that the people refused, could they be compelled? Was it the duty of the rich, or all inhabitants – rich or poor? He answered that no one can be compelled to repair it since those who refuse may have valid reasons such as they do not use it because they have a well, or that they irrigate from the *wādī* or another source. This is for their conscience to decide. However, those who contribute to its repairs can prevent someone who did not participate from using the water carried in the *qadūs* until all the participants had their share.[23]

The categories of people who used the water of a large running sources were quite diverse, and deciding who held the greatest responsibility in the upkeep of a particular sytem of water management was often more complex than a simple appeal to one's conscience. In a case involving the Wādī Masmūda near Fez, various categories of users ranging from households to businesses were described: households who used the water from the river for use in the house, those who had wells which drew from the river water, those who had latrines which emptied into the river, those who lived along streams which emanated from the river, and farmers and artisans who used the water to produce a profit. The question of who was responsible for paying for or participating in the cleaning of the channels and the *wādī* was posed. The problem was that since running water, such as that in the *wādī*, could not be owned, no one was really directly responsible. And if some of them did clean out the *wādī*, then they, on the basis of their shared labour, would have an exclusive right to the water. The decision rendered by the *qāḍī* avoided this last scenario by stipulating that only those who drew a profit from the use of the water were required to help clean out the *wādī*.[24] In another case the users of the system were taxed according to the amount of water they used. This tax could then be used for the upkeep of the water supply system.[25]

One of the most detailed cases in the *Miʿyār* involves a long-term dispute addressed by several *qāḍīs* from Fez in the thirteenth century.[26] It concerns the use of *wādī* waters for irrigation and contains a detailed description of the sloping sides of the *wādī*, the streams leading into it, and the communities which depended on it. Many *wādīs* had both perennial and seasonal water. Thus, they required an elaborate channelling of water by stone barrages, and water distribution technologies such as the *sāqiya* and *noria*; and they needed flood management and regulation of rights to flood waters. In this case, the people of one community complained that the people of a second had cut off their access to water by modifying the flow of the stream without their permission. In the decision, the *qāḍī* stated that no stream could be modified without the say of the original users, and that running water is not the property of anyone. Here two principles are evident – priority is based on first use, and running water is not property. In other cases those higher up the *wādī* have priority, however, they are supposed to leave enough for those lower down. Often *wādī* systems were very long and meandered past a dozen communities or more. Any infringement on the rights of others could lead to warfare or sabotage. And, in fact, the destruction of *wādī* irrigation systems could lead to the demise of whole communities.

Along *wādīs* the water was often lifted and channelled in canals called *sāqiya* in the Maghrib. Lifting devices such as *irḥā* and *sāniya* were often used. The participation in the construction of such a system gave the participants the right of access. Abū 'Imrān of Qayrawan (d. 1038) heard a case involving a dispute between members of a community which had terraced gardens, one above the other, all fed from such a *sāqiya* system. Each garden was watered in turn, until the last was reached. The last recipient claimed he never got enough water, and that he deserved an equal share. Abū 'Imrān stated that if they had all worked together on the *sāqiya* system, then the division should be according to participation. Each should have an equal turn and they should choose by lot who will get their water first. Thus the legal principle of *shārik* is applied to labour in water construction.

The problem of measurement in water use is quite clear in many of the cases. One particularly complex case arose among the people of Taza in the western Maghrib (Morocco).[27] In this town, the water of the canal was carried in four *qadūs*. One was for cisterns, two for general use, and the fourth to refill the water supply of three houses. One of the owners of one of the three houses was asked for permission for the use of the *sāqiya* to take some water from the *qadūs* to another street. He authorised it. After two years, the people on the two streets found that this had affected the flow of water and that in the summer it was less, and they argued about it. The right of the two streets to the water was established by producing an *'aqd*. But the question remained as to whether one resident had the right to give a third party access. It was determined that he did. This is unusual, because the joint proprietors were always consulted on water matters. In the description of this system, the use of measuring access time by the call to prayer and the openings in the *qadūs* is evident.

The result of an unresolved dispute over access to water could be years of feuding and warfare between villages or communities. Often, as in the following case, the result was decided for a long time by force. However, when an agreement was finally reached to stop fighting and resolve the problem, the local *qāḍī* or *muftī* was often asked to render his opinion or decision in the matter. Al-Māzarī was once asked about people who were fighting with their neighbours, and some of them died, and finally their leaders concluded an agreement dividing the water of the *wādī* which they used for irrigation. But some of the people protested on the grounds that the strong had grabbed the water of the river from the weak, and that this had occurred over and over until they no longer knew to whom the water belonged. How should justice be done? And he answered that if they did not know, and the strong had been taking advantage of the weak, then the water should be divided starting with those who were highest, until the water arrived at the last.[28] Here, the simple application of a long-standing legal precedent was an easy solution to what was in reality a very complex situation. Obviously the 'strong' were only willing to negotiate, call in an arbitrator, and abide by such a decision because they probably were no longer in a position of strength.

The *fatwās* in the *Mi'yār* of Wansharīsī show several patterns of development in the Maghrib. First, as urbanisation increased in the Maghrib during the Islamic period, and urban centres like Fez and Qayrawan become associated with trades and crafts and less with agriculture, the water dispute cases involving a purely agricultural economy decreased and those relating to urban disputes increased. This may be partly due to the selectivity of the author, but a preliminary study of the *fatwās* in Burzulī's *Nawāzil* also points to a similar pattern. Second, as in the case of the inhabitants of Taza, legal scholars heard complex cases of a technical nature where they needed to understand both the technological, as well as legal principles to be considered in a case. Third, they had to deal with cases where the principles laid down by Mālik were not sufficient to arrive at an adequate response. So they either looked for other principles to be applied, such as rules of partnership, or as in the case of the Wādī Masmūda, rules of equity to decide the case. In the process of developing the principles to be applied and the arguments to support it, *muftī*s and *qāḍīs* developed legal precedents.

Their *fatwās* became precedents for later jurists to choose from when necessary. It is this process of change and adaptation of Islamic legal practice which is evident in the numerous cases involving water rights in the medieval Maghrib.

Notes

1 See Saḥnūn, *al-Mudawwana al-kubrā* (Baghdad, n.d.), and Haṭṭāb, *Kitāb muwāḥib al-jalīl li-sharḥ mukhtaṣar khalīl* (Cairo, 1329)

2 Aḥmad b. Yaḥyā al-Wansharīsī, *al-Mi'yar al-mu'rib wa-l-jāmi' al-mughrib 'an al-fatāwā 'ulama Ifriqiyya wa-l-Andalūs wa-l-Maghrib* (13 vols., Rabāṭ, 1981–3).

3 See my dissertation: Patricia K. Kabra, 'Patterns of Economic Continuity and Change in Early Hafsid Ifriqiya' (University of California, Los Angeles: 1994), 106.

4 Olwen Brogan and D. J. Smith, *Ghirza: A Libyan Settlement in the Roman Period*, (Tripoli, 1984), 227.

5 See G. W. W. Barker and G. D. B. Jones, 'The UNESCO Libyan Valleys Survey 1979–1981: Paleaoeconomy and Environmental Archaeology of the Pre-Desert', *Libyan Studies*, 13 (1982), 1–8.

6 Kabra, ibid., p. 123.

7 C. Courtois et al., *Tablettes Albertini: actes privés de l'époque vandal (fin du ve siecle)* (Paris, 1955), 223; P. Trousset, 'Les oasis présahariennes dans l'antiquité: partage de l'eau et division du temps', *Antiquités africaines*, 22 (1986), 163–93.

8 There is a difference of opinion in the secondary sources over the meaning of some of these terms in the Maghrib. *Sāqiya* is defined in various ways. For example, M. Perron in his 'Précis de jurisprudence musulmane au principes de législation musulmane civile et religieuse, selon le rite malékite par Khalīl Ibn Isḥāq' in *Exploration Scientifique d'Algérie pendents les années 1840, 1841 1842* (Paris, 1848) 1: 10 defines *sāqī* as a system of a resevoir from which water is raised to irrigate by use of a machine pulled by animals with pots to fill and dump. However, the sense of the word in the *Mi'yār* and in Ch. Monchicourt, 'Règlements d'irrigation dans le haut tell (Règions du Kef, Teboursouk, Mactar et Thala)', *Extrait du Bulletin de la direction générale de l'iagriculture, du commerce et de la colonisation* (Tunis, 1911), 5 is that the term applies to an irrigation channel or canal. Monicourt also presents an interesting case of ownership of water near Sbibas in Tunisia where water is divided by tent and each tent has an automatic right to a certain quantity of water.

9 al-Bakrī, *Kitāb al-masālik wa-l-mamālik* (Tunis, 1992), vol. 2, 708–9; and al-Tijānī, *Riḥla al-Tijānī* (Tunis, 1981), 157.

10 See P. Penat, *L'Hydraulique agricole dans la Tunisie méridionale* (Tunis, 1913), 79.

11 *Kitāb al-istibṣār*, p. 153.

12 Abū al-Qāsim al-Burzulī, *Nawāzil al-aḥkām*, MSS in Maktabat al-waṭaniyya in Tunis. And Abū al-Faḍil al-Qāsim b. Muḥammad Mazūq b.

'Azzūm, *Ajwiba.*

13 For a discussion of 'Azzūm, see: Jacques Berque, *L'intérieur du Maghreb: xve–xixe siecle* (Paris, 1978), ch. 3. For a discussion of Burzulī see Muḥammad al-Hādī al-'Amrī, *Bāb al-Qaḍā' wa al-shahādāt min nawāzil al-Burzulī* (Tunis, 1979).

14 See the discussion of water law in A. M. A. Maktari, *Water Rights and Irrigation Practices in Lahj: A Study of the Application of Customary and Sharī'ah Law in South-West Arabia* (Cambridge, 1971); and *Encyclopaedia of Islam* articles on *mā'* and *bir.*

15 The manuscripts of Burzulī include water issues primarily in the sections of *al-muzar'a, al-mugharisa, ijāra, al-ḍarar, al-qism, al-wadī'a,* and *hubus.*

16 Khalīl, *Mukhtaṣar*, p. 6; pp. 16–18.

17 Saḥnūn, *Mudawwana*, vol. 4, p. 290.

18 Ibid., vol.6, p. 189.

19 al-Wansharīsī, *Mi'yar*, vol. 5, p. 86. For information on this jurist see al-Ṭāhir al-Ma'mūrī, *Fatāwā al-Māzrī* (Tunis, 1994).

20 al-Wansharīsī, *Mi'yar*, vol. 5, p. 152.

21 Ibid., vol. 5, p. 153–4

22 Ibid., vol. 5, p. 350.

23 Ibid., vol. 7, p. 11.

24 Ibid., vol. 8, pp. 20–7.

25 Ibid., vol. 7, p. 55.

26 Ibid., vol. 8, pp. 5–6.

27 Ibid., vol. 8, pp. 37–40.

28 Ibid., vol. 6, p. 518.

SIX

Ijtihād in Ibn Taymiyya's *fatāwā*[1]

BENJAMIN JOKISCH

Ijtihād is a central term in the relationship between theory and practice in Islamic Law. It is usually defined in *uṣūl* works as the greatest possible effort by a qualified jurist to reach a legal decision within the framework of the *Sharīʿa*.[2] This vague phrase, 'the greatest possible effort', has to be understood in its broadest sense. It means that the jurist, by observing the material sources of the law (Qur'ān and *sunna*), and the general principles of Islamic law, is allowed, if not obliged, to exhaust all possible avenues of inquiry in order to find an adequate legal solution. Even a *mujtahid* of a lesser degree (for example a *mujtahid fī'l-madhhab* who has agreed to regard the opinions and principles of his own law school) can chose between the contradictory prescriptions in his law school. *Al-ijtihād al-muṭlaq* (absolute or unrestricted *ijtihād*) as well as other forms of *ijtihād* offers the possibility of applying the Islamic legal system to specific circumstances and thereby determining the extent of the discrepancy between theory and practice. This is an underlying premise in what follows.

In Western accounts of Islamic law, however, the opinion that the so-called 'door of *ijtihād*' was closed in about the fourth/tenth century has predominated, and since that time, it is argued, the *Sharīʿa* has been unable to take account of changes through time because it has lost its flexibility.[3] Contrary to this opinion, and agreeing with recent research,[4] this study seeks to demonstrate that *ijtihād*, in reality, continued to exist after the fourth/tenth century. There are, on the one hand, purely theoretical arguments, such as the opinions of the Muslim jurists about the existence of *ijtihād*, the logical necessity of *ijtihād* as a *conditio sine qua non* in the science of *uṣūl al-fiqh*, and the impossibility of deciding cases purely on the basis of *furūʿ* works (since the works are contradictory, obscure and full of lacunae). On the other hand *ijtihād* was (and is), above all, the means whereby real cases in judgements (*aḥkām*) are decided and the legal opinions of a *muftī* (*fatāwā*) are reached.

The primary literary base for the present study is the *fatwās* of Taqī al-Dīn Ibn Taymiyya (d.728/1328), a famous religious and legal scholar, whose *fatwās* are characterised by well founded and detailed argumentation, perhaps more so than the *fatwās* of other jurists. Islamic legal decisions, in the majority of cases, are not deduced directly from the Qur'ān or *sunna*, but indirectly by reference to the prescriptions and principles developed and formulated by authoritative jurists. An understanding of the complexity of these decisions requires not just an analysis of the *fatwās* themselves, but also of related works of Islamic legal literature. Many of the prescriptions, principles and arguments used by Ibn Taymiyya in his *fatwās* can be found in a variety of legal or law-related works, including *uṣūl*, *furūʿ*, *qawāʿid* and *jadal* works, as well as *ḥadīth* and Quranic commentaries. One intention in the following analysis is to reveal and describe a network of legal questions, which, though unable to be located in any particular law book, serve as the back ground of the jurist's legal pronouncements.

Before analysing the *fatwās* of Ibn Taymiyya, some remarks need to be made about his *ijtihād* theory. Ibn Taymiyya is normally considered a *mujtahid muṭlaq* by his contemporaries and later scholars, even those who were critical of his doctrines.[5] This does not mean that there are no elements which might be described as *taqlīd* in his *fatwās*, for his Ḥanbalī character can unquestionably be established by the fact that he cites Ḥanbalī authors more frequently than jurists of any other *madhhab*. He often adopts the opinions of the Ḥanbalī jurists without apparently reviewing them. He seems to hold to the principle that every rule must be derived from Qur'ān and *sunna*,[6] though the means whereby this derivation occurs often remains obscure. On the other hand, one has to accept that a legal decision is often the result of several steps of reasoning. Some of these may be influenced by *taqlīd*, and others not. Hence the final result is still, on aggregate if you like, *ijtihād*. It is this coexistence of *ijtihād* and *taqlīd* which characterises Ibn Taymiyya's *fatwās*, and which sometimes leads to interesting results. The use of *ijtihād* in his *fatwās* is not restricted to the field of *furūʿ*, but extends to the field of *uṣūl* also.[7] Before deciding a case, a jurist must define his own view on the debates surrounding legal methodology. Ibn Taymiyya has a limited view of *ijmāʿ* (consensus), accepts certain forms of analogy rejected by other scholars and condemns the use of *hiyal* (legal devices) recognised by the Ḥanafis and the Shāfiʿīs.

By analysing three *fatwās* of Ibn Taymiyya in this article, the extent to which *ijtihād* was used can be determined. These three *fatwās* can be regarded as representative of his *fatwās* concerning transactions, and probably reflect real cases in sixth/thirteen and seventh/fourteenth century Damascus.

I The Purchase of an Amorous Slave Girl[8]

The first *fatwā* to be analysed here concerns the sale and purchase of slaves. Slaves played an important economic role in the time of the Mamluks.[9] It emerges not only from *furūʿ* works, but also from a number of Ibn Taymiyya's *fatwās* that slaves were often treated in connection with the 'law of deficiency'. This field of positive law was one which had been thoroughly explored by previous jurists, and provides a suitable basis for decision by *taqlīd*. As these *fatwās* demonstrate, Ibn Taymiyya, more or less explicitly, refers to the opinions of the previous jurists instead of arguing independently (i.e. using his *ijtihād*). In general he comes to conclusions which agree with the unanimous or prevailing opinion within the Ḥanbalī school.

The following case was submitted to Ibn Taymiyya:

A sells a female slave to B. The slave is in love with A. Afterwards B resells the slave to C. Is C entitled to return the slave to B with a return of the payment, (and subsequently B to A), under the argument that this love for A is a defect in the slave?

Ibn Taymiyya refers to neither Qur'ān nor *ḥadīth* not to the opinions of previous jurists in this case. However, he does define the 'amorousness' as a defect and concedes that C and B have the right to return the object to the seller and reclaim the price, unless they had knowledge of the defect when they bought the slave.

The legal aspects considered by Ibn Taymiyya in this case can be summarised in three points. Firstly, by defining 'amorousness' as a defect, Ibn Taymiyya cannot refer to a corresponding prescription in *furūʿ* works. In these works a large number of defects in slaves are mentioned, but amorousness is not included. Instead of subsuming amorousness under a specific defect already described in the *furūʿ* works, Ibn Taymiyya refers to the general principle of *ʿāda* (custom), stating that a slave girl who is in love with her previous owner usually (*fi'l-ʿāda*) has a reduced price. This principle, which should be seen in conjunction with *maṣlaḥa* (public interest), is used in *furūʿ* works together with a rich topology of defects in order to define the term *ʿayb* (defect).[10] *ʿĀda*, in fact, plays an important role in the field of contracts, though it is rarely recognised as a source in *uṣūl* works.[11] Ibn Taymiyya[12] is not the only jurist to recognise custom as having an important influence in legal-decision making; Qarāfi[13] and Zaylaʿī[14] also underline its necessity and importance. Some elements of the principle of *ʿāda* are, however, recognised and treated in detail by the *uṣūl* writers. The Uṣūlīs,[15] often under the designation of *asmāʾ ʿurfiyya*, discuss particular elements which, being part of the Quranic or prophetic precept have to be interpreted in the light of custom. Taqī al-Dīn al-Subkī [16] points out that *ʿayb* belongs to this category of 'terms which are defined in accordance with custom', implying that the meaning of *ʿayb* can change between places and through time. Ibn Taymiyya, who treats other terms such as '*ruʾya*' (seeing)[17] and '*qabḍ*' (taking possession)[18] as also dependent upon custom, used custom, and especially the *asmāʾ ʿurfiyya* as a dynamic element in Islamic law, which allows for the harmonisation of a supposedly unchanging legal system (the *Sharīʿa*) with the changing conditions of time.

Returning to the case of the slave girl, Ibn Taymiyya decrees that C is entitled to return the slave to B. This agrees with the opinion of all the law schools, which grant the buyer of a defective object the right to return it to the seller.[19] The Ḥanbalīs allow him to keep it, but pay a lower price. Both of these are dependent upon the buyer's lack of knowledge of the defect at the time of purchase.

If B has had the slave returned to him from C, he is, according to Ibn Taymiyya, permitted to return her to A, claiming the original price. This decision also agrees with the opinion of the law schools,[20] though some jurists add the condition that C must have returned the object (in this case the slave girl) to B solely because of the defect. The Ḥanafis, for instance, do not grant the first buyer any claim if he concludes a new contract and buys the defective object back from the second buyer. In this case, a new state of property would have been created. Only if the previous state of property exists will the Ḥanafis allow B to assert his claim against A.

What this case demonstrates is that Ibn Taymiyya, though he does not refer to previous jurists explicitly, is willing to utilise these sources, particularly the opinions of past jurists, to reach a *ḥukm*. He is also willing, however, to explore means whereby the law might be made more flexible to local circumstances, hence his use of custom to define *ʿayb*.

II The Purchase of Pollen[21]

The second case dealt with here deals with the so-called *mubāḥāt* (objects which belong to all Muslims equally). These include things like water, grass and fire, according to a prophetic *ḥadīth*. The debate dealt with in this *fatwā* concerns whether pollen can be also considered as *mubāḥ*. Honey, normally produced from pollen, was an important commodity in the Near East in the late Middle Ages[22] and, as emerges from the chronicle of Ibn al-Dawādārī,[23] bee-keepers often had to pay taxes on honey. Bee-keepers allowed their bees to fly in a certain region to collect the pollen from the plants there. The question which faced Ibn Taymiyya was, can landowners claim a recompense or payment for the consumption of their pollen.

Ibn Taymiyya was deciding here a case not covered in the *furūʿ* works, and hence is forced to use a certain amount of *ijtihād*. He discusses two questions relating to the case. Firstly, does pollen belong to the category of *mubāḥāt*? Although the case of pollen does not occur in the *furūʿ* works, the jurists have discussed an issue that could be relevant here. In one of the traditions of the Prophet related in Ibn Taymiyya's preferred source,[24] Aḥmad b. Ḥanbal's *Musnad*, it is related that the property of land extends to the plants growing on it.[25] It follows therefore that the plants as well as the pollen are regarded as the owners property and hence not *mubāḥ*. However, according to another tradition from Aḥmad b. Ḥanbal,[26] accepted by a majority of Ḥanbalīs as sound,[27] plants are not included in the land of the owner and therefore are categorised as public property. Ibn Taymiyya seems to follow the latter *ḥadīth*, without however mentioning any jurist or previous opinion. It is therefore most probable that he argues directly on the basis of *sunna*, since he directly refers to the prophetic utterance[28] in his definition of pollen as *res communis*. This *ḥadīth*, which Ibn Taymiyya himself accepts as *maʿrūf*[29] (weak but commonly accepted) does not occur in the collections of Bukhārī or Muslim (the two most authoritative sources, even for Ibn Taymiyya). One version of it is found in Ibn Māja's collection (considered much less authoritative), though this version has an addition (*ziyāda*) to the text (*matn*), though it does have a sound *isnād*. The version found in the *Musnad*, however, has a defective *isnad* (termed *munqaṭī*). Ibn Taymiyya is referring to the second version (with the defective *isnād*) because he does not mention the *ziyāda*. According to the Uṣūlīs[30] a weak *ḥadīth* can become sound (*ṣaḥīḥ*) if it becomes accepted by the community (*talaqqathu al-umma bi'l-qabūl*).

Ibn Taymiyya holds to this principle[31] though he does consider the term *umma* to refer solely to the *ḥadīth* experts and no the community as a whole.[32]

Ibn Taymiyya then attempts to demonstrate that the *ḥadīth* which refers to water, fire and grass as public property also applies to pollen. He does this by using what is known as an *awlā* argument (*argumentum a maiori ad minus/a minori ad maius*).[33] *Awlā* arguments are generally described by Uṣūlīs as referring to *mafhūm al-muwāfaqa* or *qiyās jalī* (sometimes also called *qiyās qaṭʿī*).[34] Ibn Taymiyya[35] seems to approve of this argument.

In this case Ibn Taymiyya uses the *awlā* argument as follows: if it is permitted for someone to take grass, fire or water, then it is even more permitted for a person to take pollen (through the agency of the bees) since the bees are the only ones able to collect it. He argues that if bee-keepers make use of pollen, the property of the landowner (providing they do not themselves own bees) is not harmed or reduced in value, and therefore the landowners rights are not infringed. In reality Ibn Taymiyya's argument is circular in that he presumes pollen is an object of public property, and then argues that only those who are able to collect the pollen have the right to do so.

He also deals with the taxation of honey. This was not part of the *mustaftī*'s question. Referring to the Prophet, his companions and a number of previous scholars, he deduces that though the pollen is public property, honey is none the less subject to taxation. It becomes clear that Ibn Taymiyya, on this issue, is not utilising *ijtihād* but following the opinions of previous scholars of the Ḥanbalī *madhhab*.[36] Other law schools uphold the opposite view,[37] exempting honey from taxation, or accepting it only with restrictions.[38] The Ḥanbalī view is based on a Prophetic *ḥadīth* which, after being mentioned by Abū ʿUbayd,[39] is only found in Ibn Māja.[40] Unlike all the other traditions on this matter, it records that the Prophet imposed taxation on honey. According to Bukhārī however there is no sound tradition in favour of this measure.[41] Even Ibn Mufliḥ, a Ḥanbalī and a pupil of Ibn Taymiyya, calls into question the veracity of this *ḥadīth*.[42] Ibn Taymiyya apparently ignores the vehement opposition to this *ḥadīth*, and the fact that highly esteemed experts like Mālik b. Anas and Shāfiʿī are recorded as having only approved of the *ḥadīth* which does not prescribe the taxation of honey.

Ibn Taymiyya here then is displaying once again his loyalty to his *madhhab*, by citing Ḥanbalī authors and by reaching conclusions in line with school doctrine. However he is also involved in a process of discovering the law and utilising *ijtihād*, as is demonstrated by his inclusion of pollen in the category of *mubāḥāt*.

III The Rent of an Orchard[43]

According to contemporary accounts, the area around Damascus during the thirteenth and fourteenth century was characterised by intensive agriculture,[44] including a number of fruit orchards.[45] Unsurprisingly then, many of Ibn Taymiyya's *fatwās* deal with the cultivation of fruits and a contract known as *ḍamān*. This type of contract also attracted the attention of a number of other jurists.[46] *Ḍamān* is conceived of a combination of *musāqā* (a share-cropping agreement) and *ijāra* (rent). Hence in a *ḍamān* agreement, the landowner (*rabb al-arḍ*) receives a fixed payment of rent whereas the worker on the land (*ʿāmil*) gets the whole crop. The landowners of Damascus, whose land often comprised of a combination of orchard and arable land, preferred a simple rent agreement, where the land and the trees were rented for a fixed price. *ʿĀmils* probably preferred a *ḍamān* agreement, so as to minimise their losses if the crop fails.

The contract though was not universally accepted as in accordance with the *Sharīʿa*. Ibn Taymiyya, however, approved of this contract and he demonstrated its legality through the use of *ijmāʿ* and *qiyās*. In one *fatwā*, A is the owner of an orchard, in which fruit trees, including apricots, grapes and pomegranates grow. He wants to sell the fruits (still on the trees) to B, though some of the fruits have not yet ripened. Ibn Taymiyya asserts that this can be done through the contract of *ḍamān*. A lets the land to B for a fixed amount, and B irrigates the trees, harvesting the fruits when they have ripened. Many jurists, amongst them Ḥanbalīs, do not accept this type of contract as *sharʿī*, or accept it but only with certain restrictions.[47] The reason being that it constitutes payment for goods which do not yet (and might not ever) exist (i.e. it is a risk) and that the seller of the fruit has to continue to tend the tree until harvest time (constituting unpaid labour and hence unfair exchange).[48]

1. *Ijmāʿ*

As with most contemporary jurists,[49] Ibn Taymiyya emphasises the legal importance of *ijmāʿ*.[50] He often utilised *ijmāʿ* in his *fatwās* in order to demonstrate the validity of his conclusions on a particular matter. At this point, it is important to note that there are different types of *ijmāʿ*, and Muslim jurists never came to an unanimous decision concerning its scope, validity and nature. The fact that there is not *ijmāʿ* about *ijmāʿ* makes it difficult, if not impossible to find out whether it has been achieved on a particular issue. This problematic character concerning *ijmāʿ* is compounded by a practical one. In one *furūʿ* work, a prescription is described as *mujmaʿ ʿalayhi*, whilst in another it is described as *mukhtalaf fihi*. Whilst other jurists avoid using *ijmāʿ* in the case of *ḍamān*, Ibn Taymiyya is willing to embrace its conclusions. However his view of *ijmāʿ* is basically the *ijmāʿ* of the companions of the Prophet. Consequently he cites a *ḥadīth* from Ḥarb al-Kirmānī and Abū Zurʿa al-Dimashqī, according to which ʿUmar Ibn al-Khaṭṭāb hired out the orchard of Usayd b. al-Ḥuḍayr (d. 20/642) after his death, for a fixed amount in order to pay off a debt which Usayd had incurred during his life. Ibn Taymiyya regards the decision of ʿUmar as *mujmaʿ ʿalayhi* because he presumes that it was known to the companions, but they did not object. Ḥanbalīs appear as proponents of this type of *ijmāʿ*,[51] though al-Ghazālī[52] and others reject it. In most cases this *ijmāʿ* is considered *ijmāʿ ẓannī*, an uncertain consensus which does not have binding force.

2. *Qiyās*

In addition to *ijmāʿ*, Ibn Taymiyya has recourse to a variety of *qiyās* arguments. *Qiyās* is recognised by most jurists[53] as the most productive instrument of deduction in Islamic Law. The contrast between the limited number of Quranic and prophetic prescriptions, and the unlimited number of cases in everyday life made *qiyās*, or more generally *ijtihād* necessary.[54] The analogy in Islamic law was obviously influenced by the epistemological approaches of Greek logic[55] and requires the universalisation of a legal principle in order to reach a definitive conclusion. This, legal speaking, is nothing more than the subsumption of a particular case under a general category (just as a Greek syllogism). The jurists developed more or less certain ways of establishing the cause (*ʿilla*) in the original case (*aṣl*); in effect this was isolating those elements of a prescription which are the cause of the ruling (*ḥukm*). When the jurist has discovered the relevant element, other contingent elements can be eliminated and a large number of assimilated cases (*furūʿ*) can be subsumed. Ibn Taymiyya accepted *qiyās*, as long as it did not contradict other rulings in Qurʾān and *sunna*.[56] It might be argued that he was willing to use *qiyās* procedures which go beyond those used by other jurists.

One of the types of *qiyās* Ibn Taymiyya uses in this case is termed *qiyās al-ṭard*. Most jurists reject it because the *ʿilla* of the *aṣl* is deduced only negatively.[57] *Qiyās al-ṭard* deduces a common element between a number of similar Quranic and Prophetic rulings with the same *ḥukm*, and declares that common element as the *ʿilla*. If there is no other ruling which contains this special element but has another *ḥukm*, then this element must be the *ʿilla*. The basis of his analogy in the case of *ḍamān* is a Quranic verse (Q65.6) according to which nurses are due compensation for suckling a child. Ibn Taymiyya deduces from this verse that usufruct (*manfaʿa*) cannot be an essential element of a contract of *ijāra*, if by usufruct is meant 'using a thing without reducing its worth for the next user or the owner'. The prevailing opinion was that usufruct in *ijāra* contracts meant just that,[58] and that renting an orchard cannot be permitted because at the start of the rental period the fruit in the orchard has a value, but when the orchard is returned to the owner the fruit has been harvested and hence the value of the orchard is reduced. According to Ibn Taymiyya, the Quranic verse demonstrates that consumable items and their usufruct can be part of an *ijāra* contract, and hence the rental element in the *ḍamān* contract is valid. It should be noted here that some jurists did not accept the opinion that consumables can be the subject of contracts similar to rent, such as *ʿāriya* and *waqf*.[59] Uṣūlīs have also argued that not every Quranic or Prophetic prescription can be used as the basis of analogy; some prescriptions are termed *rukhṣa* (a prescription in which a general prohibition is suspended due to a specific need),[60] and the contract of the wet-nurse is one such contract.

Ibn Taymiyya also utilises another type of *qiyās* to legitimise *ḍamān*. *Qiyās al-shabah* is accepted by most Uṣūlīs and consists of comparing the case in question with two other similar cases.[61] These two cases must have different rulings, but both be grounded in Qurʾān and Sunna. The jurist then decides which of the two cases his present case is most similar to. In effect *qiyās al-shabah* represents a rudimentary form of *qiyās* which does not integrate the concept of *ʿilla* because 'similarity' can never be identified with 'cause'. The fact that several cases share a similarity, and that they have the same *ḥukm*, does not mean that that similarity is the cause of the ruling. With respect to the case of renting the orchard, Ibn Taymiyya compares the rent of an orchard with firstly the rent of land (which is permitted)[62] and the purchase of unripened fruit (which is prohibited).[63] The impermissability of selling unripened fruit can be traced back to a tradition of the Prophet and there is no jurist who doubted its status as *mutawātir*.[64] According to Ibn Taymiyya, the rent of an orchard and the rent of land has a common element; that is that the tenant himself cares for the crop in each case. However, the purchaser of unripe fruits does not assume any liability for the maintenance of the fruits (on the tree) until the harvest. The similarity between renting land and renting an orchard is strong enough for Ibn Taymiyya to decide the case, and renting an orchard becomes permissible.

There is a third type of analogy used by Ibn Taymiyya in his deliberations on this case, namely *qiyās al-munāsaba*. This type of *qiyās* is widely accepted by jurists[65] and can be considered as a surreptitious form of *maṣlaḥa* (public interest). *Maṣlaḥa* itself is rejected by many jurists.[66] *Qiyās al-munāsaba* is utilised when there is no explicit indication in the sources, but that the general prescription to preserve public interest is transferred to the case in question. For example, wine is prohibited because it is intoxicating, and intoxication violates the important command to preserve the mind (*ḥafẓ al-ʿaql*) which in turn forms a part of public interest. In this case, Ibn Taymiyya refers to a *ḥadīth* according to which the Prophet allowed the selling of dried dates at the same price as the same estimated quantity of fresh dates on a tree.[67] Many jurists treat this *mutawātir ḥadīth* as an exception to the general prohibition on risk, but Ibn Taymiyya uses it as the basis for his analogy. He reasons that the suspension of the prohibition of risk in this case can be transferred to the case in question. The Prophet allowed the sale and barter of goods so that prosperity could increase, which is in the public interest. Similarly the *ḍamān* contract is legal on the grounds of its ability to increase of prosperity.

The procedure known as *ilghāʾ al-fāriq* is also utilised by Ibn Taymiyya. This procedure is also accepted by most Uṣūlīs[68] and consists of comparing the *aṣl* with the *farʿ* and all differing elements are disregarded. The remaining elements, it is then concluded, must be part of the *ʿilla*, and hence the *ḥukm* in each case is the same. Ibn Taymiyya compares the rent of land to that of an orchard and concludes that the only difference between the two is the elements 'land' and 'trees'. He then attempts to prove that this difference is irrelevant, comparing this contract with those termed *muzāraʿa* and *musāqā*. Although the rent of land and the rent of an orchard differ in regard to this one element, they must have the same *ḥukm*.

The final type of analogy which Ibn Taymiyya uses is termed *dawarān*. This procedure is also accepted as valid by the Uṣūlīs.[69] It is based upon the idea that if two cases are similar in all ways except for one element, and yet they have different *ḥukms*, then the differing element must be considered the *ʿilla*. Ibn Taymiyya refers to the aforementioned *ḥadīth*, according to which the sale of unripenned fruit is prohibited. He points out that the cause of this prescription is the fact that the seller has to take care of the fruits until the harvest, whereas someone who rents land, has to take care of the land himself. This being the only difference, and the *ḥukms* being directly opposed, it must be the *ʿilla*. This demonstrates that the rent of an orchard cannot have the same *ḥukm* as the purchase of unripened fruit since the tenant immediately begins to take care of the trees himself.

3. *Ḥiyal*

The contract of *ḍamān* has been rejected as incompatible with the *Sharīʿa* by many jurists. Nevertheless, some jurists (particularly Ḥanafis[70] and Shāfiʿīs) recognise the practical use of this contract and attempt to legalise it by use of devices (*ḥiyal*). Ḥanbalīs[71] and Mālikīs[72] reject this *ḥīla*. The suggested *ḥīla* is a contract which combines the principles *ijāra* and *musāqā*. The contracting partners conclude a contract of *ijāra* with regard to the land, and simultaneously conclude a contract of *musāqā* with regard to the fruit trees, stipulating a percentage of the crop for each of the contracting partners. The landowner requires a small percentage of the crop, but asks for a high rent. Ibn Taymiyya refuses to accept this device, which he claims aims to conceal the real intention of the jurist, which is to circumvent the *Sharīʿa*.[73]

Conclusion

These three *fatwās* on the amorous slave-girl, the purchase of pollen and the renting of an orchard, each demonstrate Ibn Taymiyya's willingness to use his own *ijtihād*. He contradicts the opinions of both his own *madhhab*, and the other *madhāhib*. In reaching these novel opinions he uses various forms of *qiyās*, and restricted definitions of *ijmāʿ*. What these *fatwās* demonstrate is that Ibn Taymiyya not only approved of *ijtihād* in theory (as one might expect from a Ḥanbalī), but also that he was willing to utilise *ijtihād* in practice, through issuing *fatwās* in specific cases. For Ibn Taymiyya, the gate of *ijtihād* was not closed, neither in theory nor in practice.

Notes

1 This article is based on my dissertation *Islamisches Recht in Theorie und Praxis. Analyse einiger kaufrechtlicher Fatwas von Taqī'd-Dīn Aḥmad b. Taimiyya*, which is not yet published.

2 Muwaffaq al-Dīn Ibn Qudāma, *Rawḍat al-nāẓir wa-jannat al-munāẓir* (Cairo, 1342/1923), vol. 2, 401; Najm al-Dīn al-Ṭūfī, *Sharḥ mukhtaṣar al-rawḍa* (Beirut, 1987–89), vol. 3, 576; Ibn al-Najjār al-Ḥanbalī, *Sharḥ kawkab al-munīr* (Cairo, 1372/1953), 602; Abū Isḥāq al-Shīrāzī, *al-Luma' fī uṣūl al-fiqh* (Cairo, 1377/1957), 73; al-Ghazālī, *al-Mustaṣfā min 'ilm al-uṣūl* (Cairo, 1322–4/1904–6), vol. 2, 350; Sayf al-Dīn al-Āmidī, *al-Iḥkām fī uṣūl al-aḥkām* (Cairo, 1966), vol. 3, 204; al-Bayḍāwī, *Minhāj al-wuṣūl ilā 'ilm al-uṣūl*, in al-Isnawī, ed, *Nihāyat al-sūl fī sharḥ minhāj al-wuṣūl ilā 'ilm al-uṣūl* (Cairo, 1316/1899), vol. 3, 284; al-Isnawī, *Nihāyat al-sūl fī sharḥ minhāj al-wuṣūl ilā 'ilm al-uṣūl* (Beirut, 1982), vol. 4, 524–29; Ibn al-Ḥājib, *Muntahā al-su'āl wa'l-'amal fī 'ilm al-uṣūl wa'l-jadal* (Istanbul, 1326/1908), 156.

3 I. Goldziher, 'Muhammedanisches Recht in Theorie und Wirklichkeit', *Zeitschrift für vergleichende Rechtswissenschaft*, 8 (1889), 406–23, esp. 409; G. Bousquet, *Du droit musulman et de son application effective dans le monde* (Algiers, 1949), 7; N. Coulson, *A History of Islamic Law* (Edinburgh, 1964), 2; ibid., 'Doctrine and Practice in Islamic Law', *BSOAS* 18 (1956), 211–26, esp. 222–3; J. Schacht, *An Introduction to Islamic Law* (Oxford, 1984), 69; P. Crone, *Roman, Provincial and Islamic Law* (Cambridge, 1987), 18; L. Sjukijajnan, *Musuljmanskoe Pravo* (Moskau, 1986), 97.

4 B. Krawietz, *Die Ḥurma. Schariatrechtlicher Schutz vor Eingriffen in die körperliche Unversehrtheit nach arabischen Fatwas des 20. Jahrhunderts* (Berlin, 1991), 323; A. Noth, 'Die Scharia, das religiöse Gesetz des Islam – Wandlungsmöglichkeiten, Anwendung und Wirkung', in Fikentscher, Franke and Köhler eds, *Entstehung und Wandel rechtlicher Traditionen* (Freiburg/München, 1980), 415–37, esp. 429; B. Johansen, *The Islamic Law on Land Tax and Rent* (London, 1988), 24; W. Hallaq, 'Uṣūl al-fiqh: Beyond Tradition', *Journal of Islamic Studies*, 3 (1992), 172–202, esp. 182.

5 'Imād al-Dīn Ismā'īl Ibn Kathīr, *al-Bidāya wa'l-nihāya* (Damascus, 1967), vol. 14, 137; 'Abd al-Hādī, *al-'Uqūd al-durriyya* (Cairo, 1938), vol. 8 , 12, 24; Zayn al-Dīn Abū al-Faraj Ibn Rajab, *al-Dhayl 'alā ṭabaqāt al-ḥanābila* (n.p., 1372/1952), vol. 2, 387; Ibn Yusuf al-Mar'ī, *al-Kawākib al-durriyya fī manāqib al-Imām Ibn Taymiyya* (Cairo, 1329/1911), 141–142, 144, 148; al-Ḥusnī, *Kitāb muntakhabāt al-tawārīkh li-Dimashq* (Beirut,1399/1979); Ibn Ḥajar al-'Asqalānī, *al-Durar al-kāmina fī a'yān al-mi'a al-thāmina* (Cairo, 1966), vol. 1, 160.

6 Taqī al-Dīn Aḥmad Ibn Taymiyya, *Majmū' fatāwā Shaykh al-Islām Aḥmad Ibn Taymiyya* (Riyad, 1381–86/1962–7), vol. 17, 443, vol. 19, 280, 285, vol. 25, 236.

7 This is explicitly pointed out by al-Ṭūfī, *Sharḥ mukhtaṣar rawḍa*, vol. 3, pp. 615–16.

8 Ibn Taymiyya, *Fatāwā*, vol. 29, p. 392.

9 Badr al-Dīn Maḥmūd al-ʿAynī, *ʿIqd al-jumān fī taʾrīkh ahl al-zamān* (Cairo, 1409/1989), vol. 3, 16.

10 Muwaffaq al-Dīn Ibn Qudāma, *al-Mughnī* (Riyad, 1401/1981), vol. 4, 168; Shams al-Dīn Ibn Qudāma, *al-Sharḥ al-kabīr* (Cairo, 1348/1930), vol. 4, 85; Shams al-Dīn Abū ʿAbd Allāh Ibn Mufliḥ, *Kitāb al-furūʿ* (Beirut, 1982–84), vol. 4, 100; ʿAlāʾ al-Dīn al-Mardāwī, *Kitāb al-inṣāf li-maʿrifat al-rājiḥ min al-khilāf* (Cairo, 1375–7/1955–7), vol. 4, 405; ibid., *al-Tanqīḥ al-mushbiʿ fī taḥrīr aḥkām al-muqniʿ* (Cairo, 1961), 129; Sharaf al-Dīn Mūsā al-Ḥujāwī, *al-Iqnāʿ* (Beirut, n.d.), 93; Ibn al-Najjār al-Ḥanbalī, *Muntahā al-irādāt fī al-jamʿ bayn al-muqniʿ maʿa al-tanqīḥ wa-ziyādāt* (Cairo, n.d.), vol. 1, 361; Ibrāḥīm Ibn Muḥammad Ibn Ḍūyān, *Kitāb manār al-sabīl* (Damascus, 1378/1959), vol. 1, 319; Abū al-Ḥusayn Aḥmad al-Qudūrī, *al-Mukhtaṣar* (n.p., 1309/1892), 39; Fakhr al-Dīn al-Ḥasan Qāḍīkhān, *Fatāwā Qāḍīkhān*, in *al-Fatāwā al-hindiyya* (Cairo, 1310/1893), vol. 2 199, 200, 201; ʿAlāʾ al-Dīn al-Samarqandī, *Tuḥfat al-fuqahāʾ* (Cairo, 1377/1958), vol. 2, 135; Shams al-Dīn al-Sarakhsī, *Kitāb al-Mabsūṭ* (Istanbul, 1982), vol. 13, 106; Abū Bakr b. Masʿūd al-Kāsānī, *Badāʾiʿ al-ṣanāʾiʿ wa-tartīb al-sharāʾiʿ* (Cairo, 1970), vol. 7, 3319; Abū Isḥāq al-Shīrāzī, *Kitāb al-tanbīh*, (Cairo, 1348/1929), 58; Abū Ḥāmid al-Ghazālī, *Kitāb al-wajīz* (Beirut, 1399/1979), vol. 1, 142; Muḥyī al-Dīn Yaḥyā al-Nawawī, *Rawḍat al-ṭālibīn* (Damascus, 1968), vol. 3, 458; sometimes *ʿayb'* is defined as everything, that causes a reduction in price: al-Nawawī, *Majmūʿ sharḥ al-muhadhdhab* (Cairo, 1966), vol. 12, 109; Shams al-Dīn al-Dimashqī, *Raḥmat al-umma fī ikhtilāf al-aʾimma* (Cairo, 1386/1967), 141; Ibn al-Qāsim Saḥnūn, *al-Mudawwana al-kubrā* (Cairo, 1906–7), vol. 4, 330; Abū al-Walīd al-Bājī, *al-Muntaqā* (Cairo, 1332/1914), vol. 4, 188; Abū al-Walīd Muḥammad Ibn Rushd al-Ḥafid, *Bidāyat al-mujtahid wa-nihāyat al-muqtaṣid* (Cairo, 1971), vol. 2, 145.

11 Shihāb al-dīn al-Qarāfi, *Anwār al-burūq fī anwāʾ al-furūq* (Beirut, n.d.), vol. 1, 174 (he rejects the principle of *ʿāda* as a primary, not however as a secondary source of Islamic law); Schacht, *Introduction*, p. 62; Abū Sinna, *al-ʿUrf waʾl-ʿāda fī raʾy al-fuqahāʾ* (Cairo, 1947), 32; N. J. Coulson, 'Muslim Custom and Case–Law', *Die Welt des Islam* 6 (1959), 13–24, esp. 13; A. Udovitch, Les échanges de marché dans l'Islam medieval:Théorie du droit et savoir local', *SI* 65 (1987), 5–30, esp. 22; Bousquet, *Droit musulman*, p. 170.

12 Ibn Taymiyya, *Fatāwā*, vol. 29, pp. 17–18; sometimes with reference to the Mālikīs: ibid., vol. 20, pp. 345–6.

13 al–Qarāfi, *Furūq*, vol. 3, p. 288; ibid., *al-Iḥkām fī tamyīz al-fatāwā ʿan al-aḥkām* (Cairo, 1938), 98.

14 al-Zaylaʿī, *Tabyīn al-ḥaqāʾiq* (Cairo, 1313/1895), vol. 4, 176.

15 al-Qarāfi, *Sharḥ tanqīḥ al-fuṣūl fī ikhtiṣār al-maḥṣūl fī al-uṣūl* (Cairo, 1393/1973), 44; Muḥammad b. ʿAlī al-Shawkānī, *Irshād al-fuḥūl* (Cairo, 1356/1937), 21; al-Shīrāzī, *Lumaʿ*, p. 6.

16 Taqī al-Dīn al-Subkī/Tāj al-Dīn al-Subkī, *al-Ibhāj fī sharḥ al-minhāj* (Cairo, 1981–82), vol. 3, 149.

17 Ibn Taymiyya, *Fatāwā*, vol. 29, p. 216.

18 Ibid., p. 448.

19 al-Ḥujāwī, *Iqnāʿ*, vol. 2, p. 95; Ibn Qudāma, *Mughnī*, vol. 4, p. 159; al-Mardāwī, *Inṣāf*, vol. 4, p. 410; ʿAwn al-Dīn Abū al-Muẓaffar Ibn Hubayra, *Kitāb al-ifṣāḥ ʿan maʿānī al-ṣaḥāḥ* (Riyad, 1980), vol. 1, 345; Majd al-Dīn Ibn Taymiyya, *al-Muḥarrar fī al-fiqh* (Cairo, 1369/1950), vol. 1, 323; al-Qudūrī, *Mukhtaṣar*, p. 39; al-Ghazālī, *Wajīz*, vol. 1, p. 142; al-Shīrāzī, *Tanbīh*, p. 58; ibid., *Kitāb al-muhadhdhab* (Cairo, n.d.), vol. 1, 284; Ibn al-Najjār, *Muntahā*, vol. 1, p. 362; al-Bājī, *Muntaqā*, vol. 4, p. 187.

20 Muḥammad Ibn al-Ḥasan al-Shaybānī, *Kitāb al-aṣl* (Cairo, 1954), vol.1, 84; ibid., *al-Jāmiʿ al-ṣaghīr*, in Yaʿqūb b. Ibrāhīm Abū Yusuf, *Kitāb al-kharāj* (Cairo, 1306/1889), 83; al-Qudūrī, *Mukhtaṣar*, p. 10; al-Sarakhsī, *Mabsūṭ*, vol. 13, p. 103; al-Kāsānī, *Badāʾiʿ*, vol. 7, p. 3337; Qāḍīkhān, *Fatāwā*, vol. 2, p. 206; Muḥammad b. Idrīs al-Shāfiʿī, *Kitāb al-umm* (Cairo, 1388/1968–69), vol. 3, 62; al-Shīrāzī, *Tanbīh*, p. 58; al-Ghazālī, *Wajīz*, vol. 1, p. 143; Ibn Rushd, *Bidāya*, vol. 2, p. 150; Ibn al-Qāsim/Saḥnūn, *Mudawwana*, vol. 4, p. 324; al-Bājī, *Muntaqā*, vol. 4, p. 192; Majd al-Dīn Ibn Taymiyya, *Muḥarrar*, vol. 1, p. 325; Shams al-Dīn Abū ʿAbd Allāh Ibn Mufliḥ, *Kitāb al-furūʿ* (Beirut, 1982–84), vol. 4, p.107; Muwaffaq al-Dīn Ibn Qudāma, *Mughnī*, vol. 4, pp. 174–5; Shams al-Dīn Ibn Qudāma, *Sharḥ kabīr*, vol. 4, pp. 92–3.

21 Ibn Taymiyya, *Fatāwā*, vol. 29, pp. 220–1.

22 S. Labib, *Handelsgeschichte Ägyptens im Spätmittelalter (1171–1517)* (Wiesbaden, 1965), 320.

23 Abū Bakr Ibn al-Dawādārī, *Kanz al-durar wa-jāmiʿ al-ghurar* (Cairo, 1969), vol. 9, 286.

24 Zayn al-Dīn Abū al-Faraj Ibn Rajab, *al-Qawāʿid al-fiqhiyya* (n.p., 1972), 202.

25 Ibn Qudāma, *Mughnī*, vol. 4, p. 90.

26 Ibid.

27 Ibn Qudāma, *Mughnī*, vol. 4, p. 90; ibid., *al-Muqniʿ* (Cairo, 1382/1962), 10; Majd al-Dīn Ibn Taymiyya, *Muḥarrar*, vol. 1, p. 368; Ibn Mufliḥ, *Furūʿ*, vol. 4, p. 42; Ḥijjāwī, *Iqnāʿ*, vol. 2, p. 387; ibid., *Zād al-mustaqniʿ fī ikhtiṣār al-muqniʿ* (Riyad, 1977), 37; al-Mardāwī, *Tanqīḥ*, p. 180; Ibn al-Najjār, *Muntahā*, 1, p. 341; al-Bahūtī, *Kashshāf al-qināʿ ʿan matn al-iqnāʿ* (Riyad, n.d.), vol. 3, 160; Muḥammad Ibn ʿAbd al-Wahhāb, *Mukhtaṣar al-inṣāf waʾl-sharḥ al-kabīr* (Cairo, 1965), 271.

28 Aḥmad Ibn Ḥanbal, *Musnad* (Cairo, 1895), vol. 4, 364; Abū Dāwūd al-Sijistānī, *Kitāb al-sunan* (Beirut, 1984), vol. 3, 278 (No. 3477); Abū ʿAbd Allāh Muḥammad Ibn Māja, *al-Sunan* (Lucknow, 1315/1897), 180; Abū ʿUbayd al-Qāsim Ibn Sallām, *Kitāb al-amwāl* (Cairo, 1401/1981), 271 (No. 729).

29 Ibn Taymiyya, *Fatāwā*, vol. 29, p. 219.

30 Muḥammad b. al-Ḥusayn Abū Yaʿlā, *al-ʿUdda fī uṣūl al-fiqh* (Beirut, 1400/1980), vol. 3, 900–1; Abū al-Khaṭṭāb al-Kalwadhānī, *al-Tamhīd fī uṣūl al-fiqh* (Mekka, 1985), vol. 3, 84; Abū al-Walīd al-Bājī, *Iḥkām al-fuṣūl fī aḥkām al-uṣūl* (Beirut, 1986), 329–30; Abū Bakr al-Shāshī, *Uṣūl al-Shāshī* (Beirut, 1402/1982), 272; Ibn al-Najjār, *Sharḥ kawkab*, p. 264; al-Shīrāzī, *Lumaʿ*, p. 40.

31 Ibn Taymiyya, *Fatāwā*, vol. 28, pp. 16–17.

32 Ibn Taymiyya, *Fatāwā*, vol. 13, p. 352.

33 Ibn Qudāma, *Rawḍa*, vol. 2, pp. 254–5; al-Shīrāzī, *Luma'*, p. 55; al-Māwardī, *Adab al-qāḍī* (Baghdad, 1971–72), vol. 1, 587–92; Ghazālī, *Mustaṣfā*, vol. 2, p. 281; Āmidī, *Iḥkām*, vol. 3, p. 95; Subkī, *Ibhāj*, vol. 3, pp. 30–2; Ibn al-Ḥājib, *Muntahā*, p. 137; Majd al-Dīn Ibn Taymiyya, *Musawwada* (Cairo, 1384/1964), 346.

34 W. Hallaq, 'Non-analogical Arguments in Sunnī Juridical Qiyās', *Arabica* 36 (1989), 286–306, esp. 289.

35 Ibn Taymiyya, *Fatāwā*, vol. 6, p. 381, vol. 15, p. 446, vol. 31, pp. 105–10, pp. 136–41.

36 Aḥmad Ibn Ḥanbal, *Masā'il al-Imām Aḥmad Ibn Ḥanbal*, (Beirut/Damascus, 1981), 165; al-Balabānī, *Kāfī al-mubtadī min al-ṭullāb* (Cairo, 1969), 150; Aḥmad Ibn 'Abadallāh al-Ba'lī, *al-Rawḍ al-nadī* (Cairo, 1969), 150; Ibn Qudāma, *Mughnī*, vol. 2, pp. 713–14; Majd al-Dīn Ibn Taymiyya, *Muḥarrar*, vol. 1, p. 221; Ibn Hubayra, *Ifṣāḥ*, vol. 1, p. 215; al-Ḥijjāwī, *Iqnā'*, vol. 1, p. 266, Ibid., *Zād*, p. 25; al-Bahūtī, *Kashshāf*, vol. 2, pp. 220–22; Ibn al-Najjār, *Muntahā*, vol. 1, p. 192; Ibn Ḍūyān, *Manār*, vol. 1, p. 192.

37 Ibn Rushd, *Bidāya*, vol. 1, p. 232; Mālik Ibn Anas, *al-Muwaṭṭa'* (Cairo, 1339/1921), vol. 1, 151; al-Bājī, *Muntaqā*, vol. 2, p. 172; al-Shāfi'ī, *Umm*, vol. 2, p. 33; al-Ghazālī, *Wajīz*, vol. 1, p. 90.

38 Abū Yusuf, *Kitāb al-kharāj*, p. 40; Burhān al-Dīn 'Alī al-Marghinānī al-Farghānī, *al-Hidāya* (Cairo, 1356/1937), vol. 2, 5–7; Ḥāfiẓ al-Dīn al-Nasafi, *Kanz al-daqā'iq* (n.p., 1887), vol. 1, 64; al-Sarakhsī, *Mabsūṭ*, vol. 2, p. 216; al-Zayla'ī, *Tabyīn*, vol. 1, p. 291.

39 Abū 'Ubayd, *Amwāl*, p. 444 (No. 1488).

40 Ibn Māja, *Sunan*, p. 132.

41 This opinion has been transmitted by Aḥmad b. al-Ḥusayn al-Bayḥaqī, *Kitāb al-sunan al-kubrā* (Haydarabad, 1952), vol. 1, 126.

42 Ibn Mufliḥ, *Furū'*, vol. 2, pp. 448–50; see also al-Mardāwī, *Taṣḥīḥ al-furū'* (Beirut, 1388/1967), vol. 4, 450.

43 Ibn Taymiyya, *Fatāwā*, vol. 29, pp. 478–83; this *fatwā* has been analysed in connexion with Ibn Taymiyya, *Fatāwā*, vol. 20, pp. 346, 547–51, vol. 29, pp. 55–78, vol. 30, pp. 151, 220–40, 240–3; see also Muḥammad Ibn 'Alī al-Ba'lī, *Mukhtaṣar al-fatāwā al-miṣriyya* (Cairo, 1368/1949), 336–8, 370–5.

44 N. Elisséeff, 'Ghūṭa', *EI2*, 2, p. 1105.

45 Ibn Baṭṭūṭa, *Tuḥfat al-nazzār fī gharā'ib al-amṣār wa-'ajā'ib al-asfār* (Paris, 1926), vol. 1, 233–6.

46 Taqī al-Dīn 'Uthmān Ibn al-Ṣalāḥ, *Fatāwā wa-masā'il Ibn al-Ṣalāḥ* (Beirut, 1986), vol.1, 327–8; Taqī al-Dīn al-Subkī, *Fatāwā al-Subkī* (Cairo, 1356/1937), vol. 1, 438–9.

47 Abū 'Ubayd, *Amwāl*, pp. 69–78; Muḥammad Ibn al-Ḥasan al-Shaybānī, *Kitāb al-ḥujja* (Beirut, 1387/1968), vol. 4, 175–8; ibid., *al-Jāmi' al-kabīr* (Cairo, 1356/1937), 336; al-Sarakhsī, *Mabsūṭ*, vol. 16, p. 33; al-Samarqandī, *Tuḥfa*, vol.

2, p. 529 (implicitly); al-Kāsānī, *Badā'i'*, vol. 5, p. 2558; al-Nawawī, *Rawḍa*, vol. 5, p. 178; Abū Ḥāmid al-Ghazālī, *Iḥyā' 'ulūm al-dīn* (Cairo, n.d.), vol. 2, 72; Ibn Qudāma, *Mughnī*, vol. 4, pp. 64, 423; Shams al-Dīn Ibn Qudāma, *Sharḥ kabīr*, vol. 5, p. 587; Ibn Mufliḥ, *Furū'*, vol. 4, p. 416; al-Mardāwī, *Tanqīḥ*, p. 162; ibid., *Taṣḥīḥ*, vol. 4, p. 416; Ibn al-Najjār, *Muntahā*, vol. 1, p. 475; al-Bahūtī, *al-Rawḍ al-murbi' bi-sharḥ zād al-mustaqni'* (Cairo, 1324/1906), vol. 2, 104.

48 Mālik Ibn Anas, *Muwaṭṭa'*, vol. 2, pp. 144–5; Ibn al-Qāsim/Saḥnūn, *Mudawwana*, vol. 4, p. 554; Bājī, *Muntaqā*, vol. 5, p. 137; Qarāfi, *Furūq*, vol. 4, p. 4.

49 Abū al-Khuṭṭāb-Kalwadhānī, *Tamhīd*, vol. 3, p. 224; Abū al-Wafā' 'Alī Ibn 'Aqīl, 'Kitāb al-jadal', *Bulletin d'études orientales*, 20 (1967), 119–204, esp. .6; Ibn Qudāma, *Rawḍa*, vol. 1, p. 335; Ibn al-Laḥḥām *al-Mukhtaṣar fi uṣūl al-fiqh* (Damascus, 1400/1980), 74; Ibn al-Najjār, *Sharḥ kawkab*, p. 226; Shawkānī, *Irshād*, pp. 78–9; Shāfi'ī, *al-Risāla* (Cairo, 1958), 403–4; Abū Bakr Aḥmad b. 'Alī al-Khaṭīb al-Baghdādī, *al-Faqīh wa'l-mutafaqqih* (Damascus, 1975), vol. 1, p. 154; al-Māwardī, *Adab*, vol. 1, p. 450; Abū Isḥāq al-Shīrāzī, *al-Tabṣira fi uṣūl al-fiqh* (Damascus, 1984), 349; ibid., *Luma'*, p. 48; Abū al-Ma'ālī al-Juwaynī, *al-Burhān fi uṣūl al-fiqh* (Cairo, 1980), vol. 1, 679; al-Ghazālī, *Mustaṣfā*, vol. 1, p. 174; ibid., *al-Mankhūl min ta'līqāt al-uṣūl* (Damascus, 1400/1980), 303; al-Āmidī, *Iḥkām*, 1, p. 150; al-Subkī, *Ibhāj*, vol. 2, p. 411; al-Isnawī, *al-Tamhīd fi takhrīj al-furū' 'alā al-uṣūl* (Beirut, 1981), 51; al-Shāshī, *Uṣūl*, pp. 287–8; Abū al-Ḥusayn al-Baṣrī, *al-Mu'tamad fi uṣūl al-fiqh* (Damascus, 1964), vol. 2, 458; Shams al-Dīn al-Sarakhsī, *Kitāb al-uṣūl* (Cairo, 1372/1953), vol. 1, 295; Ibn al-Ḥājib, *Muntahā*, p. 8; Qarāfi, *Sharḥ tanqīḥ*, p. 323.

50 Ibn Taymiyya, *Fatāwā*, vol. 7, p. 38, vol. 11, p. 341, vol. 19, pp. 176–80, vol. 27, p. 373, vol. 28, p. 125.

51 Shams al-Dīn Abū Bakr Ibn Qayyim al-Jawziyya, *I'lām al-muwaqqi'īn* (Cairo, 1970), vol. 4, 120; Ibn al-Laḥḥām, *al-Qawā'id wa'l-fawā'id al-uṣūliyya wa-mā yata'allaq bihā min al-aḥkām al-far'iyya* (Cairo, 1375/1956), 294–5; Ibn 'Aqīl, *Jadal*, p. 8.

52 al-Ghazālī, *Mustaṣfā*, vol. 1, pp. 271–2.

53 al-Shīrāzī, *Tabṣira*, pp. 424–5; ibid. *Luma'*, p. 3; al-Juwaynī, *Burhān*, vol.2, p. 753; al-Ghazālī, *Mustaṣfā*, vol. 2, p. 234; al-Āmidī, *Iḥkām*, vol. 3, p. 97; al-Subkī, *Ibhāj*, vol. 3, p. 9 ; al-Shāshī, *Uṣūl*, p. 308; Abū Ya'lā, *'Udda*, vol. 2, p. 564; Abū al-Khuṭṭāb al-Kalwadhānī, *Tamhīd*, vol. 3, p. 360; Ibn Qudāma, *Rawḍa*, vol. 2, p. 234; Ṭūfi, *Sharḥ mukhtaṣar rawḍa*, vol. 3, pp. 247–68; Ṣafī al-Dīn al-Baghdādī, *Qawā'id al-uṣūl fi ma'āqid al-fuṣūl* (Beirut, 1406/1986), 3; Ibn Qayyim al-Jawziyya, *I'lām*, vol. 1, p. 130; Ibn al-Laḥḥām, *Mukhtaṣar*, p. 142; Ibn al-Najjār, *Sharḥ kawkab*, pp. 479–80.

54 Ibn Qudāma, *Rawḍa*, vol. 2, p. 234; Ṭūfi, *Sharḥ mukhtaṣar rawḍa*, vol. 3, pp. 266–7; Abū al-Ma'ālī al-Juwaynī, *Ghiyāth al-umam fi iltiyāth al-Ẓulam* (Alexandria, 1979), p. 288; al-Isnawī, *Nihāya*, vol. 4, p. 551; Abū Ḥāmid al-Ghazālī, *Shifā' al-ghalīl* (Baghdad, 1390/1971), 23; al-Baṣrī, *Mu'tamad*, vol. 2, p. 53.

55 W. Hallaq, 'The Development of the Logical Structure in Sunnī Legal

Theory', *Der Islam*, 64 (1987), 42–67, esp. .44.

56 Ibn Taymiyya, *Fatāwā*, vol. 29, p. 88, vol. 22, pp. 331–2.

57 al-Baṣrī, *Mu'tamad*, vol. 2, pp. 786–8; al-Sarakhsī, *Uṣūl*, vol. 2, pp. 176, 227; al-Shīrāzī, *Luma'*, p. 3; al-Ghazālī, *Mustaṣfā*, vol. 2, p. 307; ibid., *Shifā'*, pp. 267–8; al-Āmidī, *Iḥkām*, vol. 3, p. 92; al-Subkī, *Ibhāj*, vol. 3, pp. 85–7; Ibn al-Ḥājib, *Muntahā*, p. 136; Ibn Qudāma, *Rawḍa*, vol. 2, pp. 291–2; Ibn al–Laḥḥām, *Mukhtaṣar*, p. 150.

58 al-Qudūrī, *Mukhtaṣar*, p. 52; al-Sarakhsī, *Mabsūṭ*, vol. 16, p. 33; Samarqandī, *Tuḥfa*, vol. 2, p. 529; Naṣr b. Muḥammad Abū al-Layth, *Khizānat al-fiqh* (Baghdad, 1385/1965), 308; al-Marghinānī, *Hidāya*, vol. 7, pp. 145–7; al-Zayla'ī, *Tabyīn*, vol. 5, p. 127; al-Shīrāzī, *Muhadhdhab*, vol. 1, p. 394; Abū Shujā', *Matn al–ghāya wa'l–taqrīb* (Cairo, 1329/1911), 4; al-Nawawī, *Rawḍa*, vol. 5, p. 178; Abū al-Walīd Ibn Rushd, *al-Muqaddamāt al-mumahhadāt li-bayān mā iqtaḍathu rusūm al-mudawwana* (Cairo, 1324/1906), vol. 3, 444; Ibn Hubayra, *Ifṣāḥ*, vol. 2, p. 39; Ibn Qudāma, *Mughnī*, vol. 5, pp. 434–5; ibid., *Muqni'*, vol. 2, p. 195; ibid., *al-'Umda fī al-fiqh al-Ḥanbalī* (Damascus, 1419/1990), 165; Majd al-Dīn Ibn Taymiyya, *Muḥarrar*, vol. 1, p. 356; Shams al-Dīn Ibn Qudāma, *Sharḥ kabīr*, vol. 6, pp. 3-4; al-Mardāwī, *Inṣāf*, vol. 6, pp. 30–2; al-Bahūtī, *Kashshāf*, vol. 3, p. 546; ibid., *Rawḍ*, vol. 2, p. 104; 'Abd al-Qādir al-Shaybānī, *Nayl al-ma'ārib* (Cairo, 1324/1906), vol. 1, 109; Ibn Ḥazm, *al-Muḥallā* (Beirut, n.d.), vol. 8, 183.

59 Abū al-Qāsim al-Khiraqī, *Mukhtaṣar al-Khiraqī* (Damascus; 1384/1964), 108; Ibn Hubayra, *Ifṣāḥ*, vol. 2, p. 52; Ibn Qudāma, *Mughnī*, p. 224; ibid, *Muqni'*, vol. 2, p. 310; ibid., *'Umda*, p. 169; Shams al-Dīn Ibn Qudāma, *Sharḥ kabīr*, vol. 5, p. 355; al-Mardāwī, *Tanqīḥ*, pp. 169, 185; al-Ḥujāwī, *Iqnā'*, vol. 2, p. 331; Ibn al-Najjār, *Muntahā*, vol. 1, p. 503; al-Bahūtī, *Rawḍ*, vol. 2, pp. 108, 119–20; al-Shaybānī, *Nayl*, vol. 1, p. 114, vol. 2, pp. 2, 4; al-Sarakhsī, *Mabsūṭ*, vol. 11, p. 133; al- Maghrinānī, *Hidāya*, vol. 7, p. 108; Abū Shujā', *Taqrīb*, p. 23; al-Ghazālī, *Wajīz*, vol.1, p. 203; al-Nawawī, *Rawḍa*, vol. 4, p. 426.

60 al-Ghazālī, *Mustaṣfā*, vol. 2, pp. 326–9; al-Āmidī, *Iḥkām*, vol. 3, pp. 13–14; al-Subkī, *Ibhāj*, vol. 3, pp. 170–3.

61 Ibn Qudāma, *Rawḍa*, vol. 2, p. 300; Ibn al-Laḥḥām, *Mukhtaṣar*, p. 149; al-Shawkānī, *Irshād*, p. 220; al-Shāfi'ī, *Risāla*, pp. 40, 479; al-Shīrāzī, *Luma'*, p. 59; ibid., *Tabṣira*, pp. 458–9; al-Juwaynī, *Burhān*, vol. 2, p. 876; al-Ghazālī, *Mustaṣfā*, vol. 2, pp. 315–18; al-Āmidī, *Iḥkām*, vol. 3, p. 90; al-Subkī, *Ibhāj*, vol. 3, p. 74.

62 Ibn Hubayra, *Ifṣāḥ*, vol. 2, p. 45; Ibn Qudāma, *Mughnī*, vol. 5, p. 482.

63 Abū 'Ubayd, *Amwāl*, p. 6; al-Shaybānī, *Aṣl*, vol. 1, p. 94 (No. 23), vol. 2, p. 95 (No. 25); ibid., *Ḥujja*, vol. 2, p. 543; al-Ṭaḥāwī, *al-Mukhtaṣar* (Cairo, 1379/1950), p. 78; Abū al-Layth, *Khizāna*, p. 234; ibid., *'Uyūn al-masā'il* (Baghdad, 1386/1967), 145; al-Qudūrī, *Mukhtaṣar*, p. 38; al-Sarakhsī, *Mabsūṭ*, vol. 12, p. 195; al-Samarqandī, *Tuḥfa*, vol. 2, p. 79; al-Kāsānī, *Badā'i'*, vol. 6, pp. 2996–7; Qāḍīkhān, *Fatāwā*, vol. 2, p. 249; al-Marghinānī, *Hidāya*, vol. 5, p. 102; al-Nasafī, *Kanz*, vol. 1, p. 208; al-Shāfi'ī, *Umm*, vol. 3, p. 41; Abū Ibrāhīm al-Muzanī, *al-Mukhtaṣar*, vol. 2 (Cairo, 1388/1968–9), 166–7; al-Shīrāẓī,

Muhadhdhab, vol. 1, p. 281; ibid., *Tanbīh*, p. 58; al-Ghazālī, *Wajīz*, vol. 1, p. 149; Abū Shujāʿ, *Taqrīb*, p. 20; al-Nawawī, *Rawḍa*, vol. 3, pp. 553, 558; ibid., *Minhāj al-ṭālibīn* (Batavia, 1882), vol. 1, 402; Taqī al-Dīn al-Subkī, *Majmūʿ sharḥ muhadhdhab* (Cairo, 1966), vol. 1, 316; Abū Ḥātim Maḥmūd al-Qazwīnī, *Kitāb al-ḥiyal fī al-fiqh* (Hanover, 1924), 13; al-Dimashqī, *Raḥma*, p. 38; Mālik Ibn Anas, *Muwaṭṭaʾ*, vol.2, p. 10; Abū al-Qāsim/Saḥnūn, *Mudawwana*, vol. 4, p. 148; Ibn Abī Zayd al-Qayrawānī, *al-Risāla* (Alger, 1980), 208; al-Bājī, *Muntaqā*, vol. 4, p. 219; al-Khiraqī, *Mukhtaṣar*, p. 4; Ibn Hubayra, *Ifṣāḥ*, vol. 1, p. 339; Ibn Qudāma, *Mughnī*, vol. 4, pp. 92, 94; ibid., *Muqniʿ*, vol. 2, p. 82; ibid., *ʿUmda*, p. 149; Majd al-Dīn Ibn Taymiyya, *Muḥarrar*, vol. 1, p. 316; Shams al-Dīn Ibn Qudāma, *Sharḥ kabīr*, vol. 4, p. 196; Ibn Mufliḥ, *Furūʿ*, vol. 4, p. 72; Ibn Rajab, *Qawāʿid*, p. 168; al-Mardāwī, *Inṣāf*, vol. 5, p. 65; ibid., *Tanqīh*, p. 137; ibid., *Taṣḥīḥ*, vol. 4, p. 72; al-Ḥujāwī, *Iqnāʿ*, vol. 2, p. 129; ibid., *Zād*, p. 42; Ibn al-Najjār, *Muntahā*, vol. 1, p. 388; al-Bahūtī, *Kashshāf*, vol. 3, p. 281; ibid., *Rawḍ*, vol. 2, p. 85; al-Shaybānī, *Nayl*, vol. 1, p. 91.

64 Muḥammad b. Ismāʿīl al-Bukhārī *al-Jāmiʿ al-ṣaḥīḥ* (Cairo, 1390/1970), vol. 4, 70 (No. 1971), vol. 4, 72–3 (No. 1978), vol. 4, 74, 75 (No. 1980); Muslim Ibn al-Ḥajjāj, *al-Jāmiʿ al-ṣaḥīḥ*, (Beirut, 1984), vol. 3, 1165–8 (No. 49, 51–2, 54, 56–8), vol. 3, p. 1174 (No. 81); al-Dārimī, *Kitāb al-sunan*, vol.2 (Beirut, n.d.), 251–2; al-Sijistānī, *Sunan*, vol. 3, pp. 252–4 (No. 3367, 3372–3); Ibn Māja, *Sunan*, vol. 3, p. 161; al-Tirmidhī, *Sunan*, vol. 3 (Cairo, 1382/1962), 520–1 (No. 1227); Abū ʿAbd al-Rahmān al-Nasāʾī, *Kitāb al-sunan*, 7 (Beirut, 1984), 262–3; Mālik Ibn Anas, *Muwaṭṭaʾ*, vol. 2, pp. 79–80; Ibn Ḥanbal, *Musnad*, vol. 2, pp. 7, 37, 41, 46, 52, 56, 59, 62–3, 75, 77, 79, 80, 123, 261–2, 363, vol. 3, pp. 372, 381, vol. 5, pp. 185, 190, 192, vol. 6, pp. 70, 105–6.

65 Ibn Qudāma, *Rawḍa*, vol. 2, pp. 277–81; al-Ghazālī, *Mustaṣfā*, vol. 2, pp. 299–306; al-Āmidī, *Iḥkām*, vol. 3, pp. 81–7; Ibn al-Ḥājib, *Muntahā*, p. 135.

66 al-Ghazālī, *Mustaṣfā*, vol. 1, p. 315; Ibn al-Ḥājib, *Muntahā*, p. 156.

67 al-Bukhārī, *Ṣaḥīḥ*, vol. 4, pp. 66–7 (No. 1963), vol. 4, pp. 70–4 (No. 1971, 1975, 1978–9), vol. 4, pp. 189–90 (No. 2136, 2137–9); Muslim, *Ṣaḥīḥ*, vol. 3, pp. 1168–71 (No. 57, 59–71), vol. 3, p. 1174 (No. 81–2), vol. 3, p. 1175 (No. 85); al-Dārimī, *Sunan*, vol. 2, p. 252; al-Tirmidhī, *Sunan*, vol. 3, pp. 585–7 (No. 1300–3); al-Nasāʾī, *Sunan*, vol. 7, pp. 267–8, 296; Ibn Māja, *Sunan*, p. 65; Ibn Ḥanbal, *Musnad*, vol. 2, pp. 8, 5, 11, 237, vol. 3, pp. 313, 360, 392, vol. 4, p. 2, 5, pp. 181, 182, 188, 190, 192, 364; Mālik Ibn Anas, *Muwaṭṭaʾ*, vol. 2, p. 80; ʿAbd al-Razzāq Ibn Hamām al-Ṣanʿānī, *al-Muṣannaf*, (Beirut, 1972), vol. 8, 103 (No. 14486); Abū Bakr al-Ḥumaydī, *al-Musnad* (Beirut/Cairo, 1383/1963), vol. 2, 280 (No. 622), vol. 2, 296 (No. 673), vol. 2, 540 (No. 1292).

68 Ibn al-Najjār, *Sharḥ kawkab*, p. 513; al-Shawkānī, *Irshād*, pp. 221–2; al-Āmidī, *Iḥkām*, vol. 3, p. 94; al-Subkī, *Ibhāj*, vol. 3, pp. 87–9; Ibn al-Ḥājib, *Muntahā*, p. 136; al-Qarāfi, *Sharḥ tanqīḥ*, pp. 388–9, 398–99.

69 Ibn Qudāma, *Rawḍa*, vol. 2, pp. 286–90; Ibn al-Laḥḥām, *Mukhtaṣar*, p. 149; Ibn al-Najjār, *Sharḥ kawkab*, pp. 529–30; al-Shawkānī, *Irshād*, p. 221; Shīrāzī, *Lumaʿ*, p. 62; al-Ghazālī, *Mustaṣfā*, vol. 2, pp. 307–9; Fakhr al-Dīn al-Rāzī, *al-*

Maḥṣūl fī 'ilm uṣūl al-fiqh (Riyad, 1979–81), vol. 2, part 2, pp. 285–98; al-Subkī, *Ibhāj*, vol. 3, pp. 78–82; al-Qarāfi, *Sharḥ tanqīḥ*, pp. 396–7.

70 al-Sarākhsī, *Mabsūṭ*, vol. 30, p. 209.

71 Abū Khāzim Ibn Abī Ya'lā, *Ṭabaqāt al-ḥanābila* (Beirut, n.d.), vol. 1, p. 104 (No. 113), vol. 1, p. 120 (No. 140), vol. 1, p. 215 (No. 282), vol. 1, p. 218 (No. 290), vol. 1, p. 332 (No. 477); 'Ubayd Allāh Ibn Baṭṭa, 'Ibṭāl al-ḥiyal', in *Min dafā'in al-kunūz* (Cairo, 1980), 19–55, esp. 34, 40–5; Ibn Qudāma, *Mughnī*, vol. 3, pp. 592–3, vol. 4, pp. 2, 97, 98; Shams al-Dīn Ibn Qudāma, *Sharḥ kabīr*, vol. 4, p. 179; Ibn Qayyim al-Jawziyya, *I'lām*, vol. 3, p. 171; ibid., *Ighāthat al-lahfān min maṣāyid al-shayṭān* (Cairo, 1381/1961), vol. 1, 403, vol. 2, pp. 67ff.; Ibn Rajab, *Dhayl*, vol. 1, p. 257.

72 al-Bājī, *Iḥkām*, pp. 689–700.

73 Ibn Taymiyya, *Fatāwā*, vol. 20, pp. 348–9, vol.29, p. 27; ibid., *Kitāb iqāmat al-dalīl 'alā ibṭāl al-taḥlīl*, in *Majmū' fatāwā Shaykh al-Islām Taqī al-Dīn Ibn Taymiyya* (Cairo, 1328/1910), 13–72.

PART 3

Minorities under Islamic Law

SEVEN

Ebū'̄s Su'ūd's Definitions of Church *vakfs*: Theory and Practice in Ottoman Law

EUGENIA KERMELI

Despite the significant role the institution of *vakf* has played in Islamic societies, research has not yet managed to fully expound its complex nature. Studies tend to either concentrate on the theoretical/juridical stipulations governing the foundation and function of *vakfs* or to examine its role in political and socio-economic structures independently of contemporary theoretical debates. In addition, as Richard van Leeuwen has argued historians following the Weberian approach have utilised the institution of *vakf* in order to characterise Islamic society as 'stagnant' and 'irrational'.[1]

Complementing this diffusion of opinions with the already diverse character of the implementation of law in the Ottoman Empire, one can understand the lack of coherence in views related to *vakf*. When examining institutions in the Ottoman Empire, one should bear in mind that custom, *'urf*, most of the time a preservation of pre-Ottoman practices, was the dominant factor in the application of law within the boundaries of the Empire.[2] Thus, attempting an overall approach which would be applicable to all regions of the Empire and throughout the centuries of Ottoman presence concerning the institution of *vakf* would be rather misleading.

In Ottoman times, people made gifts of their personal property in order to provide the means to serve the community through paying or supplementing the salaries of religious functionaries such as *imāms*, *müezzins* or teachers. They paid for the construction or maintenance of religious buildings or of schools, hotels, hospitals, *'imārets* (soup kitchens), or to support their staff. Other pious gifts were used for the construction of fountains, wells around mosques or in commercial and residential quarters of cities.[3] All the aforementioned endowments were essential for the well being of Ottoman society since they covered most aspects of public life, both religious, by the construction of mosques and *medreses* (religious schools), and lay. The purpose of all endowments, though, ought to be pleasing to God (*ḳurba*). Those endowments with a distinct religious or public nature were *vaḳf ḫairī*. Apart from those, there were other endowments where the *ḳurba* was not as apparent. These were *vaḳf ḫurrī*, family trusts for the benefit of children, grandchildren and other relatives.[4] The founder could stipulate that the income of the trust should be assigned to himself and his descendants in perpetuity.[5] Since wealthy descendants were as eligible for the trust's benefits as poor ones, the basic definition of *vaḳf* as *ṣadaḳa* was contravened.[6] By quoting an opinion, allegedly of Abū Yūsuf, that family *vaḳfs* were permissible on the ground that ultimately they benefited the destitute, Ḥanafī jurists circumvented the problem of illegality by arguing that these endowments were valid so long the ultimate beneficiary, after the extinction of the founder's line should be the indigent.[7]

Monastic trusts in mortmain were a common practice in the Balkans even before the conquest. Since the beginning of monasticism in the Mediterranean basin, a common issue of concern and negotiation between the monasteries and the regional and central authorities was that of the status of the properties owned by monastic communities and their privileges.[8] Over the centuries and, in particular, before the fall of Constantinople in 1453, influential monastic communities in the Balkans were among the most powerful landowners in the region.[9] After a period of unrest following the Ottoman conquest, most of the monasteries managed to restore part of their privileges. In certain cases monasteries undertook a more influential role, that of the representative of the *zimmī* (non-Muslim peasantry) communities within their jurisdiction.[10] It was a very favourable arrangement for both sides. The Ottoman administration managed to extract, with the least possible inconvenience taxes due to the Porte and the monasteries retained privileges held for many centuries, as well as a spiritual and political role in their communities.

Thus, since monastic/church *vaḳfs* not only continued to exist during the Ottoman period but some of them actually thrived, the main question to be addressed is that of their legal status. From the definitions of the different types of *vaḳfs*, it is certain that church *vaḳfs* could not fall into the category of *vaḳf ḫairī* since that would not constitute *ḳurba*. A number of scholars faced with the problematic term 'church *vaḳf*' have reached different conclusions. Wittek and Lemerle, in referring to a *fīrmān* for Koutloumousiou Monastery, dated 1491, argued that the word '*vaḳıf* was used to denote 'propriéte' as they translated the term with some reservations.[11] However, they were reluctant to compare it fully to a Muslim religious *vaḳf* that was the property of Allah and had a certain religious/social character. Their justification for such an awkward term was based on the privileged status of Athonite monasteries. Wittek and Lemerle argued that the Ottoman state respected practices and granted exemptions and privileges to the monasteries which they had enjoyed under the Byzantine Emperors.[12] Thus, 'the monasteries had retained the status of *ṣāḥib-i arḍ* (the master of the land) on their properties.'[13]

Fotić, on the other hand, argues that 'the Arabic term *waḳf* was used in the Ottoman Empire in its most general sense to denote every endowment (bequest), most often that made for religious, God pleasing purposes, regardless of whether it was a Muslim or a non-Muslim (Christian, Jew) who made it'.[14] He substantiated his argument that Christian *vaḳfs* were permitted in the Ḥanafī interpretation of the *Sharīʿa* with reference to A. Akgündüz. According to Akgündüz, a Christian could bequeath his property to churches/monasteries and 'he could also bequeath something for common good and other purposes considered to be God pleasing according to Islam: for fountains, hospitals etc.'[15] Fotić then quotes Boskov's documents from the Archives of the Monastery of Chilandari where the term *vaḳf* was used in a case of dispute between two monasteries in the *ḳāḍī* court in order to conclude that the term was used to 'denote even the endowments and bequests made before the establishment of Ottoman rule in the Balkans, at the time of Serbian and Byzantine rulers' in order to conclude that 'if, in the same way, we understand the term *vaḳıf* exclusively as bequeathed property, then it is quite clear how the monastery and its estates could be both a monastery *vaḳıf* and belong to a *tımar*, or even how a monastery *vaḳıf* could be on a Muslim land *vaḳıf*.[16] Akgündüz's view (adopted by Fotić) that a Christian could donate his property to a church/monastery so long as the ultimate beneficiary is the indigent is in accordance, as we will see below, with the *firmāns* from Mount Athos and the Monastery of Saint John the Theologian in Patmos.[17] However, Fotić's argument that the term *vaḳf* means bequeathed property on the basis that the term was used 'before the establishment of Ottoman rule in the Balkans' fails to take into consideration the fact that the terms were used by a monk presenting his case in the *ḳāḍī* court. Thus, it is understandable to use terms like *vaḳf* and *vaḳıfnāme* that would be familiar to the judge. In addition, Fotić's statement that if we view *vakf* 'exclusively as bequeathed property, then it is quite clear how a monastery *vakıf* could be on a Muslim land *vakıf* could rather serve better as an example of dual ownership common in the Ottoman Empire, that of the real substance (*rakaba*) of a property and of its usufruct (*taṣarruf*).[18]

Van Leeuwen, on the other hand, argues that 'in Hanafite jurisprudence the prescriptions concerning waqfs founded by Christians do not fundamentally differ from those concerning Muslim waqfs'.[19] The main limitation for these *vakfs* was that their revenues should constitute *kurba*. By declaring 'the poor' as the beneficiary of the *vakf* they were permitted. However Christian *vakfs* could never be founded for the benefit of mosques or for the repair, upkeep and expansion of religious buildings nor for the sustenance of the clergy or monks 'as these designations were clearly incompatible with the Muslim's conception of piety.'[20] Furthermore, according to van Leeuwen 'the limitations set upon the founding of Christian waqfs in the Ottoman Empire were originally intended to prevent the clergy and the church, as an institution, from acquiring a strong independent economic basis.'[21] Undoubtedly, Van Leeuwen's study is quite complex since he is dealing with the case of Christian laymen founding monasteries and registering them as *vakfs*. In his theoretical approach towards these *vakfs* he is also at pains to explain how, although the *vakfs* were following the prescriptions of Ḥanafī jurisprudence, they were considered valid and irrevocable. His argument in favour of a compromise, whereby these *vakfs* are accepted in the category of 'pious purpose' with a limitation as to the utilisation of their revenues, would seem plausible. However, he includes in the limitation *vakfs* founded for the benefit of clergy/ monks, a point contrary to information included in *firmāns* from monastic communities in Serbia, Mount Athos and the Aegean.[22] In addition, van Leeuwen's view that limitations upon the founding of these *vakfs* reveal the intention of the Ottoman administration to prevent church and clergy from acquiring a strong independent economic basis contradicts the views of the Ottoman *Şeyhü'l-islām* Ebū's Su'ūd who, in 1569, faced with the threat that monasteries in Mount Athos would be evacuated by their monks unless their demands were met, found a compromise solution that was acceptable to both sides.[23] The only way we could perhaps determine under which categorisation the *vakfs* examined by van Leeuwen were legally accepted would be through the formulae used in their *vakıfnāmes*. Since, though, his prior concern was the political struggle over the control of the *vakfs*, he does not include any such details. He only informs us that the foundation documents 'did not essentially differ from in his book documents drafted by Sunnis or others'.[24]

One final point has to be clarified before embarking upon the way an Islamic authority the *Şeyhü'l-islām* Ebū's Su'ūd, dealt with the problem of church/monastic *vaḳfs*. Although these *vaḳfs* were indeed tolerated in the Empire and efforts were made to accommodate them, they never came under the umbrella of specific privileges given to the *ẓimmīs* by the Ottoman administration.

Ebū's Su'ūd came to the office of *Şeyhü'l-islām* in October 1545 at the age of fifty-five. He was an intimate of Süleyman I and enjoyed his patronage until the latter's death. Ebū's Su'ūd continued to offer his services to Selīm II (1566–74) who succeeded his father in 1566. When Selīm came to the throne, Ebū's Su'ūd aged seventy five was still among the most powerful figures in the Empire. He controlled the senior judicial appointments and secured offices for relatives and students. He died on 23 August 1574.[25] The most important body of Ebū's Su'ūd's legal writings during his twenty eight years in office was his *fetvas*. Following the tradition of Ḥanafī jurists like Qāḍīkhān, Ibn Bazzāz and especially Kemālpaşazāde, he endeavoured to redefine the basic laws of land tenure and taxation in terms which he borrowed from the Ḥanafī legal tradition.[26] Such a task was essential since in the Ottoman Empire two systems of law were operational and had grown up independently of one another, the *Sharī'a* (Holy Law) and the *ḳānūn* (secular law) which in most cases was a systematisation of pre-existing customary law. Ebū's Su'ūd's rulings on land tenure and taxation became the predominant concepts in the Ḥanafī legal theory on land and were included in the compilation of a new land code in 1673, the *Ḳānūn-i Cedīd* which remained the official law until the promulgation of the Ottoman land Law of 1858.

His main concern was the misappropriation of land and its revenues and his first attempt to address the problem was in the *ḳānūnnāme* for Hungary in 1541.[27] However customary practices proved tenacious. The opportunity to re-enforce his rulings introduced in the *ḳānūnnāme* for Hungary and to ensure their implementation came in 1568, two years after the accession of Selīm II to the throne. Ebū's Su'ūd supervised the promulgation of a new *ḳānūnnāme* for Thessaloniki and Skopie (1568–69) and ordered the confiscation of church *vaḳfs*, at least, to our knowledge, in the Balkans. It was customary for the new Sultan to validate documents issued by his predecessors and one of his first commands was the re-registration of properties and taxes in new *defters*. As a consequence of this new registration all *firmāns* and *hüccets* validating possession, including those validating monastic property, had to be renewed. This provided the opportunity for Ebū's Su'ūd to affirm the Sultan's status as sole owner on behalf of the Fisc of arable land in the Empire.

In the introductory paragraph of the *ḳānūnnāme* Ebū's Su'ūd attacks the 'mistaken suppositions' of *re'āyā* and even *ḳādī*s on the issue of land ownership:

> But in the previous Noble Registers, no attention was paid to the detailed circumstances of the land in the Protected Realms. No investigation or clarification was made of the essence and truth of the matter: whether [these lands] are *'uşrī* or *ḫarācī*, and whether or not they are the freeholdings of the occupiers. For this reason, the *re'āyā* thought that the lands in their possession were *'uşrī* lands and disputed payment of 1/8th [of the produce in tax]. They thought that these lands were their freeholdings (*mülk*) and bought and sold them among themselves in accordance with their own [mistaken] suppositions. Governors and judges were not aware of the truth of the situation, and immense damage was done to the good ordering of affairs and to the welfare of the people by their issuing, contrary to the *Sharī'a*, certificates of sale and purchase, and *vaḳfiyes*.[28]

In this *ḳānūnnāme* Ebū's Su'ūd repeats the juristic theory of land and tax which he had formulated in the *ḳānūnnāme* for Hungary. He identified Ottoman *mīrī* land with the Ḥanafī term 'royal demesne' (*aradī'l-mamlaka*) and distinguished between the real substance of the land and the usufruct. In his theory, the real substance was *de jure* the property of the Treasury and therefore, *de facto* the property of the Sultan on behalf of the Treasury.[29] The cultivators had acquired the ownership of the usufruct as a loan (*'arīyya*).[30] The *tapu* (entry fee) a new occupant paid for land to the *sipāhī* was identified as advance rent (*ücret-i mu'accele*).

In this interpretation it was legally justifiable to confiscate monastic *vaḳfs* where the capital consisted of arable land, as the monks had only the usufruct of this by way of a loan. They could not, therefore, convert the land to *vaḳfs* since it was not their freehold. They could, nevertheless, retain their right to the usufruct by paying *tapu* for what had previously been freehold property. In this way they could by paying *tapu* to the *sipāhī*, in this case, the Sultan, acquire the ownership of the usufruct. It is for this reason that the monasteries were required to pay *tapu* before they could re-possess their former trusts.

In the *ḳānūnnāme*, Ebū's Su'ūd includes a paragraph that was also applicable to the monasteries:

> ... None of these persons has the power to dispose [of their lands] in any way contrary to what is set forth. Their giving or taking freehold possession [of them] or making them *vaḳf*, by purchase, sale, gift or any other means are all void, and the documents proving title (*hüccet*) and *vaḳfiyes* which judges have issued to this effect are, every one of them, invalid ...

The major concern here was to curtail the cultivators' practice of treating land as freehold property which they could dispose of at will. For this reason, sale, pledge and deposit were strictly forbidden.[31] The monasteries' practice of obtaining certificates of validation of the conversion for landed properties to *vaḳf* was, therefore, illegal.

The two phases of the confiscation of monastic *vaḳfs* are recorded in two *firmāns*, the first from the Saint John the Theologian Monastery in Patmos (Aa40), 6 Cemāẕī'eş-aḫīr 977/17 November 1569 that initiates the confiscation, and the second from the Mount Athos Monasteries, 13 Şaban 976/25 January 1569, dealing with negotiations between the Porte and the monks on practical issues arising from the confiscation order. The fact that the *firmān* from Athos, although anterior to the one from Patmos, deals with the second phase of the case indicates that the process was slow and it was not initiated simultaneously for all monastic communities in the Balkans.

In the *fetva* included in the *firmān* Aa40 for Patmos, Ebū's Su'ūd lays out clearly which monastic *vaḳfs* are valid and which are not:

> When a legal opinion was sought from the *Müfti* of the Age in my Protected Realms, he issued the following *fetva*: 'It can never be valid for the *ẓimmīs* to make the fields and meadows which they have the use of, or their freehold vineyards, orchards, mills, houses and shops, *vaḳf* for their churches; it is a major offence; they should be confiscated. If the *ḳādī*s give a *vaḳfiye*, that too is absolutely invalid. If their founders or heirs are alive it is their freehold; they should take it and have the use of it and pay their *şer'ī* and the *'urfi* taxes to the *mīrī*. If their founders and heirs are not alive, all of it belongs to the Treasury. It should be confiscated, and must be sold for its (true) price to anyone who requests it. If the aforementioned persons have not made the aforesaid valid freeholdings *vaḳf* for their churches, but if they have made that *vaḳf* for the monks, the indigent, or for bridges and fountains; and, if the *ḳādī*s have judged their *vaḳfiyes* to be valid; and made a valid (entry in the) *sicill*, it is valid and *şer'ī*. They have the use of them on the said conditions and pay in full the *şer'ī* and *'urfi* taxes for each one of them'.[32]

There are therefore two possible scenarios: i) Properties were made *vaḳfs* for the monks, the indigent, bridges and fountains, ii) Properties were made *vaḳfs* for the churches. In the first case the donation is valid and legal, provided the trust is recorded in a *sicill*. In the second case, all *vaḳfs* for churches are confiscated. If the *ḳāḍīs* had provided *vaḳfiyes* they were absolutely invalid. In the latter case the fate of the properties differed according to whether the founders or heirs of the *vaḳf* were alive or not: i) if the founders or heirs are alive then they could take back the properties and fulfil their tax obligations; ii) if the founder or heirs were not alive then all the properties belonged to the Treasury and should be confiscated and sold at the market price.[33] The legal arguments used to order the confiscation are evident. Monastic *vaḳfs* had offended two legal principles. Firstly, they consisted largely of rural land which, in Ebū's Su'ūd's definition, was *mīrī* land and secondly, such trusts were founded for the benefit of churches and monasteries.

Ebū's Su'ūd's ruling on the abolition of church *vaḳf* was not arbitrary: making a *vaḳf* for the benefit of a church contravenes basic Ḥanafī doctrines. As we mentioned before, there are two kinds of *vaḳf*: *vaḳf ḫairī*, endowments of a definite religious or public nature (mosques, *medreses*, hospitals, bridges, fountains), and *vaḳf ahlī* or *ḫurrī*, family endowments, for children or grandchildren or other relations.

Monastic *vaḳfs* cannot belong to the first category since their purpose was incompatible with Islam. They could therefore be created only as family *vaḳfs*, in which case, the 'heirs', besides the poor and travellers benefiting from the endowment, were the body of the monks residing in a monastery. Clearly, a definition in Islamic law of Christian religious endowments as family *vaḳfs* entails a number of problems and Ebū's Su'ūd was not wholly at ease in accepting this definition. This is evident in a *fetva* following an enquiry as to whether monks can bequeath properties to other monks residing in the same monastery:

> *Question*: Is it permissible for the monks in a monastery to bequeath the vineyards, houses and lands which they bought from the fisc, to the monks who will live in the monastery after them?
>
> *Answer*: Provided there are no heirs, and provided they bequeath all their property, apart from lands, to the monks living in the monastery; and provided the monks [in question] are limited to a well-defined group, whether they are rich or poor, their bequests are valid. No one from the fisc may intervene. If, however, they are innumerable and make up a large group, it is valid to make a bequest to all of them. It is necessary, in order that no one may intervene, to make the bequest to the poor among them. If they have heirs, these are able to refuse any [bequest] beyond the third [which the testator may freely dispose of]. They cannot interfere in the

third. In this way, no one may intervene. If their heirs accept [this arrangement], it is in its entirety a valid bequest and no one may interfere. Nevertheless, a Sultanic decree is necessary in order to prevent anyone intervening in their lands.[34]

The first hurdle to be overcome, then, was the fate of properties in case of a bequest. In this *fetva*, Ebū's Su'ūd insists on imposing the Ḥanafī laws of inheritance on the monastic community. According to the *fetva*, only if all the remaining heirs of a deceased monk forgo their portion of the property, can the monks in a monastery inherit it. This would be almost impossible since inheritance, in Ḥanafī law, is not confined to direct descendants and each heir has a canonical right to a fixed share of the deceased's property. But, then, Ebū's Su'ūd specifies that in a case where there are no heirs alive, the whole estate can be bequeathed to monks living in the monastery, regardless of whether they are rich or poor, but on the condition that they are a *limited and well defined group*. If they are a large group, he continues, the bequest should be made to *the poor among them*. Unfortunately, the *fetva* is not dated and so we cannot be certain whether it was drawn up at the beginning of the process of confiscation or as a result of complications arising from it. In either case, Ebū's Su'ūd comes as closely as possible to recognising the monks as a collectivity, within the constraints of a legal tradition which does not recognise corporations as legal entities.

However, in the *fetva* incorporated in Selīm II's *firmān*, dated 31 January 1569, to the monks of Mount Athos, Ebū's Su'ūd is more daring. The monks requested the recognition of their Byzantine right to inherit *ab indiviso* and *in common* the properties of deceased or departing monks, threatening to vacate their monasteries and to deprive the Treasury of its taxes if their request was not granted. They made this request in order to safeguard their properties and trusts from arbitrary interference by local authorities wishing to extract more money:

At the present time the monks of the monasteries on the shores of the peninsula of Ayonoroz in your *ḳadılık* have presented a petition to the exalted Porte. 'Our *çiftliks* and vineyards and orchards, fields and mills and shops, houses and wine-shops, our animals and winter pastures in the plain of Longos and goats and all we have always possessed from old days, in part and in whole, up till now in the aforementioned *ḳadılıks*, the *mülks* and animals of our monasteries [these] were [all] sold by the *mīrī*. By mutual co-operation, all of us have borrowed and acquired a debt of 14,000 golden coins. We, the monks who are living in our monastery, have taken possession of the aforementioned lands and animals which we bought in order to hold, on the following condition. According to the previous decision none of the monks in our monasteries has the freehold of our aforementioned possessions (*emlāk*), fields, vineyards, wind mills, orchards, *çiftliks* and animals. They belong in their entirety to the monasteries in order to feed travellers. *Emīns*, *emīns* of the Public Treasury, *mevḳūfātçis*, *voyvodas* and *subaşıs* should not interfere in any way whatsoever with the aforementioned possessions and animals. When one of the monks in the monasteries dies or leaves for another region, the *emīns* and employees of the Public Treasury and the *mevḳūfātçis* and *voyvodas* and *subaşıs* should not come and bother the other monks, saying 'A monk died or left for another region. His property is missing, what happened to his possessions clothes and animals?'. If the previous decision is confirmed, in accordance with the Noble Commands in our possession from the time of the late Sultan, Sultan Murād Ḫan; and if an Imperial Confirmation is granted, each one of us will go out into the world and strive to collect *aḳçes* as alms, and all of us will pay the debt of 14,000 gold coins which we have as a loan. Each year in accordance with the customary *Ḳānūn*, we will bring the 70,000 *aḳçes* fixed on us as *ḫarāc*, and deliver them each year on New Year's day (March 22) to the Imperial Treasury. We have bought for 130,000 *aḳçes* from the *il-emīni*, in the manner set forth in the Noble Decree, our *çiftliks* in Limnos and other places which are outside the aforementioned monasteries. At threshing time we will give the tithe on our tithe-lands with the knowledge of the *ḳādī*, in accordance with the *vilāyet defter*. We will take the residue to the said peninsula in accordance with the Noble Command, and provide the means of subsistence to the people of the peninsula and to travellers. And if you do not order an Imperial document of confirmation to be bestowed according to the previous decision and if we again sell the possessions and we pay back the gold which we borrowed each one of us will be scattered all around the world and it is certain that our monasteries will be deserted and our taxes, which we have been customarily paying as *maḳṭu* each year, will be lost'.

When they said this, a noble *fetva* was issued on the matter ... You should examine the *vakfs* for ... their offspring, the indigent in the monasteries and travellers who come and go and those who serve them (?). What is raised from their revenues and expenses [bestowed]? After it has [been] made *vakf*, and delivered to the *mütevelli*, and after the *vakfiye* has been judged [valid] according to the *Sharīʿa* no one may interfere ever. You should not change the conditions. But they are not their freeholdings. The fields and meadows, summer and winter pastures which they have received from the *mīrī* by *tapu* or which they have received by so-called "purchase" from the *reʿāyā*, are all on the lands of the sovereign. They may never become the freehold of anybody, whether or not they are Muslims. The *reʿāyā* have *taṣarruf* by way of rent, and are neither capable of buying or selling or pre-emptying nor of any other way. In this matter, the *vaḳfs* of the aforementioned monks and their conditions are absolutely invalid. However *mīrī* has been merciful to the aforementioned [monks]. They should sow and reap the aforementioned meadows, pay the tithe like other *re'āyā*, and graze their animals in the summer and winter pastures. No one should interfere after they have paid their *muḳaṭa'as* registered in our Imperial *defter*. If one of them dies [his share] should not be given by *tapu*, on the grounds that he has his [own] share in the said places, [but] the rest of them should have *taṣarruf* of the deceased's share. It is permissible by the *Sharī'a* to ratify in this manner and for a noble decree to be given as set out in detail. No one should interfere provided that they do not transgress the Imperial *firmān*. The reason for interfering now is that they acquired private possession[s] by selling and buying royal domains from the *re'āyā* making them into so-called *vaḳf* of the monasteries, and acquiring hüccets and the *vaḳfiyes*. They were not paying the tithes obligatory by the *şer'*, but paying a tiny *muḳaṭa'a*. It is patently obvious they have damaged the Treasury of the Muslims, clearly acted contrary to the Noble *Sharī'a* and shamefully betrayed the glory of the Sultanate.[35]

The implications of this statement are of paramount importance. By denying the possible natural heirs of the deceased their share, Ebū's Su'ūd seems, at first sight, to oppose the Ḥanafī rules of inheritance. However, since the remaining monks of a monastery do not pay an entry fine (*tapu*) to acquire the usufruct of the land, in practice they are treated similarly to the son of a deceased peasant who can inherit his father's rights to the usufruct without any entry fine. The monks are not treated as outsiders, who would have to pay a *tapu* to the *sipāhī*. This amounts to the treatment of the monks in a monastery as a family. Like in a family trust they can make *vaḳfs* for the benefit of their poor members as well as for the indigent, travellers, the dependants of the monastery and their offspring, which means, in practice, the remaining monks. This is a fine example of Ebū's Su'ūd's ingenuity. He follows the Ḥanafī doctrines of inheritance, but re-defines the monks of a monastery as a family. He thus recognises their collectivity which was a basic element of Byzantine monastic tradition while, at the same time, ordering the monks to make *vaḳfs* in their own names and not in the name of the monastery.

Ebū's Su'ūd is aware of the implications of his concessions towards the monks of Mount Athos. He recognises the pitfalls of this legal 'technasma', and so hurriedly issued a *fetva* restricting similar claims from other monasteries. When he was asked whether monks could make a trust out of flocks, vineyards, orchards and mills for the benefit of the poor and travellers, Ebū's Su'ūd answered that this was permissible provided it was not a trust for the benefit of the church and arable land was not donated.[36]

> *Question:* Some Christian subjects become monks in a monastery. The registrar of the province takes from them the flocks, vineyards, orchards and mills, which are in their ownership, and sells them back to them. If they convert the said property into a trust for the poor and travellers, can any outsider later interfere in the said trust?
>
> *Answer:* If what they have converted into a trust are things like animals, vineyards, mills or shops, and so long as they do not put them in trust for the monastery but in trust for the poor and travellers, no one may intervene. Fields and arable lands can never be [converted into] a trust, but they may receive them from the fisc on payment of a *tapu* tax, and no one may intervene, provided there is an entry in the [cadastral] register as follows: 'The monks should have possession [of the land] and, after they have paid all their dues like other subjects, no one may intervene. When monks die, the ones who take their place should have possession, and provided [the fields] are not [recorded] as trust.

In this *fetva*, Ebū's Su'ūd recognises the poor and travellers as beneficiaries of a *vakf*, which could not, however, be made out of arable land. So far, he follows the Ḥanafī rules on trusts and his own stipulations forbidding arable land to be converted into trusts. However, he then allows monks to be considered as a collective body, entitled to the same privileges as the beneficiaries of a family *vakf*, i.e. monks can receive property belonging to deceased monks without any interference by the local authorities, provided there is an entry in the cadastral *defter* stipulating that this is the case. What he does, in effect, is to disguise his ruling as if it derived uniquely from a cadastral register when, as we know, he would have been the one who advised the Sultan to include the said entry in the register, in the first place. This is the argument that must have been used to exclude small monastic communities from the privilege.

The conclusions to be drawn out of the confiscation of monastic *vakfs* in 1568–69 are quite interesting. It is obvious from the correspondence between the monks of Mount Athos and the Porte that the case we are dealing with was a mere rearrangement and redefinition of the conditions of an agreement by both sides. The issue of concern was the legal status of the monastic properties at the end of the sixteenth century in the Balkans. Of course, it was not solely an argument concerned with legalistic terms describing the ownership and the usufruct of lands and properties but mainly represented the concern of the Ottoman administration at losing financial benefits through the irregularities in obtaining and exploiting land that belonged to the *mīrī*.

Ebū's Su'ūd recognised that traditionally monasteries operated as a collective body. Thus, when the monks requested to be treated as such, in particular on the issue of whether they should pay *tapu* tax in order to acquire the usufruct of the possessions of deceased or departed monks, he ruled in favour of the monasteries. His task was difficult since, firstly, monastic *vaḳfs* were not permitted in Islamic law and he would therefore have had to categorise them differently and secondly, this new categorisation would have to recognise the collective character of a monastic community. The solution he gave was both practical and legitimate. He categorised monastic *vaḳfs* as family *vaḳfs*, treating the monks of a monastery as the offspring of the deceased monks. By this legal fiction, monks can be treated as members of a family and thus, they can enjoy benefits such as the exemption from the requirement of paying *tapu*, in the same way as a son inherits the *tapu* on his father's possessions. Ebū's Su'ūd, however, tried to make sure that monasteries could not revert to their previous 'misconceptions'. He insisted that monks could convert their *mülks* to *vaḳfs* individually, but that monastic *vaḳfs* remained invalid. Ebū's Su'ūd's legal fictions employed in the confiscation of monastic properties is proof of his willingness to treat the incident as an administrative issue and justifies his fame as the jurist who reconciled custom with Islamic legal theory.

However, following the arguments of the first part of this article, it would be rather adventurous to claim that all monastic/church *vaḳfs* in the Empire were allowed to operate on the basis of the same legal device. Further research on *vaḳfs* from different regions of the Empire would allow us to acquire a more comprehensive view of the institution of *vaḳf*, provided, of course, that we relinquish the idea that Islamic legal theory in the Ottoman Empire was stagnant and unresponsive to the call of society in general.

Notes

1 Richard Van Leeuwen, *Notables and Clergy in Mount Lebanon: The Khāzin Sheikhs and the Maronite Church, 1736–1840* (Leiden, 1994), 24.

2 Uriel Heyd, *Studies in Old Criminal Law*, V. L. Menage, ed., (Oxford, 1973); Joseph Schacht, *An Introduction to Islamic Law* (Oxford, 1966); Uriel Heyd, 'Some Aspects of the Ottoman Fetva', *British School of Oriental and African Studies*

32 (London, 1969), 35–56; Haim Gerber, 'Sharia, Kanun and Custom in the Ottoman Law: The Court Records of 17th-century Bursa', *International Journal of Turkish Studies* 2 (1981), 131–47.

3 Roland Jennings, 'Kadi Court and Legal Procedure in 17th century Ottoman Kayseri', *Studia Islamica* 48 (1978), 133–72; and Ibid., 'Limitations of the Judicial Powers of the Kadi in 17th century Ottoman Kayseri', *Studia Islamica* 50 (1979), 151–84.

4 Heffening, 'Waqf or Ḥabs', *EI1*, pp. 1096b–1098a.

5 Abū Yūsuf had accepted the endowment for oneself. The Shāfi'īs provide a legal device (*ḥīla*) to evade this condition: the thing which is to be the subject of the endowment is to be presented or sold at a low price to a third person. The latter can then create a trust in favour of the original owner. Ibn Ḥajar mentions a further subterfuge which is rejected by others: the *vakf* is created in favour of the children of the benefactor's father and in the deed he is described. Ibid., p. 1096b.

6 Joseph Schacht, 'Early Doctrines on Waqf', *60. doğum yılı münasebetiyle Fuad Köprülü Armağanı; Mélanges Fuad Köprülü* (Istanbul, 1953), 443–52.

7 Colin Imber, *Ebu'ssu'ud and the Islamic Legal Tradition* (forthcoming), 2

8 In particular, almost all the monastic archives in Mount Athos and in Patmos contain series of documents regulating the relationship between the Byzantine Emperor and the monasteries. Petitions for granting of privileges or favourable, for the monasteries, imperial intervention in case of a dispute with local clerical and lay dignitaries are commonly found. See, Era Vranousi, 'Byzantina eggrapha tes Mones Patmou' (Byzantine documents of Patmos monastery), (Athens, 1980), vol. 1; Nikolaos Oikonomidès, *Actes de Dionysiou = Archives de l'Athos* (Paris, 1968) vol. IV; Jacques Lefort, *Actes d' Esphigménou = Archives de l'Athos*, (Paris, 1973), vol. VI.

9 There is a extensive bibliography covering the role of the monastic communities as *pronoiarioi* (recipients of theoretically non-hereditary fiscal revenues in return for service) and the agricultural exploitation of monastic lands during the 13th and 14th centuries. See A. L. Thomadakis, *Peasant Society in the Late Byzantine Empire, a Social and Demographic Study* Princeton, 1977); P. Charanis, 'The monastic properties and the State in the Byzantine Empire', *Dumbarton Oaks Papers* 4 (1948), 53–118; G. Ostrogorsky, *Pour l'histoire de la féodalité byzantine* (Brussels, 1954), vol. 1; and *Quelques problèmes d'histoire de la paysanerie byzantine* (Brussels, 1956).

10 According to the *millet* system of autonomous self-government under religious leaders, the Orthodox Church found itself in a more powerful position than before. The church dignitaries were playing an important role when a delegation was sent to Istanbul to petition the Sultan. In the case of Patmos Monastery, the monks were collectively responsible for paying the taxes of all the *re'āyā* (peasant population, Christian or Muslim) of Patmos island, see, E. Zachariadou, 'Symbole sten historia tou Notianatolikou Aigaiou' (Contribution to the history of southeast Aegean) in E. Zachariadou, *Romania and the Turks, c.1300–c.1500* (London, 1985), 197.

11 P. Wittek and P. Lemerle, 'Recherches sur l'histoire et les status des monastères athonites sous la domination turque', *Archives d'histoire du Droit Oriental* 3 (1947), 428.

12 Ibid., p. 428.

13 Ibid., p. 430.

14 A. Fotić, 'The official explanations for the confiscation and sale of monasteries (churches) and their estates at the time of Selım II', *Turcica* 24 (1994), 43.

15 Ibid., p. 3. Ahmet Akgündüz, *Islâm Hukukunda ve Osmanlı Tatbikatında Vakıf Müessesesi* (Ankara, 1988), 173–4.

16 Fotić, 'Confiscation and Sale of Monasteries', p. 43.

17 See Eugenia Kermeli, 'The Confiscation of Monastic Properties by Selīm II 1568–1570' (unpublished Ph.D. thesis, Manchester, 1995).

18 The issue of dual ownership is dealt with by two *Şeyhü'l-islāms*, Ebū's Su'ūd in the *ḳānūnnāme* for Hungary in 1541 and Kemālpaşazāde in a *fetva*, both published in 'Ḳānūn-i Cedīd', Fuad Köprülü, ed., *Millī Tetebbü'ler Mecmuası* (Istanbul, 1913), 49–50 and 54–5 respectively. For the translation of the documents and the full argument see also, Imber, *Ebu'ssu'ud*, pp. 5–23.

19 Van Leeuwen, *Notables and Clergy*, p. 30.

20 Ibid., p. 30.

21 Ibid., p. 31.

22 For Serbia see Fotić, 'Confiscation and Sale of Monasteries', pp. 36–7; for Mount Athos Monasteries and Patmos Monastery see Kermeli, 'Confiscation', pp. 278–314.

23 See below, his *fetva* included in the *firmān* for Mount Athos monasteries.

24 Van Leeuwen, *Notables and Clergy*, p. 32.

25 For Ebū's Su'ūd's life see Imber, *Ebu'ssu'd*, pp. 6–19; Richard Cooper Repp, *The Müfti of Istanbul: A Study in the Development of the Ottoman Learned Hierarchy* (Oxford, 1986), 272–96.

26 Imber, *Ebu'ssu'ud*, pp. 20–44.

27 'Ḳānūn-i Cedīd,' ed Fuad Köprülü, *Millī Tetebbü'ler Mecmuası* (Istanbul, 1913), 49–50. For the islamization of Ottoman Laws see Halil Inalcik, 'Islamization of Ottoman laws on Land and Land Tax', *Festgabe an Josef Matuz: Osmanistik-Turkologie-Diplomatik* (Berlin, 1992), 101–18.

28 Ömer Lütfi Barkan, *Kanunlar*, pp. 298–9.

29 Imber, *Ebu'ssu'ud*, p. 74.

30 Barkan, *Kanunlar*, p. 298. The *ḳānūnnāme* for Thessaloniki and Skopie includes an addition to the one of Hungary. Ebū's Su'ūd tried to explain how 'tribute land' came into royal ownership. He does not follow the popular notion of the 'death of the proprietors'. Instead his interpretation depicts his strong sense of practicality attested throughout the monastic confiscation:

> There is another category which is neither *'uşrī* nor *ḫarācīye* as set forth above. It is called 'royal demesne' (*aradī'l mamlaka*), and in origin is *ḫarācīye*. However, if it were given to its owners (*ṣāḥib*), it would be divided on their

deaths among many heirs, so that each one of them would receive only a tiny portion. Since it would be extremely arduous and difficult, and indeed impossible to distribute and allocate each person's *ḫarāc*, the real substance (*raḳaba*) of the land has been kept for the Muslim Treasury (*beytü'l-māl-i Müslīmīn*), and it has been given to the *re'āyā* by way of loan (*'arīyya*). It has been commanded that they cultivate and till and tend vineyards, orchards and gardens, and pay the *ḫarāc-i mukāseme* and *ḫarāc-i muvazzaf* for the produce.

31 For a *fetva* dealing with the same problem see, 'Ḳānūn-i Cedīd', *MTM*, 57.

32 Patmos. File. Aa40.

33 This was the case for all the properties belonging to Patmos Monastery as depicted in the *hüccets* of sale, see, Kermeli, 'Confiscation', Appendix.

34 Ertuğrul Düzdağ, *Sheyhülislâm Ebussuud Efendi fetvaları ışığiuda 16. asır Türk hayatı* (Istanbul, 1972), D.452, 103.

35 For the entire text of the *firmān* see Kermeli, 'Confiscation', Appendix.

36 Düzdağ, *Fetvaları*, D.453, p. 103.

EIGHT

Halakha, *Sharīʿa* and Custom: A Legal Saga from Highland Yemen, 1900–1940[1]

ISAAC HOLLANDER

Introduction

Imām Yaḥyā b. al-Manṣūr Ḥamīd al-Dīn of Yemen (1869–1948) acknowledged the theory that Jews under Islam are accorded autonomy in jurisdictional matters.[2] Jewish community leaders in Yemen as elsewhere did their utmost to preserve their autonomy, at times penalising application to Gentile courts by excommunication:[3] such applications were considered a breaching of the moral fence protecting the community – *prīṣat gader*. Apart from the immediate implications for the authority of community institutions, such behaviour could be eyed by polemically minded observers as indicative of the superiority of one religion over its rival; this then was also a matter of self-respect. Despite the theory of autonomy and the efforts of community leaders, application to majority courts by Yemeni Jews was commonplace.[4]

A specific reason given in the literature for the profusion of Jewish applications to Muslim courts is a local Ottoman decree from 1875 restricting the jurisdiction of the Ṣanʿāʾ Jewish court to areas of marriage, divorce and ritual slaughter.[5] This is in addition to a series of situations where Jews in Yemen as in other Islamic lands are noted to have applied to the majority judiciary. Contracts were concluded in Muslim government courts to safeguard the legality of the proceedings, thereby assuring their recognition as accepted evidence should litigation at a government court ensue. Litigants would apply to a Muslim court when opponents refused to appear in the Jewish court or when unsuccessful there. Indeed, individuals by-passed Jewish courts altogether and initiated proceedings in Muslim courts when the law applied there was advantageous to them. The most cited example here is that of succession, where in Jewish law (*halakha*) females never share in an inheritance with a male and where the firstborn male is granted twice the share of any of his brothers. Daughters (or their representatives) and junior sons were tempted by the relatively beneficial provisions of Islamic law, in which daughters receive half a son's share and which does not apply principles of primogeniture.[6] The incentive was so powerful that Jewish courts are known to have amended their own judgements to approximate Islamic law in order to preserve their authority, and the instrument of bequest was widely employed by ageing fathers to prevent filial squabbling.[7] In the following pages a reconstruction of the legal experiences endured by a rural Jewish family from highland Yemen illustrates some of these situations and provides a sense both of the complexity of pressures under which such villagers lived and of the sophistication required of them in the conduct of their legal affairs.

Sources

Some preliminary information is in order regarding research material used and the method adopted for its interpretation, and the time and place of the events recounted. Legal documentation often discloses information on population segments not regularly treated in contemporary sources; but because documents by nature tend to contain information only immediately relevant to the specific proceedings, they have some drawbacks as research material. In *sijillāt*, documentation describing other court or arbitration proceedings experienced by the applicants does not normally appear. That other vast source for Jewish social and legal history, the documentary Cairo Genīza, being a depository for writings with some Jewish religious relevance, does not usually impart first-hand information as to what went on in contemporary *Muslim* courts.[8] Contracts in particular consist, to varying degrees, of set terminologies and formulae. Finally, whether or not conditions and instructions stipulated in a particular document were in fact carried out often remains unknown. In the Yemeni case, a method of research is at hand which mitigates some of these deficiencies. Messick has depicted how legal documentation was treasured by Yemenis in general and preserved by families for generations as evidence in the event of future litigation.[9] The significance of this circumstance for the researcher is that when documents of any such family cache are unrolled and laid out in chronological order, they tend to be mutually illuminating: events, identities and dimensions can be viewed in perspective, making it easier to hypothesise also as to the intentions of the personalities behind the names.

A further advantage of such documents is the fact that they focus attention on rural areas, where the great majority of Jews were distributed: more than forty years following Goitein's attempts to direct research to rural areas,[10] research on the Jews of Yemen still concentrates on Ṣanʿāʾ. This consideration also makes it possible to assess Jewish legal behaviour in a *rural* Muslim environment, in contrast with the Genīza documents, the Jerusalem *sijill* or the *musawwada* (the bound records) of the Jewish court of Ṣanʿāʾ, which primarily reflect a society situated in the majority's religious and administrative centres. The particular family bundle to which the following documents belong is part of a collection of documents gathered by the late Prof. S.D.Goitein in Israel during the early 1950s, to which I have graciously been granted access by the staff of the Ben-Zvi Institute (henceforth: B.Z.) as doctoral research material.

Time and Place

The document sequence presented here spans some forty years (1900–1940) and involves in a direct manner representatives of four generations of the Maddār clan of al-ʿAdhārib village. The players at centrestage are Sālim Yehūda al-Maddār; a son from his first wife, Yaḥyā Sālim; Sālim's second wife, Ḥanna; their daughters, Miriam and Salāma; Salāma's daughters, Miriam and Saʿīda; Yaḥyā Sālim's son, Sālim; and Yaḥyā's grandson, Ḥasan Sālim (consult Appendix III). The two villages central to the proceedings were situated on a spur of the Jabal Baʿdān massif, stretching eastwards from above the provincial centre Ibb in the direction of Qaʿṭaba, a small town situated near the border with the British protectorate of Aden. According to informants who grew up there, the village of al-ʿAdhārib of the 1930s and 1940s was relatively large, containing some forty houses belonging to Jews and some fifty belonging to Muslims; these were interspersed, there being no separate Jewish quarter or adjacent Jewish village.[11] The houses were stone built and multi-storied and owned by their inhabitants.[12] In the centre of town on the ridgeline was an elongated four-levelled field named al-Misbār,[13] and the neighbourhood adjacent to it was labelled Ḥāfat al-Misbār.[14] From the centre of town a track ran down the southern face of the ridge and lead, after a five minute walk, to Bīr Mawwān, the inhabitants' drinking-water source. Here stood a group of derelict structures, labelled Ḥāfat Bīr Mawwān (or simply Ḥāfat Mawwān), which included the remains of a synagogue and two or three other buildings. Like other Jewish communities al-ʿAdhārib had its own *morī* (learned person); but the central judicial authority recognised by Jews from the entire area resided a two-hour walk north-west in the exclusively Jewish village of Akamat Banī Manṣūr. This individual, Morī Hārūn Yaʿqūb al-Maṣrafī, held his post throughout the half century preceding the 1949 exodus.[15]

The Document Sequence

B.Z. 184 (February–March 1900); B.Z. 362.15 (May–June 1902)

The first two documents in our sequence can be viewed as representative of the first group of situations listed above, where Jews applied to Muslim courts for reasons of judicial security. Accompanied by his son Yaḥyā, Sālim Yehūda al-Maddār applies to a Muslim notary to ascertain in unequivocal wording, through an *iqrār* document (a document of acknowledgement), that buildings located in Ḥāfat Mawwān listed in the son's name and various books (including part of a *Tōra* scroll) are indeed his alone. Two years later Sālim has another notary draft a second *iqrār*, in which he updates the list of items over which he wished Yaḥyā's ownership to be recognised. These documents are indicative of a special relationship between Sālim and Yaḥyā, his son from his first wife, Qadriyya.

B.Z. 362.9 (20.6.1903)

Sālim's relationship with his second wife, Ḥanna (or Ghazāl), was more complex. When Sālim lost his sight (about the year 1896), Ḥanna took it upon herself to tend to his mundane needs until his death, in return for which he provided her with the right to the produce of a cow kept by a Muslim partner. Ḥanna also agreed that another cow she became entitled to would replace her marriage dues.[16] But Sālim survived longer than must have been expected. Ḥanna failed to fulfil her obligations, leaving Yaḥyā to pay for his father's maintenance. In 1903 the affair was brought before Morī Hārūn al-Maṣrafī's court.[17]

The proceedings open with Yaḥyā claiming that Ḥanna had neglected her obligations. She replied that that she was *prevented* from selling the produce of the first cow, and admitted that the second was sold, but the revenue was transferred to Sālim. Now turned claimant, Ḥanna propounded that Sālim was chargeable for her upkeep from the day he lost his sight. Witnesses impressed the court that Ḥanna did receive regular payments for the milk of the first cow, and that the second was indeed sold, but Sālim had duly transferred the money to Ḥanna. The court decided that no mutual obligations remained between the couple; that Sālim was to divorce Ḥanna and to provide her with two riyāls to cover any possible remaining debt; and that Sālim's maintenance should now be equally incumbent on all the children. Despite the court's advice that a divorce should take place, the couple agreed that Ḥanna would remain married, with no further rights to a *ketubba* (marriage contract); neither should any other mutual duties remain (B.Z. 362.9 *verso*). Yaḥyā could be pleased with this result: when Sālim should pass away, Ḥanna's *ketubba*, having been defrayed, would not be deducted from the estate; in the meantime, the burden of Sālim's upkeep would be mitigated.

B.Z. 362.10 (20.6.1903)

Capitalising on the court's instructions that the children should share payments for their father's upkeep, Yaḥyā advanced his case further still. Basing himself on clauses in Sālim's will as well as on two other documents, Yaḥyā now claimed that his father owed *him* sixteen riyāls, the sum he had already spent on Sālim's maintenance. Rather than denying this, Sālim promptly suggested covering the debt by providing Yaḥyā with the value of one of the two houses he owned in Ḥāfat Misbār. This suggestion did not satisfy Morī Hārūn: this particular house had been promised to Ḥanna's daughters in the will just presented. Sālim retorted that the will had been drawn up while he was on his deathbed (*shekhīv meraʿ*), and while Ḥanna was committed to his upkeep; since both conditions were no longer effectual, the bequest was null and void. Unless his other children fulfil the decree of the court, he declared, the house should be materialised in Yaḥyā's favour. This aroused Yaḥyā's half-sisters, who were now willing to do their part, on condition that the house was not transferred to Yaḥyā. More unexpectedly, they demanded also that two additional houses – those of Ḥāfat Mawwān – should be recognised as belonging to their father (and not to Yaḥyā), who according to them was doing his best to deprive them of their rightful share in his estate.[18] Following the hearing of evidence judgement was made in Yaḥyā's favour: the Ḥāfat Mawwān houses belonged to Yaḥyā by right of purchase and those of Ḥāfat Misbār too should be delivered to him, as the dutiful son. This verdict notwithstanding, the parties returned to court the next day in a more relaxed atmosphere to notarise an accord (B.Z. 362.10 *verso* [21.6.1903]), whereby Yaḥyā agreed that Ḥāfat Mawwān should after all be divided amongst his siblings, while his half-sisters agreed to submit to Yaḥyā's decision as to the size of the shares they would receive.

B.Ẓ. 'Farz' (21.6.1903)

Apportionment of an estate in Yemen may entail the preparation of three types of document. The first, called *ḥasr mukhallaf al-tarika*, is an initial listing and evaluation of the items in an estate, including a listing of the various sums to be subtracted from the estate before its apportionment – debts, widows' dowers (*mahr*), and various division-related expenses. On the second, the *tarkīz al-tarika*, appear a series of columns equal to the number of heirs, each of which describes the constitution of a particular share. A third document, coined *farz*, is prepared for submission to each heir; on it appears a detailed survey of that heir's relevant column on the *tarkīz*.[19] The *farz* handed to Qadriyya's children (Yaḥyā, 'Awāḍ and Sa'īda) states that although Yaḥyā was empowered to divide the estate as he saw fit, he followed to the letter his father's original will, according to which the half-sisters Miriam and Salāma were to be eligible for the small house in Ḥāfat Misbār. Yaḥyā also gave up his claim to the sixteen riyāls owed by his father, technically allowing the small house at Ḥāfat Misbār to be transferred to his half-sisters as ordained by the will. On the assumption, based on his forceful appearances in court, that Yaḥyā did not relinquish the small house and the debt solely out of goodwill, his courtesy may reflect his wish and perhaps that of his father, to check any further claims by his agnatic sisters: by compromising Ḥāfat Misbār they may have hoped to close the issue of Ḥāfat Mawwān permanently. Whether or not this was the intention, tempers in the Maddār family appeared to have abated.

B.Ẓ. 362.11 (7.8.1921)

Sālim eventually did pass away; some eighteen years following the events of 1903, strife surfaced again. Salāma's daughters (Ḥanna's grand-daughters) claimed from Yaḥyā their now deceased mother's portion in Sālim's estate. Although Hārūn al-Maṣrafi was still active the daughters did not turn to him – he had made his position clear. Instead they approached the local Jewish court of al-'Adhārib, listing four claims: Salāma's portion in the Ḥāfat Mawwān houses; her portion of the Ḥāfat al-Misbār houses; her portion of cash monies left by Sālim; and the return of a riyāl owed by Yaḥyā to one of the claimants. But *beyt dīn* (=the court of) al-'Adhārib did not alter Morī Hārūn's 1903 conclusions: the Ḥāfat Mawwān houses were Yaḥyā's by right of purchase, and the Ḥāfat Misbār houses had been divided between the successors by agreement. Yaḥyā did agree to pay half the cash claimed (four riyāls), but only following an exceptional showdown between Yaḥyā and the functionary – who was backed by a local *sayyid* – over proper judicial procedure: Yaḥyā had to be persuaded to take the defendant's oath.

B.Z. 319 (October–November 1925)

Four years later, Miriam (Yaḥyā's second half-sister and Sa'īda and Miriam's aunt) felt conditions were ripe to try her hand. Like her nieces, she charged that Yaḥyā was illegally in possession of the entire estate – the Ḥāfat Mawwān properties as well as those of Ḥāfat Misbār. To these she added the *Tōra* scroll, various other books, a cow given by Sālim to Yaḥyā to cover part of the debt waived by Yaḥyā, and various other items of property. She demanded that a new inventory and apportionment of the estate should take place. Unlike her nieces, she took her case to a local *Muslim* court. But most impressive is the sophistication of her double-edged claim: she succeeded first in proving to the functionary's satisfaction that Yaḥyā and his father were partners in all their financial endeavours; and second, that having taken place before their father's death, the 1903 estate apportionment was null and void. Yaḥyā produced yet a third time the series of documents he kept for such occasions, the latest addition to which was a *qāḍī*'s explicit confirmation of Morī Hārūn's 1903 verdict. But all to no avail – the functionary ordered the undertaking of a fresh inventory and division of all properties held by Yaḥyā at the time of his father's death. He took care to add a passage of annulment to the *verso* of *beyt dīn* al-'Adhārib's 1921 document, and Yaḥyā was duly returned the cash paid then to Salāma's heirs. The serious consideration of each piece of evidence brought before this functionary is noteworthy: while giving serious consideration to the contents of Jewish documentation read to him, he overruled an *iqrār* drafted by a Muslim *qāḍī* less uncompromising than himself. Miriam thus took full advantage of *sharʿī* norms, access to which until then may not have been practical.

B.Z. 138, B.Z. 172 (October–November 1925)

The lengthy litigation just described is accompanied by Yaḥyā's *farz* and by that belonging to the heirs of his brother ʿAwāḍ, who lived at the time in the British protectorate of Aden, in the border town of al-Ḍālaʿ. And an amendment added by our functionary to the *verso* of the 1903 *farz* prepared by Morī Hārūn summarises the new *furūz* handed to Yaḥyā's sister and two half-sisters. Both the Ḥāfat Mawwān buildings as well as those of Ḥāfat Misbār are now in fact taken into consideration, half their value being divided between the siblings in keeping with the partnership Miriam had uncovered. Yaḥyā was able to salvage in full only the *Tōra* scroll: half was rightfully his as part of the partnership and half he received in return for his participation in the actual labour of division. At the end of the day Yaḥyā was left with less than sixty-five percent of what he had considered his for more than thirty years. It is safe to presume that he had learned a lesson: when a 'customary partnership' (*shirka ʿurfiyya* – B.Z. 319, line 40) between father and son obliterated the financial source of a son's acquisitions, or when an estate was divided (even *de jure*) before the death of its owner, *iqrār* documents prepared by Muslim notaries no longer provided adequate security as proof of ownership. If Yaḥyā wished to ascertain that a portion of property as large as possible should remain in his son's family following his own death, he would have to consider alternative plans of action.

B.Z. 136 (January–February 1927 [Appendix II])

One year and three months following his defeat, Yaḥyā had a Muslim functionary draft what may best be described as a hybrid of a gift (*hiba*) and a bequest (*waṣiyya*). On the one hand, unequivocal terminology constituting declaration of offer (*ījāb*), acceptance (*qabūl*) and taking of possession (*qabḍ*)[20] makes it clear that this is a *sharʿī* gift taking effect on the spot. On the other hand, additional features suggest that this perhaps was not the case at all. First, although a gift is not limited in size,[21] this one is structured as an order of bequest – up to one third of the estate only may be bequeathed, and no bequest to *sharʿī* heirs is permitted.[22] Yaḥyā here 'donates' a third of his estate to his son's son, Ḥasan. Second, use is made of the term *mukhallaf*, estate. Third, while the nature of a gift must be precisely designated,[23] here the relevant 'donated' third is not depicted.

B.Z. 301, B.Z. 320, B.Z. 304 (March–April 1940)

Our suspicions are substantiated: in practice, the 1927 hybrid was treated as a testamentary disposition. It played a central role in the 1940 apportionment of Yaḥyā's estate following his death. A comparison between the shares listed in the three final documents of our series – the *farz* pertaining to the son (B.Z. 301), that of the grandson (who only now received his 'donated' third – B.Z. 320) and that of one of four daughters (B.Z. 304) – demonstrates that each item of property was surgically dissected into the relevant *sharʿī* shares. We also incidentally learn of an additional stratagem successfully implemented by Yaḥyā. He had instructed that a testamentary *waqf* be formed of that property which could least suffer fragmentation – such as the *Tōra* scroll which had accompanied him through half a century – to be administered, unsurprisingly, by Ḥasan. Yaḥyā seems to have learned his lesson in full – and to have acted on it.

Synthesis

The Maddār saga contains material pertinent to legal procedure, female initiative in court applications and representation in court, and execution of court judgements. The current discussion is restricted to an attempt at assessing events in terms of the circumstances explaining Jewish activity in the majority courts.

Attribution of Maddār activity in Muslim courts to an Ottoman decree is not satisfying.[24] Ottoman administration (which was only nominal in rural areas such as that which concerns us here) ceased in 1918, before the events of 1925–40. And Morī Hārūn's court was undeniably authoritative during the period of Ottoman rule. Moreover – as is below attested by B.Z. 188 – the Maddārs were active in Muslim courts well before the early 1870s, when Ottoman administration established itself in Yemen.

Can the remaining situations explaining Jewish application to Muslim courts account for the Maddārs' behaviour? That Jews applied to Muslim courts to avail themselves of favourable *sharʿī* norms is indisputable. Miriam's claim, which necessitated a clear understanding of the relevant *sharʿī* principle according to which an estate can be apportioned only upon the death of the praepositus,[25] is a case in point. Yet it is a mistake to presuppose that application to a Muslim functionary was invariably accompanied by strict application of Islamic law – as is exemplified by the *iqrār* document of 1902 (B.Z. 362.15). In the second half of that document, Sālim elaborates on how his property should be divided after his death. This is not a will in the *sharʿī* sense, which is limited to a third of one's property and restricted to those who are not legal heirs. Nor is this a *sharʿī* gift: the requisite wording is missing and Sālim obviously does not intend to relinquish his property on the spot (cf. above, B.Z. 136). It seems that just as the Muslim notaries of our *iqrār* documents do not make it their business to question Sālim as to the accuracy of his statements, so too this particular notary makes no apparent effort to have Sālim's instructions conform to *sharʿī* principles. We know that Sālim prepared a will in a Jewish court of law (see above, B.Z. 362.10); it is a reasonable supposition that the second part of this document is intended to provide legal sanction – customary legal sanction – to that will. As a form of evidence creating an obligation without regard to the cause of its origin,[26] the *iqrār* was the obvious tool to employ in providing such sanction.

More outstanding still is B.Z. 136, the document anchored in scrupulous *sharʿī* terminology yet defying a single *sharʿī* definition. This document brings to mind a situation observed by Prof. N. Anderson amongst the Shāfiʿī population of southern Arabia. The irrevocable undertaking (*nadhr*) of a gift (*hiba*) made to become operative three days before the death of the *nādhir* was widely used as an improved mechanism in outflanking *sharʿī* succession laws and directing the division of one's property.[27] The advantages of such a *nadhr* over a *sharʿī* bequest (*waṣiyya*) to that end are those of the promised gift: the sum transferable is unlimited and transfer of property to a legal heir is allowed. Its relative attractiveness over *waqf dhurrī* (family *waqf*) is likewise similar to that of a gift: rights of disposal (*taṣarruf*) over the property remain unaffected. The advantage of the *nadhr* over the *hiba* itself lies in the fact that there is no immediate effectuation: the *nādhir* enjoys complete ownership for practically his entire life. Yaḥyā Sālim's version of *hiba* seems even more advantageous than Anderson's *nadhr*: in the event the *hiba* itself should not take effect for any reason (the annulment of the 1903 apportionment here comes to mind), it would still be possible to relate to the document as a bequest – as indeed was done in 1940.

But if Yaḥyā's primary intention was reflected by the 1940 treatment of the document as a *waṣiyya*, why was the *hiba* terminology necessary at all?[28] A reasonable explanation is at hand. Were it not for his past experiences, Yaḥyā presumably would have preferred drafting a Jewish bequest, which is considered a form of donation in that an entire estate can be apportioned by the praepositus (and during his lifetime) and in which the praepositus retains the right to the fruits of the property until his death.[29] Indeed, Yaḥyā is likely actually to have prepared such a will (just as his father had drafted a will and an *iqrār* to the same effect); but a *Sharīʿa* court could not be expected to effectuate such broad instructions. Yaḥyā may here be using Islamic terminology to accommodate the Jewish notion of bequest, taking care to keep to conditions and limitations enforceable by a *Sharīʿa* court: the 1940 treatment of the document then need not reflect Yaḥyā's primary intention at all.[30] According to this explanation, our Islamic document defies a single *sharʿī* definition because it reflects the *rabbinic* idea of bequest, which offers the testator, in a manner of speaking, the best of both worlds.[31]

It is claimed that as far as the matter was dependent on the Yemeni Jewish courts, Jewish law was adhered to.[32] Was customary behaviour restricted to Muslim functionaries, or would Jewish courts diverge from pertinent normative directives even where this *cannot* be attributed to an effort to prevent application of one of the parties to a Muslim court? There was nothing blatantly amiss from a halakhic viewpoint with the legal proceedings which took place in Morī Hārūn al-Maṣrafī's courtroom as elaborated in B.Z. 362.10. As has just been mentioned, in contrast to Islamic law, an entire estate *can* be apportioned by the praepositus, and during his lifetime. The court is justifiable also in approving the cancellation of Sālim's will so as to be able to transfer to Yaḥyā the house promised to Ḥanna's daughters: maintenance of a father is indeed incumbent on the children, out of his own capital, if available;[33] a death-bed bequest is retractable upon recovery of the ill man;[34] and if a properly stipulated condition upon which a gift was made contingent is not fulfilled, the gift is null and void.[35] As for the following day's renewed apportionment, when a man deeds all his property as a gift to one of his sons, he '… has merely appointed him by this act as the administrator … the father meant merely to have his brothers abide by that son's decision'.[36]

In B.Z. 362.9 too, Morī Hārūn appeared to have been following rabbinic tradition, when having heard that Ḥanna had been living without a *ketubba* he decided that Sālim must divorce her and make her a token payment, even though he had already paid her dower. It is an iron rule that a man ' … is forbidden to abide with his wife even for one hour without a *ketubbah*',[37] and that a *ketubba* is payable only upon divorce or the husband's death.[38] Indeed, some Gaonic authorities accorded a minimalist 'statutory *ketubba*' sum (*'iqqar ketubba*) even to wives ineligible for their *ketubba* moneys, such as those denying themselves to their husbands ('recalcitrant' wives, or *mōrdōt* [s. *mōredet*]); amongst other reasons this was done so as to dispel any doubts that the marriage retroactively be considered illicit or that the husband's consummations during the marriage should be considered fornication.[39] Yet contrary to these principles, Morī Hārūn immediately following his decision sanctioned an agreement arrived at by the couple stating that the woman should remain married and at the same time stating that no legal obligations, financial or physical, remained between them. In deference to the principles just listed, should not payment of the two riyāls have been deferred until death or divorce? The tendency of judges to sanction agreements between disputants, even when these were contrary to normative law, is identifiable in courts serving tribal Muslims.[40] It appears that a similar state of affairs existed in Morī Hārūn's court as well.

How does *beyt dīn* al-ʿAdhārib fare here? Morī Yaḥyā seems justifiable in his protests as to the procedure followed there. An appearance made by his sister in court opposed the *Halakha* on any of three counts: she was a lone witness,[41] next of kin,[42] and a woman.[43] In addition, following Yaḥyā's refusal to take an oath, the court was able to transfer the onus of the oath to the claimant,[44] and instead chose to exert more pressure on Yaḥyā. Finally, following his oath, instead of being freed from payment,[45] Yaḥyā found himself agreeing to pay half of the claimed sum.

Clearly, the Maddārs encountered tensions between theory and practice in both Muslim and Jewish courts. An assumption that Muslim and Jewish courts each acted according to standard codes would thus be oversimplistic. The realisation of this point is crucial to our debate: when in practice – by way of example – the majority society itself does not regularly offer daughters their rightful *sharʿī* share, 'pull' and 'push' factors explaining applications to the majority judiciary tend to be neutralised. Care must therefore be taken to identify the 'level of normativity' offered by any specific court or functionary in practice at a particular point in time, before appeal is made to the common presumption that Jews would apply to Muslim courts to take advantage of relatively favourable *sharʿī* principles.

Do our documents reflect the fact that Jewish courts sometimes provided women with their *sharʿī* shares in an estate so as to pre-empt application to Muslim courts? To a limited extent. Such a motive may afford additional insight into Yaḥyā's behaviour in 1903 (when he dropped his claim of the sixteen riyāls and re-apportioned the Ḥāfat Misbār edifices even though the court ruled that these should revert to him alone), but is insufficient as an explanation for later Maddār activity. In the face of the Maddār women's steadfastness (or that of their backers), Yaḥyā's preliminary actions in 1927 were aimed not at placating his daughters but at reinforcing the share of his male issue. Moreover, these actions were performed from the start in Muslim courts. (The same is true of Sālim's three *iqrār* documents.) The irony is plain: only by conducting his affairs in Muslim courts could Yaḥyā hope to salvage something of the basic halakhic axiom that females do not inherit in the presence of males.

Goitein has remarked in his article on the village of al-Gades that rural Jews and Muslims were drawn together in the face of increased government interference with tribal law.[46] Can intensified Maddār activity in Muslim courts as of the mid-1920s be attributed to changes in what the Muslim courts themselves were offering applicants, Muslims and Jews alike? Chronologically, the assertion of *sharʿī* principles attested to does coincide with Imām Yaḥyā's policy of enforcement of Islamic law as the only legal code in Yemen, reflecting the political and military efforts made throughout his reign to strengthen his hold on remote rural areas.[47] A clear and increasing bias towards the *Sharīʿa* can be detected over the years in the proceedings experienced by the Maddārs. The 1925 functionary justifiably did not recognise the validity of a division carried out before the property owner's death; but even he applied *sharʿī* principles selectively. While the property was divided into the correct *sharʿī* shares (sevenths in this case), an effort was at the same time made to preserve the integrity of each individual item: no mention is made of one of the two Ḥāfat Misbār houses in the 1925 *furūz* pertaining to the two brothers. One can only conjecture that Salāma's heirs and Miriam accepted joint ownership of this house in return for a smaller share (if any) in the Ḥāfat Mawwān houses. This is supportable by the functionary's explicit statement (on the *verso* of the 1903 *farz*) that the two houses of Ḥāfat Misbār were redivided between the sisters. In the 1940 division of Yaḥyā's property, by way of comparison, each item was surgically divided (into ninths). Again, there is no insistence on Muslim witnesses in the 1925 documents; in one of the documents no document witnesses are mentioned at all. This contrasts with the events of 1940, where Jewish witnesses (when they appear) only complement the Muslim ones. The more active part played by central institutions is evident again in the fact that the 1940 division of the estate was ordered by the Ibb *ḥākim*, whereas the 1925 re-apportionment resulted from the initiative of one of the litigants. Finally the *iqrār*, the document genre classically providing legal security and through which such practices as 'customary partnerships' found support in legal documentation, no longer appears in the Maddār papers, presumably in keeping with its diminishing value under the new conditions.

There is another reason why it may be most realistic to consider even such classic applications as Miriam's in a more localised, inter-confessional context of practices, rather than in terms of clear-cut contrasts between Islamic and Jewish law. The explanations given for Jewish applications to Muslim courts are similar to those encouraging tribal Muslims to apply to the official government or *Sharīʿa* courts of law in the twentieth century Middle East. In Libya, heirs who felt wronged (and others whose position in tribal society was weak) preferred government courts over the traditional methods of arbitration.[48] In that same society the *Sharīʿa* court was applied to for reasons of legal security: when divorce occurred out of court, the parties applied to the court to acquire declaratory judgements to pre-empt future claims in the *Sharīʿa* court.[49] More specifically, the hypothesis is corroborated in Yemen itself by Martha Mundy's observations in Wādī Ḍahr (Hamdān): 'Where women challenge men, the cases ... are fought primarily before Islamic legal authority.'[50] On another plane too, Miriam's actions recall patterns of behaviour typical of rural Yemeni Muslims. Rarely is the share of a daughter in her father's estate transferred to her at an early stage of her marital career; but during her middle life she would fight to move her property from under her brother's management.[51] The Maddār testators' actions too are consistent with behaviour patterns in tribal Muslim societies in the present century. Thus, for example, Judean desert Bedouin would evade *sharʿī* inheritance laws by the division of property between the sons, with their agreement, during the father's lifetime.[52] Such behaviour is observable amongst Yemeni Muslims as well.[53] And this was precisely what Sālim Yehūda attempted to do in 1903. As for the *hiba*, *waṣiyya* and *waqf* – the more sophisticated methods Yaḥyā employed to the same end following the constraint of customary freedom of movement – these are the time-proven techniques by which *sharʿī* laws of inheritance were avoided by Muslims.[54]

Conclusions

The reconstitution of the Maddār saga using the dormant document cache salvaged by Goitein demonstrates the relevance of Yemeni legal documentation for historical research: even deeds and contracts consisting largely of set formulae take their place in the narrative. But there are more specific impressions. First, neither the theory that Jews were accorded legal autonomy or the moralistic charge of *prīṣat gader* accurately depict matters in al-ʿAdhārib. In practice, application to Muslim functionaries was *necessary*; there often was no satisfactory alternative. Second, prior to the increasing accessibility of *sharʿī* norms in the courts in particular, both rural Jews and rural Muslims tended to transfer property to their issue in keeping with patriarchal ideals. This complements other shared customary practices which have been identified in the field of marriage and divorce.[55] Most impressive is the range of interacting and conflicting principles and practices encountered in al-ʿAdhārib village, and the associated fact that litigating individuals were sufficiently appreciative of the subtleties and dynamics of this interplay of *Sharīʿa*, *Halakha* and custom to make the most of a given situation at any point in time. But even this statement fails to accord the Maddārs their full due: one last Maddār document (B.Z. 188 [Appendix I]) suggests that some of these villagers knew how to put to use normative differences between the Islamic schools of law themselves. This adds a further dimension to an observation made above: before appeal is made to the model in which Jews applied to Muslim courts to avail themselves of favourable *sharʿī* principles, not only must the 'level of normativity' of the particular functionary be identified, but so must the school of law the norms of which ostensibly are being applied.

Appendix I: B.Z. 188 (January–February 1845)

This document involves rights of 'pre-emption' (*shufʿa*), according to which an individual may substitute himself for a buyer of land over which he is accorded priority, while refunding the price of the land to the buyer. For pre-emption to take effect, no adjudication is necessary beyond the pre-emptor's statement of intent, the money need not yet have been transferred and the outside buyer's presence is not required.[56] Sālim Yehūda's father – Yehūda – was intent on exercising his right of pre-emption over the purchase by another Jew of parts of a building adjacent (*bi-jiwār*) to his own. Because of difficulties posed by the outside buyer, Yehūda turned to a Muslim legal expert who was able both to pass judgement and to order that buyer's imprisonment. At first sight this seems to be no more than a further example of the classic axiom that Jews applied to the Muslim judiciary because of its executive capabilities: Jewish law is similar here to the Zaydī principle recognising the right of a neighbour to pre-emption.[57] This explanation would have been sufficient were it not for the fact that the proceedings took place in an exclusively Shāfiʿī area of Yemen; and according to that school, neighbourhood is meaningless in the context of pre-emption – the right of pre-emption is applicable only for a co-owner of the sold property.[58] Plausibly, Yehūda al-Maddār needed to have made an extra effort to appeal to a functionary applying Zaydī principles;[59] this is suggestive of an awareness of differences between the two Islamic schools of law.

Appendix II: B.Z. 136[60]

Arabic Transcription

عبد [اللـ]ـه بن محمد المنصوب وفقه ا[لـ]ـله

وقع صدور الهبة من الواهب
لدي بتأريخ شهر رجب سنة

١٣٤٥

الحمد لله

[١] حضر لدي الذمي يحيى سالم المدار طايعا مخطار ساعيا علا قدميه جايز تصرفه
[٢] فيما هوا شرعا ووهب لولد ولده الذمي حسن سالم وذلك من ثلث مخلفه
[٣] جميع من كل ما يملكه وهبا صحيحا واذن الواهب لولد ولده بالقبض
[٤] والتصرف بالطوع والرضا والنفوذ والامضا بقول الواهب
[٥] وهبته وقول الموهوب له الذمي حسن سالم لنفسه قبلت وتخلا
[٦] الواهب عن ثلث مخلفه وصار ثلث مخلفه ملكا وحقا ويدا
[٧] لولد ولده الذمي حسن سالم وهبا لا يرد ولا يستثنا عليه
[٨] بتأريخ شهر رجب الاصب سنة خمسة واربعين وثلاث ماءة والف
[٩] سنة ١٣٤٥ بحضر من شهد الولد صالح عبد [اللـ]ـه المنصوب ومحمد ناجي
[١٠] يحيى السميري وخالد مانع السميري وآخرون وكفا با[لـ]ـله شهيدا

بسم الله
[١١] هذا خط عبد [اللـ]ـه محمد المنصوب معروف
[١٢] عندي خطه وشخصه علا شروط
[١٣] القسمة[؟] في الهبة المعتبرة[؟] شرعا
[١٤] بتأريخه رجب سنة ١٣٤٥
[١٥] عبد الله [الجلال...؟]

Translation

[Signature:] ʿAbd [Alla]h b. Muḥammad al-Manṣūb – may A[llah] grant him success

The effectuation of the gift (*hiba*) on the part of the donator (*wāhib*) transpired before me on the date: the month of Rajab, year 1345 [=January–February 1927].[61]

Praise be to Allah

1. Yaḥyā Sālim al-Maddār the *dhimmī* appeared before me willingly, of his own free choice, moving on his own two feet [and] able to dispose freely
2. in such matters as are lawful;[62] and he granted his son's son, Ḥasan Sālim the *dhimmī*, out of a third of his estate (*mukhallaf*)
3. [which consists of] everything he owns, a valid gift. The donator authorised his son's taking of possession (*qabḍ*)[63]
4. and [right of] disposal. [This was effectuated] of [his own] free will and agreement and [his] executive ability and endorsement, by means of the donator's utterance
5. 'I have donated it' (*wahabtuhu*) and the first hand utterance of the donatory, the *dhimmī* Ḥasan Sālim, 'I have received' (*qabaltu*).[64] The
6. donator relinquished a third of his estate; the ownership, rights and physical possession of a third of his estate reverted
7. to his son's son, the *dhimmī* Ḥasan Sālim, [as] a donation which may not be returned and from which nothing may be extracted.[65]
8. [The document was written] on the date: the month of Rajab 'The Pouring' (*al-aṣabb*),[66] year thirteen hundred and forty five
9. – the year 1345 – in the presence of those who testified: the youth[67] Ṣāliḥ ʿAbd [Alla]h al-Manṣūb and Muḥammad Nājī
10. Yaḥyā al-Sumayrī and Khālid Mānīʿ al-Sumayrī and others. Allah is a sufficient witness.

[Top right corner:][68] In the name of Allah

11. This is the script of ʿAbd [Alla]h Muḥammad al-Manṣūb whose
12. script and person are known to me, concerning the conditions
13. of the apportionment [and] relating to the donation that must be considered lawful.
14. [Written] on its date: Rajab, year 1345.
15. [Signature:] ʿAbd Allah [al-Jalāl ... ?]

Appendix III – the Maddār Family Tree[69]

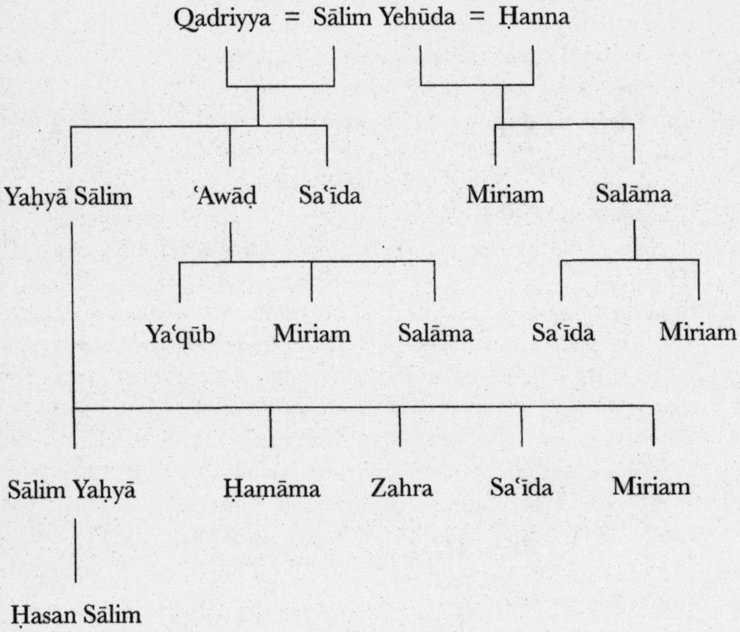

Notes

Archival Sources

Ben-Zvi Institute, Jerusalem (Goitein collection) 136; 138; 172; 184; 188; 301; 304; 319; 320; 362.9; 362.10; 362.11; 362.15; '*Farz*' (not numbered)

Informants

Mrs. Shūdhia Maddār (Elyakhin, 21.9.94)
Mr. Abraham Ṣā'igh (Elyakhin, 21.9.94)

1 This essay is a rendering of a seminar paper written under the supervision of Prof. Aharon Layish (I. Hollander, *Halakha, Sharīʿa ū-Minhag: Sīpūr Mishpaṭī me-Harey Teyman* [unpublished seminar paper, Hebrew University of Jerusalem, 1994]). I wish to thank him for taking the time to read the essay and for his suggestions. I also wish to acknowledge financial support extended by the Morris M. Pulver scholarship fund and by the Prof. S.D. Goitein memorial prize commitee. Special thanks are due to the informants who provided background information on al-ʿAdhārib village. Finally, I extend my gratitude to the directors of the Ben-Zvi Institute in Jerusalem for allowing me to study the Yemeni documentation gathered by the late Prof. S.D. Goitein; to my teacher, Prof. Menahem Ben-Sasson for introducing me to the collection; and to Mr. Robert Attal of the institute library for his encouragement and for his expert assistance.

2 Y. Tobi, 'Ha-Qehilla ha-Yehūdīt be-Teyman', in Y. Tobi (ed.), *Mōreshet Yehūdey Teyman: ʿĪyyūnīm we-Meḥqarīm (Legacy of the Jews of Yemen: Studies and Researches)* (Jerusalem, 1976), 106, 109–10.

3 S. D. Goitein, *A Mediterranean Society, Vol. 2: The Community* (Berkeley and Los Angeles, 1971), 401; I. Hollander, '*Ibrā*' in Highland Yemen: Two Jewish Divorce Settlements', *Islamic Law and Society*, 2 (1995), 14–15 notes 44–5.

4 S. D. Goitein, "Al ha-Ḥayyīm ha-Ṣībūriyyim shel ha-Yehūdīm be-Ereṣ Teyman', in M. Ben-Sasson (ed.), *Ha-Teymanīm: Hīsṭorya, Sidrey Ḥevra, Ḥayyey ha-Rūaḥ (The Yemenites: History, Communal Organisation, Spiritual Life)* (Jerusalem, 1983), 204; Y. Nini, *Teyman we-Ṣiyyōn: ha-Reqaʿ ha-Medīnī, ha-Ḥevratī we-ha-Rūḥanī le-ʿAliyyōt ha-Rīʾshōnōt mi-Teyman, 1800–1914* (Jerusalem, 1982), 133–4.

5 Y. Ratzaby, 'Yehūdey Teyman Taḥat Shilṭōn ha-Tūrkīm', *Sinai*, 64 (1969), 53–77; Y. Tobi, *Yehūdey Teyman ba-Meʾa ha-19 (The Jews of Yemen in the 19th Century)* (Tel-Aviv, 1976), 95; Y. Tobi, 'Qehīlat Yehūdey Teyman Taḥat Shilṭōn ha-Tūrkīm (1872–1918)', *Kiwwunīn*, 15 (1982), 137–9; Nini, *Teyman we-Ṣiyyōn*, pp. 80–4.

6 Goitein, *The Community*, pp. 398–9; cf. H. Z. Hirschberg, "Arka'ot shel Goyyim Bīmey ha-Ge'ōnīm', in Z. Werheftig and S. Y. Zavin (eds), *Mazkeret le-Zekher Maran ha-Rav Yiṣḥaq Isaac ha-Lewī Hertzog* (Jerusalem, 1962), 494; see Hollander, '*Ibrā*' in Highland Yemen', pp. 6–9, for additional incentives.

7 Goitein, *The Community*, p. 399; Tobi, 'Ha-Qehilla ha-Yehūdīt be-Teyman', pp. 114–15.

8 S. D. Goitein, 'The Interplay of Jewish and Islamic Laws', in Bernard S. Jackson (ed.), *Jewish Law in Legal History and the Modern World* (Leiden, 1980), 76.

9 B. Messick, 'Literacy and the Law: Documents and Document Specialists in Yemen', in Daisy Hilse Dwyer (ed.), *Law and Islam in the Middle East* (New York, 1990), 62–5.

10 Goitein, "Al ha-Ḥayyīm ha-Ṣībūriyyim', p. 199.

11 This description of al-ʿAdhārib is a synthesis of information transmitted to me by Mr. Abraham Ṣāʾigh and Mrs. Shūdhia Maddār in separate interviews (21.9.94).

12 Cf. the situation in nearby al-Nādib village, where buildings were leased from landlords (Hollander, '*Ibrā*ʾ in Highland Yemen', p. 12 note 33).

13 *Misbār*: level (ground) – M. Piamenta, *Dictionary of Post-Classical Yemeni Arabic, pt. 1* (Leiden, 1990), 213.

14 *Ḥāfa*: neighbourhood, quarter – Piamenta, *Dictionary, pt.1*, p. 99.

15 See a divorce settlement drafted by him in 1948, in Hollander, '*Ibrā*ʾ in Highland Yemen', pp. 10–15.

16 These could have included maintenance payments (*nafaqa*) during the marriage and the sums listed in the *ketubba* (the marriage contract), normally payable by the husband upon his demise or divorce.

17 Morī Hārūn had arrived in al-ʿAdhārib to conduct the proceedings.

18 It should be recalled that in the presence of a son daughters have no 'rightful' share in an estate (Maimonides, *The Code of Maimonides, book thirteen: The Book of Civil Laws*, translated by Jacob J. Rabinowitz [New Haven and London, 1949], 260 [=*Naḥalōt* (laws of inheritance), 1:2]), though rabbinic law grants unmarried daughters the right to maintenance (ibid., p. 273 [=*Naḥalōt*, 5:2]).

19 B. Messick, *Transactions in Ibb: Economy and Society in a Yemeni Highland Town* (Ph.D. dissertation, Princeton University, 1978), 370–6.

20 See Y. Linant de Bellefonds, *Traité de droit musulman comparé, Vol. 3* (Paris et La Haye, 1973), 319–20; 359.

21 Yaḥyā b. Sharaf b. Murī al-Nawawī, *Minhāj al-ṭālibīn*, edited by L. W. C. van den Berg, with French translation (Batavia, 1883), vol. 2, 194; Linant de Bellefonds, *Traité*, p. 356.

22 N. Coulson, *Succession in the Muslim Family* (London, 1971), 213–14.

23 Linant de Bellefonds, *Traité*, p. 346.

24 Indeed, the nature of the decree itself remains obscure; I have seen deeds of sale drawn up in the early 1880s by the Jewish court of Ṣanʿāʾ.

25 Coulson, *Succession*, p. 195.

26 J. Schacht, *An Introduction to Islamic Law* (Oxford, 1964), 151.

27 J. N. D. Anderson, *Islamic Law in Africa* (London, 1972), 17 note 2; 30, 370.

28 I thank Dr. Mohammad Fadel for pressing this point.

29 J. Caro, *Shulhan Arukh*, edited by Z. Preisler and S. Havlin (Jerusalem,

1993), 664 (=*Shulḥan ʿArūkh, Ḥōshen Mishpaṭ*, 257:1).

30 In fact, the 1940 *furūz* themselves perceivably may not even be accurate reflections of what actually occurred. Martha Mundy's call for caution about assuming that *furūz* reflect the precise way in which property was transmitted between family members must be kept in mind (Martha Mundy, 'Women's Inheritance of Land in Highland Yemen', *Arabian Studies*, 5 [1979], 174). In the absence of post–1940 Maddār documents, a conclusive picture of the way the property was divided in practice is evasive here – in contrast to the 1903 and 1925 allocation and re-allocation of Sālim Maddār's estate: there the document sequence supplies ample evidence that several of the functionaries' rulings had not been carried out (Hollander, *Halakha, Sharīʿa ū-Minhag*, p. 140).

31 The expertise of Jews applying to Muslim courts in couching Jewish legal theory in Islamic terms is also discernable in divorce settlements drafted in majority courts (consult Hollander, '*Ibrāʾ* in Highland Yemen', p. 6).

32 Y. Tobi, 'Yerūshat Nashīm ba-Ḥevra ha-Yehūdīt we-ha-Mūslimīt', in S. Seri (ed.), *Bat-Teyman (Daughter of Yemen)* (Riʾshōn le-Ṣiyyōn, 1994), 39.

33 Maimonides, *The Code of Maimonides, book fourteen: The Book of Judges*, translated by Abraham M. Hershman (New Haven, 1949), 154–155 (=*Mamrīm* [laws concerning rebels], 6:3).

34 Maimonides, *The Code of Maimonides, book twelve: The Book of Acquisition*, translated by Isaac Klein (New Haven and London, 1951), 141 (=*Zekhiyya ū-Matana* [laws concerning original acquisition and gifts], 8:23).

35 Ibid., p. 118 (=*Zekhiyya ū-Matana*, 3:6).

36 Ibid., p. 128 (=*Zekhiyya ū-Matana*, 6:2).

37 Maimonides, *The Code of Maimonides, book four: The Book of Women*, translated by Isaac Klein (New Haven and London, 1972), 64 (=*Īshūt* [laws of marriage], 10:10).

38 Ibid., p. 99 (=*Īshūt*, 16:3).

39 M. A. Friedman, 'Divorce upon the Wife's Demand as Reflected in Manuscripts from the Cairo Geniza', in Bernard S. Jackson (ed.), *The Jewish Law Annual [vol. 4]* (Leiden, 1981), 108.

40 A. Layish, *Divorce in the Libyan Family* (Jerusalem, 1991), 187.

41 Maimonides, *The Book of Judges*, p. 91 (=ʿ*Edūt* [laws concerning evidence], 5:1).

42 Ibid., p. 110 (=ʿ*Edūt*, 13:1).

43 Ibid., p. 100 (=ʿ*Edūt*, 9:2).

44 Maimonides, *The Book of Civil Laws*, p. 191 (=*Ṭōʿen we-Niṭʿan* [laws concerning pleading], 1:4).

45 Ibid., pp. 190–1 (=*Ṭōʿen we-Niṭʿan*, 1:3).

46 S. D. Goitein, 'Portrait of a Yemenite Weaver's Village', *Jewish Social Studies*, 17 (1955), 16–17.

47 M. M. Wenner, *Modern Yemen* (Baltimore, 1967), 65–6.

48 J. Davis, *Libyan Politics: Tribe and Revolution* (London, 1987), 223.

49 Layish, *Divorce in the Libyan Family*, pp. 182–3.

50 Martha Mundy, *Domestic Government: Kinship, Community and Polity in North Yemen* (London, 1995), 53.

51 Mundy, 'Women's Inheritance', pp. 165–70.

52 A. Layish and A. Shmueli, 'Custom and Sharīʿa in the Bedouin Family According to Legal Documents from the Judaean Desert', *Bulletin of the School of Oriental and African Studies*, 42 (1979), 39.

53 I. Hollander, 'Parashat "Araṣa mi-Ḥujariyya', in Y. Tobi (ed.), *Le-Rosh Yōsef: Meḥqarīm be-Ḥokhmat Yisraʾel* (Jerusalem, 1995), 537 note 90.

54 A. Layish, 'The Family *Waqf* and the *Sharʿī* Law of Succession', in G. Baer and G. Gilbar (eds), *Studies in the Muslim Waqf* (Oxford, forthcoming), 16–17; Messick, *Transactions in Ibb*, pp. 378–84.

55 See Hollander, '*Ibrāʾ* in Highland Yemen', p. 9.

56 Al-Nawawī, *Minhāj*, pp. 122–3.

57 Maimonides, *The Book of Acquisition*, p. 198 (=*Shekhenīm* [laws concerning neighbours], 12:4–5); cf. the Zaydī principle in Ḥusayn b. Aḥmad al-Ḥusayn al-Sayāghī al-Ḥaymī, *Kitāb al-rawḍ al-naḍīr sharḥ majmūʿ al-fiqh al-kabīr* (Cairo, 1348), vol. 3, 335–9. For a description of how the 1962 Republican replacement of Zaydī rule affected *shufʿa* claims in the Ibb area see Messick, *Transactions in Ibb*, p. 358.

58 Al-Nawawī, *Minhāj*, p. 120.

59 The events occurred during what was a period of drastically weakened Imāmic control over Shāfiʿī Lower Yemen (see B. Messick, *The Calligraphic State: Textual Domination and History in a Muslim Society* [Berkeley and Los Angeles, 1993], 49).

60 In transcribing the document, for the reader's convenience, I have added diacritics where omitted by the scribe. Inconclusive readings of text are indicated by a question mark. Noteworthy is the writer's inconsistent use of Yemeni script: the lower diacritics added to the dentals *dāl* and *ṭāʾ* (lines 6–7, 9); the stroke above the *ḍād* (line 4); and the symbol above the *sīn* (lines 2, 5, 7, 8). For more details on Yemeni Arabic script, consult Piamenta, *Dictionary, pt.1*, viii–x. In the English translation, terms of special interest are transliterated and parenthesized.

61 This is the functionary's own summary of the contents of the document.

62 The donator's capacity to contract and dispose (*taṣarruf*) is a precondition for the validity of a gift (Linant de Bellefonds, *Traité*, p. 327).

63 Another condition for the validity of a gift is the authorization extended by the donator to the donatee to take possession of the donated object (ibid., p. 361).

64 *Ījāb* (offer) and *qabūl* (acceptance) are two of the three terminological requisites validating a contract, the third being the taking of possession (*qabḍ/yad*) (al-Nawawī, *Minhāj*, p. 193 and p. 195; al-Ḥaymī, *Kitāb al-rawḍ al-naḍīr*, 381, 383), which is twice mentioned in this document (lines 3 and 6).

65 In principle, a donation is irrevocable (Linant de Bellefonds, *Traité*, p. 388; al-Ḥaymī, *Kitāb al-rawḍ al-naḍīr*, p. 384). One exception to this rule

according to the Shāfiʿīs is the gift to a grandchild (Linant de Bellefonds, *Traité*, p. 406): the instructions specified in the text possibly indicate that our functionary was not trained in the Shāfiʿī tradition.

66 This epithet is said to relate to God's bestowment of mercy upon his servants during the month of Rajab (see M. J. Kister, 'Rajab is the Month of God ... : A Study in the Persistence of an Early Tradition', *Israel Oriental Studies*, 1 [1971], 200).

67 The term *walad* is a common honorific title (M. Piamenta, *Dictionary of Post-Classical Yemeni Arabic, pt. 2* (Leiden, 1991), 532); it particularly becomes Ṣāliḥ ʿAbd Allah al-Manṣūb, in that he seems to have been the son of our functionary, ʿAbd Allah Muḥammad al-Manṣūb.

68 The following passage is an attestation as to the identity of the functionary, added by a personality who must have been more widely acknowledged than the writer himself. Messick ('Literacy and the Law', p. 70) explains that 'Documents seem to stand alone as pieces of evidence, only because of the judge's intimate acquaintance with the local men who produce them'. See Messick, *The Calligraphic State*, pp. 231–7 for an analysis of the Yemeni 'spiral text'.

69 The diagram includes the names only of those household members alluded to in the essay.

PART 4

Modern Islamic Law

NINE

Ḍarūra In Modern Islamic Law: The Case Of Organ Transplantation

BIRGIT KRAWIETZ

Scanning through twentieth-century *fatwā* collections, we encounter a remarkable number of modern developments which call for new legal solutions (*ijtihād*). The occurrence of these kinds of problems is discernable throughout various fields of law under which these new topics are subsumed by the religious legal experts.

Although there is the voluminous official collection *al-Fatāwā al-islāmiyya min dār al-iftā' al-miṣriyya*[1] which contains legal dicta of the Egyptian Great *Muftīs* and also some Saudi Arabian *fatwā* collections[2] which comprise single or collective *fatwās* given by the most eminent religious scholars of the country like Ibn Bāz and Ibn Jibrīn, the great majority of legal dicta produced within the framework of state-run *iftā'* institutions which have been set up in different Arab countries since the last century are still not available for convenient extensive research. Therefore, a systematic analysis of this *fatwā* material with regard to *ijtihād* topics[3] in general is yet to appear. Furthermore, a comparison of the treatment of these issues in different countries, between *muftīs* and between statements of other scholars, is also needed. The *fatwā* material – official or non-official – available up to now nevertheless allows us to recognise certain general developments.

For instance a two-volume, thousand-page PhD thesis under the title 'The Tunisian *Fatwās* of the Fourteenth Islamic Century' was submitted to the Shariah Faculty of Zaytūna University in 1406/1986. The author, Muḥammad b. Yūnus al-Swīsī, included all the official Tunisian *fatwās* of the period between 1883 and 1979 which he could acquire from the government authorities. Besides an ongoing preoccupation with traditional topics, the impact of the modern world – accelerated by the presence of French colonial power – is much in evidence throughout the work. The 'keeping up of the *fatwās* with the modern novelties (*musāyarat al-fatāwā li'l-mustaḥdathāt al-ʿaṣriyya*, also referred to as *mubtakarāt*, *mukhtaraʿāt* and *muktashafāt*)[4] is detectable in four major fields: novelties concerning food consumption and drinking; modern financial transactions; modern medical practices and technical novelties.[5]

The various developments constantly arising in these fields generally met and continue to be met with great public interest; however, in some cases there is also hesitation, doubt and even resistance. Swīsī's collection, as with the *fatwās* of the famous Muḥammad Rashīd Riḍā which he edited in *al-Manār*, bear testimony to the fact that public interest (*maṣlaḥa*) plays a considerable role in legitimising many of the products and procedures of modern life. This trend has been repeatedly noticed. Discussing modern reformers like Rashīd Riḍā, Kerr underlines that the 'element in their jurisprudence which the modernists have particularly seized upon as the basis for dynamism and humanism is the notion of *maṣlaḥa* (welfare, benefit, utility)'.[6] The question is whether we can go so far as to regard *maṣlaḥa* as a sort of universal means whereby all kinds of modernisation are sanctioned. Some authors seem to regard *maṣlaḥa* as a dangerous opening for human value judgements or as the principal weak point within the Islamic legal system. Not seldomly they accuse the 'modernists' of its abuse: 'Their claim is to regard public interest as a source of law which could only serve to reduce the position of Divine Law to that of man-made laws'.[7] It should be recalled that, as an elaborate concept, *maṣlaḥa* – with *ḍarūra* or necessity as its most essential component – is a relative latecomer to legal theory (*uṣūl al-fiqh*).[8] After al-Shāfiʿī's intervention on behalf of the tradition of the Prophet and his confinement of *ijtihād* to analogical reasoning (*qiyās*) the elaboration of the concept of *maṣlaḥa* seems to be the major development which has brought decisive new elements to the rather static world of classical legal theory.[9] *Maṣlaḥa* offered a balance to the virtually 'positivistic' character of classical legal theory which 'is very source based' and 'does not provide a hospitable environment for considerations' of general ethics. That means that any ruling could be regarded to be law as long as it could be technically deduced from the sources.[10] *Maṣlaḥa* on the other hand propagates the evolution of legal growth along general detectable guidelines. Nevertheless, there are several topics that could be chosen to characterise these discussions and to trace the exact weight accorded to 'necessity and need'. For example, the twentieth-century phenomenon of the penetration of the Islamic world by photography, news media and European art posed and partly still poses problems with regard to the exact conception of the so-called Islamic '*Bilderverbot*'. On reflection, of the central areas of modernisation named by Swīsī, the medical one is certainly the most important for discussions about *ḍarūra/maṣlaḥa* , necessity and need. In the Tunisian *fatwās* of the last Islamic century and in related documents, there is a broad array of questions discussed under the heading of 'medical necessity' ranging from artificial insemination to dental surgery and blood transfusion.[11]

I want to confine myself here to the case of organ transplantation (*naql al-aʿḍāʾ*) because it may serve as a good example with which to test a number of aspects of the theory of *ḍarūra/maṣlaḥa.* It comprises of a variety of interests and needs including the aspect of life-saving, life-prolonging or merely life-improving, the weighing of concurrent rights between living people but also between the living and the dead. I cannot imagine a comparable test case which offers such a scope of issues with regard to conceptions of *maṣlaḥa.* Nevertheless, looking at Western literature that deals with *ijtihād* cases, it seems to me that there is a great neglect of aspects of legal theory. For instance Rispler-Chaim tells us that 'all medical *fatāwā* seem to demonstrate a pragmatic approach. The most frequent principle employed by the *muftīs* is *al-ḍarūrāt tubīḥ al-maḥẓūrāt* ("necessities render the prohibited permitted")'.[12] She even claims that 'Islamic Law permits all organ transplants'[13] and that a certain set of 'general statements, which are so often quoted in relation to organ transplants, have furthered the willingness of Islamic medical ethics to overlook Sharʿī prohibitions when saving life is at stake'.[14] On the whole, there is hardly any detailed analysis in the Islamic scientists' literature of the exact *ijtihād* mechanisms with regard to organ transplantation as with regard to similar topics.[15] I doubt that there would be such a careless use or collective misuse of the principle of 'necessity and need' to sanction the medical blessings of modern civilisation. The whole topic of organ transplantation actually calls for a detailed treatment by Islamic scientists. Leaving aside intricate problems such as the acceptability of brain death in Islamic law,[16] I shall confine myself to the removal of organs from the dead on behalf of the living. These acts are much more controversial than, for example, kidney donations to relatives (which are by now practised all over the Islamic world) and the taking of transplants from animals or transplantation within the same human body. There are at least two Arabic monographs on organ transplantation which fiercely and diligently argue against the taking of organs from the dead.[17] But this does not mean that the other *fatwās* or *fatwā*-based studies which are mostly in favour of this type of transplantation display a neglect of the requirements of *ijtihād*.

The first impression, even with regard to rather short *fatwās*, is that no topic can be so novel that some sort of precedent cannot be found in the Islamic legal tradition. Below, I outline the main elements of the legal reasoning found in these *fatwās*.[18]

1. At the start, the scholars often lay down the principal Islamic sanction of medical treatment found in the tradition literature. This is merely a basic orientation and does not mean that all new medical facilities pass unquestioned as *sharʿī* practices. That is to say, medical needs do not automatically represent a valid necessity (*ḍarūra*).
2. Medical necessity (as a special case of necessity) is a topic with a pedigree in Islamic legal literature. It is usually discussed under the topic *al-tadāwī bi'l-muḥarram(āt)*, treatment with forbidden things.[19] The principle is based upon the Qur'ān itself.[20] For example, to the legal scholars, when a person might die of thirst, he is allowed to drink wine to save his life, or when he is starving to death, to eat pork or carrion. These Quranic concessions are of utmost importance for the sanctioning of, for example, anaesthetics (*mukhaddirāt*) during medical operations.
3. Nevertheless, the *tadāwī bi'l-muḥarram* principle cannot serve as a comprehensive solution for the question of organ transplantation. In Sunni law the corpse is not ritually impure (*najis*) and therefore forbidden to be touched, but the slightest – even verbal – interference is forbidden because of the basic principle of *ḥurma*, the sanctity of the human body; a principle which is diligently upheld in Islamic law.[21] Given the importance of human *ḥurma*, it is more difficult, in the case of organ transplantation, to overcome the Quranic dicta than in the case of alcohol consumption, which has concessions in special situations. Some authors attach such great importance to the *ḥurma* principle that they totally disapprove of organ transplantation, even of a cornea.[22]
4. Most jurists, though acknowledging and underlining the great importance of the *ḥurma* concept, do not interprete it in such an absolute and categorical way. They consider it necessary to take the *ijtihād* a further step, because the physical integrity of the living is at stake. Because there is no definite or detailed instruction in Quran and Sunna, the legal scholars discuss traditional cases

that might serve as a basis for analogical reasoning. A certain set of classical cases usually appear in these discussions, the most important ones being: the opening of the deceased pregnant woman to save the life of her child; the opening of a corpse to rescue a valuable object;[23] the injuring of a Muslim family used by the enemies as a protective shield in war; the consumption of parts of the dead.[24]

The last topic is treated in the literature as representing the best case upon which an analogy can be based with regard to organ transplantation. Its discusion is found under headings such as *al-intifāʿ bi-ajzāʾ al-mayyit* (the use of parts of a deceased person's body) or *istiʿmāl aʿḍāʾ al-mayyit fī muʿālajat al-ḥayy*.[25] It is a much discussed issue and no consensus has emerged. That the person starving to death is allowed to eat from a corpse as long as nothing else is available is not automatically implied in the Quranic concession about the eating of carrion (*mayta*). However, the reason for the concession is the saving of life, one of the five essential values acknowledged by Islamic law. The main thing is not the eating as such but the use of carrion (*mayta*), in this case, the use of human corpse (*mayyit*).

Further, the discussion of transplants from a deceased donor is linked to former *ijtihād* cases, particularly relating to post-mortem examination (*tashrīḥ al-juthath*) which set an important precedent.[26] Post-mortems are usually legitimised for three purposes in Islamic law: for medical purposes, to detect the exact cause of death e.g. a dangerous infectious disease; with the aim of discovering criminal acts; for scientific purposes (e.g., as part of the education of students of medicine).[27]

The consumption of parts of the dead serves directly to save lives, and the three purposes for which post-mortems are permitted serve, at least indirectly, the same aim. This aim undoubtly represents a *ḍarūra*. However, things get more complicated when the encroachment on the dead does not serve the saving of life but merely serves as a means of prolonging life for a short while or 'improving' it. In such cases the necessary restrictions of necessity (*shurūṭ al-ḍarūra*)[28] may be lacking and it may be that a medical technique concerning certain organs is not yet fully developed. In such cases the *muftīs* need up-to-date knowledge about the actual chances of recovery after surgery. Without a definite expectation of recovery which outweighs the command not to interfere with a corpse, there is no way for a scholar to consent to an attack on the *ḥurma*.[29] Some *muftīs* overcome the strong barrier of *ḥurma* by declaring a destructive intent (*niyya*) to hurt as an essential part of an attack on the *ḥurma*. In such cases where the impulse is laudable, as in the case of a doctor who is guided by his willingness to heal, one could not really speak of an onslaught on the integrity of the human body.[30]

A special reservation is nevertheless expressed by some authors concerning the storing of human organs in special organ banks. From the viewpoint of Islamic legal theory the difficulty lies in the lack of a specified case of *ḍarūra*. Al-Dhahabī even mocks that if organ banks are permitted, it would be licit for a man to carry with him carrion, alcohol and pork so that he might consume them in times of necessity.[31] What he is referring to is the lack of an individually specified case of *ḍarūra*. Also connected with the topic of organ banks is the classical discussion concerning how much *mayta* or other forbidden things a starving man might consume. A further question is whether it is permitted that he supplies himself with rations (*tazawwud*) of forbidden things, be they carrion, a corpse or something else when, for example, he is making his way out of a desert[32]

Organ transplantation is connected 'with a myriad of legal and ethical problems'.[33] It seems to me that the majority of Muslim scholars diligently deal with the instruments of *ijtihād*, taking the strongly casuistic character of Islamic law into account along the way.[34] That means that there is no such thing as a general permission for organ transplantation. Instead there is a careful exploration of the various aspects of organ transplantation, especially of the conditions of *maṣlaḥa* – without which the *ḍarūra/maṣlaḥa* concept would indeed create the opportunity for human value judgements. Unexpected difficulties in legal theory may appear at any stage of the *ijtihād* process. In this sense organ banks are not a logical consequence of a general consent to transplantation. The apodictic brevity of some *fatwās* is easily misinterpreted as giving an irrevocable ruling. Nevertheless the *fatwās* are but the first step of differentiated *ijtihād* procedures which are by now followed by more detailed and diligent studies on the side of the Muslim scholars. A warning is in order not to draw conclusions too quickly about the content of Islamic law and the character of its reasoning by just referring to *fatwā* literature. There is no such thing as an unrestricted general permission; instead there is the constant possibility of modification or even withdrawal of a principal concession which is granted by *ijtihād*. This is possible through constant attention by the *muftīs* to what is going on – in this case in the field of medicine. For example, post-mortems for educational purposes may, to an extent, become obsolete with the advent of new technology like computer simuation.[35] These considerations lead to another point; the general necessity for the knowledge of secular experts – whether the *muftī* himself attains this knowledge or whether he incorporates 'secular *fatwās*' so to speak within his dicta. I do not know of any independent study of this especially twentieth-century phenomenon. This has important consequences for the process of *ijtihād* because it is unrealistic to hope for individual outstanding *mujtahid*s of the highest degree who also have expertise in this area. This increases collective *fatwās*, not only among *fiqh* scholars but also in co-operation with secular experts. For a study of the importance of *ḍarūra/maṣlaḥa* one should first turn to the call for *ijtihād*. It is here that we can expect to grasp the modern dimensions of *ḍarūra*, such as the role of psychological distress (for example, in the case of cosmetic surgery, music therapy,[36] sex change surgery and artificial insemination).[37] These issues have also been expressed in theoretical writings on *ḍarūra/maṣlaḥa* or on the *Sharīʿa*'s adaptability towards modern life in general.[38]

Taking this into account, we are perhaps not witnessing blind imitators of al-Shāṭibī, with some scholars operating on the brink of secularism, but instead, we are seeing the development of a rich tapestry of Islamic legal theory which operates in the area of *fatwās* and ensuing special studies. Whether the government authorities in Muslim countries dominate the *muftī*'s findings, or at least influence his rulings, is quite a different matter. For their part, the Muslim legal experts continue to offer solutions to problems of modern life.

Notes

1 *al-Fatāwā al-islāmiyya min dār al-iftāʾ al-miṣriyya* (Cairo, 1980). See also Rudolph Peters, 'Muḥammad al-ʿAbbāsī al-Mahdī (d. 1897), Grand Muftī of Egypt and his al-Fatāwā al-Mahdiyya', *Islamic Law and Society* 1 (1994), 66–82.

2 For example, *Fatāwā islāmiyya li-majmūʿa min al-ʿulamāʾ wa-hum: al-shaykh ʿAbd al-ʿAzīz Ibn Bāz, al-shaykh Muḥammad Ibn al-ʿUthaymīn, al-shaykh ʿAbd Allāh Ibn Jibrīn bi'l-iḍāfa ilā fatāwā li'l-lajna al-dāʾima li'l-iftāʾ*, ed. Qāsim al-Rifāʿī al-Shammāʿī (3 vols., Beirut, 1988).

3 The publication of the findings of Jakob Skovgaard-Petersen in the *Dār al-Iftāʾ* in Cairo is awaited. An initial outline of Saudi Arabian *fatwās* is given by Gerd-Rüdiger Puin, 'Der moderne Alltag im Spiegel ḥanbalitischer Fetwas aus ar-Riyad', *Zeitschrift der Deutschen Morgenländischen Gesellschaft*, Suppl. 3 (1977), 589–97.

4 Muḥammad b. Yūnus al-Swīsī, *Al-Fatāwā al-tūnisiyya fī al-qarn al-rābiʿ ʿashara al-hijrī*, to the best of my knowledge still unpublished, 257.

5 al-Swīsī, *Fatāwā*, p. 258.

6 Malcolm H. Kerr, *Islamic Reform: The Political and Legal Theories of Muḥammad ʿAbduh and Rashīd Riḍā* (Berkeley/Los Angeles, 1966), 55

7 Mohammad Muslehuddin, 'Islamic Jurisprudence and the Rule of Necessity and Need', *Islamic Studies* 11 (1973), 37–52, especially 37.

8 For fundamental contributions prior to al-Shāṭibī (d. 790/1388) see Muhammad Khalid Masud, *Islamic Legal Philosophy: A Study of Abū Isḥāq al-Shāṭibī's Life and Thought* (Delhi, 1989), 149–72.

9 Ihsan A. Bagby, 'The Issue of *Maṣlaḥah* in Classical Islamic Legal Theory', *International Journal of Islamic and Arabic Studies* 2 (1985), 1–11, especially 3.

10 Ibid., p. 5.

11 For an overview see Vardit Rispler-Chaim, *Islamic Medical Ethics in the Twentieth Century* (Leiden, 1993); Birgit Krawietz, *Die Ḥurma: Schariatrechtlicher Schutz vor Eingriffen in die körperliche Unversehrtheit nach arabischen Fatwas des 20. Jahrhunderts* (Berlin, 1991).

12 Rispler-Chaim, *Ethics*, p. 145.

13 Ibid., p. 42.

14 Ibid., p. 30.

15 One laudable exception and a step in the right direction is Mohammad Naeem Yaseen, 'The Rulings for the Donation of Human Organs in the Light of Sharīʿa Rules and Medical Facts', *Arab Law Quarterly* 5 (1990), 49–87.

16 Jād al-Ḥaqq ʿAlī Jād al-Ḥaqq, *Buḥūth wa-fatāwā islāmiyya wa-qaḍāyā muʿāṣira* (Cairo, 1900), vol. 2, 491–530.

17 Muṣṭafā Muḥammad al-Dhahabī, *Naql al-aʿḍāʾ bayn al-ṭibb wa'l-dīn* (Cairo, 1414/1993). ʿAqīl b. Aḥmad al-ʿAqīlī, *Ḥukm naql al-aʿḍāʾ maʿa al-taʿqībāt al-bayyina ʿalā man taʿaqqaba Ibn Taymiyya* (Jedda, 1412/1992).

18 When there is no detailed mentioning of a source I refer to the findings of my chapter on organ transplantation as derived from twentieth-century *fatwās*: Krawietz, *Die Ḥurma*, pp. 169–202.

19 ʿAbd al-Fattāḥ Maḥmūd Idrīs, *Ḥukm al-tadāwī bi'l-muḥarramāt* (Cairo, 1414/1993). For a modern discussion of the *tadāwī bi'l-muḥarram* principle and *ḍarūra*, Miklos Muranyi, 'Untersuchungen zu *šarīʿa* -rechtlichen Entwicklungen der Gegenwart. I: Ein Rechtsgutachten (fatwā) über das Chininverbot im Islam', *Arabica* 27 (1980), 223–56.

20 Qur'ān 2:168; 3:5; 6:119; 16:116.

21 For details about this legal principle see Krawietz, *Die Ḥurma*, pp. 317–26 *et passim*.

22 For example, Muḥammad Burhān al-Dīn al-Sanbuhaylī, *Qaḍāyā fiqhiyya muʿāṣira* (Beirut/Damascus, 1408/1988), 67f.

23 These two cases are treated in Krawietz, *Die Ḥurma*, pp. 139–42.

24 For example, Ibrāhīm al-Yaʿqūbī, *Shifāʾ al-tabārīḥ wa'l-adwāʾ fī ḥukm al-*

tashrīḥ wa-naql al-a'ḍā' (Damascus, 1407/1986), 50, 53f., 82–4, 87.

25 'Abd al-Karīm Zaydān, *Majmū'at buḥūth fiqhiyya* (Baghdad, 1402/1982), 188.

26 For post-mortem examinations in general, Rispler-Chaim, *Ethics*, pp. 72–83; Krawietz, *Die Ḥurma*, pp. 147–52.

27 For details 'Abd al-'Azīz Ibn Bāz, *Ḥukm tashrīḥ juthath al-muslimīn* (n.p., 1976).

28 Muḥammad Sa'īd Ramaḍān al-Būṭī, *Ḍawābiṭ al-maṣlaḥa fī al-sharī'a al-islāmiyya* (Beirut, 1412/1992).

29 Bilḥājj al-'Arabī, 'Ḥukm al-sharī'a al-islāmiyya fī a'māl al-ṭibb wa'l-jirāḥa al-mustakhdama', *Revue algérienne des sciences juridiques économiques et politiques* 31 (1993), 564–606, especially 585.

30 Krawietz, *Die Ḥurma*, p. 177.

31 Al-Dhahabī, *Naql al-a'ḍā'*, p. 72.

32 al-Ya'qūbī, *Shifā'*, p. 60, p. 73, p. 82, p. 87. For details about the principle *al-ḍarūra tuqaddar bi-qadrihā*, see Wahba al-Zuḥaylī, *Naẓariyyat al-ḍarūra al-shar'iyya* (Beirut, 1405/1985), 245–54.

33 Badar Durrez Ahmad, 'Organ Transplant and the Right to Die', *Islamic and Comparative Law Quarterly* 7 (1987), 121.

34 In this way al-Ya'qūbī, (*Shifā'*, pp. 106–8), finally arrives at sixteen conditions or considerations that are to be fulfilled before granting permission to a certain case of transplantation.

35 Al-'Aqīlī, *Ḥukm naql al-a'ḍā'*, p. 18. Al-Dhahabī, *Naql al-a'ḍā'*, p. 12.

36 Idrīs, *Ḥukm al-tadāwī*, pp. 349–56.

37 Krawietz, *Die Ḥurma*, pp. 210–21; Rispler-Chaim, *Ethics*, pp. 19–27.

38 Jād al-Ḥaqq 'Alī Jād al-Ḥaqq, *Al-Fiqh al-islāmī: Murūnatuhu wa-tāṭawwuruhu* (Cairo, 1987), 210–87.

TEN

Family Law in Algeria before and after the 1404/1984 Family Code[1]

RUTH MITCHELL

The Impact of French Colonial Rule on the Practice of Family Law for Algerian Muslims

Prior to the imposition of French colonial rule in Algeria from 1246/1830 onwards, family law was not applied in a unified way over the whole country. Most Muslims under the jurisdiction of the Dey of Algiers followed the Mālikī rite. However, in the Berber areas of Kabylie, the law was largely inspired by *'ādāt* (local custom). In the Mzab, the inhabitants followed the Ibāḍī rite. The Toureg, too had their own customary law.

The French authorities attempted to centralise the legal system in Algeria, and progressively stripped power away from Muslim courts. *Qāḍī* courts (courts presided over by a single Muslim judge) were retained, but their powers were reduced by a decree of 16 Sha'bān 1306/17 April 1889 to matters of family law and personal status only. Muslims were allowed to put themselves under the jurisdiction of French law by express declaration. French *colons* (settlers) in the 1880s made a full-scale attempt to eliminate Muslim courts and law schools. However, after strong opposition was voiced by Muslims, the French colonial authorities decided to retain Muslim courts, and created a Chambre de Revision Musulmane (Muslim Appeal Court) to hear appeals from *qāḍī* courts.[2]

Not content with restricting Islamic Law to personal status and family law matters, the French appeal courts sometimes gave judgements inconsistent with traditional Mālikī law. In Mālikī Law, *khiṭba* (betrothal) is an important part of the marriage process. If someone is betrothed to one person, yet contracts a marriage to a second person, Mālikī law states that the second marriage is null and void before consummation. However, the French Cour d'Alger (Court of Algiers) sometimes refused to annul the second marriage of women if the first *khiṭba* could not be proved. The Court demanded proof of negotiations over dower, rather than mere promises of marriage. Indeed, in 1309/1892, the Cour d'Alger went so far as to proclaim that marriage promises had no legal effect and did not exist in Muslim law.[3]

The French authorities also objected to the exercise of *ijbār* (power of constraint) by the father over his virgin daughter's marriage. In traditional Mālikī law, a father may contract a marriage for his virgin daughter even against her wishes. Until 1298/1881, French jurists in these cases would object to the marriage if they felt *ṣadāq* (dower) was insufficient, or if the person exercising *ijbār* was not qualified to do so. After 1298/1881 French judges began to annul the marriages of young girls contracted by their fathers if the marriage seemed contrary to the girl's interest. They justified this on the basis of Ḥanifi law, which allows a girl to exercise *khiyār al-bulūgh* (the option of puberty) to dissolve an unconsummated marriage.

A first attempt at codification of Muslim Family Law was made by a commission under the French jurist Morand in 1324/1906. However, no final law was passed because of fierce opposition from the Muslim jurists who felt that they had been insufficiently consulted. The Commission responsible for drafting the code had included 10 French administrators and jurists, but only five Algerian Muslims.

However, Mālikī law was also changed in piecemeal fashion by statute and by decree. Registration of marriages was included in the law of 3 Dhū al-Qaʿda 1348/2 April 1930 concerning the civil status of Muslim Algerians. The procedure for registration proved so cumbersome that most Muslims did not bother to register their marriages. If cases concerning marriage came to court, the Law of 13 Dhū al-Ḥijja 1396/1 July 1957, and the subsequent decree of 14 Rabīʿ al-Awwal 1379/ 17 September 1959, required the parties to produce a certificate of registration. Under traditional Mālikī law, marriages did not have to be registered by a civil authority to be valid. As long as offer and acceptance had taken place in front of two witnesses, and the marriage had been publicised, the *qāḍī* would accept the testimony of the witnesses that the marriage had indeed taken place.

An ordinance of 25 Rajab 1378/4 February 1959 deviated from traditional Mālikī law. It fixed the age of marriage of all Muslim Algerians at 18 years for men and 15 years for women. Marriages not concluded before a *qāḍī* or civil court were not considered valid. The express consent of both spouses was required, thus suppressing the father's right of *ijbār*. The husband's right of *ṭalāq* could only take effect through the courts. In Mālikī law the husband had the right to repudiate his wife unilaterally at any time without needing a good reason, and without court intervention. The decree of 14 Rabīʿ al-Awwal 1379/17 September 1959 also stipulated that on divorce both spouses must contribute to the maintenance and education of their children in proportion to their ability. Mālikī law makes it incumbent upon the husband alone to maintain his children after divorce.

Changes to Family Law in Independent Algeria from 1962 to 1984

After independence the Government decided to codify family law in order to regularise court judgements and end confusion on certain points of law. However, attempts to codify family law in 1962, 1966, 1973, 1980 and 1982 were all rejected by the Government or by the National Assembly. Changes to family law evoked strong arguments between traditionalists and modernisers. Traditionalists pushed for a code that would reflect traditional Mālikī law and believed that during the colonial period family law had been modified to express European ideas of marriage and divorce. Modernisers wanted to bring family law into line with modern social and economic changes, in particular, women's increasing participation in the work-force.

While debate was continuing on the family law code, some changes were effected through legislation. The age for marriage for girls was raised from 15 to 16 under law No. 63–224 of 6 Ṣafar 1383/29 June 1963 (known as Loi Khémisti). However, a judge could give a dispensation of age if good reasons were shown. If girls did marry before 16 without a judge's dispensation, the marriage would be null and void before consummation; however, such a marriage could not be attacked once the spouses had attained the legal age or when the woman conceived. On registering of marriages, Ordinance No. 71–65 of 1 Shaʿbān 1391/22 September 1971 stated that unregistered marriages could be registered subsequently with the president of the court in the area in which the marriage was contracted, and would be considered valid from the date recognised by the court as the date of the marriage.

Despite legislation, an analysis of 23 cases published in the *Revue Algérienne* in 1387/1968 show confusion in the courts over registration provisions. In a case before the Tribunal de Grande Instance d'Alger (High Court of Appeal of Algiers), the judge decided that a marriage before a *jamāʿa* (public assembly) was invalid because exchange of consent had not been expressed in front of a *qāḍī* or public official (Ait Adir v Nabti 1385/1965). However, in similar case, the Cour d'Alger (Court of Appeal of Algiers) ruled that a marriage contracted according to Muslim rites could be proved by Muslim law provisions (Dame Harrache v Zouaoui 1386/1966).

Divorce cases also show diverse judgements. In a case before the Cour de Tlemcen (Tlemsen Court) on 6 Shawwāl 1386/18 January 1967, the judge stated that the husband had an absolute right at any time to repudiate his wife (Dame Kara-Ali v Smir 1386/1967). This is in conformity with traditional Mālikī law. However, in a court case in Tizi-Ouzou on 11 Ramaḍān 1387/13 December 1967 the judge refused the husband's request for a divorce, since it was unjustified and did not have a serious motive.[4]

Custody of children after divorce was an issue debated by many courts. Under traditional Mālikī law, *ḥaḍāna* (custody) was granted to the mother until a boy reached puberty, and until a girl reached the age of marriage. Custody could be taken away from the mother if she remarried someone who was not close relative. In independent Algeria, courts began to take into account the interests of the child. One ex-wife refused to allow her ex-husband to visit the child, claiming the child needed constant maternal attention because of his ill-health. The court finally ordered a medical report on the child in his interest (Dame Bouyad-Allem v Briki 1387/1967). One maternal grandmother, passed over when custody of her grandson was awarded to the paternal grandparents, petitioned the Cour Supreme (High Court) to award her custody instead. In view of the maternal grandmother's great age, it was decided to confer custody on the paternal grandparents, in the interests of the child (Kazi-Tani v T 1385/1965).

Theory and Practice of the 1404/1984 Algerian Family Code

Law No. 84–11 was approved by the Algerian National Assembly on 9 Ramaḍān 1404/9 June 1984. The governmental commission which drafted the law stated that it was based on the Qur'ān, *sunna* (tradition of the Prophet), *ijmāʿ* (consensus), *qiyās* (analogy), *ijtihād* (effort of interpretation) and *fiqh* (jurisprudence), according to the four Sunni schools, as well as personal status legislation in Syria, Egypt, Morocco and Tunisia. Having established its Islamic credentials, the law does depart from the strict letter of Mālikī law in certain areas. Indeed, the 1404/1984 Family code can be seen as a compromise between traditionalists who wanted to restore *Sharī'a* in its entirety, and the modernists who wished to make some concessions to modern social conditions.

Some provisions of traditional Mālikī law have been completely overturned. Article 7 puts the age of marriage for men at 21 and for women at 18, but allows the judge to give a dispensation of age for an important reason or in the case of necessity. Under Mālikī law, marriage can be contracted at any age, with consummation taking place at puberty. When contracting a marriage, the woman must be represented by her *walī* (guardian), usually her father or a close relative, in conformity with Mālikī law. However, article 13 forbids the *walī* to contract a marriage for his ward without her consent, thus suppressing the father's right of *ijbār*. Article 12 prevents the *walī* from forbidding his ward's marriage if she wants it and if it is profitable for her. However, a father can oppose the marriage of his virgin daughter if his opposition is in her interest.

According to the commission which drafted the law, polygamy was a matter of some controversy. The commission concluded that polygamy was sanctioned by the Qur'ān, if the spouses were treated equally, in times of wars, natural disasters, and for certain specific illnesses or sterility of the first wife. The 1404/1984 law, therefore, permits polygamy (in contrast to some earlier drafts of the law). However, it puts certain restrictions on the husband's right under traditional Mālikī law to marry up to four wives at one time. Article 8 permits a second wife if the motive is justified, if the conditions and intentions of equity are supplied and after informing first and subsequent wives. However, either wife can take legal action against the husband in case of deception, or demand divorce in the absence of consent.

The respective rights and duties of the spouses generated much debate. Under the 1404/1984 Family Code, it is the husband's duty to maintain his wife according to his means, unless she abandons the marital home. The wife had a duty to obey her husband, and to bring up his children. She has a right to visit and receive visits from her relatives, and can dispose of her own property freely. These provisions are in conformity with Mālikī law. However, the 1404/1982 draft code had contained an article stipulating the woman's right to work outside the marital home – a point of importance to modernisers. This point was left out of the 1404/1984 law on the grounds that such a condition could be stipulated in the marriage contract.

Divorce was a topic of much debate. Some modernisers argued for the same grounds for divorce to be applied to both sexes. However, both the 1402/1982 draft and the 1404/1984 Family Code allow the husband to exercise an exclusive right of *ṭalāq* in conformity with Mālikī law. However, divorce must take place through a court after a three month reconciliation period; and if the judge believes the husband has abused his right of divorce, he may award damages to the wife. The wife may apply for a divorce (*taṭlīq*) from her husband on very limited grounds: non-payment of maintenance, husband's infirmity or his refusal to share his wife's bed for more than four months, husband's prison conviction of more than one year, husband's absence for more than one year without valid excuse or maintenance, any legally recognised prejudice (such as the husband taking a second wife) and for any proven grave immoral fault. It is unclear whether this last category includes physical or mental cruelty, which had sometimes been grounds for divorce under Mālikī law using the concept of *ḍarar* (harm).

Upon divorce, the wife must observe the *ʿidda* (legal waiting period) before she may remarry; three months or three periods of menstrual purity, or in the case of a pregnancy, until birth. During this time, she is entitled to maintenance and to stay in the marital home. These provisions are in conformity with Mālikī law.

The 1404/1984 Family Code gives the right of custody of the children to the mother first, with custody passing to the father when boys reach the age of 10 (or 16 if the mother has not remarried). Girls stay with the mother until the age of capacity to marry. If the mother remarries someone not a close relative, custody passes to the father. However, in a departure from traditional Mālikī law, Article 65 states that the interest of the child must be taken into account in the decisions concerning custody.

It is noteworthy with that the 1402/1982 draft allowed mothers with custody of the children to remain in the marital home after divorce. Under traditional Mālikī law, the divorced wife has no right to the marital home, and would return to her parents'. In practice, judges had been granting divorced wives with three or more children the right to stay in the rented marital dwelling, under Article 467 of the 1395/1975 Civil Code. However, the 1404/984 Family Code takes away this right, presumably because it is not in conformity with Mālikī law provisions.

The provisions in the 1404/1984 code on *nafaqa* (maintenance) state that the husband must maintain his wife from the date of consummation of marriage, and his children until the age of majority for males and until marriage for females. However, contrary to traditional Mālikī law, the wife is made responsible for maintaining her children if the husband is incapacitated.

Traditional Islamic law forbids *tabannā* (adoption) completely, both the 1402/1982 draft and the 1404/1984 law remain faithful to this prohibition. However the commission drafting the law introduced *kafāla* (legal sponsorship) as a partial solution for childless couples who wished to 'adopt' children. However, *kafāla* has some important limitations compared with adoption. The sponsored child may not take the surname of the sponsoring father. He is not entitled to a fixed share of inheritance, although the sponsor may make a legacy of up to one third of his property in his favour. The natural mother or father may claim back the sponsored child, but only with the child's permission if he has reached the age of discernment.

The 1404/1984 Law in Practice

Information about how the 1404/1984 law worked in practice was obtained from several different sources. Articles in the Algerian press and interviews with journalists and academics working in the field gave an overview of the main areas of controversy. Details of 26 individual cases were obtained from Algerian lawyers working in family law; and 82 unpublished cases from Jumādā al-Ūlā and Jumādā al-Ākhira 1406/January and Febuary 1986 were analysed from the archives of the Majlis al-Qaḍā' al-Jazā'ir (First Appeal Court of Algiers).

The sample of cases allows us to draw some preliminary conclusions about the application of the 1404/1984 Family Code. However, since all the cases analysed come from the first two years after the 1404/1984 law was passed, there have been few precedent-setting cases from the Supreme Court in the interpretation of certain clauses in the law.

There has been confusion and inconsistency in judgements in such areas as: the registering of marriages, polygamy, divorce and its effects, and the custody of children. Some issues were repeatedly mentioned by lawyers and others as being detrimental to women.

How free is the woman to choose her husband, since her father can oppose the marriage 'in her interest'? Is the wife to be called *nāshiza* (disobedient) if she continues to work outside the home after marriage in defiance of her husband's wishes? Will she subsequently be held responsible if her husband divorces her, and thus lose her right to damages? How fair are the provisions on divorce to women? Faced with the severe housing crisis in Algeria, where are a divorced mother and her children supposed to live, if they can no longer stay in the marital home? Is *kafāla* really an acceptable alternative to adoption?

The Algerian courts seem fairly lenient in their decisions to register marriages retrospectively. They generally grant permission for registering *fātiha* marriages (traditional marriage celebrations where the opening *sūra* of the Qur'ān is recited), as long as the celebration included all the constituent elements of a valid marriage, even if the parties were under-age at the time of the marriage. However, Algerian courts did not extend registering to couples who merely cohabited. In case no. 680 from the Majlis al-Qaḍā' al-Jazā'ir, dated 25 Rabī' al-Ākhir 1406/7 January 1986, the judge refused to agree to a wife's request for registration since there had been no proper contract and no traditional celebrations. In case no. 1205 from the same court, dated 22 Jumādā al-Ūlā 1406/2 February 1986, the judge refused permission for registration on the grounds that the four witnesses produced were not acceptable. Two had only witnessed the fact that the couple lived together, and a third had not been present at the ceremony. The judge ruled that two witnesses present at the actual ceremony were needed to prove the marriage.

The lawyers interviewed agreed that polygamy is rare in Algeria, but may be more common in the countryside. The 1404/1984 Family Code does allow polygamy, but only for a valid reason. This has been strictly interpreted by an unpublished juridical circular as the wife's sterility or incurable illness. In the sample of cases studied, two wives were granted a divorce with damages on the grounds that their husbands had married a second wife.

By far the largest number of cases in the sample examined involved divorce and its effects. Most of these divorces were requested by the husband. The 1404/1984 Family Code gives the husband an absolute right to divorce, but the judge may grant damages to the wife for any harm (*ḍarar*) she has suffered. The notion of 'fault' currently plays a large part in Algerian court decisions, mainly to determine whether the wife is entitled to damages. Even though many husbands tried to prove that the divorce was their wife's fault, in practice the courts mostly decided that divorce was the husband's fault. Out of the 27 cases where the husband requested divorce, or appealed a decision attributing the divorce as his fault, 26 were pronounced as the husband's fault.

Many husbands justified their demand for divorce by stating that the wives neglected their marital duties stipulated by Article 39. Especially common was the complaint that the wife left the marital home or worked outside it without the husband's permission. In reply to the husband's accusations, wives often complained that their husbands neglected them or the children, or beat them, or had sent them away from the marital home.

In case no. 84 from the Majlis al-Qaḍā' al-Qālima (Guelma First Appeal Court) the judge refused a husband's request for divorce. His reasons for refusal were that the man's wife was four months pregnant, and divorce was not in the interest of the child. This decision seems to be an incorrect application of the 1404/1984 law, since the husband has the absolute right to divorce.

The amount of damages awarded to the wife on divorce varied from between 500 dinars to 20000 dinars in the sample of 48 divorce cases. The damages do not really represent a large sum of money, especially since the husband keeps the marital home on divorce. In order to deter husbands from capricious divorce, courts could raise the amount of damages payable on divorce.

Several lawyers said that it was rare for the wife to ask for divorce, and that if she did so, she would be deprived of damages and custody of the children. It was surprising, therefore to find 17 cases where the wife requested a divorce under Article 53. Divorce was granted in 13 cases, refused in two cases and in the other two cases a commissioner was appointed to investigate the wife's complaints. All 13 divorces were pronounced as the husband's fault. In six cases, the wife was awarded damages, in 10 cases she was given an *'idda* payment and in six cases she was awarded custody of the children.

The 1404/1984 Family Code states that the interest of the child must be taken into account when determining custody. From the sample of cases studies, it does not seem that the courts are systematically considering the interest of the child. In most cases, custody is automatically given to the mother. However, where the mother is deemed to be at fault in divorce, custody may be given to the father. In case no. 2205/85, from Majlis al-Qaḍā' al-Jazā'ir, dated 1 Jumādā al-Ākhira 1406/ 11 February 1986, the court awarded custody to the father, since the mother had abandoned the marital home.

The courts systematically awarded the right of access to the other parent when deciding custody. There were four cases where the person having custody of the child tried to prevent the other parent from visiting the child, but in each case the courts decided that the other parent had right of access. In case no. 1637 from Majlis al-Qaḍā' al-Jazā'ir, dated 29 Jumādā al-Ūla 1406/9 February 1986, a father with custody tried to prevent his ex-wife from visiting children on the grounds of her bad conduct. She apparently visited hotels with foreign men. The court refused his request, since her right of access did not harm the children.

Conclusions

The 1404/1984 Family Code was designed to resolve a number of contentious issues in the realm of family law. However some important social and legal problems remain unsolved, particularly as they affect women's status in marriage and in society as a whole. The National Union of Algerian Women had campaigned on several issues, notably against polygamy, and for a woman's right to work outside the home after marriage. The 1404/1984 law appears to uphold the traditional view of women within society and the family, which may not always accord with social reality.

Women's right to work was established in Article 39 of the 1383/1963 Constitution. In Algeria's professional class, many women were working as lawyers, doctors, teachers, nurses and pilots. However, it remains unclear whether a woman must give up her work if her husband demands it, or be considered *nāshiza*, and thereby lose her right to maintenance. The charge in the law over a woman's right to the marital home on divorce has created severe hardship for a number of divorced women. Sometimes they have had to give up custody of their children, since they cannot provide the children with decent housing. If a husband used his unilateral right of divorce for no good reason, this burden is doubly hard to bear.

Another issue of concern has been that of children born outside marriage. It is difficult to calculate how serious a problem this is, since there are severe social sanctions imposed on women who 'shame' the family by having children outside marriage, and the subject is still largely taboo. It appears that such children born to unmarried mothers are usually cared for in orphanages. Sometimes childless couples care for such children under the provisions of *kafāla*. However, the legal clauses on *kafāla* provide an inadequate solution to the problem of abandoned illegitimate children, allowing the natural parents to reclaim the child and forbidding the abandoned child to take the sponsor's name. This last provision perpetuates the social stigma of both the abandoned child and the childless couples who wish to care for such children as their own. Hélène Vandevelde suggests that in the absence of a more acceptable solution, many childless couples may be tempted to adopt an abandoned child secretly and forge his birth certificate.[5]

As an attempt to fill a legal vacuum in family law matters and end the diversity of opinions surrounding different aspects of the law, the 1404/1984 Family Code represents a serious initiative. However, since it ignores some basic contradictions between the traditional Mālikī view of marriage and women's status and the changing role of women in society in independent Algeria, the code is flawed in key areas. In future, there may need to be further amendments to clarify certain important issues on divorce, polygamy and the woman's right to work outside the home.

Notes

1 The Research for this paper was carried out at SOAS, London.

2 See A. Christelow, *Muslim Law courts and the French Colonial state in Algeria* (Princeton, 1985) and ibid., 'Jugements et arrêts sur le droit de la famille', *Revue Algérienne*, 5 (1968), 1193–244.

3 See C. Bontemps, 'L'influence française dans le projet de la code de la famille algérienne', *Revue Algérienne* 19 (1982), 625–45.

4 See M. Issad, 'Le rôle du juge et la volonté des parties dans la rupture du lien conjugal', *Revue Algérienne* 5 (1968), 1065–90.

5 See H. Vandevelde, 'Quelqes remarques sur la nature et la fonction du droit à propos de l'article 46 du code de la famille', unpublished conference paper from Institut du Droit d'Oran, (1986)

ELEVEN

Qāḍīs and the Implementation of Islamic Law in Present Day Israel[1]

YITZHAK REITER

Approximately one-sixth of the population of Israel is Muslim. The Islamic judicial system in Israel serves about 700,000 Muslims (including the population of East Jerusalem which, since 1967, has been dependent on the Israeli-Islamic judicial system).[2] In addition to religious differences between minority and majority populations, Israel has been immersed in a political conflict with the Palestinians and the Arab world as a whole. This conflict has taken on the additional element of confrontation between the adherents of the respective faiths. Israel has maintained the Islamic judicial system more or less as it was prior to 1948, i.e., as it had coalesced during the British Mandate in Palestine.[3] The Islamic courts retained their powers in areas of personal status and *waqf* affairs, even after 1948, although the Islamic judicial system was integrated into the general juridical system. *Qāḍīs* (judges) are appointed in accordance with civil law, by civil authorities, at the recommendation of a committee headed by the minister of religious affairs and staffed by another member of cabinet, three members of Knesset (parliament) at least two of whom are Muslims, two *qāḍīs* and two members of the Israeli Bar Association (these may also be Muslims). The *qāḍīs* take an oath of allegiance in the presence of the president of the state and operate Muslim law within the limits of the civil laws legislated by the Knesset.[4]

Intervention by the Knesset in areas within the jurisdiction of the Islamic courts has usually been done indirectly and in an effort to establish social norms, particularly in regard to social legislation designed to improve the status of women. This intervention has occurred in areas such as the prohibition of polygamy, the establishment of a minimum marriage age, guardianship and custody of minor children, relations between spouses and the prohibition of divorcing a woman against her will.[5] Israeli legislation on these issues did not interfere directly with the *Sharīʿa* (Islamic law); rather, it amended the penal law to stipulate criminal sanctions for transgressors. This intervention has at times created constraints in the application of Islamic law in Israel.

In addition to intervention through legislation, one may also examine the civil court's attitude towards the *Sharīʿa* Courts. Usually Israeli courts do not intervene in Muslim personal affairs, which are the jurisdiction of the *Sharīʿa* Courts according to the British Order-in-Council of 1922 (arts. 52–53). The civil courts tend to overrule the religious courts only when the later display a particularly unjust approach to a certain issue. Such is the case in paternity suits, which in Western and Israeli civil society are determined by biological relation; Islamic law recognises paternity only within marital relations. In one such case, a Muslim woman gave birth to a daughter, outside of marriage, fathered by a married Muslim man (she claimed that he promised to marry her and based on that promise she had agreed to enter into a sexual relationship with him). The woman brought the biological father before the *Sharīʿa* Court in order to force him to recognise his paternity and to pay child maintenance for the daughter. The *Sharīʿa* court did not agree to obligate the father to submit to genetic testing in order to prove his paternity. The Supreme Civil Court, comprised of seven judges, with Judge Mishael Heshin as Chief Justice, found that there was a distinction between civil and religious paternity. Civil paternity is biologically determined and is subject to the Israeli civil law concerning maintenance and inheritance; thus it as found that this paternity suit would fall under the jurisdiction of the district court. Heshin proposed that the jurisdiction of the district court would be parallel to that of the religious court in all essential matters. This judgement from 1995 altered the previous legal rule, which had been established by the Supreme Court twelve years earlier (known as the ʿUmarī rule), according to which, even after a decision had been reached under Israeli legal regulations, an Israeli district court did not have the exclusive jurisdiction to decide in matters of conflicts over child maintenance between Muslims: the *Sharīʿa* Court had exclusive jurisdiction in this area.[6]

Another of Heshin's judgements was to narrow the scope of the law, decided upon by the Supreme Court more than 30 years ago, which gave the *Sharīʿa* Court exclusive authority to discuss conflict between Muslims in the question of paternity. The president of the

Supreme Court, Meir Shamgar, suggested that the district court would have authority parallel to that of the religious court, in any essential matter, if the Supreme Court were to accept this proposal the religious courts in Israel would lose their exclusive authority.

One may regard the fact that every Israeli civil lawyer can represent clients before the *Sharīʿa* court according to the law regulating the operation of *Sharīʿa* courts (1961 Qāḍīs Law), as a tool which assists the Islamic judiciary in becoming familiar with civil law.

The shadow cast by the Israel–Arab conflict, coupled with Israeli policies which view the country's Arab citizens as potential security risks because of their Palestinian national identity, have prevented Israeli Muslims from forming their own, overarching religious institutions, such as the Supreme Muslim Council, which operated under the British Mandate. Furthermore, the office of the *muftī* has not been reinstated in Israel. Practically speaking, there is no institution within Israel's sovereign borders that is capable of issuing legal opinions based on the *Sharīʿa*. The president of the Supreme Muslim Council and the *muftī* of Jerusalem until 1937, Ḥājj Amīn al-Ḥusaynī, was one of Zionism's greatest adversaries, and used his position at the head of the Palestinian religious system to serve his political struggle thus provoking wariness on the part of the government of Israel in 1948 in establishing autonomous, Islamic agencies.

The factor with the greatest bearing on the application of Islamic law in Israel is the education of *qāḍīs*. Specifically the fact that Muslims in Israel cannot pursue advanced studies of the *Sharīʿa* at a recognised institution such as al-Azhar in Egypt. Even after Israel and Egypt reached terms of peace, at which time Israeli Muslims were able to enrol at al-Azhar, the post of *qāḍī* was not among the most sought after among young Muslims in Israel; it was not one to which they were willing to devote their future and for which they would invest their money. In contrast, young Arabs in Israel prefer to study civil law at universities in Israel and abroad.[7] After 1967, Israeli Muslims gained the opportunity to enrol in Islamic religious colleges in the West Bank and the Gaza Strip. The scholastic standards of these institutions, however, are poor, and their graduates have ended up as founders of radical Islamic movements in Israel rather than as learned *qāḍīs*. In the absence of higher Islamic education, no institution of *ʿulamāʾ* or scholars has come into being in Israel to provide legal rulings based on the *Sharīʿa*. The lack of competent teachers of Islamic law in the Israeli Arab educational system is a contributing factor to poor standards of Islamic education in schools.[8]

Because it is the *qāḍīs* who apply Islamic law in matters of personal status and *waqf* affairs, it is of the utmost importance to recognise their educational background – where and how they acquired their knowledge of Islamic law, the level of their general education, and their command or ignorance of statutory law.

The Israeli Muslim community does not hold the *Sharīʿa* judicial system in very high esteem, but opinion polls among Muslim Arabs show a strong respect for the Israeli judicial system.[9] Nevertheless, Muslims generally maintain *Sharīʿa* and customary norms, and are disinclined to adjudicate matters of personal status in the civil courts, although this option is available to them. In matters of succession and probate, for example, few Muslims in Israel register civil bequests with the courts, and few ask civil courts to adjudicate their entitlement to succession.[10] Israeli Muslims do not tend to challenge Quranic instructions with regard to inheritance, however, the *Sharīʿa* judiciary is held in low regard because of the *qāḍīs*' lack of training in Islamic law. Five of the seven *qāḍīs* who were appointed to their positions immediately after 1948, were graduates of al-Azhar. Two of them, Shaykh Amīn al-Ḥabash and Shaykh Mūsā al-Ṭabarī, had served as *qāḍīs* in the late Mandate period. One *qāḍī* was a graduate of the Aḥmadiyya College in Acre, and another served as a lawyer prior to his nomination (see table). None of the subsequent *qāḍīs* graduated from a higher institute for Islamic studies. They had acquired their knowledge of the *Sharīʿa* on their own, some of them from their *qāḍī* fathers, or during their terms as secretaries of *Sharīʿa* Courts. The second generation of *qāḍīs*, lacking Islamic or any other academic education, carried on with the judicial customs of the first generation and made the *qāḍī*'s work a technical, clerical activity. Members of the third generation, appointed as *qāḍīs* in the last decade, are better schooled; although they lack advanced training in *Sharīʿa* law. They have secular educations in the humanities, the social sciences and, in some cases, modern law, and make an effort to study Islamic law by themselves directly from the sources. Three of the seven present *qāḍīs* graduated from Israeli law faculties, another three graduated with degrees in the humanities, while the remaining *qāḍī*, whose father served as *qāḍī* during the first generation, has only high school education.

Public criticism of the *Sharīʿa* judicial system focuses on fact that the 1961 Qāḍīs Law does not stipulate minimum educational criteria for prospective *qāḍīs*. Recently, Muslim members of the Knesset have presented draft legislation that would limit the candidacy for appointment to the position of *qāḍī* to persons with a legal education. The sponsors of these bills do not, however, stipulate a level of expertise in Islamic law because Israel has no institutions of advanced Islamic studies. One may ask if such legislation will bring about the secularisation of Islamic law. It appears that the legislation's initiators are interested mainly in bringing more justice into the Muslim religious judicial system and assume that law school graduates will have a better understanding of Islamic texts and jurisprudence.

Qāḍīs in Israel by generation and education

Generation	Name of *qāḍī*	Education
First	Ḥasan al-Ḥabash	al-Azhar graduate
	Mūsa al-Ṭabarī	al-Azhar graduate
	Ḥusnī al-Zuʿbī	law school graduate
	Ṭāhir al-Ṭabarī	al-Azhar graduate
	Tawfiq ʿAsaliyya	al-Azhar graduate
	Ṭāhir Ḥammād	al-Azhar graduate
	Amīn Midlij	al-Aḥmadiyya College
Second	Muḥammad Ḥubayshī	high school graduate
	Yūsuf al-Dasūqī	high school graduate
	Ḥasan al-Asadī	law school graduate
	Farīd Wajdī al-Ṭabarī	BA in Humanities
Third	Aḥmad al-Nāṭūr	BA in Arabic, MA in Communication and Law studies
	Zakī Midlij	high school
	Salīm Samāra	BA in Humanities
	Farūq al-Zuʿbī	law school graduate
	Muḥammad Tilāwī	BA in Humanities
	Dā'ūd al-Zaynī	BA in Humanities
	Ziyyād ʿAsaliyya	BEd

The *Sharīʿa* judiciary has for many years been the object of discrimination *vis-à-vis* the Jewish religious judiciary in Israel. Because the *Sharīʿa* system is subordinate to the Ministry of Religious Affairs, which has always been administered by Jewish religious parties (chiefly the National Religious Party), it has not received adequate funding, staff, or attention.[11] Until 1994, the Sharīʿa Court of Appeals did not have a full complement of judges. All of its *qāḍīs,* with the exception of the president of the court, were rotating judges from the lower courts. Under these circumstances, the Court of Appeals could neither function as a norm-setting institution nor guide the *qāḍīs* of the lower courts in matters that required policy decisions. Not until 1994 did it become possible to complete the *Sharīʿa* judiciary by appointing three permanent *qāḍīs* to the Court of Appeals and a young, academically trained *qāḍī*, Shaykh Aḥmad al-Nāṭūr, as president of the Court of Appeals.

Shaykh Aḥmad al-Nāṭūr was appointed in 1985, at the age of thirty-three, to the position of *qāḍī* of Jaffa and Beersheva. At that time, al-Nāṭūr had a bachelor's degree in Arabic language and Islamic studies and a master's degree in social sciences, both from the Hebrew University of Jerusalem, in addition to a bachelor's degree in law from Tel Aviv University. Before his appointment as *qāḍī*, he was a licensed pleader in the *Sharīʿa* court system. He acquired his expertise in *Sharīʿa* studies independently, by direct study of the Islamic sources. After his appointment, he continued studying for a master's degree in law and began teaching *Sharīʿa* law in several higher-education institutions in Israel. Al-Nāṭūr took up his position as *qāḍī* with the aim of reforming the *Sharīʿa* judicial system.

The purpose of this essay is to examine the influence of modern legal education, and general academic studies, on the practical application of Islamic law by the third generation of *qāḍīs* in Israel. A selection of al-Nāṭūr's rulings from the two courts serve as a basis for the study. Rulings given by al-Nāṭūr during his ten years in office, especially those issued during his tenure as president of the Court of Appeals, point to several trends.

Rejection of State Legislation as a Source of Inspiration

When a graduate of a law school, who has not attended a traditional Islamic college, is appointed to the presidency of the Sharīʿa Court of Appeals, one might expect him to consider state legislation as a source of inspiration for various modifications of *Sharīʿa* jurisprudence. Layish found that some of the first-generation *qāḍīs* favoured the adoption of certain provisions of Knesset legislation, and even advocated further initiatives in civil law with respect to Muslims' personal status.[12] We do not know if this was part of their *weltanschaung* or whether they wished to appease the Jewish establishment. The rulings of the Sharīʿa Court of Appeals under Shaykh al-Nāṭūr exhibit a bias of the opposite kind. In many of his verdicts, al-Nāṭūr reproaches *qāḍīs* for relying excessively on civil law instead of anchoring their decisions in the *Sharīʿa*. His rulings express his anger with the lower court *qāḍīs* who quote civil law as reference for their court decisions (for example, in the case of temporary maintenance, they base their ruling on the Israeli Maintenance Law of 1959). He refers them to the Islamic sources as if they use civil law out of ignorance. Al-Nāṭūr's guidelines to this effect originate in his *weltanschauung*, which asserts the all-embracing nature of Islamic law. The *qāḍī*, when administering justice, must refer to the sources of Islamic law and find his answers there. An example of this tendency is found in the issue of the custody of minors.

Ḥanafī law recognises the mother's right to custody of minor children (*ḥaḍāna*) up to the age of seven for a boy and nine for a girl. Israeli legislation intervened in this matter and set forth a universal norm in child custody, following the principle of the child's welfare. Concurrently, the 1962 Capacity and Guardianship Law reduced the term of child custody with the mother (unless there are reasons to rule otherwise) to age six for children of both sexes. When the civil courts attempt to resolve the issue of a child's welfare, they tend to rely on the opinion of a welfare officer, an institution anchored in yet another civil law: the Welfare Law (Procedure in Matters of Minors, Mentally Sick Persons, and Absent Persons), 1955. It had been the *qāḍīs*' custom to base their *ḥaḍāna* rulings on the child's age, unless suit had been filed to deprive the mother of custody for whatever reason. In such suits, most *qāḍīs* regarded the child's welfare as a norm worthy of adoption and usually availed themselves of the services of welfare officers who operate by force of secular law. Layish found that welfare officers' opinions usually discriminate against women.[13]

There are few precedents in which the Sharīʿa Appeals Court ruled in favour of a woman's custody of her minor children when considering the child's welfare, however, in these cases, the Court based its ruling on the civil laws. In one such case, as an example, a woman claimed that her husband wanted custody of their children only in order to avoid paying child support to them. She pointed out that the civil law (*al-qawānīn al-waḍʿiyya)* grants the woman authority equal to that of the father (natural custody). Moreover, she claimed that the lower court had ruled in opposition to the opinion of the welfare officer. The husband answered that the decision of the Sharīʿa Court of Appeals should not be based upon civil law. The court ruled that the welfare of the child was the basis of child custody (*ḥaḍāna*), and quoted from a judgement of the Supreme Civil Court, according to which it is not permitted to find in opposition to the wishes of a child over the age of eight.[14]

The following case illustrates a new approach toward understanding a principle of *Sharīʿa* law in light of a principle derived from modern law. After the divorce of a couple from the village of Mazraʿa, the ex-husband sued for custody of his son, arguing that the boy was now seven years old and the mother's *ḥaḍāna* period had expired. The Sharīʿa Court solicited the opinion of a welfare officer and ruled that although the mother worked on the night shift as a hospital nurse, the child's welfare mandated that he stay with his mother. The ruling did not spell out the welfare officer's arguments, so when the father appealed, the president of the Appeals Court called the *qāḍī*'s attention to this lacuna. As for the merits of the case itself, al-Nāṭūr ruled that there was no need to rely on civil law, for the *Sharīʿa* also includes the principle of child's welfare.[15] However, the determining age stipulated by the Ḥanafi jurists (seven for boys and nine for girls) was a long-standing convention that could be overruled. This convention, meant to ensure the child's welfare, was rooted in the assumption that the child needed his mother until this cut-off age but needed his father more afterwards in order to prepare for adult life. This entire premise was an outgrowth of customary considerations. Because the *qāḍī* of the first instance had said nothing in his ruling about the child's welfare and offered no reason for his decision to award custody of the child to his mother after age seven, even though she worked at night, al-Nāṭūr culled a term from modern law – a 'questionable assumption' to interpret the Muslim jurists' ruling and adapt it to current norms. He construes the Ḥanafi jurists' age stipulation as an assumption (*iftirāḍ*), and because any assumption can be challenged, custody may be extended beyond the age limit if one of the litigants can bring proof that this will serve the child's welfare.

Al-Nāṭūr showed, for example, that in contrast to the age stipulations, the *Sharīʿa* prescribes the separation of custody over a brother and sister of different ages. In this case, however, the age stipulations should be overridden and custody of both children given to one of the two parents, because the separation would harm the sibling relationship.[16]

In another case, a divorced husband sued to assure his visitation rights with respect to children who were in their mother's custody. The *qāḍī* of the lower court referred to Article 25 of the Capacity and Guardianship Law, 1962. The president of the Court of Appeals took note of this and wrote in his ruling:

The Capacity and Guardianship Law is a civil law, whereas a *qāḍī* should rely on the *Sharīʿa* only. Needless to say, the *Sharīʿa* is a complete, all-inclusive judicial system that can provide a response to any question or issue.[17]

The Sharīʿa Court in Nazareth misunderstood al-Nāṭūr's inclination to sanctify the principle of child's welfare irrespective of the age of the minor. In one case, the court ruled that the child's welfare would be determined in accordance with the age set forth in Islamic law, even though a welfare officer had presented the court with a contrasting opinion. The Court of Appeals struck down the ruling of the first instance, stating that the *qāḍī* should have given the child's welfare greater consideration irrespective of his age. In his criticism of the Appellate Court's verdict, the *qāḍī* of Nazareth argued: 'The president of the court has ruled on several occasions that we should not rely on civil law and should not disregard Islamic law.' The president deflected this criticism by arguing that the Nazareth court had, on its own initiative, solicited the opinion of the welfare officer, an agent of a civil institution, but had ruled against the opinion given. The court could have rendered judgement according to the *Sharīʿa* without soliciting any opinion. Having asked for the welfare officer's opinion, the *qāḍī* could not disregard it and rule in a manner contrary to it without providing a good reason or marshalling evidence to justify his decision.[18] Here again the principles of procedures, as learned in law school, influenced al-Nāṭūr's rulings.

The president of the Sharīʿa Court of Appeals objects to the use of Israeli law. He wishes to serve as an example to other *qāḍīs* by referring to Islamic legal sources, which he reinterprets in light of the 'spirit of the law', or the 'lawmaker's intentions'. If, for example, a medieval or Ottoman lawmaker determined that it is in the child's best interests to stay with the mother until a certain age and only then to be transferred to the custody of the father, then this 'lawmaker's intention' and the 'spirit of the law' is tantamount to the child's well-being. If one of the litigants can convince the *qāḍī* that the child's well-being warrants a ruling that overrules the age factor, then that principle replaces the child's age as the determining factor. Rather than calling on the welfare officer, the president of the Sharīʿa Court of Appeals urges the *qāḍī* to make more sophisticated use of the tools available to him, and to determine the child's welfare by examining and cross-examining witnesses. The *qāḍī*'s unmediated impression is more important than the welfare officer's professional opinion. Here the influence of a legal education has inspired al-Nāṭūr to introduce civil procedures in the Sharīʿa Court; such as examination and cross-examination of witnesses instead of the *Sharʿī tazkiyya* method, in which the court examines only the purity of the witness, not his testimony.

The Use of Arbitrators and Well-informed Persons

Qāḍīs in Israel make frequent use of arbitrators (*ḥakam* or *muḥakkam*) in cases involving the dissolution of marriages, and of experts (*mukhbirūn* or *ahl al-khibra*) in setting levels of alimony. In al-Nāṭūr's opinion, *qāḍīs* in Israel overuse the institution of family arbitration. The arbitrators themselves are not only oblivious to the limits of their authority and therefore frequently exceed them, but they also lack the requisite skills. They are unaware that theirs is a juridical task that requires compliance with juridical norms.[19]

According to Article 130 of the Ottoman Family Rights Law of 1917, which continues to be implemented in Israel, in the case of a marital dispute the *qāḍī* shall appoint two arbitrators, one from the husband's family and one from the wife's, who will serve as a family council (*majlis ʿāʾilī*) in an effort to effect a reconciliation. The Ḥanafi school recognises the institution of arbitration and its jurists have ruled that the arbitrators are authorised to dissolve a marriage if both spouses empower them to do so.[20] Ottoman law effected an innovation by inserting a Mālikī principle allowing the arbitrators, in cases where reconciliation is impossible, to determine which spouse is at fault. If it is the wife, she is entitled to her dowry or to the portion thereof, as stipulated by the arbitrators as her entitlement, commensurate with the extent of her guilt. If the arbitrators cannot reach an agreement between themselves, the *qāḍī* may replace them or appoint a third arbitrator who is not related to either spouse. This arbitrators' decision (whether based on an agreement or on a majority) is final and cannot be appealed. The first generation of *qāḍīs* in Israel disagreed as to how to apply the Ottoman law.[21] According to Layish, this provision of the Ottoman legislation was used chiefly by women who wished to take the initiative to dissolve their marriage.[22] In the second and third generations, this provision was also invoked extensively by men who wished to divorce their wives and feared the sanction of the penal law if they took this action against their wives' will.[23] Consequently, arbitration came into very wide use, and none of the second- or third-generation *qāḍīs* objected to the application of this law.

The following case gave the president of the Sharīʿa Court of

Appeals the justification to point out irregularities in the use of arbitration for the dissolution of marriages, and to instruct *qāḍīs* of the first instance (lower court) to wield this power in a different fashion than it had been applied hitherto.

Following a marital quarrel, a husband in the village of Majd al-Kurūm disposed of his wife's possessions, and she relocated to a house owned by her father in Haifa. The Sharīʿa Court in Haifa appointed two arbitrators under Article 130 of Ottoman Family Rights Law. They ordered that the marriage be dissolved but disagreed on the financial arrangements. The arbitrator appointed by the husband allowed the wife only one-fifth of the deferred dowry (which, according to the marriage contract, was $30,000). The wife's arbitrator held the husband solely responsible for the failure to reconcile and, consequently, ordered him to remit the full deferred dowry. The wife's arbitrator then exceeded his authority by ordering the husband to pay his wife an additional sum, equal to her dowry, in compensation for the suffering he had caused her. Finally, he stated that according to the Israeli civil Law on Property Relations between Spouses (1973), the combined property accrued by the spouses during their marriage should be divided equally between them.[24] After hearing both arbitrators' opinions, the Sharīʿa Court of Haifa appointed a third arbitrator, as prescribed by Article 130 of the Ottoman law. This arbitrator ordered the husband to return two-fifths of his wife's dowry, twice the share stipulated by the husband's arbitrator. When the latter was appraised of the third arbitrator's decision, he revised his opinion to conform to that of the third arbitrator. The wife's arbitrator knew nothing of the third arbitrator's decision. The *qāḍī* of Haifa issued a ruling in accordance with the decision of two of the three arbitrators.

When the wife appealed to the Sharīʿa Court of Appeals, its president, al-Nāṭūr, recognised a phenomenon familiar to him from his term as *qāḍī* of Jaffa: the *qāḍī*'s ignorance of the rules of arbitration. He therefore decided to use a legal ruling in this case to refresh his subordinates' familiarity with these rules. First, he stated that none of the arbitrators represent any specific litigant. An arbitrator is a judicial trustee who is answerable to the rules of jurisprudence, as is the *qāḍī* who appointed and empowered him. An arbitrator cannot change his mind after having heard the decision of another arbitrator. Furthermore, the role of the third arbitrator is to choose one of the options proffered by the other two arbitrators, not to add a third opinion which would aggravate the confusion and disagreement. In this particular case, the arbitrator from the woman's side did not understand his powers and limitations and therefore exceeded them. He was not competent to make any decision for the wife other than the award of her full dowry, and he certainly was not empowered to serve in a *Sharīʿa* institution and apportion the couple's property in accordance with the law of Property Relations between Spouses (1973), a civil statute based on a civil norm. Here, al-Nāṭūr drew the *qāḍī*'s attention to his duty to choose reliable arbitrators and apprise them of their guidelines and powers. Finally, the Court of Appeals revoked the ruling of the first instance and returned the case to the first instance for rehearing.[25] The president of the *Sharīʿa* Courts expects the *qāḍīs* to act as judges of Islamic law and not as agents of customary norms.

Mention of a civil law – Property Relations between Spouses (1973) – in a *Sharīʿa* court is particularly interesting. This statute, a standard feature in Israeli civil courts, prescribes that upon termination of marriage, the wealth accrued by the spouses during the marriage be divided between them. Israeli civil law, influenced by European norms, has long accepted the norm of combined and community property. When the Knesset debated the bill, all of the *qāḍīs* opposed it for two reasons. First, the idea of combined and community property is alien to Islamic law because Muslim women keep a separate account of their dowry, property, jewellery and earnings. A Muslim husband must support his wife even if her earnings are greater than his. If the civil law on Property Relations between Spouses were applied to Muslim husbands, they would be paying their divorced wives, relatively speaking, more than non-Muslim husbands would pay theirs: dowry and alimony first, and half of the combined property afterwards. Second, in the absence of an agreement between spouses, the *Sharīʿa* Court, according to the statutory law, has to rule for an equal division of the combined property. After the Knesset passed the law, despite the *qāḍī's* objections, the *qāḍīs* began to circumvent it by advising marriage registrars to propose to future spouses, when drawing up marriage contracts, to insert a stipulation committing them, in the case of divorce, to apply only *Sharīʿa* law, not the law of Property Relations between Spouses. A hint to this circumvention is found in the *Sharīʿa* Court Director's words, 'the practice has been that at the time of contracting a marriage, the couple are asked to state their conditions in the pertinent entry in the marriage contract. It is here that they can opt for the law to be applied with regard to their property relations and for the form of division of wealth should the opt for the secular law'.[26] The actual situation was more extreme; the spouses would sign first on a blank marriage contract, and only afterwards the *ma'dhūndhūn* (registrar of marriage) would fill out the details. It was found that the registrars were then acting on their own initiative in entering the conditions of the marriage contract. The bride does not sign on the marriage contract, rather her father or brother signs as patron to the marriage. This phenomenon is widespread, and based on it courts in Israel have ruled in a large number of cases that there is no validity to the above described condition in the marriage contract: property must be divided equally between the parties.[27]

Al-Nāṭūr orders the *qāḍīs* to instruct the *ma'dhūn* not to compile the marriage contracts but to record the parties' words, and to provide both parties with a copy of the contract within three days of its signing.[28]

By mentioning the civil legislation, the wife's arbitrator in the above-mentioned case gave the president of the Sharīʿa Court of Appeals an opportunity to call the attention of the lower court to the fact that marriage registrars, who derive their authority from the *qāḍī*, are empowered only to record the parties' statements; they may not propose the insertion of additional provisions in the contract. According to the *Sharīʿa*, such an official, known as the *ma'dhūn* is solely a registrar and cannot be a party to the contract. The President's remark reflects his judicial opinion, not his principles. As a matter of principle, al-Nāṭūr opposed the application of the civil Property Relations between Spouses Law to Muslim couples. As a jurist well versed in civil law, he argues that financial agreements integrated into marriage contracts, and not as separate agreements approved by a court, are invalid. *Qāḍīs* and *ma'dhūn*s who propose such agreements believe they are helping husbands by providing them with a remedy against the application of the Property Relations between Spouses Law. This practice, however, is actually detrimental to husbands because wives can easily enforce the civil law against them.[29] This is because the law stipulates that any financial agreement between the parties must be separate from the marriage contract, thus invalidating an agreement embedded within the contract itself.[30] The Tel Aviv District Court demonstrated this in February 1995 in the case of a divorced woman from Taybe – 'Āṭifa Jābir – pronouncing her right to one half of the house purchased by her husband Farīd after their marriage. The Court indicated that the household upkeep and raising of the child is regarded as an equal contribution made by the wife to the common effort of acquiring property.

The case was raised by the personal initiative of a member of Knesset in an effort to amend the law of Financial Relations between Spouses in such a way that minors cannot certify the financial agreement between themselves at the time of their marriage. When 'Āṭifa Jābir separated from her husband, Farīd, after the fifteenth year of marriage, she left the house that he had acquired after their marriage, in Taybe, and had registered under his name. According to the 'Rābī Legal Rule' of the Supreme Court, from 1977 all partners are entitled to the communal right to property. The judge, Goren, accepted 'Āṭifa's claim that the marriage contract was not a valid financial agreement, because there was no certification from either the District Court or the religious court. Certification can only be given if it can be proved that both partners entered into the contract freely and with understanding of its meaning and implications. In this case 'Āṭifa did not sign, rather her father did. Furthermore, she was a minor and therefore did not understand what was being signed. Accordingly, Goran ruled on a 'balance of resources'. Goran pointed out that even if 'Āṭifa did not invest money in the purchase of the house, 'maintenance of the house and raising the children are contributions equal in value to contribution of the husband in the co-operative efforts of the couple in the purchase of property.'[31]

The above-mentioned law is the most indirect intervention of the Israeli parliament in the personal status affairs of Muslims. Unlike inheritance cases, where women do not tend to use civil law for their benefit, as customary norms prevail and family inheritance disputes are rare, many divorce cases reflect an emotional dispute between the parties which sometimes result in a suit being brought against the ex-husband, in civil courts in order to implement the Property Relations between Spouses Law. The low number of such actions results from the lack of awareness of Muslim women of the existence of legislation.[32]

Al-Nāṭūr's method of improving the *Sharīʿa* judicial system draws on two devices. The conventional method is to use appeal rulings, and al-Nāṭūr indeed invokes these extensively in order to teach *qāḍīs* how to approach their work. The *qāḍīs* of the lower court, noticing that their decisions are subject to the judicial review of the appeals instance, usually make an effort to bring their rulings into conformity with the intentions of the court above them. This conventional *modus operandi*, which is widely used in secular civil law, was adopted by al-Nāṭūr and is invoked more extensively than in the past. However, unlike civil law, in which Supreme Court verdicts are sources of law because they interpret the law, Islamic law does not treat rulings as binding precedents. The Appeals Court may rescind, amend or reverse the decisions of a lower court, or may return the case to the *qāḍī* of the lower court for rehearing.

In the absence of an institution of *ʿulamāʾ* or an Islamic legal institute, al-Nāṭūr decided to introduce binding procedures modelled after the Sudanese system, according to which the Grand Qāḍī is vested with the authority to issue legal circulars (*manshūrāt qaḍaʾiyya*), some of them reforming the *Sharīʿa* law.[33] Al-Nāṭūr published a collection of judicial regulations (*marsūm qaḍāʾī*) on various subjects and made sure that the *qāḍīs* signed a commitment to honour them. This innovation was carried out without seeking state legislation backing it, as was the Sudanese case of the Grand Qāḍī. As a result, anyone who regards himself as injured by these 'regulations' can challenge their validity by applying to the higher court of justice. Al-Nāṭūr himself is aware of this. He claims that what he needs most is the co-operation of his *qāḍī* colleagues. The first *marsūm* dealt with the prohibition upon *qāḍīs* forbidding them to produce legal opinions (*fatāwā*), or to approve transactions in *waqf* (endowments) assets or plots of land which formerly served as a mosque or a cemetery. The second *marsūm* was aimed at abolishing a judicial practice of the *mukhbirūn,* the well-informed people whom the *qāḍīs* appoint to advise them in alimony cases before they determine the husband's liability. The *marsūm* was necessary because *qāḍīs* in Israel had adopted the custom of allowing *mukhbirūn* to determine the level of alimony by themselves, thus effectively waiving their own power.[34] Al-Nāṭūr considered this practice irregular. Moreover, in order to reach a final ruling in cases of alimony, *qāḍīs* often set their secretaries to find two Muslims at random to act as 'well informed people'. They would then determine the level of alimony without any knowledge of the husbands economic situation.[35] According to the *Sharīʿa*, it is the *qāḍī* who sets alimony if the spouses cannot reach agreement on this point during the divorce proceedings. The *qāḍī* may appoint an adviser only in order to help him assess the husband's economic situation.[36] The President of the *Sharīʿa* Court noted that the empowerment of *mukhbirūn* proved detrimental to women because *mukhbirūn* were exclusively men and for this reason, would tend to perpetuate male social attitudes. The custom of relying on *mukhbirūn* had become so widespread that in the past the Court of Appeals, in its ignorance, had been wont to strike down alimony rulings simply because the *qāḍīs* had made them without consulting *mukhbirūn*. In his *marsūm*, Shaykh al-Nāṭūr scolds the *qāḍīs* and describes their alimony decisions as non-reflective of norms of justice. Pointing to public criticism that had surfaced about this issue, he warns that voices calling for the transfer of jurisdiction of alimony and maintenance to civil courts will be heeded if the public loses confidence in the *qāḍīs*' rulings. Tracing the source of the institution of *mukhbirūn* in the Ḥanafi school and in civil legislation in Arab countries, al-Nāṭūr asserts that the *mukhbir*'s sole function is to ascertain the husband's economic capacity. A *qāḍī* should appoint *mukhbirūn* only if the wife demands an aberrant, above-average level of alimony on the grounds that her husband is affluent but she is unable to prove it. Shaykh al-Nāṭūr points out that a *mukhbir* has no standing either as an arbitrator or as an expert witness, that his appointment is not subject to any criteria, and that he has no liability. The *mukhbir*, according to al-Nāṭūr, is an 'informant' only. It is therefore absurd, al-Nāṭūr concludes, to entrust such people, some of whom are illiterate or dishonest, with a *de facto* judicial function. Shaykh al-Nāṭūr believes there is no better expert in setting alimony than the *qāḍī*, and therefore he should not delegate his judicial authority to anybody else. He then advises *qāḍīs* to invoke the administrative tools that the modern state makes available to them, which are far more reliable than the opinion of a *mukhbir*: the husband's payslips, the income tax authorities' assessment of his income and documents from the National Insurance Institute, the Welfare Bureau, or the Employment Service.[37] In those cases where the *qāḍīs* followed the *marsūm*, the sums of alimony and maintenance granted rose dramatically.

The Reinterpretation of *Sharīʿa* Terms in Accordance with Current Conditions

Some of al-Nāṭūr's rulings attest to a thorough exploration of religious sources in an attempt to interpret and adjust them to modern conditions. One example is the definition of *maskan sharʿī* (legal domicile). A legal domicile, according to the Ḥanafi codex of laws compiled by Qadrī Pāshā, is a separate house (i.e. separate from the house of the husband's family) if the couple are well off, and a separate apartment within the husband's family's house if they are not. The dwelling must have all the legally required facilities, as well as neighbours of a social level that accords with the couple's standing. If the husband installs his wife in a separate dwelling in his family's house, she is not entitled to demand a different dwelling unless his relatives 'harass her by word or deed'.[38]

In a suit filed by a husband against his wife in the Sharī'a Court of Jaffa, the plaintiff petitioned for obedience (*ṭā'a*) in order to compel his wife to resume her domicile in their matrimonial residence in Lod. The woman, represented by her brother, asserted that she was willing to comply on three conditions: that the residence meet the criteria of *maskan shar'ī*, that her husband treat her properly and that members of his family refrain from meddling in her affairs. The principal issue was how to define the conditions of the dwelling, i.e. whether they met the criteria of *maskan shar'ī* as stipulated in the *Sharī'a*. The court secretary, sent by the court to examine the residence, found that the residence met the requirements. As for neighbours, the secretary pointed out that the dwelling was a condominium apartment, in which the husband's parents lived in the adjacent flat. The kitchen of the apartment overlooked the parents' flat. The house had a common entrance to the condominium; however, each apartment was separate. The husband's brother had built a house two metres from the husband's apartment, but the house was untenanted.

The woman claimed that the windows of the apartment were positioned such as to deny the possibility of conjugal privacy (*tuṣarrab asrār al-zawjiyya*). When the *qāḍī* asked her to substantiate this allegation, she described an incident in which she left the house one day when her husband was out, clutching a wrapped object. When her husband returned from work, he asked her what she had been holding when she left the house. She inferred from this that her husband's relatives had apprised him of what they had seen. In her suit, the wife, through her brother, argued that *maskan shar'ī* denoted a house separate from her husband's family, and that the presence of no neighbours other than her husband's relatives intimidated her.

The court had to decide whether the husband's dwelling met the definition of *maskan shar'ī* as *bayt lahu ghalaq min dār* (a room in a dwelling unit that can be locked). An especially important question was whether, as some jurists believed, 'a woman of the upper class must be provided with an unshared residence' (unlike a middle- or lower-class woman, who may settle for a dwelling shared with her husband's second wife or his parents).[39] In his ruling, the *qāḍī* writes that it is inappropriate under current conditions to stipulate the criteria of a legal domicile in view of economic circumstances. In the past, living conditions were harsh and economic class mobility was virtually non-existent. Today, rental housing is available and one's economic situation can change quickly; the rich may suddenly become poor and *vice versa*. Therefore, the stipulation that an affluent woman requires a separate dwelling is no longer valid. As for defining a legal domicile as a *bayt* (house), al-Nāṭūr consulted the classical dictionaries and jurists' definitions. He quotes the *Lisān al-ʿArab* Dictionary, which defines a *bayt* as a unit within a *dār* and defines a *dār* as a plot of land with rooms and an unroofed yard. At the present time, the *qāḍī* explains, the original meanings of *bayt* and *dār* as 'room' and 'house' are no longer tenable. An apartment in an urban condominium is tantamount to a *bayt*. He adds that if *dār* denotes a separate dwelling, one would have to declare entire towns as comprised of illegal dwellings. After searching for the 'legislator's intention' he concluded that the logic of *maskan sharʿī* is the woman's right to privacy in conjugal life. Thus, the discovery of conjugal secrets through the windows depends solely on the couple. Therefore, the court found the dwelling legal and ordered the wife to obey her husband in his apartment, on pain of being declared a rebellious wife and, as such, not entitled to alimony from the time she left home.[40] This ruling by al-Nāṭūr as the *qāḍī* of Jaffa marked a departure from the decisions of other *qāḍīs* who, in similar suits, had construed *maskan sharʿī* as defined by Qadrī Pāshā.[41] According to this definition, *qāḍīs* had tended to rule that a dwelling was illegal if the husband's family lived in a condominium that lacked a separate entrance. Al-Nāṭūr interpreted the term 'separate entrance' differently, i.e. not as a separate entrance to the condominium, but rather a separate entrance (front door) to each apartment. What distinguishes al-Nāṭūr from his predecessors is his tendency to look for a just solution for questions raised under modern current conditions. As a law school graduate who was trained to consider the 'legislator's intention', he tends to enquire and to interpret the classical legal sources according to reasoning.

Introduction of Ethical Norms in the *Sharīʿa* Judiciary

In one of his first rulings as *qāḍī* of Jaffa, al-Nāṭūr did not hesitate to level direct criticism at his superiors, the Court of Appeals and its president. Below is a description of this case and its subsequent ruling.[42]

A woman from Jaffa stipulated in her 1973 marriage contract with her fiancé who was from Haifa, that if he abandoned or divorced her, he would pay her 1,500 Israeli pounds per month. This is an exceptional stipulation in marriage contracts,[43] but the bride-to-be evidently anticipated such an event and insisted on the inclusion of this stipulation in her contract as a deterrent. After her husband abandoned her in 1980, she asked the court to order him to tender maintenance for herself and child support for their daughter, a minor. After she obtained a ruling ordering her husband to pay maintenance, she sued again to invoke the stipulation in her marriage contract, i.e. monthly payments of 1,500 Israeli pounds per month since the date of marriage in 1973, linked to the consumer price index. The Sharīʿa Court of Jaffa heard the case in 1984, before Shaykh Aḥmad al-Nāṭūr was appointed *qāḍī*. In the proceedings, the husband argued that his wife's stipulation should be regarded as a condition for tendering of maintenance, which he had already been ordered to pay. The woman insisted that the stipulation was in fact a condition of desertion (*sharṭ al-hajr*) and left the matter in the court's hands. The court ruled that she should receive the exact sum stipulated in the contract, 1,500 Israeli pounds without adjustment to the Index, to be paid from the day of the ruling, which was seven months after her husband deserted her. It should be noted that Israel experienced triple-digit inflation from the late 1970s to the mid-1980s. During this period, the pound was replaced by the sheqel at the rate of 10:1. The basis for this ruling was Article 38 of the Ottoman Family Rights Law,[44] which states that a woman may stipulate that if her husband takes another wife, then she or her rival would be considered divorced. The woman appealed against the ruling and argued that the payments should be adjusted to the Index and calculated from the day her husband abandoned her. The Court of Appeals, with a panel of two judges, ruled that if the alimony stipulated by the Jaffa court was insufficient, she could sue for a larger amount. However, if her intention was to construe the stipulation in the marriage contract as a fine to impose on her husband, her claim was only able to be judged in a civil court, for the *Sharīʿa* Court did not have the jurisdiction to impose fines. The Court of Appeals rejected the petition but rescinded the decision of the lower court and ordered the latter to rehear the case.[45] When the Jaffa Court reheard the case, it asked the plaintiff to clarify the nature of the stipulation. She answered that her stipulation was not alimony but rather 'compensation for desertion' (*taʿwīḍ ʿalā al-hajr*). In its ruling, the court found that such a stipulation came under the jurisdiction of the civil courts. The *qāḍī* of Jaffa wishing to assist her in transferring the case to the civil judiciary, attached a letter to his verdict, addressed 'to whom it may concern', describing the judgement as final and not subject to appeal. The woman then sued in Haifa District Court, which ruled that the *Sharīʿa* Court was indeed empowered to adjudicate breaches of marriage-contract stipulations. In its ruling, it cited a list of matters under *Sharīʿa* court jurisdiction according to Article 51 of His Majesty's Order in Council for Palestine.[46]

The woman wrote to the president of the Sharīʿa Court of Appeals, enclosing the decision of Haifa District Court. The president sent her the following reply:

> I inform you that you may file a new suit with the Jaffa Sharīʿa Court with respect to the letter you have sent me, demanding the effectuation of said stipulation at an indexed sum. The Sharīʿa Court of Jaffa will adjudicate the case in accordance with the rules. After judgement is handed down, you may appeal it to me in order to bring the matter to a close …

In the first session, the Qāḍī of Jaffa tried to persuade the sides to reach a reconciliation. By the second session, Qāḍī al-Nāṭūr had taken office. Al-Nāṭūr began by criticising the Haifa District Court. His dispute over the correct interpretation of the law of a secular state was unusual and highly atypical of a *qāḍī* in a *Sharīʿa* court. In his critique, the Qāḍī of Jaffa informed the District Court that it had based its decision on the wrong article of His Majesty's Order in Council: Article 51 instead of Article 52. The British parliament, he explained, differentiated between Muslims, who had constituted an *umma* (nation) in the Ottoman state, and members of other *millets*, to whom Article 51 pertains. Article 51 lists only all issues of personal status, whereas Article 52 relates specifically to the exclusive jurisdiction of the *Sharīʿa* Court.[47]

In the remainder of al-Nāṭūr's ruling, he criticises the instance above him. First, he writes that the Court of Appeals had erred in treating the case as a suit for damages. The suit had been brought in order to invoke a stipulation in the marriage contract; as such, the *Sharīʿa* Court was fully empowered to adjudicate it. Second, the Court of Appeals had erred in allowing the plaintiff to refile her suit. Using terms of modern jurisprudence, al-Nāṭūr cites an unequivocal rule in Islamic law: verdicts handed down are final, *res judicata*, because of a *bar*, with the exception of a certain type of suit in which the circumstances have changed, as in alimony and child support cases.

Because the stipulation in the marriage contract was *res judicata* and the plaintiff had exhausted all her remedies including the right to appeal, she should not have been allowed to submit a new claim and reopen the case. Third, al-Nāṭūr criticises the legal ethics of the president of the Appeals Court. He quotes the letter that the president sent the plaintiff, after the decision of the lower court in Jaffa, instructing her how to act: 'After judgement is handed down, you may appeal it to me in order to bring the matter to a close ...' Al-Nāṭūr then subjects the president to further criticism. In his opinion, the president, who had served on a two-judge panel in the appeal decision, should have at least expanded the panel of judges hearing the appellant's case instead of having decided at his own discretion to reopen the case. Al-Nāṭūr pointed out that the president had no authority to instruct the *qāḍī* to reopen the case. The appellant's only remedy after receiving the final ruling of the Sharīʿa Court of Appeals was to petition the Supreme Court of Israel, sitting as the High Court of Justice. Only this instance, he noted, had the authority to rescind the ruling of a religious court and order it to rehear the case.

Finally, al-Nāṭūr analysed the claim on its own merits, citing a variety of Islamic sources. He ruled that the woman's stipulation in her marriage contract was null and void. It is a principle in *Sharīʿa* nuptial law that no stipulation in a marriage contract may contradict the *Sharīʿa* itself. For example, a woman may not forbid her husband to divorce her, but she may stipulate that if he takes another wife, he must divorce either her or her rival.[48]

The aforementioned court ruling reflects the inter-generational contrast among the *qāḍīs*, as illustrated by a *qāḍī* of the third generation and the justices on the Court of Appeals who still belong to the first generation. This is without doubt an exceptional verdict. With full command of the rules of modern jurisprudence, al-Nāṭūr, the third-generation *qāḍī*, has the confidence to criticise even the Haifa District Court. His familiarity with the principles of judicial ethics and norms, acquired at law school, made him aware of the extent of the ethical flaws in the *Sharīʿa* system, and he chose to effect change by means of his verdicts. Al-Nāṭūr's appointment in 1994 as president of the Sharīʿa Court of Appeals gave him an opportunity to promote dynamic change throughout the system.

Another example is a suit that was brought before the Sharīʿa Court in Haifa for the termination of housing payments for two minors as part of the settlement that a divorced father had been ordered to pay for his children. The *qāḍī* accepted the father's argument and absolved him from payment on the grounds that, as the father had insisted, they could live with *his* mother and did not have to live with *their* mother. The mother appealed the ruling, alleging *inter alia* that the *qāḍī* was the brother-in-law of the plaintiff's counsel. The latter acknowledged the relationship and admitted that he and the *qāḍī* spent much time in each other's company. In his defence, however, he stated that this was well known to the defendant from the start of the case, and she had not complained about it in the first instance. In his ruling, the president of the Court of Appeals asked:

> How can the public trust a judicial system that adjudicates cases and issues verdicts when one of the litigants is represented by the brother-in-law of the judge who is hearing the case? The *qāḍī* should have recused himself. Moreover, no reasons were given for the *qāḍī*'s decision.[49]

In another ruling on appeal, al-Nāṭūr again pointed to the absence of reasons in a verdict by the Sharīʿa Court of Nazareth:

> A judiciary that administers justice between people derives its power from the public's trust, but it cannot win the public's trust unless the public is convinced that justice is seen to be done. This can be accomplished only if the *qāḍī* explains the rationale and evidence that underlie his rulings.[50]

Conclusions

Under the conditions prevailing in Israel, a basically secular non-Muslim state that has no institution for higher Islamic education for Muslims who wish to study Islamic law, the education of *qāḍīs* is an important factor in determining their juridical orientation. *Qāḍīs* in Israel can be divided into four categories, depending on their educational background: graduates of al-Azhar (most *qāḍīs* of the first generation), those with high-school education only, university graduates in the humanities and social sciences, and graduates of law faculties. This paper has examined the way a *qāḍī*'s education at a law faculty in a modern university affects his attitude toward the *Sharīʿa*, state law, and the interplay between them.

Since 1948, three of the eighteen *qāḍīs* appointed to the *Sharīʿa* judicial system have been graduates of Israeli law faculties. Only one, the incumbent president of the Sharīʿa Court of Appeals, has taken an original approach. This article has described his novel attitudes as reflected in several of his rulings. A grounding in modern law alone is not sufficient to affect the *qāḍīs*' rulings significantly. It may have this effect only when coupled with a desire to effect changes in the *Sharīʿa* judicial system .

The president of the Sharīʿa Court of Appeals, whose rulings form the basis of this article, rejects state legislation as a source of inspiration for rulings in the *Sharīʿa* Court. It is not surprising that he and other *qāḍīs* categorically reject secular Israeli legislation because it reflects European legal norms that contradict the principles of Islamic culture. One example is the principle of combined and community property, as adopted by the Israeli legislature, as opposed to the principle of separate property existing in Islamic law. However, the president of the Sharīʿa Court of Appeals also rejects civil laws that do not contradict the tenets of the *Sharīʿa* and that may even help the *qāḍī* arrive at the truth and administer fair justice. In the matter of child custody, for example, Israeli law, like Islamic law, considers the child's well-being the determining factor. Israeli law allows consultation with a welfare officer to determine the child's well-being.

In this specific case, it was not the *qāḍī*'s legal education but rather his 'reformist' orientation that guided his attempt to reinterpret the sources of Islamic law. As the head of the *Sharīʿa* judicial system in Israel, Shaykh Aḥmad al-Nāṭūr would like to see *qāḍīs* abandon their predecessors' judicial customs and be more active in rendering judgements. The *qāḍī* should strive to interpret the Islamic legal sources as they apply to contemporary issues, such as the meaning of *maskan sharʿī* as applied to modern urban housing. The *qāḍī* should also set the level of alimony or child support, as opposed to delegating this prerogative to *mukhbirūn*, and should ensure that the arbitration process in marital disputes follows appropriate judicial rules. Finally, the *Sharīʿa* judicial system should be free of biases and should operate within a normative ethical context, as befits a judicial system.

Al-Nāṭūr's appeal to his colleagues to invoke Islamic sources and disregard Israeli legislation is based on his view of the *Sharīʿa* as an all-embracing, living body of law that can be interpreted and adapted to changing realities. The introduction of ethical norms in the *Sharīʿa* judicial system and reinforcement of the *qāḍī*'s judicial function should enhance the public's trust in the *Sharīʿa* judicial system. These ethical norms make the *qāḍī* an active judge who uses methods influenced by modern law, such as examination and cross-examination of witnesses and substantiation of decisions. As al-Nāṭūr expresses this in his second *marsūm qaḍāʾī* (collection of judicial guidelines):

The *Sharī'a* court is the only official Islamic institution that Muslims in Israel still retain. It is incumbent upon us to make it an institution that applies Islamic law in practice, in order to inculcate religious faith and strengthen the rule of Allāh on earth. Therefore, the preservation of the *Sharī'a* courts is a basic Islamic imperative, provided that these courts serve as bastions of justice and truth.

Notes

1 Author's note: The author thanks the Harry S. Truman Institute for Research and the Advancement of Peace at the Hebrew University of Jerusalem for the research grant that made this research possible. I am indebted to Professor Aharon Layish for his guidance and encouragement since my graduate studies, and Shaykh Aḥmad al-Nāṭūr for his insightful comments.

2 On the *Sharī'a* judiciary in East Jerusalem, see L. Welchman, 'Family Law under Occupation: Islamic Law and the *Sharī'a* Courts in the West Bank' in Ch. Mallat and J. Connors, eds, *Islamic Family Law* (Dordrecht/Boston/New York, 1990), 93–115; Y. Reiter, *Islam in Jerusalem* (forthcoming), chapter 2.

3 On the *Sharī'a* judiciary during the Mandatory period, see U. M. Kupferschmidt, *The Supreme Muslim Council: Islam under the British Mandate for Palestine* (Leiden, 1987), 78–98; A. Layish, 'Muslim Religious Jurisdiction in Israel', *AAS* 1 (1965), 49–79; R. H. Eisenman, *Islamic Law in Mandate Palestine and Modern Israel* (Leiden, 1978).

4 On the *Qāḍīs* in Israel and the Islamic judiciary see Ibid.; Layish, '*Qāḍīs* and *Sharī'a* in Israel', *AAS* 7 (1971), 237–72; Layish, *Women and Islamic Law in a Non-Muslim State* (New York/Toronto/Jerusalem, 1975); Layish, 'Maḥkama', *EI* vol. 2, p. 6, fasc. 99–100: 30; Eisenman, *Islamic Law*; S. Sha'ashu'a, *Islamic Courts in Israel* (Hebrew) (Tel Aviv, 1981).

5 On the Knesset legislation, see Layish, *Women and Islamic Law*, pp. 1–4; Layish, 'The Status of the *Sharī'a* in a Non-Muslim State; The Case of Israel', *AAS* 27 (1993), 171–87.

6 Moshe Reinfeld, "Beit Ha-Mishpat", *Ha'aretz*, 22.6.95.

7 There are about 1000 Israeli Muslim law school graduates. In 1995 there were about 80 Muslim students in the law schools.

8 On education in Arab schools in Israel, see M. al-Hajj, *Education among the Arabs in Israel* (Jerusalem, 1996); S. Mar'ī, *Arab Education in Israel* (New York, 1978).

9 Opinion polls show that 59 per cent of Arabs trust the state courts compared to only 38 per cent who trust the government. H. Levinson, E. Katz and M. al-Hajj, *Jews and Arabs in Israel: Common Values and Mutual Images* (Hebrew) (Jerusalem, 1995), 16.

10 Suha 'Arraf, 'Aba kvar hatam', *Ha'aretz magazine*, 21.7.95. The Succession Law of 1965 provides in civil courts for complete equality between the sexes

in all categories of property, and it secures complete freedom of testation, whereas the *Sharīʿa* permits one third of the estate to be disposed of by will. See Layish, 'The Status of the *Sharīʿa*', p. 175; Ibid., 'Bequests as an Instrument for Accomodating the Inheritance Rules: Israel as a Case Study', *ILS* 2, 3 (1995), 282–319.

11 See Lilly Galeely, 'Be-Sha'arey ha-'i-tzedeq', *Ha'aretz*, 16.12.94.

12 Layish, *Women and Islamic Law*, p. 335.

13 Ibid., pp. 256–7.

14 Appeals, 12/78 from 22.1.79.

15 Appeals 28/94.

16 On the child's welfare as a principle of the first generation of *Qāḍīs* see Layish, *Women and Islamic Law*, pp. 256–7.

17 Appeals 48/94. For rulings of the appeals court prior to al-Nāṭūr, based on civil law, see *Appeals* 7/82 of 14.3.82, 42.86 of 25.11.86 and 37/87 of 20.8.87

18 *Appeals* 23/94.

19 See as an example, a case in which the arbitrators determined the property relations betwee spouses; *Appeals* 48/86 of 27.12.86.

20 For arbitration in the Ḥanafi school see Layish, *Women and Islamic Law*, p. 169.

21 Ibid., pp. 206–8.

22 Ibid., pp. 169–71.

23 On divorce against the wife's will, see ibid., pp. 35ff. The phenonmenon of men using Article 130 as a means of by-passing puishment according to Article 181 of the 1977 Penal Law regarding divorce against a woman's will, is mentioned by the *Sharīʿa* Court of Appeals in case 63/87 o 25.1.88 and in case 2/88 of 30.3.88 i which a man sued for the establishemt of a family council because his wife could not deliver children.

24 *Sefer Hahuqim* (*Book of Laws*) 712, 24 July 1973.

25 *Appeals* 50/93; 54/94.

26 Subhi Abu Gosh, 'The *Sharīʿa* Courts from the Perspective of Israeli Pluralism', in K. O. Cohen and J. S. Gerber, eds, *Perspectives on Israeli Pluralism: Proceedings of a Conference on Pluralism in Israel* (New York, 1991), 50.

27 Yossi Elgazi, 'Lama Lish'ol et hakkala kesheyyesh la av o-aḥ', *Ha'aretz*, 23.8.95.

28 Suha ʿArraf, 'Aba kvar hatam', *Ha'aretz magazine*, 21.7.95.

29 Interview dated 3 April 1995.

30 Abū Zahra reveals that the principle of custody age for a boy is that he is capable of eating, drinking and dressing on his own and is no more in need of a woman to raise him, and for a girl when she arrives physical maturity. In order to prevent disputes it layed down a definite age for these descriptions. Muḥammad Abū Zahra, *al-Aḥwāl al-Shakhṣiyya* (2nd ed., Cairo, 1950), 483–4. In another verdict pertaining to the institution of arbitration, the Court of Appeals ruled that a court of first instance may not rely on the opinions and decisions of one arbitrator only. Yet another verdict stipulated that wherever

two arbitrators fail to agree, the *qāḍī* of the first instance should appoint a third arbitrator instead of choosing the opinion of the arbitrators whom he had appointed. Al-Naṭūr also ruled that arbitrators may not overstep their powers by setting compensation that wives must pay their husbands. *Appeals* 37/92; 38/94; 50/94.

31 H"P, 490/90 of 28.2.95. See Moshe Reinfeld, 'Yahasey mamon bein qtinim', *Ha'aretz*, 3 July 1995.

32 Claimed by lawyer Hadass Tagri of the Civil Rights' Association, Suha 'Arraf, 'Aba kvar hatam', *Ha'aretz magazine*, 21.7.95.

33 A. Layish and G. R. Warburg, *The Implementation of the Sharī'a in Sudan under Numayri: 1983–85* (forthcoming), 105–8.

34 On the task of *mukhbir* during the first generation of *qāḍīs* see Layish, *Women and Islamic Law*, p. 91.

35 See as an example, *Appeals*, 18/81 of 16.9.81.

36 Suha 'Arraf, 'Aba Krar halam', *Ha'aretz magazine*, 21.7.95

37 *Marsūm Qaḍā'ī*, no. 2, dated 24 January 1995.

38 Layish, *Women and Islamic Law*, p. 3 based on Muḥammad Qadrī Pāshā, *Kitāb al-Aḥkām al-Shar'iyya fi al-Aḥwāl al-Shakhṣiyya 'alā Madhhab al-Imām Abī Ḥanīfa al-Nu'mān* in Rushdī al-Sarrāj, *Kitāb Majmū'at al-Qawānīn al-Shar'iyya* (Jaffa, 1944), 80ff., articles 184–8.

39 Ibn 'Ābidīn quotes from Multaqāt Abū al-Qāsim: '*al-sharīfa dhāt al-yasār lā budd min ifrādihā bi-dār*'.

40 Jaffa *sijill* 82/85.

41 For rulings of the first generation of *qāḍīs* see Layish, *Women and Islamic Law*, pp. 3ff., pp. 108ff.

42 Jaffa *sijill* 388/84.

43 It originates from the development of a customary norm to compensate a women for divorcing her without a legal ground. See Layish, *Women and Islamic Law*, pp. 145–6.

44 Jaffa *sijill* 829/80.

45 *Sharī'a* Court of Appeals 1/81.

46 Haifa District Court 1743/81.

47 On the Order-in-Council with regard to *Sharī'a* Court jurisdiction see S. D. Goitein and A. Ben Shemesh, *Muslim Law in Israel* (Hebrew) (Jerusalem, 1957), 274. Abu Gosh, 'The *Sharī'a* Courts', p. 46.

48 On the stipulations in marriage contracts, see as an example al-Shalabī, 'Ḥāshiyyat al-Durr' in Muḥammad Ibn 'Ābidīn, *Radd al-Muḥtār 'alā al-Durr al-Mukhtār* (2nd ed., Cairo, 1979), vol. 3, 241.

49 Appeals 64/94. On a case in which the Supreme Court of Justice ruled out a *qāḍī's* decision for his friendship with the plaintiff's father see *Ha'aretz* , 13 September 1991. The Supreme Court ruled also against the *Sharī'a* Court of Appeals who claimed that friendship between the *qāḍī* and one of the parties is not included in article 62 of the Ottoman Civil Procedure Law as a ground for a *qāḍī* to recuse himself . The Supreme Court interpreted this article by

saying that the grounds listed in that article are only exemplary. However, whenever fear exists that the principle of natural justice can not be honoured, or a case of judicial authority's bias is at hand, or a judge in particular can not be honoured, this is a good reason for a judge to recuse himself. *Ha'aretz*, 3 July 1995. For criticizing the *qāḍī's* ethical norms see 'Alī Rāfi', 'al-Maḥākim al-Shar'iyya', *al-Ittiḥād*, 18 August 1991.

50 Appeals 68/94.

Bibliography

Primary Sources

'Abd al-Ḥāmid, *Kitāb al-istibṣār fī 'ajā'ib al-amṣār* (Alexandria, 1958)
Abū al-Layth, Naṣr b. Muḥammad, *'Uyūn al-masā'il* (Baghdad, 1386/1967)
——*Khizānat al-fiqh* (Baghdad, 1385/1965)
Abū Shujā', Aḥmad b. Hasan, *Matn al-ghāya wa'l-taqrīb* (Cairo, 1329/1911)
Abū Ya'lā (al-Qāḍī), *al-'Udda fī uṣūl al-fiqh*, (5 vols, vols 1–3, Beirut, 1980; vols 4–5, Riyadh, 1990)
Abū Yusuf, Ya'qūb b. Ibrāhīm, *Kitāb al-kharāj* (Cairo, 1306/1889)
Abū Zahra, Muḥammad, *al-Aḥwāl al-Shakhṣiyya* (2nd ed., Cairo, 1950)
al-Āmidī, *al-Iḥkām fī uṣūl al-aḥkām* (4 vols, Beirut, 1984)
al-'Amrī, Muḥammad al-Hādī, *Bāb al-Qaḍā' wa al-shahādāt min nawāzil al-Burzulī* (thesis, Tunis, 1979)
al-'Aqīlī, 'Aqīl b. Aḥmad, *Ḥukm naql al-a'ḍā' ma'a al-ta'qībāt al-bayyina 'alā man ta'aqqaba Ibn Taymiyya* (Judda, 1412/1992)
Arab League Manuscript Institute, *al-Ḥadīqa al-mustaqilla al-naḍra fī al-fatāwā al-ṣādira 'an 'ulamā al-ḥaḍra*, Fiqh Mālikī, no. 5.
al-'Asqalānī, Ibn Ḥajar, *al-Durar al-kāmina fī a'yān al-mi'a al-thāmina* (Cairo, 1966)
al-'Aynī, Badr al-Dīn Maḥmūd, *'Iqd al-jumān fī ta'rīkh ahl al-zamān* (Cairo, 1409/1989)
Bābā, Aḥmad, *Nayl al-ibtihāj bi-taḥrīz al-Dībāj* (Beirut, n.d.)
al-Baghdādī, Ṣafī al-Dīn, *Qawā'id al-uṣūl fī ma'āqid al-fuṣūl* (Beirut, 1406/1986)
al-Baḥrānī, Yūsuf b. Aḥmad, *Al-Ḥadā'iq al-Nāḍira* (25 vols, Qum, 1377)
——*al-Durur al-Najafiyya* (Qum, n.d.)
al-Bahūtī, Manṣūr b. Yūnus, *Kashshāf al-qinā' 'an matn al-iqnā'* (Riyad, n.d.)
——*al-Rawḍ al-murbi' bi-sharḥ zād al-mustaqni'* (Cairo, 1324/1906)
al-Ba'lī, Aḥmad Ibn 'Abd Allāh, *al-Rawḍ al-nadī* (Mecca 1969)
al-Ba'lī, Muḥammad Ibn 'Alī, *Mukhtaṣar al-fatāwā al-miṣriyya* (Cairo, 1368/1949)
al-Bājī, Abū al-Walīd, *al-Muntaqā* (Cairo, 1332/1914)
——*Iḥkām al-fuṣūl fī aḥkām al-uṣūl* (Beirut, 1986)
al-Bakrī, *Kitāb al-masālik wa-l-mamālik* (Tunis, 1992)
al-Baṣrī, Abū al-Ḥusayn, *al-Mu'tamad fī uṣūl al-fiqh* (2 vols, Damascus, 1963)
—— *Sharḥ al-'umad* (2 vols, Medina/Cairo, 1989)

al-Bayḍāwī, ʿAbd Allāh, *Minhāj al-wuṣūl ilā ʿilm al-uṣūl*, in al-Isnawī, *Nihāyat al-uṣūl fī sharḥ minhāj al-wuṣūl ilā ʿilm al-uṣūl* (Cairo, 1316/1899)
—— *Minhāj al-wuṣūl fī maʿrifa ʿilm al-uṣūl* (Beirut, 1985)
al-Bayḥaqī, Aḥmad b. al-Ḥusayn, *Kitāb al-sunan al-kubrā* (Haydarabad, 1952)
El-Bujārī, *Les Traditions islamiques*, trans. O. Houdas (Paris, 1943)
al-Bukhārī, Muḥammad b. Ismāʾīl, *al-Jāmiʿ al-ṣaḥīḥ* (Cairo, 1390/1970)
al-Būtī, Muḥammad Saʿīd Ramaḍān, *Ḍawābit al-maṣlaḥa fī al-sharīʿa al-islāmiyya* (Beirut, 1412/1992)
Caro, J., *Shulhan Arukh* (Jerusalem, 1993)
al-Dardīr, Aḥmad b. Muḥammad b. Aḥmad, *al-Sharḥ* (4 vols, Cairo, 1986)
al-Dārimī, ʿAbd Allāh b. ʿAbd al-Raḥmān, *Kitāb al-sunan* (Beirut, n.d)
al-Dhahabī, Mustafā Muḥammad, *Naql al-aʿḍāʾ bayn al-tibb waʾl-dīn* (Cairo, 1414/1993)
al-Dimashqī, Shams al-Dīn, *Raḥmat al-umma fī ikhtilāf al-aʾimma* (Cairo, 1386/1967)
Ebn Acem, *Traité de droit musulman: La Tohfat d'Ebn Acem,* Houdas, O. and Martel, F. trans., (Algiers, 1882)
al-Garnāṭī, Abū Isḥāq, *Al-Wathāʾiq al-Mukhtaṣa-ra* (Rabat, 1987)
al-Ghazālī, Abū Ḥāmid, *Shifāʾ al-ghalīl* (Baghdad, 1390/1971)
—— *Iḥyāʾ ʿulūm al-dīn* (Cairo, n.d.)
—— *Kitāb al-wajīz* (Beirut, 1399/1979)
—— *al-Mustaṣfā min ʿilm al-uṣūl* (Cairo, 1322–4/1904–6)
—— *al-Mankhūl min taʿlīqāt al-uṣūl* (Damascus, 1400/1980)
al-Hāʾirī, Muḥammad, *Muntahā al-Maqāl* (Tehran, n.d.)
al-Ḥajawī, Muḥammad b. al-Ḥasan, *al-Fikr al-sāmī fī tārīkh al-fiqh al-islāmi* (Medina, 1396)
al-Ḥanbalī, Ibn al-Najjār, *Sharḥ kawkab al-munīr* (Cairo, 1372/1953)
—— *Muntahā al-irādāt fī al-jamʿ bayn al-muqniʿ maʿa al-tanqīḥ wa-ziyādāt* (Cairo, n.d.)
al-Ḥaqq, Jād al-Ḥaqq ʿAlī Jād, *Buḥūth wa-fatāwā islāmiyya wa-qaḍāyā muʿāsira* (Cairo, 1900)
—— *al-Fiqh al-islāmī: Murūnatuhu wa-tatawwuruhu* (Cairo, 1987)
al-Ḥaṭāb, Muḥammad b. Muḥammad, *Kitāb mawāhib al-jalīl li-sharḥ Mukhtaṣar Khalīl* (3rd ed., 6 vols, Beirut, 1412/1992)
al-Ḥaymī, Ḥusayn b. Aḥmad al-Ḥusayn al-Sayāghī, *Kitāb al-rawḍ al-naḍīr sharḥ majmūʿ al-fiqh al-kabīr* (Cairo 1348)
al-Ḥujāwī, Sharaf al-Dīn Mūsā, *al-Iqnāʿ* (Beirut, n.d.)
—— *Zād al-mustaqniʿ fī ikhtiṣār al-muqniʿ* (Riyad, 1977)
al-Ḥumaydī, Abū Bakr, *al-Musnad* (Beirut/Cairo, 1383/1963)
Ibn ʿAbd al-Wahhāb, Muḥammad, *Mukhtaṣar al-inṣāf waʾl-sharḥ al-kabīr* (Cairo, 1965)
Ibn Abī Yaʿlā, Abū Khāzim, *Ṭabaqāt al-ḥanābila* (Beirut, n.d.)
Ibn ʿAqīl, Abū al-Wafāʾ ʿAlī, ʻKitāb al-jadal,ʼ *Bulletin d'études orientales*, 20 (1967)
Ibn al-ʿAṭṭār, *Kitāb al-Wathāʾiq waʾl-sijillāt* (Madrid, 1983)
Ibn Baṭṭa, ʿUbayd Allāh, ʻIbṭāl al-ḥiyalʼ, in *Min dafāʾin al-kunū* (Cairo, 1980)

Ibn Baṭṭūṭa, Shams al-Dīn Abū 'Abd Allāh, *Tuḥfat al-naẓẓār fī gharā'ib al-amṣār wa-'ajā'ib al-asfār* (Paris, 1926)
Ibn al-Dawādārī, Abū Bakr, *Kanz al-durar wa jāmi' al-ghurar* (Cairo, 1969)
Ibn Ḍūyān, Ibrāḥīm Ibn Muḥammad, *Kitāb manār al-sabīl* (Damascus, 1378/1959)
Ibn Farḥūn, Ibrāhīm b. 'Alī, *Kashf al-nuqāt al-Ḥājib min Muṣṭalaḥ Ibn al-Ḥājib* (Beirut, 1990)
Ibn Māja, Abū 'Abd Allāh Muḥammad, *al-Sunan* (Lucknow, 1315/1897)
Ibn Mufliḥ, Shams al-Dīn Abū 'Abd Allāh, *Kitāb al-furū'* (Beirut, 1982–4)
Ibn Fūrak, *Mujarrad maqālāt al-shaykh abī al-Ḥasan al-Ash'arī* (Beirut, 1987)
Ibn al-Ḥājib, Jamāl al-Dīn Abū Amr, *Muntahā al-su'āl wa'l-'amal fī 'ilm al-uṣūl wa'l-jadal* (Istanbul, 1326/1908)
Ibn Ḥanbal, Aḥmad, *Masā'il al-Imām Aḥmad Ibn Ḥanbal*, (Beirut/Damascus, 1981)
—— *Musnad* (Cairo, 1895)
Ibn Ḥazm, Abū Muḥammad 'Alī, *al-Muḥallā* (Beirut, n.d.)
Ibn Hubayra, 'Awn al-Dīn Abū al-Muẓaffar, *Kitāb al-ifṣāḥ 'an ma'ānī al-ṣaḥāḥ* (Riyad, 1980)
Ibn Kathīr, 'Imād al-Dīn Ismā'īl, *al-Bidāya wa'l-nihāya* (Damascus, 1967)
Ibn Muḥammad, al-Nu'mān (al-Qāḍī), *Ikhtilāf uṣūl al-madhāhib* (Beirut, 1983)
Ibn al-Qāḍī, *Jadhwat al-iqtibās fī dhikr man ḥalla min al-a'lām madīna Fās* (Rabat, 1974)
Ibn Qayyim al-Jawziyya, Shams al-Dīn Abū Bakr, *Ighāthat al-lahfān min maṣāyid al-shayṭān* (Cairo, 1381/1961)
—— *I'lām al-muwaqqi'īn* (Cairo, 1970)
Ibn Qudāma, Muwaffaq al-Dīn, *al-Mughnī* (Riyad, 1401/1981)
—— *Rawḍat al-nāẓir wa-jannat al-munāẓir* (Cairo, 1342/1923)
—— *al-Muqni'* (Cairo, 1382/1962)
—— *al-'Umda fī al-fiqh al-Ḥanbalī* (Damascus, 1419/1990)
Ibn Qudāma, Shams al-Dīn, *al-Sharḥ al-kabīr* (Cairo, 1348/1930)
Ibn Rajab, Zayn al-Dīn Abū al-Faraj, *al-Dhayl 'alā ṭabaqāt al-ḥanābila* (n.p., 1372/1952)
—— *al-Qawā'id al-fiqhiyya* (n.p., 1972)
Ibn Rushd, Abū al-Walīd Muḥammad, *Bidāyat al-mujtahid wa-nihāyat al-muqtaṣid* (Cairo, 1971)
——*La Bidaya: Manuel de l'interprète des lois et traité complet du jurist. Du mariage et de sa dissolution*, trans. A. Laïmèche (Algiers, 1926)
—— *al-Muqaddamāt al-mumahhadāt li-bayān mā iqtaḍathu rusūm al-mudawwana* (Cairo, 1324/1906)
Ibn al-Ṣalāḥ, Taqī al-Dīn 'Uthmān, *Fatāwā wa masā'il ibn al-Ṣalāḥ fī al-tafsīr wa'l-ḥadīth wa'l-uṣūl wa'l-fiqh wa ma'ahu adab al-muftī wa l-mustaftī* (2 vols, Beirut 1986)
Ibn Sallām, Abū 'Ubayd al-Qāsim, *Kitāb al-amwāl* (Cairo, 1401/1981)
Ibn Taymiyya, Majd al-Dīn, *al-Muḥarrar fī al-fiqh* (Cairo, 1369/1950)
—— *Musawwada.* (Cairo, 1384/1964)

Ibn Taymiyya, Taqī al-Dīn Aḥmad, *Majmūʿ fatāwā Shaykh al-Islām Aḥmad Ibn Taymiyya* (Riyad, 1381–86/1962–7)

——*Kitāb iqāmat al-dalīl ʿalā ibṭāl al-taḥlīl* in *Majmūʿ fatāwā Shaykh al-Islām Taqī al-Dīn Ibn Taymiyya* (Cairo, 1328/1910)

Idrīs, ʿAbd al-Fattāḥ Maḥmūd, *Ḥukm al-tadāwī biʾl-muḥarramāt* (Cairo, 1414/1993)

ʿIyāḍ, Abū Faḍl, *Tartīb al-Madārik wa-taqrīb al-masālik li-maʿrifat aʿlām madhhab Mālik* (Rabat, 1983)

al-Jīdī, ʿUmar, *Muḥāḍarāt fī tārīkh al-madhhab al-mālikī fī al-gharb al-islāmī* (Rabat, 1407/1987)

Jumhūriyyat Misr al-ʿArabiyya, *al-Fatāwā al-islāmiyya min dār al-iftāʾ al-miṣriyya* (Cairo, 1980)

al-Juwaynī, Abū al-Maʿālī, *Ghiyāth al-umam fī iltiyāth al-ẓulam* (Alexandria, 1979)

—— *al-Waraqāt* (Cairo, 1977)

—— *al-Burhān fī uṣūl al-fiqh* (2nd ed., 2 vols, Cairo 1980)

——*Kitāb al-ijtihād (min Kitāb al-talkhīṣ)* (Damascus/Beirut, 1987)

al-Kalwadhānī, Abū al-Khaṭṭāb, *al-Tamhīd fī uṣūl al-fiqh* (4 vols, Mecca, 1985)

'Ḳanūn-i Cedīd' in *Millī Tetebbüʿler Mecmuası* (Istanbul, 1913)

al-Kāsānī, Abu Bakr b. Masūd, *Badāʾiʿ al-ṣanāʾiʿ wa-tartīb al-sharāʾiʿ* (Cairo, 1970)

Kashmirī, Muḥammad ʿAlī, *Nujūm al-Samāʾ* (Lucknow, 1303/1885),

al-Khaṭīb al-Baghdādī, Abū Bakr Aḥmad b. ʿAlī, *al-Faqīh wa al-Mutafaqqih* (Damascus, 1975)

al-Khiraqī, Abū al-Qāsim, *Mukhtaṣar al-Khiraqī* (Damascus; 1384/1964)

al-Khwānsārī, Muḥammad Bāqir, *Rawḍāt al-Jannāt* (8 vols, Qum, 1970–72)

al-Kinānī, Abū Muḥammad ʿAbd Allāh b. ʿAbd Allāh b. Salmūn, *al-ʿIqd al-munaẓẓam lil-ḥukkām* (2 vols, Beirut, n.d.)

Maimonides, *The Code of Maimonides, book thirteen, The Book of Civil Laws,* trans. Jacob J. Rabinowitz (New Haven and London, 1949)

Maimonides *The Code of Maimonides. book fourteen: The Book of Judges,* trans. Abraham M. Hershman (New Haven, 1949)

Maimonides, *The Code of Maimonides. book twelve: The Book of Acquisition,* trans. Isaac Klein (New Haven and London, 1951)

Maimonides, *The Code of Maimonides, book four, The Book of Women,* trans. Isaac Klein (New Haven and London, 1972)

Mālik Ibn Anas, *al-Muwattaʾ* (Cairo, 1339/1921)

Makhlūf, *Shajarāt al-Nūr al-Zakiyya fī ṭabaqāt al-Mālikiyya* (Cairo, 1350)

al-Mālaqī, al-Shaʿbī, *al-Aḥkām* (Beirut, 1992)

al-Mardāwī, ʿAlāʾ al-Dīn, *Taṣḥīḥ al-furūʿ* (Beirut, 1388/1967)

—— *Kitāb al-inṣāf li-maʿrifat al-rājiḥ min al-khilāf* (Cairo, 1375–7/1955–7)

——*al-Tanqīḥ al-mushbiʿ fī taḥrīr aḥkām al-muqniʿ* (Cairo, 1961)

al-Marghīnānī al-Farghānī, Burhān al-Dīn ʿAlī, *al-Hidāya* (Cairo, 1356/1937)

al-Marʿī, Ibn Yusuf, *al-Kawākib al-durriyya fī manāqib al-Imām Ibn Taymiyya* (Cairo, 1329/1911)

al-Māwardī, Abū al-Ḥasan ʿAlī, *Adab al-qāḍī* (Baghdad, 1971–2)

Muslim, Ibn al-Ḥajjāj, *al-Jāmiʿ al-ṣaḥīḥ* (Beirut, 1984)

al-Muzanī, Abū Ibrāhīm, *al-Mukhtaṣar* (Cairo, 1388/1968–9)

al-Nasafi, Ḥāfiẓ al-Dīn, *Kanz al-daqā'iq* (n.p., 1887)

al-Nasā'ī, Abū 'Abd al-Raḥmān Aḥmad, *Kitāb al-sunan* (Beirut, 1984)

al-Niẓām, al-Shaykh, *al-Fatāwā al-hindiyya*, (6 vols, repr. Beirut, 1980)

al-Nawawī, Muḥyī al-Dīn Yaḥyā, *Minhāj al-ṭālibīn*, (Batavia, 1882)

—— *Rawḍat al-ṭālibīn* (Damascus, 1968)

—— *Majmū' sharḥ al-muhadhdhab* (Cairo, 1966)

Pasha, Muhammad Qadri, *Kitab al-Aḥkām al-Shar'iyya fī al-Aḥwāl al-Shakhṣiyya 'ala Madhhab al-Imām Abī Ḥanīfa al-Nu'mān* in Rushdi al- Sarraj, *Kitāb Majmu'at al-Qawānīn al-Shar'iyya* (Jaffa, 1944)

Qāḍīkhān, Fakhr al-Dīn al-Ḥasan, *Fatāwā Qāḍīkhān* in *al-Fatāwā al-hindiyya* (Cairo, 1310/1893)

al-Qazwīnī, Abū Ḥātim Maḥmūd, *Kitāb al-ḥiyal fī al-fiqh* (Hannover, 1924)

al-Qarāfi, Shihāb al-Dīn Aḥmad b. Idrīs, *Kitāb al-iḥkām fī tamyīz al-fatāwā 'an al-aḥkām wa taṣarrufāt al-qāḍī wa al-imām* (Aleppo, 1387/1967)

—— *Anwār al-burūq fī anwā' al-furūq* (Beirut, n.d.)

—— *Sharḥ tanqīḥ al-fuṣūl fī ikhtiṣār al-maḥṣūl fī al-uṣūl* (Cairo, 1393/1973)

al-Qayrawānī, Ibn Abī Zayd, *al-Risāla* (Alger, 1980)

—— *La Risāla ou Epître sur les éléments du dogme et de la loi de l'Islām selon le rite mālikite*, ed. and trans. Léon Bercher (5th ed., Algiers, 1968)

al-Qudūrī, Abū al-Ḥusayn Aḥmad, *al-Mukhtaṣar* (n.p., 1309/1892)

al-Rāzī, Fakhr al-Dīn, *al-Maḥṣūl fī 'ilm al-uṣūl* (6 vols, Beirut, 1992)

Saḥnūn, *al-Mudawwana al-kubrā* (Baghdad, n.d.)

al-Samarqandī, 'Alā' al-Dīn, *Tuḥfat al-fuqahā'* (Cairo, 1377/1958)

al-Sanbuhaylī, Muḥammad Burhān al-Dīn, *Qaḍāyā fiqhiyya mu'āsira* (Beirut/ Damascus, 1408/1988)

al-Sarakhsī, Shams al-Dīn, *Kitāb al-Mabsūṭ* (Istanbul, 1982)

—— *Kitāb al-uṣūl* (Cairo, 1372/1953)

al-Shāfi'ī, Muḥammad b. Idrīs, *Jimā' al-'ilm* (Beirut, n.d.)

——*Kitāb al-Umm*, (7 vols, Cairo, n.d.)

——*al-Risāla*, (Beirut, n.d.)

al-Shalabī, *Hashiyyat al-Durr* in Muhammad Ibn 'Abidin, *Radd al-Muhtar 'ala al-Durr al-Mukhtar* (2nd ed., Cairo, 1979)

al-Shammā'ī, Qāsim al-Rifā'ī, *Fatāwā islāmiyya li-majmū'a min al-'ulamā' wa-hum: al-shaykh 'Abd al-'Azīz Ibn Bāz, al-shaykh Muḥammad Ibn al-'Uthaymīn, al-shaykh 'Abd Allāh Ibn Jibrīn bi'l-iḍāfa ilā fatāwā li'l-lajna al-dā'ima li'l-iftā'* (3 vols, Beirut, 1988)

al-Shāshī, Abū Bakr, *Uṣūl al-Shāshī* (Beirut, 1402/1982)

al-Shawkānī, Muḥammad b. 'Alī, *Irshād al-fuḥūl* (Cairo, 1356/1937)

al-Shaybānī, 'Abd al-Qādir, *Nayl al-ma'ārib* (Cairo, 1324/1906)

al-Shaybānī, Muḥammad Ibn al-Ḥasan, *Kitāb al-aṣl* (Cairo, 1954),

—— *al-Jāmi' al-ṣaghīr*, in al-Shīrāzī, *Kitāb al-muhadhdhab* (Cairo, n.d.)

——*Kitāb al-ḥujja* (Beirut, 1387/1968)

——*al-Jāmi' al-kabīr* (Cairo, 1356/1937)

al-Shīrāzī, Abū Iṣḥāq, *al-Tabṣira fī uṣūl al-fiqh* (Damascus, 1980)

——*al-Luma' fi uṣūl al-fiqh* (Beirut, 1985)
—— *Sharḥ al-luma'* (2 vols, Beirut, 1988)
—— *Kitāb al-tanbīh* (Cairo, 1348/1929)
al-Sijistānī, Abū Dāwūd, *Kitāb al-sunan* (Beirut, 1984)
al-Subkī, 'Alī and Tāj al-Dīn, *al-Ibhāj fi sharḥ al-minhāj* (3 vols, Beirut, 1984)
al-Subkī, Taqī al-Dīn, *Fatāwā al-Subkī* (Cairo, 1356/1937)
——*Majmū' sharḥ muhadhdhab* (Cairo, 1966)
al-Swīsī, Muḥammad b. Yūnus, 'Al-Fatāwā al-tūnisiyya fī al-qarn al-rābi' 'ashara al-hijrī' (Ph.D. thesis, Zaytūna University, 1986)
al-Ṭaḥāwī, 'Abd al-Jalīl, *al-Mukhtaṣar* (Cairo, 1379/1950)
al-Ṭāhir, al-Ma'mūrī, *Fatāwā al-Māzrī* (Tunis, 1994)
Tanukābānī, Muḥammad, *Qiṣaṣ al-'Ulamā'* (Tehran, n.d.)
al-Tijānī, *Riḥla al-Tijānī* (Tunis, 1981)
al-Tirmidhī, Abū Īsā Muḥammad, *Sunan* (Cairo, 1382/1962)
al-Ṭūfī, Najm al-Dīn, *Sharḥ mukhtaṣar al-rawḍa* (Beirut, 1987–9)
1377/1957)
al-Ṭulayṭulī, Ibn Mughīth, *al-Muqnī' fi 'ilm al-shurūṭ* (Madrid, 1994)
al-Wansharīsī, Aḥmad b. Yaḥyā, *al-Mi'yar al-mu'rib wa'l-jāmi' al-mughrib 'an al-fatāwā 'ulamā Ifriqiyya wa'l-Andalūs wa'l-Maghrib* (Rabat/Beirut, 1981–3)
al-Ya'qūbī, Ibrāhīm, *Shifā' al-tabārīḥ wa'l-adwā' fi ḥukm al-tashrīḥ wa-naql al-a'ḍā'* (Damascus, 1407/1986)
al-Zarqā, Muṣṭafā Aḥmad, *al-Fiqh al-islāmī fi thawbihi al-jadīd: al-madkhal al-fiqhī al-'āmm, al-juz al-awwal* (6th. ed., Damascus n.d.)
Zaydān, 'Abd al-Karīm, *Majmū'at buūḥth fiqhiyya* (Baghdad, 1402/1982)
al-Zuḥaylī, Wahba, *Naẓariyyat al-ḍarūra al-shar'iyya* (Beirut, 1405/1985)
al-Zurqānī, 'Abd al-Bāqī, *Sharḥ al-zurqānī 'alā khalīl* (4 vols, Beirut, n.d.)

Secondary Sources

Abu Gosh, Subhi, 'The *Sharia* Courts from the Perspective of Israeli Pluralism', in K. O. Cohen and J. S. Gerber, eds, *Perspectives on Israeli Pluralism: Proceedings of a Conference on Pluralism in Israel* (New York, 1991)
Abu Zahra, Muhammad, 'Family Law', in M. Khadduri and H. J. Liebesny, eds, *Law in the Middle East* (Washington DC, 1955)
Ahmad, Badar Durrez, 'Organ Transplant and the Right to Die', *Islamic and Comparative Law Quarterly* 7 (1987)
Ajetunmobi, M. A., 'An Analytical Survey of *Kafā'ah* (Equality in Islamic Marriage) at the Dawn of Islam', *Journal of Arabic and Religious Studies* 1 (1984)
Akgündüz, Ahmet, *Islâm Hukukunda ve Osmanlı Tatbikatında Vakıf Müessesesi* (Ankara, 1988)
Amar, E., 'La Pierre des touches de consultations juridiques', *Archives Marocaines* 12 (1908)
—— 'La Pierre de touche des fétwas de Aḥmad al-Wanscharīsī (Choix de

consultations juridiques des Faqīhs du Maghreb, traduites et analysées)', *Archives Marocaines* 12 (1908); 13 (1909)

Anderson, J. N. D., *Islamic Law in Africa* (London, 1972)

al-ʿArabī, Bilḥājj, "Ḥukm al-sharīʿa al-islāmiyya fī aʿmāl al-tibb wa'l-jirāḥa al-mustakhdama', *Revue algérienne des sciences juridiques economiques et politiques* 31 (1993)

al-Azmeh, Aziz, 'Islamic Legal Theory and the Appropriation of Reality', in Aziz al-Azmeh, ed., *Islamic Law: Social and Historical Contexts* (New York, 1988)

Bagby, Ihsan A., 'The Issue of *Maṣlaḥah* in Classical Islamic Legal Theory', *International Journal of Islamic and Arabic Studies* 2, 2 (1985)

Barker, G. W. W. and Jones, G. D. B., 'The UNESCO Libyan Valleys Survey 1979–81: Paleaoeconomy and Environmental Archaeology of the Pre-Desert', *Libyan Studies* 13 (1982)

Beck, H. L., *L'Image d'Idris II, ses descendants de Fās et la politique Sharīfienne des sultans marīnides (656–869/1258–1465)* (Leiden, 1989)

Berque, Jacques, *L'Intérieur du Maghreb: xve-xixe siecle* (Paris, 1978)

Bontemps, C., 'L'influence française dans le projet de la code de la famille algérienne', *Revue Algérienne* 19 (1982)

Botiveau, B., *Loi islamique et droit dans les sociétés arabes* (Paris, 1993)

Bousquet, G.-H., *Du droit musulman et de son application effective dans le monde* (Algiers, 1949)

——*Abrégé de la loi musulmane selon le rite de l'Imām Mālek* (Paris/Algiers, 1958)

Brogan, Olwen and Smith, D. J., *Ghirza: A Libyan Settlement in the Roman Period* (Tripoli, 1984)

Brunschvig, R., 'Métiers vils en Islam', *Studia Islamica* 16 (1962)

Calder, N., 'Doubt and Prerogative: The Emergence of an Imāmī Shīʿī Theory of *Ijtihād*', *Studia Islamica* 70 (1989)

Charanis, P., 'The monastic properties and the State in the Byzantine Empire', *Dumbarton Oaks Papers* 4 (1948)

Chaumont, É., 'La Problématique classique de l'*ijtihād* et la question de l'*ijtihād* du Prophète', *Studia Islamica* 75 (1992)

——"Tout chercheur qualifié dit-il juste?' (*hal kull mujtahid muṣīb*) La Question controversée du fondement de la légitimité de la controverse en Islam', in A. Le Boulluec, ed., *La Controverse religieuse et ses formes* (Paris, 1995)

——'al-Shāfiʿiyya', *EI2*

Coulson, N. J., 'Doctrine and Practice in Islamic Law', *Bulletin of the School of Oriental and African Studies* 18 (1956)

——'Muslim Custom and Case-Law', *Die Welt des Islams* 6 (1959–61)

—— *A History of Islamic Law* (Edinburgh, 1964)

——*Succession in the Muslim Family* (London, 1971)

Courtois, C., et al, *Tablettes Albertini: actes privés de l'époque vandal (fin du ve siecle)* (Paris, 1955)

Christelow, A., 'Jugements et arrêts sur le droit de la famille', *Revue Algérienne*, 5 (1968)

—— *Muslim Law courts and the French Colonial state in Algeria* (Princeton, 1985)
Crone, P., *Roman, Provincial and Islamic Law* (Cambridge, 1987),
Davis, J., *Libyan Politics: Tribe and Revolution* (London, 1987)
Düzdağ, Ertuğrul, *Şeyhülislâm Ebussuud Efendi fetvaları ışığında 16. asır Türk hayatı* (Istanbul, 1972)
Eisenman, R. H., *Islamic Law in Mandate Palestine and Modern Israel* (Leiden, 1978)
Elisséeff, N., 'Ghūṭa', *EI2*
van Ess, Josef, 'La Liberté du juge dans le milieu basrien du VIIIe siècle', in G. Makdisi, ed., *La Notion de liberté au Moyen-Âge* (Paris, 1985)
Fischer, A., 'Ḳais-'Ailān',*EI2*
Fotić, A., 'The official explanations for the confiscation and sale of monasteries (churches) and their estates at the time of Selım II', *Turcica* 24 (1994)
Frank, Jerome, *Law and the Modern Mind* (Gloucester, Ma., 1970)
Friedman, M. A., 'Divorce upon the Wife's Demand as Reflected in Manuscripts from the Cairo Geniza', in Bernard S. Jackson, ed., *The Jewish Law Annual (Vol. 4)* (Leiden, 1981)
García-Arenal, M., 'The Revolution of Fās in 869/1465 and the Death of Sultan 'Abd al-Ḥaqq al-Marīnī', *Bulletin of the School of Oriental and African Studies* 41, 1 (1978)
—— 'Algunos manuscritos de *fiqh* andalusíes y norteafricanos pertenecientes a la Real Biblioteca de El Escorial', *al-Qanṭara* 1 (1980)
Gerber, Haim, 'Sharia, Kanun and Custom in the Ottoman Law: The Court Records of 17th–century Bursa', *International Journal of Turkish Studies* 2 (1981)
Gleave, R., 'Akhbārī Shī'ī Jurisprudence in the Writings of Yūsuf b. Aḥmad al-Baḥrānī (d.1186/1772)' (Unpublished PhD thesis, University of Manchester, 1996)
—— 'The Akhbārī-Uṣūlī Dispute in *Ṭabaqāt* Literature: An Analysis of the Biographies of Yūsuf al Baḥrānī and Muḥammad Bāqir al-Bihbihānī', *Jusur* 10 (1994)
Gimaret, D., *La doctrine d'al-Ash'arī* (Paris, 1990)
Goitein, S. D., and Ben Shemesh, A., *Muslim Law in Israel* (Hebrew) (Jerusalem, 1957)
Goitein, S. D., *A Mediterranean Society. Vol. 2: The Community* (Berkeley and Los Angeles, 1971)
—— "Al ha-Ḥayyīm ha-Ṣībūriyyim shel ha-Yehūdīm be-Ereṣ Teyman,' in H. M. Ben-Sasson, ed., *Ha-Teymanīm: Hīsṭorya, Sidrey Ḥevra, Ḥayyey ha-Rūaḥ (The Yemenites: History Communal Organisation, Spiritual Life)* (Jerusalem, 1983),
—— 'The Interplay of Jewish and Islamic Laws', in Bernard S. Jackson, ed., *Jewish Law in Legal History and the Modern World* (Leiden 1980)
—— 'Portrait of a Yemenite Weaver's Village', *Jewish Social Studies* 17 (1955)
Goldziher, I., 'Muhammedanisches Recht in Theorie und Wirklichkeit', *Zeitschrift für vergleichende Rechtswissenschaft* 8 (1889)
Guidi, I. and Santillana, D., *Il 'Mukhtaṣar' o Sommario del diritto Malechita di Khalīl b. Isḥāq* (Milan, 1919)

al-Hajj, M., *Education and Social Change among the Arabs in Israel* (Tel Aviv, 1991)
Hallaq, Wael B., 'Was the Gate of Ijtihād Closed ?', *International Journal of Middle East Studies* 16 (1984)
—— 'From *Fatwā* to *Furū'*: Growth and Change in Islamic Substantive Law', *Islamic Law and Society* 1, 1 (1994)
—— 'The Development of the Logical Structure in Sunnī Legal Theory', *Der Islam* 64 (1987)
—— 'Non–analogical Arguments in Sunnī Juridical Qiyās', *Arabica* 36 (1989)
—— 'Uṣūl al-fiqh: Beyond Tradition', *Journal of Islamic Studies* 3 (1992)
—— 'Murder in Cordoba: *Ijtihād, Iftā'* and the Evolution of Substantive Law in Medieval Islam', *Acta Orientalia* 55 (1994)
—— 'Model *Shurūṭ* Works and the Dialectic of Doctrine and Practice', *Islamic Law and Society* 2, 2 (1995)
Hart, H. L. A., *The Concept of Law* (Oxford, 1961)
Harvey, L. P., *Islamic Spain 1250–1500* (Chicago, 1990)
Heffening, W., 'Waqf or Ḥabs', *EI1*
Heyd, Uriel, *Studies in Old Criminal Law*, V. L. Menage, ed., (Oxford, 1973
—— 'Some Aspects of the Ottoman Fetva,' *British School of Oriental and African Studies* 32 (1969)
Hollander, I., '*Ibrā'* in Highland Yemen: Two Jewish Divorce Settlements', *Islamic Law and Society* 2 (1995)
—— 'Parashat "Araṣa' mi-Ḥujariyya', in Y. Tobi ed., *Le-Rosh Yôsef: Meḥqarīm be-Ḥokhmat Yisra'el* (Jerusalem, 1995)
Humphreys, R. Stephen, 'Islamic Law and Islamic Society', in *Islamic History: A Framework for Inquiry* (revised ed., Princeton, 1991)
Hirschberg, H. Z., "Arka'ot shel Goyyim Bīmey ha-Ge'ōnīm', in Z. Werheftig and S. Y. Zavin, eds., *Mazkeret le-Zakher Maran ha-Rav Yiṣḥaq Isaac ha-Lewī Hertzog* (Jerusalem, 1962)
Idris, Hady Roger, 'Le Mariage en Occident musulman d'après un choix de fatwàs médiévales extraites du *Mi'yār* d'al-Wansharīsī', *Studia Islamica* 32 (1970)
—— 'Le Mariage en Occident musulman: Analyse de fatwās médiévales extraites du 'Mi'yār' d'al-Wansharīsī', *ROMM* 17–18 (1974)
Inalcik, Halil, 'Islamization of Ottoman laws on Land and Land Tax', *Festgabe an Josef Matuz: Osmanistik–Turkologie–Diplomatik* (Berlin, 1992)
Issad, M. , 'Le rôle du juge et la volonté des parties dans la rupture du lien conjugal', *Revue Algérienne* 5 (1968)
Jennings, Roland, 'Kadi Court and Legal Procedure in 17th century Ottoman Kayseri', *Studia Islamica* 48 (1978)
——'Limitations of the Judicial Powers of the Kadi in 17th century Ottoman Kayseri', *Studia Islamica* 50 (1979)
Johansen, B., *The Islamic Law on Land Tax and Rent* (London, 1988),
Kabra, Patricia K., 'Patterns of Economic Continuity and Change in Early Hafsid Ifriqiya' (Unpublished Ph.D. thesis, University of California, Los Angeles, 1994)

Kermeli, Eugenia, 'The Confiscation of Monastic Properties by Selīm II 1568–1570' (unpublished Ph.D thesis, Manchester, 1995)

Kerr, Malcolm H., *Islamic Reform: the Political and Legal Theories of Muḥammad 'Abduh and Rashīd Riḍā* (Berkeley/Los Angeles, 1966)

Kohlberg, E., 'Aspects of Akhbārī Thought in the Seventeenth and Eighteenth Century' in J. O. Voll and N. Levtzion, eds, *Eighteenth Century Renewal and Reform in Islam* (New York, 1987)

Kohlberg, E., 'Some Imāmī Views on *Taqiyya*', *JAOS* 95.3 (1975)

Kierkegaard, S., *La Reprise,* trans. N. Viallaneix (Paris, 1990)

Kister, M. J., 'Rajab is the Month of God ... A Study in the Persistence of an Early Tradition', *Israel Oriental Studies* 1 (1971)

Krawietz, Birgit, *Die Ḥurm: Schariatrechtlicher Schutz vor Eingriffen in die koerperliche Unversehrtheit nach arabischen Fatwas des 20. Jahrhunderts* (Berlin, 1991)

Kupferschmidt, U. M., *The Supreme Muslim Council: Islam under the British Mandate for Palestine* (Leiden, 1987)

Labib, S., *Handelsgeschichte Ägyptens im Spätmittelalter (1171–1517)* (Wiesbaden, 1965)

Lagardère, V., *Histoire et société en Occident musulman au Moyen Age: Analyse du 'Mi'yār' d'al-Wansharīsī* (Madrid, 1995)

Layish, A., 'Muslim Religious Jurisdiction in Israel', *AAS* 1 (1965)

—— '*Qāḍīs* and *Sharīa* in Israel', *AAS* 7 (1971)

—— *Women and Islamic Law in a Non-Muslim State* (NewYork/Toronto/Jerusalem, 1975)

——*Divorce in the Libyan Family* (Jerusalem, 1991)

—— 'The Status of the *Sharīa* in a Non-Muslim State; The Case of Israel', *AAS* 27 (1993)

—— 'Bequests as an Instrument for Accomodating the Inheritance Rules: Israel as a Case Study', *Islamic Law and Society* 2, 3 (1995)

—— 'Mahkama', *EI2*

——'The Family *Waqf* and the *Shar'ī* Law of Succession', in G. Baer and G. Gilbar (eds), *Studies in the Muslim Waqf* (Oxford, forthcoming)

Layish, A. and Shmueli, A., 'Custom and Sharī'a in the Bedouin Family According to Legal Documents from the Judaean Desert', *Bulletin of the School of Oriental and African Studies,* 42 (1979)

Layish, A., and Warburg, G. R., *The Implementation of the Sharīa in Sudan under Numayri: 1983–85* (forthcoming)

van Leeuwen, Richard, *Notables and Clergy in Mount Lebanon: The Khāzin Sheikhs and the Maronite Church, 1736–1840* (Leiden, 1994)

Lefort, Jacques, *Actes d' Esphigménou = Archives de l'Athos,* (Paris, 1973)

Levi Provençal, 'al-Andalus', *EI2*

Levinson, H., Katz E., and al-Hajj, M., *Jews and Arabs in Israel: Common Values and Mutual Images* (Jerusalem, 1995)

Linant de Bellefonds, Y., *Traité de droit musulman comparé* (Paris/La Haya, 1965)

—— 'Kafā'a', *EI2*

López Ortiz, J., *Derecho musulmán* (Barcelona, 1932)

—— 'Fatwas Granadinas de los Siglos XIV y XV', *al-Andalus* 6 (1941)

Madelung, W., 'Imamism and Mu'tazilite theology' in Colloque de Strasbourg, *Le Shi'isme Imamate* (Paris, 1970)

Maktari, A. M. A., *Water Rights and Irrigation Practices in Lahj: A Study of the Application of Customary and Sharī'ah Law in South-West Arabia* (Cambridge, 1971)

Mar'i, S., *Arab Education in Israel* (New York, 1978)

Masud, Muhammad Khalid, *Islamic Legal Philosophy: A Study of Abū Isḥāq al-Shāṭibī's Life and Thought* (Delhi, 1989)

Mediano, Fernando R., 'Fez en los siglos XV-XVII: Aproximación a un estudio de la literatura bio-bibliográfica fesí' (unpublished, Universidad Complutense de Madrid, 1991)

Messick, B., 'Transactions in Ibb: Economy and Society in a Yemeni Highland Town' (unpublished Ph.D dissertation, Princeton University, 1978)

——'Literacy and the Law: Documents and Document Specialists in Yemen', in Daisy Hilse Dwyer (ed.), *Law and Islam in the Middle East* (New York, 1990)

——*The Calligraphic State: Textual Domination and History in a Muslim Society* (Berkeley and Los Angeles, 1993)

Monchicourt, Ch., 'Règlements d'irrigation dans le haut tell (Règions du Kef, Teboursouk, Mactar et Thala)' in *Extrait du Bulletin de la direction générale de l'agriculture, du commerce et de la colonisation* (Tunis, 1911)

Morizot, P., 'Awerba', *Encyclopedie Berbère*

Mundy, Matha, 'Women's Inheritance of Land in Highland Yemen', *Arabian Studies*, 5 (1979)

——*Domestic Government: Kinship, Community and Polity in North Yemen* (London, 1995)

Muranyi, Miklos, 'Untersuchungen zu *sharī'a* -rechtlichen Entwicklungen der Gegenwart. I: Ein Rechtsgutachten (fatwā) über das Chininverbot im Islam', *Arabica* 27 (1980)

Muslehuddin, Mohammad, 'Islamic Jurisprudence and the Rule of Necessity and Need', *Islamic Studies* 11 (1973)

Newman, A., 'The Nature of the Akhbārī/Uṣūlī Dispute in Late Ṣafawid Iran. Part 1: 'Abdallāh al-Samāhijī's '*Munyat al-Mumārisīn*', *Bulletin of the School of Oriental and African Studies* 55 (1992)

Newman, A., 'The Nature of the Akhbārī/Uṣūlī Dispute in Late Ṣafawid Iran. Part 2: The Conflict Re-assessed,' *Bulletin of the School of Oriental and African Studies* 55 (1992)

Nini, Y., *Teyman we-Ṣiyyōn: ha-Reqa' ha-Medīnī, ha-Ḥevratī we-ha-Rūḥanī le-'Aliyyōt ha-Ri'shōnōt mi-Teyman, 180–914* (Jerusalem, 1982)

Noth, A., 'Die Scharia, das religiöse Gesetz des Islam – Wandlungsmöglichkeiten, Anwendung und Wirkung', in Fikentscher, Franke and Köhler, eds, *Entstehung und Wandel rechtlicher Traditionen* (Freiburg/München, 1980)

Oikonomidès, Nikolaos, *Actes de Dionysiou = Archives de l'Athos* (Paris, 1968)

Ostrogorsky, G., *Pour l'histoire de la féodalité byzantine* (Brussels, 1954)

—— *Quelques problèmes d'histoire de la paysanerie byzantine* (Brussels, 1956)
Penat, P., *L'Hydraulique agricole dans la Tunisie méridionale* (Tunis, 1913)
Perron, M., 'Précis de jurisprudence musulmane au principes de législation musulmane civile et religieuse, selon le rite malékite par Khalīl Ibn Ishaq' in *Exploration Scientifique d'Algérie pendents les années 1840, 1841, 1842*, vol. 1 (Paris, 1848)
Peters, Rudolph, 'Muḥammad al-ʿAbbāsī al-Mahdī (d. 1897), Grand Muftī of Egypt and his al-Fatāwā al-Mahdiyya', *Islamic Law and Society* 1, 1 (1994)
Piamenta, M., *Dictionary of Post-Classical Yemeni Arabic* (Leiden 1990–91)
Powers, David S., '*Fatwās* as Sources for Legal and Social History: A Dispute over Endowment Revenues from Fourteenth-Century Fez', *al-Qanṭara* 11 (1990)
Puente, C. de la, 'Esclavitud y matrimonio en *al-Mudawwana al-kubrā* de Saḥnūn', *al-Qanṭara* 16 (1995)
Puin, Gerd-Rüdiger, 'Der moderne Alltag im Spiegel ḥanbalitischer Fetwas aus ar-Riyad', *ZDMG*, Suppl. 3, 1 (1977)
Ratzaby, Y., 'Yehūdey Teyman Taḥat Shilṭôn ha-Tūrkīm', *Sinai*, 64 (1969)
Repp, Richard Cooper, *The Müfti of Istanbul: A Study in the Development of the Ottoman Learned Hierarchy* (Oxford, 1986)
Rispler-Chaim, Vardit, *Islamic Medical Ethics in the Twentieth Century* (Leiden, 1993)
Schacht, J., 'Early Doctrines on Waqf', *60. doğum yılı münasebetiyle Fuad Köprülü Armağanı; Mélanges Fuad Köprülü* (Istanbul, 1953)
——*An Introduction to Islamic Law* (Oxford, 1964)
——'Classicisme, traditionalisme et ankylose dans la loi religieuse de l'Islam', in *Classicisme et déclin culturel dans l'histoire de l'Islam* (Paris, 1977)
Shaʿashuʿa, S., *Islamic Courts in Israel* (Hebrew) (Tel Aviv, 1981)
Sjukijajnan, L., *Musuljmanskoe Pravo* (Moskau, 1986),
Spectorsky, S. A., *Chapters on Marriage and Divorce: Response of Ibn Ḥanbal and Ibn Rāhwayh* (Austin, 1993)
Thomadakis, A. L., *Peasant society in the Late Byzantine Empire, a Social and Demographic Study* (Princeton, 1977)
Tobi, Y., 'Yerūshat Nashīm ba-Ḥevra ha-Yehūdīt we-ha-Mūslimīt', in S. Seri, ed., *Bat-Teyman (Daughter of Yemen)* (Ri'shôn le-Ṣiyyôn, 1994)
——'Ha-Qehilla ha-Yehūdīt be-Teyman', in Y. Tobi, ed., *Mōreshet Yehūdey Teyman: ʿĪyyūnīm we-Meḥqarīm (Legacy of the Jews of Yemen: Studies and Researches)* (Jerusalem, 1976)
——*Yehūdey Teyman ba-Meʾa ha-19 (The Jews of Yemen in the 19th Century)* (Tel-Aviv, 1976)
——'Qehīlat Yehūdeh Teyman Taḥat Shilṭōn ha-Tūrkīm (1872–1918)', *Kiwwunīn*, 15 (1982)
Toledano, Henry, *Judicial Practice and Family Law in Morocco: The Chapter on Marriage from Sijilmāsī's al-ʿAmal al-Muṭlaq* (Boulder, 1981)
Trousset, P., 'Les oasis présahariennes dans l'antiquité: partage de l'eau et division du temps', *Antiquités africaines* 22 (1986)

Turner, Bryan S., *Weber and Islam* (London, 1974)
Udovitch, Abraham, 'Theory and Practice of Islamic Law', *Studia Islamica* 32 (1970)
——'Les échanges de marché dans l'Islam medieval:Théorie du droit et savoir local', *Studia Islamica* 65 (1987)
Vandevelde, H., 'Quelqes remarques sur la nature et la fonction du droit à propos de l'article 46 du code de la famille', unpublished conference paper from Institut du Droit d'Oran, (1986)
Vidal Castro, F., 'Aḥmad al-Wansharīsī (m. 914/1508): Principales aspectos de su vida', *al-Qanṭara* 12 (1991)
—— 'Las obras de Aḥmad al-Wansharīsī (m.914/1508): Inventario analítico', *Anaquel de Estudios Arabes* 3 (1992)
—— 'El Miʿyār de al-Wansharīsī (m. 914/1508), I: Fuentes, manuscritos, ediciones, traducciones', *Miscelánea de Estudios Arabes y Hebraicos* 42–3 (1993–4)
Vila, S., 'Abenmoguit: Formulario Notarial', *Anuario de Historia del Derecho Español* 8 (1931)
Vranousi, Era, *Byzantina eggrapha tes Mones Patmou (Byzantine documents of Patmos monastery)* (Athens, 1980)
Watt, W. M., 'The Closing of the Door of Ijtihad', *Orientalia Hispanica* (Leiden, 1974)
Watson, Alan, *The Nature of Law* (Edinburgh, 1977)
Welchman, L., 'Family Law under Occupation: Islamic Law and the *Sharīa* Courts in the West Bank', in Ch. Mallat and J. Connors, eds, *Islamic Family Law* (Dordrecht/Boston/New York, 1990)
Wenner, M. M., *Modern Yemen* (Baltimore, 1967)
Wensinck, A. J., et al., *Concordance et Concordance de la Tradition Muslamane* (8. vols, Leiden, 1936–88)
Wittek, P. and Lemerle, P., 'Recherches sur l'histoire et les status des monastères athonites sous la domination turque', *Archives d'histoire du Droit Oriental* 3 (1947)
Yaseen, Mohammad Naeem, 'The Rulings for the Donation of Human Organs in the Light of Sharīʿa Rules and Medical Facts', *Arab Law Quarterly* 5, 1 (1990)
Zachariadou, E., 'Symbole sten historia tou Notianatolikou *Aigaiou (Contribution to the history of southeast Aegean)*', in Zachariadou, E., *Romania and the Turks, c.1300–c.1500* (London, 1985)
Ziadeh, F. J., 'Equality (*kafāʾah*) in the Muslim Law of Marriage', *The American Journal of Comparative Law* 6 (1957)
Zysow, Aron, 'The Economy of Certainty' (unpublished PhD thesis, Harvard University, 1984)

Index of Personal Names

Index of Technical Terms